Mind and Context in Adult Second Language Acquisition

METHODS, THEORY, AND PRACTICE

CRISTINA SANZ
EDITOR

GEORGETOWN UNIVERSITY PRESS
Washington, DC

Georgetown University Press, Washington, DC

Printed in the United States of America

10 9 8 7 6 5 4 3 2 1 2005

This book is printed on acid-free paper meeting
the requirements of the American National Standard
for Permanence in Paper for Printed Library Materials.

Library of Congress Cataloging-in-Publication Data

Mind and context in adult second language acquisition : methods, theory, and practice / Cristina Sanz, editor.
p. cm.
Includes bibliographical references and index.
ISBN 1-58901-070-1 (pbk. : alk. paper)
1. Second language acquisition. 2. Cognitive learning. 3. Psycholinguistics.
4. Computational linguistics. I. Sanz, Cristina.
P118.2.M56 2005
418—dc22 2005008372

To my mother,
María Antonia Alcalá Aroca
(1936–2003)

Contents

Acknowledgments

THIS VOLUME EMERGED from my course Instructed SLA, which in spring 2001 included a series of lectures generously given by several of my Georgetown University colleagues and Bill VanPatten of the University of Illinois, each on their current research. Gail Grella of Georgetown University Press discerned in the course and lectures the seeds of this volume, and the rest is history. Since then some of us have invited our students and alumna to coauthor the chapters. I believe that this volume provides a good picture of the work in cognitive second language acquisition that we do here at Georgetown, which results from collaboration between faculty and graduate students, the main and medical campuses, and the language and linguistics departments.

I am most thankful for the detailed comments and insights provided by the following reviewers on individual chapters: David Birdsong, Harriet Bowden, Joaquim Camps, Andrew Farley, Shinichi Izumi, Renee Jourdenais, Hiram Maxim, Kara Morgan-Short, Nuria Sagarra, Bill VanPatten, Paula Winke, Winnie Wong, and two reviewers who wish to remain anonymous. I also acknowledge the helpful feedback I received from the two anonymous reviewers who evaluated the volume. My thanks also go to Georgetown's Faculty of Languages and Linguistics and Graduate School of Arts and Sciences, and especially to Gerry Mara and Gail Grella of Georgetown University Press for their support. Finally, many thanks must go to the students in Instructed SLA who suffered the first draft of this volume: Mariona Anfruns, Chris Barley, Beatriz Lado, Hui-Ju Lin, Almitra Medina, and Iñigo Yanguas; special thanks go to Mariona Anfruns and Beatriz Lado, who painstakingly proofread the manuscript.

Introduction

CRISTINA SANZ

INFORMATION-PROCESSING APPROACHES to second language acquisition (SLA) attempt to explain how nonnative languages are learned—usually by adults—and how knowledge of such second languages is used. The perspective on language acquisition presented in this volume is multifactorial and interactionist: It takes into account external and internal variables and the multiple interactions among them. This approach has attracted the attention not only of researchers but also of practitioners, since the pedagogical implications of such a perspective are readily seen. The last ten years have seen a surge in the number of research articles and book chapters on the topic. A few volumes on specific issues related to processing approaches have also appeared. However, an avid reader or a course instructor would have to consult a variety of sources and attempt to integrate all that information. This volume seeks to provide, in one place, a coherent, well-structured picture of the latest research on processing approaches to SLA.

The volume is divided into four parts, which differ in contents as well as goals. All chapters follow the same structure: key words, an introduction, main body, summary, suggestions for further reading, and references. Chapters 2 through 8 also include exercises requiring a data analysis and a guided critique, which exemplify and develop some of the constructs and operationalizations in each chapter. Familiarity with the contents of chapters 2 and 3 is required for succesful completion of most of the exercises in the volume.

The first part, "Theory and Methodology," provides an introduction to the main concepts and to the most popular procedures for data gathering and data analysis to be found in information-processing approaches to SLA research. I hope this part prepares those without a strong background in information-processing approaches to critically read the chapters in the two parts that follow. Chapter 1 defines the scope of SLA research and contextualizes processing approaches within current language acquisition theories. It also establishes the relationship between processing approaches and advances in cognitive psychology. After a discussion of the what and the how of SLA, it summarizes the last thirty years of SLA research by focusing on the role that different lines of research have assigned to internal and external factors and their interaction. Chapters 2 and 3 present information on quantitative and qualitative approaches to data gathering and analysis. The information contained in these two chapters is fundamental to understand reports of empirical research and even more to develop any data-based study. Readers with a strong background in research methodology might choose to skip them.

In chapter 2, Rusan Chen includes the statistical procedures that are typically implemented in empirical SLA research, such as *t* tests, ANOVA, chi-square tests, correlation and regression, and nonparametric tests. The chapter emphasizes conceptual understanding over mathematical formula derivation in the hope that the reader will understand the basic principles and logic of statistical methods.

Chapter 3, by Rebecca Adams, Akiko Fujii, and Alison Mackey, provides an introduction to qualitative approaches to research in instructed SLA. First, definitions in qualitative paradigms are discussed, including theoretical assumptions and methodological characteristics. An overview of research issues in instructed SLA that have been addressed through qualitative methods is then provided, followed by commonly used qualitative methods for data gathering in instructed SLA. These include classroom observations, uptake charts, verbal protocols, case studies, surveys, diaries, and journals. The chapter concludes with a discussion of practical considerations in conducting qualitative research, including issues such as coding of data, quantification, credibility, transferability, and dependability.

The second and third parts of the volume are really its heart. Part 2, "Internal Factors," includes a review of specific subfields within processing approaches to SLA: attention and awareness, brain-based views of SLA, and individual differences.

In chapter 4, Harriet Wood Bowden, Cristina Sanz, and Catherine Stafford contrast old and new processing-based approaches to the study of individual differences (IDs) and their role in SLA. Lately the field has experienced renewed theoretical interest as developments in cognitive psychology suggest differences in brain structure and behavior in relation to IDs, especially age, aptitude, sex, and the role of experience (bilingualism) in the acquisition of nonprimary languages. Age is seen as the crucial variable distinguishing between acquisition processes led by an internal universal grammar and those led by problem-solving strategies. Likewise, aptitude has been deconstructed and broken up into smaller, more measurable components like working memory and phonological short-term memory. Sex has been selected because there are new experimental and theoretical approaches to sex-based differences that had until now been anecdotally observed. And with the increase in migration and the creation of supranational entities, the need to explain the effects of bilingualism on cognition has become more pressing.

In chapter 5, Michael Ullman discusses theoretical and empirical aspects of the neural bases of the mental lexicon and the mental grammar in first and second language (L1 and L2). It presents a retrospective examination of lesion, neuroimaging, and electrophysiological studies investigating the neural bases of L2 and argues that these data support the predictions of the declarative/procedural model. After a review of predictions of the model for L1 acquisition, the chapter elaborates predictions made by the model for L2 acquisition, including those related to age, sex, and other individual differences.

Chapter 6, by Ronald Leow and Melissa Bowles, provides a summary of the major attentional frameworks in SLA, followed by a review of research investigating the issue of awareness in SLA. The chapter carefully analyzes constructs and measurements, especially think-aloud protocols, instructions, and coding.

The third part of the volume, "External Factors," includes two chapters on external factors in SLA, with focus on input, interaction, and pedagogical research conducted within a cognitive framework. In chapter 7, Alison Mackey and Rebekha Abbuhl describe the role of input and interaction in the L2 learning process. The chapter outlines the interaction hypothesis of SLA, describes empirical work suggesting a link between conversational interaction and L2 learning, and provides a brief discussion of the connections between input, interaction, and task-based language teaching and learning.

Chapter 8, by Cristina Sanz and Kara Morgan-Short, surveys empirical research on the effects of pedagogical interventions on acquisition, defined as provision of manipulated input, explicit rule explanation, or feedback in combination with practice. Whether preemptive or reactive, provision of pedagogical interventions is one of the main distinctions between acquisition of an L1 and an L2. Some studies suggest that pedagogical interventions can enhance language acquisition, making it a more efficient process. There are also studies that have identified negative effects, such as rule overgeneralization, while others have not identified any effects at all. This chapter details the theoretical and methodological differences among the studies to account for their at times contradictory results. A great deal of attention is devoted to practice, a key variable.

The fourth part, "Pedagogical Implications," presents examples of pedagogical implications of the major constructs outlined in parts 2 and 3. These two chapters differ in the breadth of the pedagogical object to which they apply processing principles. The focus of Bill VanPatten's chapter 9 is a pedagogical technique known as processing instruction that has proven worthy of scrutiny in any discussion of focus on form, pedagogical intervention, computer-assisted language learning, or explicit instruction. The chapter presents the model of input processing that motivates processing instruction and sets forth its basic characteristics in contrast with other approaches.

In contrast, chapter 10, by Heidi Byrnes, uses some of the theoretical concepts presented in previous parts to focus on the curricular program and the development of advanced literacy and to motivate content-based instruction. It introduces the cognitive dimensions of negotiating form and meaning and the role of tasks, specifically genre-based tasks that integrate cultural knowledge and language.

In its four parts on theory and methods, internal factors, external factors, and pedagogical implications, this volume presents an overview of work in a multifactorial, interactive approach to adult SLA that should be of help for both researchers and practitioners.

PART 1

Theory and Methodology

ONE

Adult SLA: The Interaction between External and Internal Factors

CRISTINA SANZ

KEY WORDS

External and internal factors ▪ individual differences ▪ interactive approach ▪ interlanguage ▪ level of ultimate attainment ▪ nativism ▪ neurolinguistics ▪ rate of acquisition ▪ universals ▪ variation.

1. Introduction

Like their counterparts in the field of first language (L1) acquisition, scholars in the field of second language acquisition (SLA) need to explain both the nature of language and how it is acquired, that is, what is learned and how it is learned. Unlike researchers in the field of L1 acquisition, however, SLA researchers need to explain the enormous variation found both in the rate of acquisition and in the level of ultimate attainment that characterizes adult language learning. Their goal is to identify universals of adult SLA as well as to explain the role of individual differences (IDs) in the process of acquiring a second language (L2). Researchers agree that L2 learners follow a predictable path in their acquisition process irrespective of their L1, aptitude, and context of acquisition and that language learners vary in the efficiency with which they go through the stages. There is no doubt that the learning context is in part responsible for this situation: Graduates from immersion programs learn faster and attain higher proficiency levels than L2 learners in foreign language programs. In addition, IDs such as motivation, aptitude, and attitude account for differences among learners in the same contexts. It is the interaction between internal processing mechanisms and IDs on the one hand, and external factors, such as quality and quantity of input on the other, that explain why some adult language learners learn faster than others and get further ahead in the acquisition process.

This volume is concerned with the adult L2 learner and the interaction between external and internal factors that determines and ultimately explains adult L2 learning processes. It therefore contributes to the general picture of language acquisition in a context that is different from child bilingualism and skilled adult bilingualism (i.e., adults who started learning an L2 at a young age and who have reached a high level of proficiency). Given the fact that adult L2 acquisition takes place after cognitive development is basically complete, adult language learners need to make the most of their cognitive resources in order to compensate for the limitations that have been imposed both externally (linked to the nature of the input, generally poorer in quality and frequency than L1 input) and internally (related to depleted cognitive resources). Key topics to be explored regard (a) the nature of the language, which is the input that feeds the learning process (Mackey and Abbuhl, this volume, chapter 7; Sanz and Morgan-Short, this volume, chapter 8), (b) the mechanisms that process information and the role of attention and awareness in explicit and implicit processing of information (Leow and Bowles, this volume, chapter 6), (c) how properties of the brain may account for differences in child and adult SLA (Ullman, this volume, chapter 5), and (d) how age, sex, and prior language experience interact with cognitive limitations to explain differential success in the acquisition of nonprimary languages (Bowden, Sanz, and Stafford, this volume, chapter 4).

Although the volume takes a cognitive approach to L2 learning, it also accepts the importance of social context in both L1 and L2 acquisition. All knowledge, especially but not exclusively linguistic knowledge, is the result of learners' interaction with their social context, and acquisition is thus both social and cognitive. Mackey and Abbuhl's work on input and interaction as well as Bowden, Sanz, and Stafford's discussion of bilingualism and the acquisition of nonprimary languages provide insights into these issues. The latter chapter in particular distinguishes between individual and societal bilingualism and defends the proposition that the first cannot be understood without the second. Psycholinguistics may explain the positive effects that the ability to read and write in two languages has on subsequent language learning (Sanz, 2000), but biliterate bilingualism results from specific external conditions, for example, language policies leading to bilingual education.

The motivation behind adult SLA research is in large part theoretical. L2 learning is pervasive throughout the world today, as it has been throughout history. An understanding of SLA processes adds to a greater understanding of that which makes us human, our minds. Scholars will one day explain the cognitive processes underlying adult SLA and thus contribute to the larger understanding of human cognition. But the motivation behind SLA research is also practical. Practical applications of adult SLA research are not always necessary, but most SLA research can inform language teachers, language learners, and administrators involved in language policy and language program direction.

More and more, thanks to advances in neurolinguistics, findings from SLA research also have implications for clinical treatment, for example, helping bilingual aphasics.

The SLA field has borrowed both theory and research methodology from the fields of linguistics and psychology, both of which have posited theories attempting to explain what language is and how it is learned. Although descriptive accounts are important, a theory that has explanatory power is indispensable. Given a solid theoretical foundation, SLA researchers can make predictions, elaborate hypotheses, test them, and explain their results. This process ultimately tests, and if necessary, changes, the theory itself. Ullman (this volume, chapter 5) presents an example of such a process. His model, based on observations that have accumulated from psycholinguistic, developmental disorder, neurological, and neuroimaging studies, makes predictions that are now being tested.

SLA research methodology has largely been borrowed from L1 acquisition research, which is carried out primarily by scholars trained in psychology departments. Some methods more common to theoretical linguistics and sociolinguistics are also popular. Research methodology can be classified as quantitative or qualitative and may be either cross-sectional or longitudinal, though mixed designs are increasingly common. Chen's chapter (this volume, chapter 2) on quantitative methods and Adams, Fujii, and Mackey's (this volume, chapter 3) on qualitative methods provide an excellent overview of basic SLA methodological tools. Becoming familiar with SLA research tools is necessary not only for those who carry out data-based studies but also for language practitioners who need to read the research with a critical eye.

Thus the purpose of this chapter is to introduce the reader to adult SLA from an information-processing perspective, to contextualize its focus within general SLA and its connections with other disciplines. The chapter often makes reference to relevant chapters in the volume, but the reader is referred to the introduction at the beginning of the volume for summaries and details on chapter structure and volume organization. The remainder of the chapter is divided into three sections. The first presents two competing approaches to adult SLA, namely, generative and general nativist approaches, the latter of which includes information-processing approaches. The second section briefly provides a historical perspective on adult SLA research and the different emphases that a number of models and theories have assigned to external and internal factors to explain L2 acquisition. The final section introduces key issues and terms discussed in depth in the volume, which include external factors, such as input and interaction, and IDs, such as cognitive capacity (working memory) and its relation to attention.

2. Two Competing Approaches to Language Acquisition

The present section explores the contrast between two major approaches to adult SLA: grammatical nativism or generativism (Schwartz, 1993; White, 1989), connected to generative linguistic theory, and more psychology-based approaches, including information-processing approaches, grouped under the umbrella of general nativism (Anderson, 1983; McLaughlin, 1987). Both approaches attempt to explain *what* is learned (rules and representations, associations, or both) and *how* it is learned, but differ in scope, methods, and assumptions. General nativism posits domain-general mechanisms, such as those responsible for all skill learning, while grammatical nativism or generativism posits a language acquisition device—an innate grammar (termed *Universal Grammar*) that both expands with exposure and sets limits on learners' predictions. The theories agree on a basic definition of what constitutes language knowledge: a lexicon with information about properties of words, such as categories (nouns, verbs, etc.), and a computational system that allows words to be combined to produce and interpret language. The disagreement between the theories begins with the nature of the computational system. Generativists propose that such a system is a hierarchical set of rules, whereas connectionists characterize the system as a nonhierarchical set of mental associations. More disagreement between approaches is found in relation to how language is learned (see Ullman, this volume, chapter 5).

Generativists propose a language acquisition device (LAD) exclusively devoted to language in order to explain the speed and sophistication of language acquisition (i.e., modularity). The LAD consists of an innate grammar that grows in contact with input triggering its development and that limits the otherwise infinite possibilities that a purely computational system would generate. The LAD is posited in order to explain how the L1 is acquired rapidly and efficiently based on degenerate input and lacking negative feedback. This is known as Plato's paradox or the logical problem of language acquisition. The key question in SLA for this approach is whether L2 grammars are like L1 grammars and whether interlanguage (i.e., the developing L2 system) is the result of access to Universal Grammar. There are three basic positions: the full access–full transfer account (Schwartz and Sprouse, 1996); the weak transfer–valueless features hypothesis (Eubank, 1996) and the lexical transfer–minimal trees hypothesis (Vainikka and Young-Scholten, 1996).

Since generativists see knowledge or competence as internally driven and universal, their research gives only minimal attention to external factors, including input and IDs. Elegance (a theory's ability to explain phenomena with the fewest possible constructs) is a fundamental principle for generativists and is always preferred over inclusiveness. General nativists (cognitive nativists, connectionists, and emergentists) posit the existence of domain-general mechanisms responsible for all learning, not just language learning. Acquisition is input driven and takes place through interaction and experience. The goal of nativist theory is to explain all language behavior. From input characteristics, such as complexity and frequency and the factors intervening in its processing (strategies and attention), to knowledge representation and access, their approach is inclusive. SLA research of this type is interactive in nature since it looks at both internal and external factors in language acquisition and at the way they affect each other. While it must be recognized that generativist approaches to language acquisition, including SLA, have made contributions to the advancement of knowledge of the human mind, administrators, teachers and practitioners in general find it difficult to relate them to their needs.

Although it may appear contradictory, most SLA researchers do not adhere to one theory alone. For example, in Gass (2003) the first section is a defense of the primary role of an innate program (nature) over input (nurture) in acquisition, but the rest of the chapter focuses exclusively on topics within processing approaches, such as types of input, the role of output and interaction, and mechanisms (primarily attention) that are responsible for input processing. Although Gass accepts a less restrictive definition of negative feedback (one that includes recast and other forms of implicit feedback), thus reducing the importance of Plato's paradox, she accepts the limited role of negative feedback in effectively promoting change in the learner's grammar. She thus returns in the end to a defense of the role of nature, that is, innate grammar, in SLA. Similarly, VanPatten (1996) assumes a limited processor—positioning himself squarely within processing approaches to SLA—but admits to modularity. Ullman (this volume, chapter 5), unlike the generativists, assumes that the mechanisms that drive language acquisition are shared by other types of learning, but like the generativists, he sees grammar as a set of rules rather than associations. It is possible to conclude that for SLA researchers, generativism offers a widely accepted theory of language that addresses the *what* of language acquisition, but when it comes to the *how,* most SLA scholars turn to cognitive, information-processing models.

3. A Brief History

This section presents a brief overview of SLA theories from the 1970s to the present, with a focus on the importance that each assigns to external and internal factors. In the last thirty years, a number of models and theories have appeared that have been more or less successful at generating research. The theories have been connected mostly to advances in linguistics (Lenneberg's, 1967, functional-typological model) and psychology, including social psychology (Gardner's, 1985, motivational-social psychological model), but also in neurocognition (Paradis, 1994). The purpose of this section is to briefly describe a number of approaches to SLA that exemplify the different emphases assigned to internal and external factors as well as to their interaction.

The combination of structural linguistics and behavioral psychology (Skinner, 1957), which relied only on observable behavior and viewed learning as the result of repeated responses to stimuli that led to habit formation, sits on the most extreme end of a continuum that assigns importance to external variables. In the L2 classroom, this approach to learning translated into the audiolingual method, with its stress on overt correction and imitation through drills. Instructors and book authors created drills informed by contrastive analysis to prevent or correct the effects of negative transfer from the L1. The behaviorist period is considered to have ended with Chomsky's (1965) publication of *Aspects of the Theory of Syntax.*

This publication was the beginning of a new period in SLA research, one that emphasized internal factors with almost total disregard for those external to the language learner. It also privileged explanation over description and theory over data. Simultaneously, Roger Brown's work in child language acquisition also influenced SLA, specifically his work on acquisitional orders (1973). In contrast to previous positions, errors were now seen as a natural part of the learner's interlanguage or L2 grammar, which was posited to be different from the learner's L1 and the target language. Errors acquired new significance as they provided a window onto this interlanguage.

Krashen's (1985) monitor theory, of great influence at the time and in following years, is a performance model that attempted to explain precisely the results of morpheme studies in both L1 and L2, which had identified a natural order of acquisition. This order of acquisition was found to be constant in adults and in children, in the classroom and in naturalistic contexts, and in learners of English as a second language (ESL) from different backgrounds. Krashen interpreted this as evidence of an internal map that neither age, L1, nor external context could alter. According to Krashen, this internal map was fed by input that fulfilled certain conditions, namely, that it be comprehensible and that it contain language beyond the learners' current level ($i + 1$). Most morpheme studies used the Bilingual Syntax Measure (Burt, Dulay, and Hernández-Chávez, 1975) to elicit data. When other tests and tasks were implemented, however, they yielded different acquisitional orders. Krashen explained these differences as resulting from two different sources of knowledge, implicit and explicit knowledge, which he called *acquired* and *learned* knowledge. While the former was considered true competence ready for use in comprehension and production, Krashen posited that the latter could be used only for self-correction. According to this position, exposure to explicit input (that is, grammatical explanation and correction) could result only in learned knowledge, which functioned as a monitor. These ideas, articulated in five hypotheses, comprised Krashen's monitor theory: (a) the natural order hypothesis, (b) the input hypothesis, (c) the affective filter hypothesis, (d) the monitor hypothesis, and (e) the acquisition-learning hypothesis.

McLaughlin (1987) criticized the monitor theory on methodological grounds; a primary requirement of a theory is that it has to be testable. In Krashen's case, $i + 1$ as a construct could not be operationalized and therefore could not be measured. Moreover, the hypotheses were not independent but instead depended on each other, making them difficult to test. The view that the monitor was either on or off was rather simplistic, and the natural order hypothesis lacked explanatory power. Finally, Long's (1983) review of the pedagogical research conducted at the time provided evidence against the monitor hypothesis. On the other hand, White (1991) defended the role of incomprehensible input in promoting L2 development, arguing that incomprehensible input can prompt L2 learners to realize the need to restructure their system in order to capture missed information.

The reaction to the monitor theory was important both in the quantity of publications it spawned and in the quality, or nature, of the issues it identified. Consequently, it represents, despite its shortcomings, a milestone in SLA theory. Terms such as input, interaction, explicit versus implicit learning, awareness, processing, and knowledge, which are key in SLA today and in this volume, emerged at that time. Krashen's influence on the language teaching profession was perhaps even stronger than it was in SLA research. For the first time, the power of explicit teaching (i.e., grammar explanation and overt error correction) was seriously questioned, causing instructors and administrators to reconsider some important assumptions. The monitor theory also motivated in part the development of immersion programs. It is ironic that an approach which in principle emphasized what is internal and universal in L2 learning resulted in directing the attention of both researchers and practitioners towards external factors like input and interaction.

While Chomskyan linguistics considered language acquisition in isolation, sociolinguistic approaches to SLA were interested in the relationship between language acquisition and the social context in which it takes place. Heavily influenced by Labov's (1972) paradigm, Tarone's (1988), Preston's (1989), and Young's (1991) work on variation has been one of the most fruitful areas of research within sociolinguistic approaches to SLA. Variationists distinguish between random and systematic variation. Their goal is to predict systematic variation, which is part of the interlanguage grammar rather than the result of performance limitations and is caused by both internal and external factors, the latter being both linguistic and social in nature. Variationist studies implement quantitative, correlational analyses in their designs in order to identify the relationship between variable interlanguage forms and the context in which they occur. With all their emphasis on external factors, variationists rely on one internal variable—attention to form or attention to content—to explain variation. The place of this framework on the internal-external continuum falls therefore between structuralist-behaviorist views of L2 learning at the external end of the continuum and generativist approaches at the internal end.

The ZISA project (Meisel, Clahsen, and Pienemann, 1981) generated the multidimensional model, an excellent example of an interactive approach to SLA. Based on cross-sectional and longitudinal data from Italian and Spanish guest workers (L2 speakers of German) and their children (L1 speakers) in Germany, the multidemensional model has two axes. One axis is developmental and explains fixed stages of development (e.g., in German word order) that result from processing constraints, which are basically short-term memory limitations. The other axis is variational and addresses forms such as articles, the copula, and prepositions that are acquired in less predictable orders depending on IDs, mostly the L2 learner's motivation. A highly motivated learner, one who wants to integrate into the L2 group, will supply the forms earlier and more often in the correct contexts than a less motivated learner. One of the strengths of this model is that unlike Krashen's monitor theory, it is falsifiable: The concrete stages identified make the predictions testable. The model generates two hypotheses, the learnability and the teachability hypotheses (Pienemann, 1984), which predict and set limits on the effects of instruction and thus have important implications for language teaching and syllabus design. The model has been criticized for its lack of detail about what is acquired (Is it rules? What are those rules?), and it is difficult to find much research on acquisitional orders beyond word order. The greatest strength of the multidimensional model is that it truly is an interactive approach, as it brings in both social (e.g., motivation) and psychological (e.g., processing constraints set by working memory) variables to explain how second languages are learned.

To summarize, from the 1970s until today the field has become aware that SLA, like all human accomplishments, is a complex phenomenon that cannot be explained by looking at only one aspect of it. Today programs from conferences such as the American Association for Applied Linguistics' annual meeting, the Second Language Research Forum, and EuroSLA reflect the complexity of the field. While some scholars call for a more flexible perspective that incorporates the social context and that is more qualitative in its approach (see Byrnes, this volume, chapter 10), others like Doughty and Long (2003) take a strong stand and see SLA as falling squarely within cognitive science. For years now, an important line of research within SLA has focused on the acquisition of pragmatics, which looks at language in context. This is in contrast with the almost exclusive attention paid to form (syntax and some morphology) by generativists and with the lack of interest in discourse, context, meaning, and content of the information-processing approaches that have in general preferred to focus instead on sentence-level phenomena. So whether it is the *how* or the *what* of L2 learning, contextual factors and internal variables still compete for the scholar's attention with variable success. Language practitioners, and more specifically language program administrators, would like to see SLA research move in the direction of more qualitative and longitudinal designs over the ever-popular quantitative short term study, but even more they would prefer a focus on textual-level processing, task, and genre (as an example of such tension, see Byrnes, this volume, chapter 10).

4. External and Internal Factors in Adult SLA

The remainder of the chapter is devoted to a discussion of internal and external variables in SLA and should serve as an introduction to the chapters that follow, providing in-depth coverage in each specific topic. The section will first address external variables in SLA, covered in more depth by Mackey and Abbhul (this volume, chapter 7) and Sanz and Morgan-Short (this volume, chapter 8). Subsequently, the discussion turns to internal variables examined in more detail by Bowden, Sanz, and Stafford (this volume, chapter 4); Ullman (this volume, chapter 5); and Leow and Bowles (this volume, chapter 6).

4.1. EXTERNAL FACTORS

As mentioned earlier, it is ironic that an extraordinary proliferation of descriptive studies on external factors such as input followed the appearance of Krashen's monitor theory, which itself focused on internal universal constraints leading to predictable orders of acquisition undisturbed by external factors such as learning contexts. In fact, research on input, its characteristics, and its ability to affect acquisition continues to thrive, although in a far more sophisticated way, in terms of both theory and research methods. This focus on input should be of no surprise; no matter the framework—generativist or general nativist—there is absolute agreement that input is essential for acquisition to take place. It is when we consider what is necessary, what is sufficient, and what kind of input is relevant for language acquisition that disagreement ensues.

The term *comprehensible input* generated early research that provided descriptions of the language that L2 learners (mostly ESL) were exposed to: teacher talk (the language that teachers use when addressing their students) and foreigner talk (the language native speakers use when addressing nonnative speakers). This work was heavily influenced by earlier L1 research on caretaker speech (the language that adults use when addressing children), and its goal was to understand the mechanisms that made the input comprehensible to the learner. Other qualities of the input, such as frequency and saliency, also attracted the attention of scholars. Chaudron (1988) provides an excellent review of this early literature. With ample descriptive studies completed, Long (1996) proposed the interaction hypothesis and a research agenda for the next two decades. Its goal was to explain how interaction facilitates comprehension and what the mechanisms are that lead from comprehensible input to acquisition. Thus, current SLA research examines the issue of what is relevant for the learner's developing interlanguage system, that is, what kind of input is capable of altering the learner's grammar.

Generativist perspectives on language acquisition (e.g., Schwartz, 1993) assume that the stimulus, that is, the input, is too poor in both amount and quality to account for acquisition. This perspective, however, does not deny the importance of input, which is posited to crucially interact with Universal Grammar. Furthermore, research carried out in the 1960s on caretaker speech showed minimal instances of negative feedback, with the exception of feedback related to the lexicon and pragmatics (i.e., the child is told what is socially inappropriate). However, in the case of L2 acquisition, especially in formal contexts, feedback is omnipresent. Still, within the generative framework only positive evidence—no feedback, no explicit input—feeds the system. Chapters 7 and 8 will address this issue of feedback. Chapter 8 also provides an in-depth review of research on explicit input (grammar explanation).

Regarding negative feedback of the implicit type, its effects may be due to the positive evidence inherently provided. For instance, recasts do not include explicit information about the language, but they do provide a correct reformulation of the learner's utterance (see Gass, 2003, for an overview). From an information-processing perspective, the power of recasts may lie in their immediacy; because only milliseconds separate the learner's original sentence from its interlocutor's reformulation, there is a cognitive window of opportunity within which an input-output comparison is possible (Doughty, 2001), leading the learner to realize the need for a change in the system. These and other related issues are covered in greater depth by Mackey and Abbuhl (this volume, chapter 7).

In regards to whether provision of explicit input facilitates the acquisition of an L2, the jury is still out. The issue has been investigated within an information-processing perspective in highly controlled laboratory studies and in relation to such constructs as intake, noticing, implicit and explicit learning, and memory for instances (chunks) and associations (see N. C. Ellis, 1994, and Hulstijn, 1997). For obvious reasons, the issue is especially relevant for classroom SLA, although research on the topic conducted in the classroom is scarce. Interest in explicit input grew after results from Canadian immersion studies started yielding somewhat surprising results (Swain and Lapkin, 1982). When reading and listening skills were considered, graduates from such programs showed nativelike command of the L2. However, their productive skills, although highly advanced, were not nativelike, despite years of exposure to vast amounts of very rich input. So while it is universally accepted that input—instances of language, positive evidence—is necessary for SLA, these studies cast doubt as to whether it is sufficient. It might be the case that provision of explicit information about how the language works enhances the rate and the final attainment level of learners, especially adult language learners. The following paragraphs provide a brief introduction to this topic, which is discussed in greater detail by Sanz and Morgan-Short (this volume, chapter 8).

In generative approaches, only raw data—instances of language—can feed the system. Krashen's monitor theory and its acquisition-learning hypothesis predicted that explicit input fed only the monitor and was therefore useful only for self-correction (under very specific circumstances), not for language generation. On the basis of these hypotheses, the teaching profession started questioning its own usefulness. Beginning with Long's (1983) publication, summaries, reviews, and meta-analyses comparing naturalistic and classroom learners, as well as different types of instruction, have concluded that acquisition can happen without instruction but that instruction helps. Instructed and naturalistic learners appear to follow the same acquisitional route, but formal learners seem to learn faster and reach higher levels of final attainment. Furthermore, comparisons of different types of instruction show that not all instruction is the same. Norris and Ortega's (2000) meta-analysis of empirical studies comparing differential effects of instruction showed not only that instruction makes a difference but that the more explicit the instruction, the more effective it is.

However, four limitations identified by these authors are important enough to call their results into question. First, the tasks used in some of these studies to evaluate the effects of the treatment were biased toward explicit knowledge. Second, participants in the implicit conditions did learn, although not as much or as efficiently as those in the explicit conditions. Third, treatments were short, which puts the implicit groups at an inherent disadvantage. Finally, the long-term effects of explicit conditions are not known. Apart from these limitations, counterevidence to Norris and Ortega's conclusion also exists. Sanz and Morgan-Short (2004), among other studies reviewed there, found no effects for explicit information on language development beyond those of practice with implicit feedback.

Interestingly, Doughty (2003) concluded that the default mode of processing in both children and adults is implicit (without attention) and that input processing for acquisition in adults should be optimized through means other than provision of explicit input. As an example, she pointed to PI research (VanPatten, 2004, and this volume, chapter 9), which examines task-essential practice and the effects of a pedagogical technique that includes in its design input that has been manipulated in different ways to make it more salient. Pedagogical treatments have typically been classified based on presence or absence of rule presentation and type of feedback (explicit or implicit), but the input and the task itself have not been considered. In chapter 8 in this volume, Morgan-Short and I argue for the need to refocus the research with a new emphasis on practice.

4.2. INTERNAL FACTORS

Due in part to the influence of Chomskyan approaches to language, SLA research has focused most of its energy on identifying universals rather than IDs that may influence SLA. In information-processing approaches, however, attention, memory, and IDs are seen as key variables in determining input processing. How much linguistic information feeds the system depends on cognitive capacity (memory) and attention, which themselves are also related to IDs such as sex and previous experience with language learning. This section provides a brief introduction to IDs, memory, and attention and lays out the major points developed by Bowden, Sanz, and Stafford (this volume, chapter 4); Ullman (this volume, chapter 5); and Leow and Bowles (this volume, chapter 6).

From a methodological standpoint, research on IDs is difficult to conduct. As in other areas, constructs are not precise enough for clear operationalization, and designs are often correlational in that relationships between the ID and outcome are established, but a cause-effect or even directionality cannot be identified. (Does increased proficiency lead to higher motivation or do more motivated learners reach higher levels of acquisition?) Other prominent questions also remain unanswered. How much is universal and how much is individual? Much of the focus has been on the effects of IDs on outcomes, but how do IDs affect processes? The specific IDs are many, even too many to enumerate in a paragraph; for this reason, Bowden, Sanz, and Stafford have in chapter 4 limited their discussion to four IDs: age, memory, sex, and prior language experience.

There is general agreement that IDs seem to have a greater effect on the acquisition of an L2 than an L1. The nature of the specific IDs and the degree to which they affect individual aspects of the acquisition of the L2—for example, syntax versus vocabulary—are still debated in the literature. In addition to neurological maturation effects (see Ullman, this volume, chapter 5), there are cognitive and social-affective factors that covary with age and that may contribute to age effects. Moreover, not enough is known about how and to what degree these factors affect different components of L2 development (i.e., the lexicon, morphosyntax, and phonology). Chapter 4 reviews the literature, giving special attention to those studies that show that age effects are not inescapable and that successful adult L2 learning is possible.

Sex differences (but not gender; see Bowden, Sanz, and Stafford, this volume, chapter 4) in L2 learning previously have attracted little attention. Perhaps their study is regarded as politically incorrect, but current research indicates that there is indeed a processing difference between males and females when processing both native and second languages. As is the case with age effects, these differences in processing seem related to verbal memory and the influence of estrogen upon it (see this volume, chapter 4, for references and a detailed discussion of IDs).

Clearly, recent advances in cognitive research represent a promising direction for the study of aptitude, posited to be a largely stable trait and the ID most predictive of L2 learning. The most commonly used test of L2 aptitude is Carroll and Sapon's (1959) Modern Language Aptitude Test (MLAT), developed when behaviorist learning theory was prevalent. Current processing approaches to SLA, however, underscore the role of working memory as the place where input is perceived, attended to, and processed for subsequent representation in the developing system. Measures of working memory could potentially be better predictors of L2 success than the MLAT and could offer more explanatory power than the MLAT, which resulted from combining five components. The review of the literature on working memory measurement in chapter 4 concludes that much remains to be done to bring measurement into line with theoretical developments.

Finally, the study of multilingual acquisition is an ideal area for those interested in the role of IDs in language learning since no two bilinguals are the same. For example, bilinguals differ in age of L2 acquisition, context and frequency of use of both languages, and degree of bilingualism. Classroom and laboratory studies have shown a positive relationship between bilingualism and acquisition of subsequent languages, and a number of factors have been posited to explain it. Research is needed on the effects of prior linguistic experience on representation of new L3 knowledge (see Ullman, this volume, chapter 5). Furthermore, recent advances in the field of attention and awareness in cognitive psychology and SLA distinguish between awareness at the level of noticing and awareness at the level of understanding. Some evidence exists that it is heightened awareness at the level of noticing that gives experienced language learners the edge.

The role of attention in SLA is a relatively new area of research. VanPatten (1990) was one of the first studies to explore attention. Based on early cognitive capacity theories, this study viewed adult learners as limited capacity processors of incoming information. On this view, form and meaning compete for attentional resources, which explains why beginning language learners process language for meaning alone, that is, they pay attention to what is said, not how it is said. Since this initial research, SLA researchers have built stronger ties with cognitive psychology and have produced three competing approaches to the role of attention and awareness (Robinson, 1995; Schmidt, 1990, 2001; Tomlin and Villa, 1994). These approaches agree on the key role of attention in acquisition of an L2 but disagree on whether awareness, "a particular state of mind in which an individual has undergone a specific subjective experience of some cognitive content or external stimulus" (Tomlin and Villa, 1994, p. 193), facilitates or is necessary for processing. Empirical studies that have investigated the relationship between awareness and learning have employed both off-line (postexposure questionnaires, retrospective verbal reports) and online (concurrent think-aloud protocols) data-gathering procedures. However, the reliability of these measures should be carefully considered. With off-line procedures, there is potential memory decay, which may lead participants to provide erroneous information. Online procedures, however, may suffer from ecological validity (i.e., it may not be normal to think aloud while performing language tasks) and reactivity (thinking aloud may affect task performance, positively or negatively). Leow and Bowles (this volume, chapter 6) provide in-depth discussion and references.

In conclusion, early language acquisition, whether for single or multiple first languages, goes hand in hand with cognitive development, but cognitive development is essentially complete by the time exposure to the L2 starts in adult L2 learning. Consequently, while L1 researchers work on pathologies such as Down and Williams syndromes to investigate the relationship between cognition and language development, the dissociation between language and cognitive development is the main characteristic of adult SLA. The goal of SLA scholars is to uncover the cognitive abilities that make L2 acquisition and use possible and the potential differences between linguistic representations and processing in L1 and adult L2, differences that may disappear after a certain acquisitional level has been reached. This is our field's contribution to the understanding of human cognition.

5. Summary

This chapter has provided an introduction to the present volume, whose domain is the acquisition of nonprimary languages by adults. Consequently, it is concerned with the internal and external factors that interact and explain adult L2 learning processes and that are different from those involved in child and skilled adult bilingualism.

The goal of adult SLA research is to explain both the nature of language and how language is acquired: what is learned and how it is learned. Two current perspectives in language acquisition address these questions. On the one hand, the generativist approach, embraced generally by SLA researchers with linguistic training, contends that L2 input is too poor to bring about acquisition in and of itself; instead, language acquisition is held to be internally driven. Proponents of this approach view the mind as modular, with different areas of the brain dedicated exclusively to language. SLA researchers using this approach are still discussing whether adults have full, partial, or no access to their posited LAD. On the other hand, general nativists, usually trained in psychology departments, believe that humans are born ready to identify patterns and draw generalizations and that this ability facilitates the learning of any complex skill, including language. Under this approach, SLA research is concerned with the nature of the input that feeds the learning process through interaction, the mechanisms that process the information (attention in particular), reliance on brain structures, and the role of IDs in explaining differential success in learning.

The benefit of a historical perspective that illuminates present concerns is significant, especially in a young field that seems to revisit issues without ever achieving closure. The brief review offered here exemplifies the differential importance attached to internal and external variables under different approaches and underscores the need to look at both individually as well as at their interaction.

Finally, there are a number of key issues and terms that the reader should be familiar with and that are discussed in depth in the rest of the chapters. First is input, an external variable and an absolute requirement for acquisition. What are the mechanisms that facilitate comprehension of input? Does comprehended input lead to acquisition? Early research followed by studies conducted under Long's interaction hypothesis attempt to provide answers to these questions. But is comprehensible input sufficient? It might be that adults need more. Most empirical studies on the effects of explicit evidence show that explicit input provided before or during exposure enhances language development. Thus this kind of input becomes relevant for language acquisition. However, given the existence of limitations within this line of research and certain counterevidence, the field should now direct its attention to the nature of the practice—especially input and task characteristics—that may well interact with explicit input and account for the contradictory results discussed above. The implications of these issues for language pedagogy are obvious.

Other issues that the reader should be familiar with relate to internal variables. What are the cognitive abilities that make L2 acquisition and use possible? How much of L2 learning is universal, how much is individual, and what is behind IDs? How do these IDs interact with instruction? SLA research has focused more on universals than on IDs and more on the effects of IDs on outcomes than on processes. IDs are now being approached differently. Methodologically, the tools provided by neurolinguistics, such as ERPs and fMRIs, are helping make fine-grained distinctions not possible before. Also, large-scale constructs such as aptitude are being broken down into smaller ones (e.g., working memory) that are easier to operationalize. The importance of working memory has increased with the current emphasis on attention as a key factor determining acquisition. Most pedagogical research relies on the concept of attention to explain its effects. Another important ID, the sex of the learner, is also worthy of further consideration. A new view of the role of sex is proposed that links hormonal differences with changes in brain structure and specific types of memory (see Bowden, Sanz and Stafford, chapter 4; and Ullman, chapter 5).

A further ID, previous language experience (bilingualism) makes for experienced language learners and leads to improved acquisition of subsequent languages. Following Sanz (2000), it is posited that experience shapes the way in which new incoming information is processed and that experienced language learners naturally pay attention to key surface features in the input, very much like what pedagogical techniques under focus on form attempt to induce. Finally, age, the variable that differentiates adult from child language acquisition, is of decided import. The research does not agree on whether there is a critical period or a sensitive period, or on the possible reasons for these periods—access to universal grammar, changes in mental and neurological mechanisms, or even changes in external factors such as amount of input. As with most topics in SLA, much more needs to be accomplished before we can reach any conclusions about these and other issues related to the learning of nonprimary languages by adults. This volume will, however, present research related to each of these issues and draw informed initial conclusions based on the research that has been conducted thus far.

Further Reading

Carroll, S. E. (2000). *Input and evidence: The raw material of second language acquisition.* Amsterdam: John Benjamins.

Doughty, C., & Long, M. H. (Eds.) (2003). *The handbook of second language acquisition.* Oxford, UK: Blackwell.

Mitchell, R., & Myles, F. (1998). *Second language learning theories.* London: Edward Arnold.

References

Anderson, J. R. (1983). *The architecture of cognition.* Cambridge, MA: Harvard University Press.

Brown, R. (1973). *A first language.* Cambridge, MA: Harvard University Press.

Burt, M., Dulay, H., & Hernández-Chávez, E. (1975). *Bilingual syntax measure.* New York: Harcourt Brace Jovanovich.

Carroll, J. B., & Sapon, S. M. (1959). *Modern language aptitude test.* New York: Psychological Corporation.

Chaudron, C. (1988). *Second language classrooms: Research on teaching and learning.* Cambridge, UK: Cambridge University Press.

Chomsky, N. (1965). *Aspects of the theory of syntax.* Cambridge, MA: MIT Press.

Doughty, C. (2001). Cognitive underpinnings of focus on form. In P. Robinson (Ed.), *Cognition and second language instruction* (pp. 206–257). Cambridge, UK: Cambridge University Press.

Doughty, C. (2003). Instructed SLA: Constraints, compensation, and enhancement. In C. Doughty & M. H. Long (Eds.), *The handbook of second language acquisition* (pp. 256–310). Oxford, UK: Blackwell.

Doughty, C., & Long, M. H. (Eds.) (2003). *The handbook of second language acquisition.* Oxford, UK: Blackwell.

Ellis, N. C. (1994). *Implicit and explicit learning of languages.* New York: Academic Press.

Eubank, L. (1996). Negation in early German-English IL: More valueless features in the L2 initial state. *Second Language Research, 12,* 73–106.

Gardner, R. C. (1985). *Social psychology and second language learning: The roles of attitude and motivation.* London: Edward Arnold.

Gass, S. M. (2003). Input and interaction. In C. Doughty & M. H. Long (Eds.), *The handbook of second language acquisition* (pp. 224–255). Oxford, UK: Blackwell.

Hulstijn, J. H. (1997). Second language acquisition research in the laboratory: possibilities and limitations. *Studies in Second Language Acquisition, 19*(2), 131–143.

Krashen, S. D. (1985). *The input hypothesis: Issues and implications.* London: Longman.

Labov, W. (1972). *Sociolinguistic patterns.* Philadelphia: University of Pennsylvania Press.

Lenneberg, E. (1967). *Biological foundations of language.* New York: John Wiley.

Long, M. H. (1983). Does second language instruction make a difference? A review of research. *TESOL Quarterly, 17*(3), 359–382.

Long, M. H. (1996). The role of the linguistic environment in second language acquisition. In W. C. Ritchie & T. K. Bhatia (Eds.), *Handbook of second language acquisition. Vol. 2. Second language acquisition* (pp. 413–468). New York: Academic Press.

McLaughlin, B. (1987). *Theories of second language learning.* London: Edward Arnold.

Meisel, J., Clahsen, H., & Pienemann, M. (1981). On determining developmental stages in natural second language acquisition. *Studies in Second Language Acquisition, 3*(1), 109–135.

Norris, J. M., & Ortega, L. (2000). Effectiveness of L2 instruction: A research synthesis and quantitative meta-analysis. *Language Learning, 50*(3), 417–528.

Paradis, M. (1994). Neurolinguistic aspects of implicit and explicit memory: Implications for bilingualism and SLA. In N. C. Ellis (Ed.), *Implicit and explicit learning of languages* (pp. 393–419). New York: Academic Press.

Pienemann, M. (1984). Psychological constraints on the teachability of languages. *Studies in Second Language Acquisition, 6*(2), 186–214.

Preston, D. R. (1989) *Sociolinguistics and second language acquisition.* Oxford, UK: Blackwell.

Robinson, P. (1995). Attention, memory and the 'noticing' hypothesis. *Language Learning, 45,* 283–331.

Sanz, C. (2000) Bilingual education enhances third language acquisition: Evidence from Catalonia. *Applied Psycholinguistics, 21:* 23–44.

Sanz, C., & Morgan-Short, K. (2004). Positive evidence versus explicit rule presentation and explicit negative feedback: A computer-assisted study. *Language Learning, 54*(1), 35–78.

Schmidt, R. (2001). Attention. In P. Robinson (Ed.), *Cognition and second language instruction* (pp. 3–32). Cambridge, UK: Cambridge University Press.

Schmidt, R. W. (1990). The role of consciousness in second language learning. *Applied Linguistics, 11,* 129–158.

Schwartz, B. D. (1993). On explicit and negative data effecting and affecting competence and 'linguistic behavior.' *Studies in Second language Acquisition, 15,* 147–163.

Schwartz, B. D., & Sprouse, R. (1996). L2 cognitive states and the full transfer/full access model. *Second Language Research, 12,* 40–72.

Skinner, B. (1957). *Verbal behavior.* New York: Appleton-Century-Crofts.

Swain, M. & Lapkin, S. (1982). *Evaluating bilingual education: A Canadian case study.* Clevedon, UK: Multilingual Matters.

Tarone, E. (1988). *Variation in interlanguage.* London: Edward Arnold.

Tomlin, R. S., & Villa, V. (1994). Attention in cognitive science and second language acquisition. *Studies in Second Language Acquisition, 16,* 183–203.

Vainikka, A., & Young-Scholten, M. (1996). Gradual development of L2 phrase structure. *Second Language Research, 12,* 7–39.

VanPatten, B. (1990). Attending to form and content in the input: An experiment in consciousness. *Studies in Second Language Acquisition, 12,* 287–301.

VanPatten, B. (1996). *Input processing and grammar instruction in second language acquisition.* Norwood, NJ: Ablex.

VanPatten, B. (2004). *Processing instruction: Theory, research, and commentary.* Mahwah, NJ: Lawrence Erlbaum.

White, L. (1989). *Universal Grammar and second language acquisition.* Amsterdam: John Benjamins.

White, L. (1991). Adverb placement in second language acquisition: Some effects of positive and negative evidence in the classroom. *Second Language Research, 7,* 133–161.

Young, R. (1991). *Variation in interlanguage morphology.* New York: Peter Lang.

TWO

Research Methodology: Quantitative Approaches

RUSAN CHEN

KEY WORDS

Chi-square test of independence ▪ correlation coefficient ▪ factorial ANOVA ▪ goodness-of-fit test ▪ hypothesis testing ▪ independent-samples *t* test ▪ multiple regression ▪ normal distribution ▪ one-sample *t* test ▪ one-way ANOVA ▪ paired-samples *t* test ▪ repeated-measures ANOVA ▪ simple regression.

1. Introduction

A typical quantitative study includes quantification of constructs related to a research interest, data collection through experimental or nonexperimental designs, statistical data analysis, and presentation of findings related to research hypotheses. This chapter introduces commonly applied statistical procedures, with the logic of hypothesis testing as the major focus of the chapter. Hypothesis testing has traditionally been the main statistical tool used by practitioners and is still widely used by researchers in many areas, including second language acquisition (SLA).

This chapter introduces statistical procedures typically covered in a one-semester introductory statistics course. It starts with an introduction of the basic concepts of statistics that serve as prerequisites to understanding the logic of statistical hypothesis testing. These concepts will be presented within contexts relevant to SLA research to facilitate SLA students' understanding of inferential statistics. The logic of hypothesis testing will be addressed through a procedure summarized in three simple steps without mathematical derivations. This procedure will be illustrated with all statistical tests presented in subsequent sections of the chapter.

The commonly used *t* tests, including the one-sample *t* test, the paired-samples *t* test, and the independent-samples *t* test, will be introduced with numerical examples in section 3. Analysis of variance (ANOVA), including the one-way ANOVA, the factorial ANOVA, and the repeated-measures

ANOVA, will be introduced in section 4. Since SLA researchers frequently use the repeated-measures ANOVA with pretest, posttest, and possible delayed tests to compare different groups, this type of design will be addressed with more detail relative to other ANOVA tests.

Section 5 is devoted to linear correlation and regression procedures, the methods investigating the relationships among variables. Simple regression is presented first and will provide the basis for the subsequent presentation of multiple regression, including stepwise and hierarchical regressions. Section 6 deals with the goodness-of-fit chi-square test and the chi-square test for independence. Chi-square tests are often used when the data are categorical.

After learning the statistical procedures introduced in this chapter, the reader may need a guide to selecting the appropriate test for a specific research topic. As a summary of this chapter, guidelines for choosing an appropriate test based on measurement scales are presented in section 7.

Due to space limitations, the introduction to each statistical procedure is kept as concise as possible, with an emphasis on conceptual understanding rather than formula derivations. In addition, some important issues, such as violation of assumptions, nonparametric tests, and power analysis for study designs, are not included in this chapter. Readers who wish to learn more about these important topics may refer to the list for further readings provided at the end of the chapter.

All examples and exercises in this chapter were taken from studies recently published in SLA journals. However, the numerical data used as examples and for exercises were generated by simulation for illustrative purposes, in most cases using the means and the standard deviations presented in published articles. The SPSS (SPSS Inc. 2003, version 11.5) statistics package was used for analyzing data and presenting findings.

2. Statistics Basics and the Logic of Hypothesis Testing

Most universities offer statistics courses at various levels, especially in graduate programs. Why is statistics such a popular tool that researchers in different disciplines all find it useful in their professional careers? One of the answers is that statistical procedures allow researchers to generalize the findings from their samples to the population. Researchers conducting empirical studies usually collect data from samples, but the research interests are always in the population. Using statistical procedures based on the logic of hypothesis testing, we are able to generalize the findings from the samples to the population of interest. Researchers also use statistics to summarize, present, and communicate their research findings. In this section some basic statistical concepts are introduced within the following setting.

Limited English Proficiency (LEP) is a legal term for students who are not native speakers of English and who often have trouble participating in regular classroom activities because of difficulties in speaking, understanding, reading, and writing English. According to one estimate, there are more than 3.4 million LEP students attending U.S. schools (Macias, 1998). Compared with their Fluent English Proficiency (FEP) peers, LEP students have disadvantages in academic achievement because they have to master both the content of a subject area and the language used in classrooms. Administrators and teachers nationwide face great challenges in designing effective classroom teaching strategies to help LEP students.

Klingner and Vaughn (2000) developed a classroom instructional approach called *collaborative strategic reading* (CSR) to help LEP students improve their reading comprehension in English as well as learn the content-area knowledge. During CSR, the LEP students worked with their bilingual and FEP peers in small, cooperative groups to assist each other while applying instructed reading strategies to facilitate comprehension. One advantage to this approach was that when the LEP students had difficulty with English vocabulary, peers would assist with their shared native language (L1, which was Spanish in this study). Klingner and Vaughn (2000) found that LEP students' English vocabulary improved significantly using the CSR approach.

2.1. BASIC CONCEPTS

The researchers conducting this study were interested in showing that the CSR approach was more effective than the traditional approach used by elementary schools with LEP students. The population for this study may be defined as all students in U.S. elementary schools that enroll LEP students. However, it is almost impossible for researchers to collect data from an entire population, so Klingner and Vaughn conducted the study using a sample of 37 fifth-grade students in an elementary school. To make statements concerning the population, the researchers needed to use a valid procedure to generalize the findings from the sample to the population.

A numeric summary obtained from a sample is called a statistic. Assuming that 72% of the 37 students were LEP students, the number 72% is a statistic because it was obtained from the sample. A numeric summary that concerns a population is called a parameter. Using the above example, the percentage of LEP students in U.S. elementary schools is a parameter. In most cases, parameters are unknown and need to be estimated from statistics.

One assessment in this study was a vocabulary definition test in which the students were required to define a set of English words. Each child took the test before and after a CSR session. The researchers were interested in examining whether the average of the posttest was higher than that of the pretest. This design had two variables: pretest and posttest. A variable is defined as the property of an event that may have different values. Taking the variable pretest as an example, the 37 students may have different scores on the pretest due to their different knowledge of English vocabulary. Variables can be either numeric or nonnumeric. In this study, both pre- and posttest are numeric variables, so that arithmetic calculations can be carried out on these variables. For nonnumeric variables, such as gender, L1, and learning strategies used by second language (L2) students, frequency tables can be used to present the number of raw occurrences and the percentages of the occurrences. For example, if the variable LEP indicates the status of students in the sample with *yes* indicating a LEP student and *no* indicating a non-LEP student, the variable LEP is a nonnumeric variable. The occurrences and percentages of the LEP students can be obtained from the sample.

In general, variability exists among individuals and within an individual over time. Descriptive statistics summarize and present such variability. Important summary statistics include mean, median, mode, variance, and standard deviation. Mean, median, and mode measure the central tendency of a variable, while variance and standard deviation summarize how much the data are spread out. The concepts and calculations for mean, median, mode, variance, and standard deviation are illustrated using the following numerical example. Suppose that we replicated Klingner and Vaughn's (2000) study and obtained a sample of 10 students with scores on the pretest and posttest as presented in Table 2.1.

The mean is the average from the scores. The formula calculating the sample mean is $\overline{X} = \Sigma X/N$, where X represents the original scores and N is the sample size. For the pretest in our example, $\overline{X} = (18 + 34 + 19 + 22 + 15 + 28 + 10 + 21 + 16 + 20)/10 = 20.3$. Likewise, we can calculate the mean for the posttest as 25.

The median is the score that lies in the middle if the data are arranged in an increasing or decreasing order. For example, we may arrange the data for the pretest in an increasing order: 10, 15, 16, 18, 19, 20, 21, 22, 28 and 34. The middle score lies between 19 and 20. Therefore, the median for the pretest is

TABLE 2.1
Simulated Scores on the Vocabulary Definition Test for the 10 Students

Student	*1*	*2*	*3*	*4*	*5*	*6*	*7*	*8*	*9*	*10*
Pretest	18	34	19	22	15	28	10	21	16	20
Posttest	23	31	19	28	21	36	20	24	26	28

(19 + 20)/2 = 19.5. Using same method, we find that the median for the posttest is (24 + 26)/2 = 25. When sample size N is an odd number, the median is the actual score in the middle.

The mode is the score with the highest frequency in the data. In the posttest data, we have two scores equaling 28 and all other scores appear only once. The score 28 has the highest frequency, and therefore the mode for the posttest is 28. In the pretest, all scores appear only once. Since no score has the highest frequency in the pretest, no mode exists.

The formula for obtaining the variance of a variable is $\Sigma (X - \bar{X})^2/(N - 1)$. For the pretest, $\bar{X}$ is 20.3. We can calculate the variance for the sample: $((18 - 20.3)^2 + (34 - 20.3)^2 + \ldots + (20 - 20.3)^2)/(10 - 1) = 45.57$. The standard deviation is the square root of the variance. For the pretest, the standard deviation is $\sqrt{45.57} = 6.75$. In published literature, the standard deviation is often reported along with the mean to indicate how much the data deviated from the central point. As an exercise, the reader may verify that the variance and standard deviation for the posttest are 28.27 and 5.32, respectively.

The statistical procedures introduced in this chapter belong to the area of inferential statistics. Inferential statistics allow researchers to generalize their findings from a sample to a population through the process of hypothesis testing. For example, if CSR is found to be more effective than the traditional classroom approach for the 37 students in the sample, can the researchers confidently infer that CSR is more effective for classes with LEP students in all U.S. elementary schools? Inferential statistics play an important role in this decision-making process.

Researchers may design a study to examine the effectiveness of CSR between students in classes using CSR and students in traditional classes. To start with, they should randomly select two classes in the same elementary school and implement CSR in one of the classes. To show the effectiveness of CSR, the two selected classes should be as similar as possible at the outset of the study. For example, it is better for the two classes to be chosen from the same grade, to be similar in class size, and to have similar percentages of LEP students. The logic here is that since the students in the two classes are similar at the beginning of the experiment, if the students in the CSR class score higher on the vocabulary test at the end of the semester than the students in the traditional class, it can be assumed that the CSR method is relatively more effective than the traditional method.

An independent variable is the factor that the experimenter can manipulate or arrange. In our example, the instructional method (CSR vs. the traditional method) is the independent variable because the experimenter has arranged the two teaching methods for comparison. On the other hand, the values of a dependent variable cannot be arranged by the experimenter but only obtained from the participants. In our example, the scores on the vocabulary test for the students are the values of the dependent variable.

2.2. MEASUREMENT SCALES

Researchers conducting quantitative studies often ask the question, "What statistical test should I use for this particular research topic?" Understanding the measurement scales underlying the variables will help the researcher to select the appropriate statistical tests. The issue of choosing correct tests is addressed in detail in section 7 as a summary to this chapter.

Nominal scales name values for a variable without indicating any order or hierarchy for those values. A nominal scale is a name system in nature. Variables with nominal scales are also called categorical variables. Examples of categorical variables are gender (male vs. female), treatment groups (CSR vs. teacher-directed), learning strategies for vocabulary acquisition (keyword, semantic, and keyword-semantic), and types of L1 languages (English, Japanese, and Korean). When a variable with nominal scale has only two categories, such as native speakers versus nonnative speakers, it is called a dichotomous variable. Numbers are sometimes used to indicate categories, such as 1 meaning *male* and 2 *female.* In such cases, the numbers are just names for the categories without implying that 2 is greater than or superior to 1.

As the name suggests, an ordinal scale assigns ordering or ranking for the values of a variable, but the differences between the values may not have the same interval. Examples of ordinal variables include language proficiency levels (high, intermediate, and low), the Likert-type scale with choices ranging from *strongly disagree* to *strongly agree,* and education status (high school, college, and graduate). Notice that the difference, for example, between high and intermediate language proficiency levels is not necessarily the same as the difference between intermediate and low proficiency levels.

Interval scales not only give ordering for the objects but also assume equality between scale values. Listening comprehension ability indicated by the number of multiple-choice items answered correctly is an example of an interval scale. In this example, if three students took the listening comprehension test and received scores of 10, 20, and 30, we can say that the difference in comprehension ability between the first and the second students is the same as that between the second and the third students. One characteristic of an interval scale is that a value of zero on the scale does not indicate nothing. For example, a score of zero on the listening comprehension test would not imply that the student had absolutely no ability in listening comprehension.

Ratio scales have all the characteristics of ordinal scales, with an additional requirement that a zero value on the scale indicates truly nothing. Examples of ratio scales include the number of years a learner has studied an L2, the number of new words introduced during one learning session, and the response time in milliseconds to a new stimuli.

It should be noted that a nominal scale is not strictly speaking a measurement scale; it is no more than a naming system, and in this sense it is inherently different in nature from the other three scales. Sometimes when we say that a variable is on a measurement scale, we just mean that it is a numerical variable on an ordinal, interval, or ratio scale.

2.3. INTRODUCTION TO HYPOTHESIS TESTING

Hypothesis testing is a decision-making process to determine whether the findings from a sample can be generalized to a population. Hypothesis testing is the central theme for the statistical procedures introduced in this chapter. The logic of hypothesis testing is based on the distribution of statistics. Imagine that we draw samples again and again from the same population and calculate the statistics from each sample. The distribution of all of the statistics relates the characteristics of the sample to those of the population. In a very simplified version of the process, hypothesis testing involves three steps:

- Step 1: State a null hypothesis concerning the population under investigation.
- Step 2: Find out the probability that the null hypothesis is true.
- Step 3: If the probability is low, say, less than 5% (or 1%), the null hypothesis is rejected. Otherwise, the null hypothesis is retained.

In the first step of hypothesis testing a null hypothesis is stated. The null hypothesis may not be the same as the research interest. Researchers usually make statements for their research interests according to the results they expect to find. For example, research interests are often stated positively: Students of English as a second language (ESL) who have received training using the keyword method will perform better on a vocabulary definition test than students who have not received such training. Null hypotheses are always statements that imply null expectations, such as no difference for the comparisons or no relationships among the variables in the population. For the research interest mentioned above, the null hypothesis would be that there is no difference in scores on vocabulary definition tests for students with and without keyword training in the population. Please note that null hypotheses always concern the population, not the sample.

How do we find out the probability that the null hypothesis is true in the second step of hypothesis testing? The probability can be calculated from known theoretical functions. Imagine that we draw random samples (with the same sample size) again and again from a population where the null hypothesis is true and calculate the statistics from each sample. The statistics will be distributed as the normal distribution, a known function from which we are able to obtain the probability that the null hypothesis is true. Numerical calculations for obtaining the probability from a theoretical distribution can be cumbersome, but you can find the probability from tables in most statistics textbooks or from a statistical package such as SPSS. The probability that a null hypothesis is true is often called the *p* value of the test. In this chapter, methods for obtaining the *p* value from a table and from SPSS output will be illustrated.

The third step in hypothesis testing is a decision-making step. Assume that the *p* value you obtained from a particular study is less than 0.05. Now consider the following fact: If the null hypothesis were true in the population and you had enough resources to repeat the same study 100 times using different samples (with the same sample size) from the population, only five or fewer studies would be likely to have a *p* value less than 0.05. Since you already have a sample with a *p* value less than 0.05, the null hypothesis is not likely to be true in the population. Therefore if a *p* value is less than 0.05, we make a decision that the null hypothesis is rejected. In most cases, the rejection of a null hypothesis confirms the research interest.

When the *p* value is greater than 0.05, the null hypothesis is retained. Retaining a null hypothesis indicates that based on the information from the available data, the null hypothesis cannot be declared as false. The case is inconclusive because we cannot make a decision about the null hypothesis based on the information we have.

There are several commonly used terms related to the hypothesis-testing procedure that warrant discussion. A type I error is made if you reject a true null hypothesis. For example, assume that the CSR method used in classrooms with LEP students in general does not improve performance compared with the traditional instructional method. If you draw a conclusion that CSR is significantly more effective than the traditional method, you make a type I error. The probability of making a type I error is denoted as α (alpha), which is conventionally set at the 0.05 or 0.01 level. These are the levels at which the researcher is willing to take the risk of making a type I error. You make a type II error when you retain a false null hypothesis. For example, if the CSR method is truly more effective in general but you conclude that there is no difference, you make a type II error. The probability of making a type II error is called β (beta).

Let's use a hypothetical study to illustrate the three steps of hypothesis testing. Assume that the average total scaled score for the TOEFL test for students admitted to U.S. graduate programs from the year 2000 to 2001 is 620, with a standard deviation of 50.[1] A TOEFL training school in China claims that anyone who takes its three-month program is guaranteed to meet the TOEFL scores required for U.S. graduate schools. A student who attended the training school took the TOEFL and reported that her total scaled score was 560. In this hypothetical study, the research interest is to evaluate the school's assertion that anyone who attends the training program will meet the TOEFL requirements of graduate programs in the U.S. Although the sample size in this study is very small (only one student), we can still conduct legitimate hypothesis testing.

The first step in hypothesis testing is to state a null hypothesis. In our hypothetical study, the null hypothesis is that students who complete the three-month TOEFL training program are not different from the students admitted into U.S. graduate programs. Please note that null hypotheses always make statements concerning populations, not samples. We have two populations in this study: all students who were admitted into U.S. graduate programs in 2000 to 2001 and all students who completed the three-month TOEFL training program. The null hypothesis states that the two populations are not different in TOEFL scaled scores.

The second step in hypothesis testing is to find out the probability that the null hypothesis is true. We have only one subject available who had a total scaled score of 560. We also know that the mean for TOEFL scaled scores for U.S. graduate programs is 620 with a standard deviation of 50. Based on this information, we can calculate a *z* score (also called standardized score) for the student. Using the formula $z = (\mu - X)/\sigma$, where μ is the population mean and σ the population standard deviation, the *z* score for this student is $(620 - 560)/50 = 1.20$. From a *z* table that most statistics textbooks provide in the appendix, we find that a *z* score of 1.20 has a corresponding *p* value of 0.115. The interpretation of *p* equaling 0.115 is that if the null hypothesis is true, the probability of obtaining a score of 560 or less after completing the training program is 0.115.

With the *p* value known, we are ready to proceed to the third step of hypothesis testing, to make a decision about the null hypothesis. Since the *p* value is greater than 0.05, we are not able to reject the null hypothesis. The null hypothesis is then retained. As discussed previously, a *p* value greater than 0.05 is inconclusive, indicating that we do not have enough information to conclude that the two populations are different in their TOEFL scores. Had the *p* value been less than 0.05, we would have rejected the null hypothesis with a conclusion that students who completed the three-month training program were different from the students admitted to graduate programs in the United States. Because the score 560 is lower than the population mean of 620, we may further conclude that students who completed the program are significantly lower in TOEFL scores than the students admitted to the graduate program in the United States.

In the following sections, we will introduce the statistical procedures most commonly used by SLA researchers, including *t* tests, *F* tests, and chi-square tests. Although the tests are applied to different research topics, the logic of hypothesis testing is the same for all tests: State a null hypothesis first, find out the *p* value, and then make a decision based on the *p* value to reject or retain the null hypothesis.

3. The *t* Tests Applied to Means

In the previous section, we learned that for testing a null hypothesis, we need to find out the *p* value, the probability that the null hypothesis is true. When the *p* value is obtained from the *t* distribution, we call it a *t* test. Three *t* tests are introduced in this section for comparing the means in populations. The one-sample *t* test compares the mean of one population to a particular known value. The paired-samples *t* test tests the null hypothesis that the mean of the difference from two related populations is zero. The independent-samples *t* test is used to compare the means of two independent populations.

3.1. THE ONE-SAMPLE *t* TEST

The hypothetical study about TOEFL scores in the previous section had one unusual characteristic: The standard deviation of the TOEFL scores in the population was known. We knew the parameter because the Educational Testing Service reports TOEFL test summaries on an annual basis. However, in most circumstances the population standard deviation is never known, and it has to be estimated from the sample standard deviation. In such cases, the *p* value should be obtained from a *t* table instead of from a *z* table as we did in the previous example.

Assume that 10 students completed the three-month training program and took the TOEFL test. The mean of the total scaled score for the 10 students is 560 with a standard deviation of 30. The null hypothesis of interest for this study is the same as that in the previous case: students who completed the three-month training program are not different from students admitted to U.S. graduate programs in their TOEFL scores. In this study, we will use the one-sample *t* test because we have one sample ($N = 10$) and the standard deviation for the population of students who completed the program has to be estimated from the sample standard deviation. We wish to test if the mean of the population is different from a particular value, 620 in this study.

After stating the null hypothesis, we need to obtain the *p* value to determine the probability that the null hypothesis is true. To obtain the *p* value, we need to calculate the *t* value first, and then look for the *p* value from a *t* table. The formula to calculate the *t* value is given in (1):

$$(1) \quad t = \frac{\overline{X} - \mu}{s/\sqrt{N}}$$

Here, $\overline{X}$ is the sample mean, *N* the sample size, *s* the sample standard deviation, and μ the population mean, the specific value to test. In our example, $t = (560 - 620)/(45/\sqrt{5}) = -2.98$.

To obtain the *p* value from a known *t* value, we also need to know the degrees of freedom, abbreviated *df*, for a particular *t* test. For the one-sample *t* test, $df = N - 1 = 10 - 1 = 9$. A typical *t* table would look like the one presented in Table 2.2. If the absolute value of the obtained *t* value is greater than the value listed in the *t* table, the null hypothesis is rejected at the corresponding α level. The values in a *t* table are called critical values.

In this study, the obtained *t* value is −2.98 with *df* at 9. From Table 2.2, we can find the critical value 2.262 at the cross of the row with *df* at 9 and the column with the heading of α equaling 0.05. Since the absolute value of the obtained *t* value is $|-2.98| = 2.98$, and it is greater than the critical value of 2.262, the null hypothesis is rejected at α equaling the 0.05 level. We conclude that the students who completed the three-month program are not the same as the students admitted into U.S. graduate programs in terms of their TOEFL scores. Since the obtained sample mean is 560, which is less than 620, we further conclude that students who completed the three-month program had lower TOEFL scores than students admitted into U.S. graduate programs.

One issue related to the use of a *t* table is the choice of a two-tailed test versus a one-tailed test. This choice should be based on the specific null hypothesis to

TABLE 2.2
Critical Values for the *t* Distribution

df	*.30*	*.20*	*.10*	*.05*	*.02*
3	1.250	1.638	2.352	3.182	4.541
4	1.190	1.533	2.132	2.776	3.747
9	1.100	1.383	1.833	2.262	2.821
10	1.093	1.372	1.812	2.228	2.764
11	1.088	1.363	1.796	2.201	2.718
12	1.083	1.356	1.782	2.179	2.681
18	1.067	1.330	1.734	2.101	2.552
19	1.064	1.328	1.729	2.093	2.539

be tested. In our hypothetical study, the null hypothesis (that the population mean is not different from 620) is nondirectional because we do not state that the mean is either greater or less than 620. Upon the rejection of the null hypothesis, we accept the alternative hypothesis that the population mean *is* different from 620. A one-tailed test is used only when the outcome is absolutely one directional. In our study, the sample mean 560 is less than 620, the value of interest to test. But for another sample, the sample mean could be higher than 620. Therefore, a two-tailed test is an appropriate choice. It should be noted that the issue of one-tailed test versus two-tailed test is only relevant to *t* tests and the *z* test. The *F* tests and chi-square tests introduced later in this chapter are always two-tailed tests.

3.2. THE PAIRED-SAMPLES *t* TEST

In the previous section, we introduced the one-sample *t* test for situations in which only one population is of interest. Quite often we wish to compare the mean difference in two sets of scores. When the two sets of scores are obtained from the same group of people, such as from a pretest and a posttest, we use the paired-samples *t* test. If the two sets of scores are taken from two different groups of individuals, such as native speakers and nonnative speakers, we use the independent-samples *t* test.

The paired-samples *t* test applies to situations in which each participant contributes two test scores and the participants are considered to belong to the same group. A common scenario in SLA research is a group of participants with a pre- and a posttest and a treatment or intervention between the two tests. The research interest is to examine whether the treatment has any effect. The null hypothesis tested by the paired-samples *t* test is that there is no difference between the pretest and the posttest scores in the population. To test this, we first calculate the difference between the pre- and the posttest scores for each participant. Then we test the null hypothesis that the mean of the difference score is zero in the population. This null hypothesis is similar to the one tested using the one-sample *t* test previously discussed. What follows is an example of a published study that used the paired-samples *t* test.

One advantage of learning an L2 is understanding and learning another culture. The desire to know a target culture is likely to promote the learning of an L2. Bateman (2002) was interested in evaluating whether students of Spanish who conducted ethnographic interviews would become more open to learning culture. Thirty-five college students in second-year Spanish classes conducted ethnographic interviews of native Spanish speakers during the semester. In an ethnographic interview, the interviewer does not have preplanned questions. The goal of the interview is to determine what cultural

TABLE 2.3
Attitude Scores on the Pretest and the Posttest for the 10 Subjects

Subjects	*1*	*2*	*3*	*4*	*5*	*6*	*7*	*8*	*9*	*10*
Pretest	34	28	36	42	35	37	41	23	42	28
Posttest	37	35	34	44	42	40	40	33	45	35
Difference	03	07	–2	02	07	03	–1	10	03	07

categories are maintained by the interviewee. Two tests consisting of Likert-type questionnaires measuring students' attitudes toward Spanish and Spanish speakers were conducted at the beginning and at the end of the semester. It was expected that the mean of the posttest would be significantly higher than the mean for the pretest.

In this study, each participant contributed two scores, one on the pretest and another on the posttest; therefore, the paired-samples *t* test was the appropriate procedure to apply. To illustrate the use of the paired-samples *t* test with a numerical example, assume we replicated the same study with 10 participants. The attitude test consisted of 10 questions with higher scores indicating more positive attitudes toward Spanish culture and Spanish people. The scores on the pretest and the posttest for the 10 subjects are presented in Table 2.3.

By eyeballing the difference scores, we can see that 8 out of 10 subjects had positive scores, indicating that most of the students had more positive attitudes toward Spanish culture at the end of the semester. To generalize the results to the population, we need to undertake hypothesis testing. The null hypothesis can be stated in terms of the difference scores: The mean of the difference scores is not different from zero in the population. By using the difference scores, the paired-samples *t* test is equivalent to the one-sample *t* test with the null hypothesis stating that the population mean is not different from zero. To find out the probability that the null hypothesis is true, we can use the same formula used for the one-sample *t* test to calculate the *t* value. Since $\bar{X} = 3.9$, $s = 3.81$ and $N = 10$, $t = 3.9/(3.81/\sqrt{10}) = 3.23$, with $df = N - 1 = 10 - 1 = 9$. From Table 2.2, we find that the critical value for *df* equaling 9 and α equaling 0.05 for a two-tailed test is 2.262. Since the observed *t* value is 3.23, which is greater than the critical value, we obtain $p < 0.05$. The null hypothesis is rejected. From the fact that the mean of the difference score equals 3.9, which is greater than 0, we conclude that the students' attitudes toward the Spanish culture and Spanish people were significantly more positive at the end of the semester, and that this, in turn, may have been due to the ethnographic interviews conducted during the semester.

3.3. THE INDEPENDENT-SAMPLES *t* TEST

One frequently encountered design in SLA research is a comparison of the performance between an experimental group and a control group to evaluate the effectiveness of a certain treatment. For example, Arnold (2000) examined whether visualization would reduce anxiety in L2 listening comprehension. Leow (2000) tested the effects of awareness on L2 learners' subsequent intake and written production. Mackey (1999) examined whether conversational interaction would facilitate L2 development. A common research interest in these studies was to evaluate whether language learners who received a certain treatment were different from those who did not undergo the treatment. The independent-samples *t* test is appropriate in such research designs with two groups of participants and each participant contributing one score in the test. Hayasa's (2002) study will be used to illustrate the application of the independent-samples *t* test.

Hayasa (2002) investigated whether a time lag in teaching Japanese scripts would make a difference for early learners of Japanese as a second language. The theory behind the delayed introduction of Japanese scripts is that beginners will concentrate on the development of oral-aural skills first (using the Roman alphabet) and then learn the Japanese scripts. But supporters of the early introduction of Japanese scripts maintain that Japanese scripts (hiragana and katakana, but not kanji) represent basic phonological units in Japanese, and therefore an early introduction of the scripts will give learners more time to familiarize themselves with basic Japanese components.

The participants in Hayasa's (2002) study were native English speakers who were randomly assigned to two groups, an experimental (lag) group ($N = 33$) and a control group ($N = 19$). In the experimental group, there was an eight-week delay in the introduction of Japanese scripts. The dependent variables included speaking, pronunciation, grammar, and reading comprehension measured at the end of the first semester. To illustrate the use of the independent-samples *t* test with a numerical example, let us assume we have replicated the same study with 10 participants in each group and the reading comprehension test is the dependent variable for comparison. Simulated reading comprehension scores for the two groups are presented in Table 2.4.

TABLE 2.4
Reading Comprehension Scores for the Lag and Control Groups

Students	*1*	*2*	*3*	*4*	*5*	*6*	*7*	*8*	*9*	*10*
Lag Group	37	35	34	44	42	40	40	33	45	35
Control Group	34	28	36	42	35	37	41	23	42	28

The null hypothesis for this test is that there will be no difference in reading comprehension scores at the end of the first semester for Japanese learners with delayed introduction of scripts and for those without delay. This can also be written as H_0: $\mu_1 = \mu_2$, where μ_1 and μ_2 are the population means for the comprehension scores for Japanese learners with and without delayed introduction of scripts, respectively. The alternative hypothesis is H_1: $\mu_1 \neq \mu_2$. The next step is to find out the probability that the null hypothesis is true. For the independent-samples *t* test, the formulae are as in (2) and (3):

(2) $$t = \frac{\overline{X}_1 - \overline{X}_2}{S_D}$$

$\overline{X}_1, \overline{X}_2$ = sample means for the two groups, S_D = sample standard deviation pooled from the two groups

(3) $$S_D = \sqrt{\left(\frac{1}{N_1} + \frac{1}{N_2}\right)\frac{(N_1 - 1)(S_1^2) + (N_2 - 1)(S_2^2)}{N_1 + N_2 - 2}}$$

N_1, N_2 = the sample sizes for experimental and control groups respectively; S_1, S_2 = standard deviations for the two groups.

Based on the scores in Table 2.4, we have $N_1 = N_2 = 10$, $\overline{X}_1 = 38.5$, $\overline{X}_2 = 34.5$, $S_1 = 4.3$, and $S_2 = 6.5$. Therefore, $S_D = 2.464$, and $t = (38.5 - 34.6)/2.464 = 1.58$. The degrees of freedom for the independent-samples *t* test is $N_1 + N_2 - 2 = 18$. From Table 2.2, we locate the critical value for a two-tailed *t* test with *df* at 18 is 2.10. Since the observed *t* value 1.58 is less than the critical value 2.10, we obtain $p > 0.05$ and retain the null hypothesis. From the data we collected, we cannot conclude that the delayed teaching of Japanese scripts will facilitate reading comprehension.

4. ANOVA Comparing Two or More Than Two Means

ANOVA stands for *analysis of variance.* ANOVAs are also called *F* tests because the *p* values from the ANOVAs are derived from theoretical *F* distributions. Like the *t* tests discussed in the previous section, ANOVA also compares population means. Unlike a *t* test, which compares only two means, the ANOVA compares two or more than two means. In situations where only two means are involved, the *p* value obtained from the ANOVA is exactly the same as that from a *t* test.

In one-way ANOVA, only one independent variable is involved. Factorial ANOVA deals with the effects of two or more than two independent variables and their interactive effects on the dependent variable. Factorial ANOVA with two independent variables is called a two-way ANOVA. SLA researchers often use repeated-measures ANOVA to compare pre-, post- and delayed test scores obtained from different groups.

4.1. ONE-WAY ANOVA

Brown and Perry (1991) compared the effectiveness of three learning strategies for ESL vocabulary acquisition: keyword, semantic, and keyword-semantic. Three groups of Arabic-speaking students received four days of training in each of the vocabulary learning strategies. The effects of the three strategies were measured one day after the treatment. The research interest was to examine whether the combined method was more effective for English vocabulary learning relative to the methods used separately.

Using the keyword strategy, learners choose a keyword that is acoustically similar to the word to be learned. The meaning of the keyword is independent of that of the new word. Learners make a visual association between the keyword and the new word. For example, to remember that *carlin* means 'an old woman,' the keyword could be *car* and the visual image could be an old woman driving a car. The semantic technique requires deeper processing of the meaning of the new word, especially building relationships between the meanings of new words with the learners' existing semantic systems. The combined method advocates that the best strategy for learning new English words is to have both visual and semantic connections.

One of the dependent variables to measure the learning effects for the three strategies is a test with 40 multiple-choice items, each designed for a new word. Suppose we replicated the experiment with 10 subjects in each of the three groups. After the three groups learned the 40 new words using different learning strategies, the multiple-choice test was administered. The scores for the three groups are presented in Table 2.5.

The major research interest in this study was to examine whether the combined method was more effective than the methods used separately. The null hypothesis corresponding to the research interest is that the three vocabulary learning strategies are not different in their effects on vocabulary learning for ESL students. To test this null hypothesis, we need to find out the p value. Detailed calculations for ANOVA can be found elsewhere (e.g., Howell, 1992), but we will rely on a statistical package for obtaining the p value to test this null hypothesis. Table 2.6 presents the SPSS output using the data in Table 2.5 showing that $F(2, 27) = 5.9, p = 0.007$. Since the p value is less than 0.05, the null hypothesis is rejected. We accept the alternative hypothesis that the three vocabulary learning methods are not the same in terms of their effectiveness. The significance of the ANOVA indicates that at least one of the three methods is significantly different from the others, but it is not clear which one it is. We

TABLE 2.5
Scores on the Multiple Choice Test for the Three Vocabulary Learning Groups

Students	*Keyword*	*Semantic*	*Combined*
1	18	20	29
2	19	22	22
3	13	25	20
4	21	15	20
5	22	25	31
6	9	6	26
7	17	13	36
8	9	18	40
9	30	18	17
10	12	24	25

need to conduct a post hoc test (e.g., the Scheffé Test, one of the post hoc tests offered by SPSS) to identify which specific method is significantly more effective than the others. We are especially interested in knowing if the combined method is significantly better than either of the two methods used separately.

The SPSS output from the Scheffé test for the hypothetical study is presented in Table 2.7. Since the mean for the combined method (26.60) is listed in a different column from the other two means and is greater than the other two means, this shows that the combined method is significantly more effective than the methods used separately, with p less than 0.05. The Scheffé test also indicates that the keyword and the semantic methods are not significantly different in their effectiveness for vocabulary learning because the two means are listed in the same column.

4.2. FACTORIAL ANOVA

The previous study using one-way ANOVA had one independent variable, the method of learning new words. Quite often it is more interesting to investigate the combined effects of two independent variables relevant to the

TABLE 2.6
SPSS Output for One-Way ANOVA Using the Data in Table 2.5

	Sum of Squares	df	*Mean Square*	F	*Significance*
Between Groups	529.067	2	264.533	5.909	0.007
Within Groups	1,208.800	27	44.770		
Total	1,737.867	29			

TABLE 2.7
SPSS Output from the Scheffé Test for Comparing Three Vocabulary Learning Methods

		Subset for alpha = .05	
Group	N	*1*	*2*
Keyword	10	17.00	
Semantic	10	18.60	
Combined	10		26.60

research interests. For example, we may extend the previous study by adding another independent variable, proficiency, with two levels, high and low. Previously, the research interest was to examine whether the combined vocabulary learning method was more effective than either of the methods used separately. By adding proficiency as a second independent variable, we are able to examine whether the effects of learning method are the same for students at different proficiency levels. Is it likely that the combined method is more effective only for students with high proficiency? An ANOVA with two independent variables is called a two-way ANOVA. In general, ANOVAs with two or more independent variables with all levels of the independent variables crossed are called factorial ANOVAs.

The number of the values that an independent variable has is also called the number of levels of the independent variable. In the previous example, the variable *method* had three levels since it had three values: keyword, semantic, and combined. The variable *proficiency* has two levels, high and low. This two-way ANOVA is called a 2×3 factorial ANOVA. A factorial ANOVA requires that each level of one independent variable cross with all levels of the other independent variables. In our example, this requirement means that for the three vocabulary learning groups, each group includes students at both high and low proficiency levels. It is also true that at both proficiency levels, students are divided into three learning groups. We now use a study reported by Oh (2001) as an example to illustrate the use of two-way ANOVA.

In teaching reading skills for ESL, the conventional wisdom is that using simplified texts is desirable for improving target language comprehension, especially for learners at low proficiency levels. However, some researchers have pointed out the disadvantages of using simplified texts (e.g., Yano, Long, and Ross, 1994; Honeyfield, 1977) and advocate the use of elaborated versions as teaching material for ESL learners at all proficiency levels.

Oh (2001) investigated the effects of two input modifications, simplification versus elaboration, on ESL reading comprehension abilities. In this study, Korean high school students were divided into high and low proficiency levels with each proficiency level further divided into two groups: One received simplified passages and the other received elaborated passages. After reading the passages, the students were required to answer 18 multiple-choice questions with the texts available for students to refer back to during the comprehension test.

There were two independent variables in this study: input modification with two levels (simplified vs. elaborated) and proficiency with two levels (high vs. low). The dependent variable was the scores on the comprehension test coded as the percentages of total items answered correctly. The main research interest for this study was to evaluate whether the two types of input modification had different effects on reading comprehension for students with high and low proficiency levels. One particular interest was to examine whether one type of modification (elaboration or simplification) was more effective than the other for high-proficiency students. Assume that we have replicated the study with 10 subjects in each group and obtained the reading comprehension scores presented in Table 2.8.

A factorial ANOVA with two independent variables assesses two main effects and one interaction effect. A main effect is defined as the effect of one independent variable regardless of the effect of another independent variable. In our example, the main effect of input modification is the effect of modification types on reading comprehension without taking proficiency levels into account (i.e., using scores with both proficiency levels combined). The main effect of proficiency is the effect of different proficiency levels on reading comprehension scores regardless of the type of input modification.

The interaction effect is usually the most interesting issue for the researcher. The interaction effect is defined as the effect of one independent variable depending on the levels of another independent variable. In our study, a significant interaction effect would indicate that the effect of input modification on reading comprehension depends on the proficiency level of the students. The null hypotheses for testing the two main effects and the interaction effect are stated in (4):

(4) Null hypothesis 1 (for the main effect of input modification): There is no difference in the effects of the two input modifications on reading comprehension across proficiency levels.

Null hypothesis 2 (for the main effect of proficiency): There is no difference in the effects of proficiency level regardless of the type of input modification.

Null hypothesis 3 (for the interaction): The effect of input modification on reading comprehension does not depend on proficiency levels.

TABLE 2.8
Reading Comprehension Scores for Proficiency and Input Modification Groups

	Scores	
	High Proficiency	*Low Proficiency*
Elaborated input	68	28
	67	44
	72	28
	74	33
	69	33
	71	25
	65	22
	75	31
	57	35
	65	29
	M 68.3 (5.27)	30.8 (6.07)
Simplified input	65	31
	69	41
	77	34
	68	33
	69	38
	63	35
	57	24
	65	46
	58	35
	57	42
	M 64.8 (6.37)	35.9 (6.23)

Note: Standard deviations are in parentheses.

Table 2.9 presents the SPSS output for the results from the two-way ANOVA based on the data in Table 2.8. From Table 2.9, we retain null hypothesis 1 with $F(1, 36) = 0.178$, $p = 0.676$, indicating no significant effect for input. Null hypothesis 2 is rejected at $F(1, 36) = 306.13$, $p < 0.001$, showing a significant effect for proficiency. From the means presented in Table 2.8, we conclude that high English proficiency students had significantly higher comprehension scores as compared to the students with lower English proficiency regardless of the type of input modification.

The interaction effect often reveals more substantively interesting findings. Null hypothesis 3 for the interaction term is rejected with $F(1, 1) = 5.135$, $p = 0.03$, indicating that the input effect is different for students at different proficiency levels. To facilitate the interpretation from a significant interaction term, researchers usually draw an interaction plot for visual

TABLE 2.9
SPSS Output for the Results from the Two-Way Factorial ANOVA

Source	*Type III Sum of Squares*	df	*Mean Square*	F	*Significance*
Corrected model	11,213.700	3	3,737.900	103.815	0.000
Intercept	99,800.100	1	99,800.100	2,771.797	0.000
INPUT	6.400	1	6.400	0.178	0.676
PROF	11,022.400	1	11,022.400	306.131	0.000
INPUT * PROF	184.900	1	184.900	5.135	0.030
Error	1,296.200	36	36.006		
Total	112,310.000	40			
Corrected total	12,509.900	39			

presentation of the results. The interaction plot produced using SPSS is presented in Figure 2.1.

The interaction plot reveals that for low-proficiency students, the group receiving simplified passages scored higher on the comprehension test than the group receiving passages with elaborated input modification. But for the students with high proficiency, the opposite is shown. The findings may have practical implications for designing classroom instructional materials for students learning second languages.

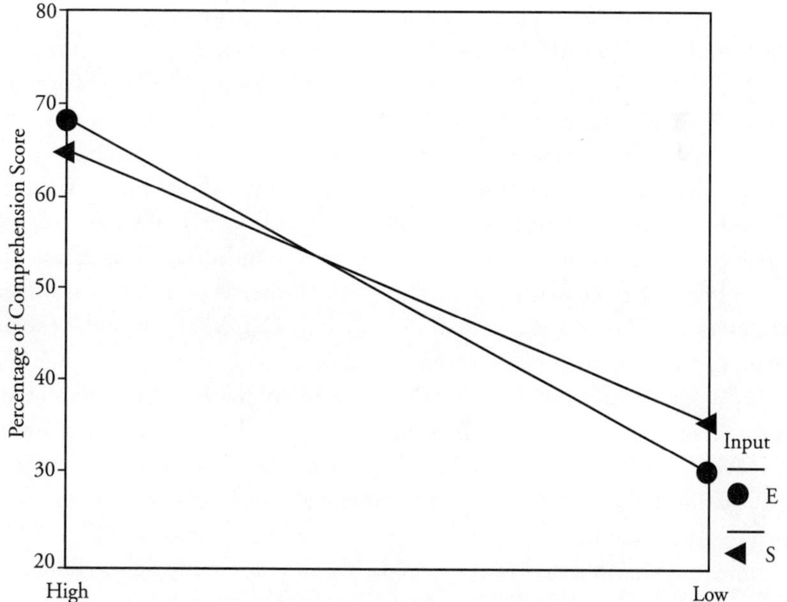

FIGURE 2.1 *Interaction Plot for Input Modification and Proficiency Levels*

With a significant main effect having more than two levels, a subsequent test (post hoc or planned) should be conducted to identify the specific group differences. When the interaction term is significant, the researcher would be interested in comparing the cell means for the interpretation of the interaction. Using the previous example, it is of interest to compare the scores for the four groups: high proficiency with elaborated input, high proficiency with simplified input, low proficiency with elaborated input, and low proficiency with simplified input. A one-way ANOVA can be used to compare the four means to facilitate the interpretation of the findings.

4.3. REPEATED-MEASURES ANOVA

In the examples illustrating one-way ANOVA and two-way ANOVA in previous sections, each participant contributed only one score to the data analyzed. However, SLA researchers often collect more than one score from each participant. For instance, scores on pretest, posttest, and delayed tests are usually collected from each participant to examine possible treatment and delayed effects. Repeated-measures ANOVA applies to designs where each participant contributes more than one score.

In SLA studies, the repeated-measures ANOVA has been frequently used in situations where two or more groups are compared, with each group assessed several times. Suppose, for instance, that a researcher is interested in examining whether a treatment effect is the same for L2 learners with different proficiency levels. The researcher administers three tests: a pretest (before the treatment), a posttest (immediately following the treatment), and a delayed test (some time later). If proficiency has three levels (e.g., low, intermediate, and high), the design is called a 3×3 Repeated Measures ANOVA. There are two independent variables in this design, with three levels for each independent variable. The independent variable *proficiency* is a between-subjects variable because the scores on this variable are taken from different participants. The other independent variable, which we may call *time,* is a within-subjects variable because the three scores (on pre-, post-, and delayed tests) are obtained from the same participants. This repeated-measures ANOVA is similar to a two-way ANOVA except that for two-way ANOVA, both independent variables are between-subjects variables.

We used Brown and Perry's (1991) study comparing three vocabulary learning strategies in the previous section to illustrate the use of one-way ANOVA. Imagine that we redesign this study using pre-, post-, and delayed tests administered 9 days after the treatment for each group. The pretest is included to establish a baseline to examine group difference prior to the treatment. Simulated test scores for this hypothetical study are presented in Table 2.10.

TABLE 2.10
Scores on the Pre-, Post-, and Delayed Tests for the Three Learning Groups

	Pretest	*Posttest*	*Delayed Test*
Keyword	5	18	17
	5	19	21
	4	13	19
	4	21	18
	3	22	19
	5	9	10
	5	17	20
	3	9	8
	5	30	29
	3	12	10
Mean =	4.2 (0.92)	17.0 (6.53)	17.1 (6.30)
Semantic	5	20	26
	3	22	23
	4	25	28
	5	15	22
	5	25	25
	4	6	8
	4	13	11
	5	18	26
	4	18	20
	1	24	16
Mean =	4.0 (1.25)	18.6 (6.04)	20.5 (6.77)
Keyword & Semantic	4	29	23
	4	22	38
	3	20	28
	4	20	16
	4	31	30
	5	26	29
	4	36	33
	3	40	38
	3	17	18
	4	25	32
Mean =	3.8 (0.63)	26.6 (7.43)	28.5 (7.55)

Note: Standard deviations are in parentheses.

TABLE 2.11
SPSS Output for Between-Subjects Comparison

Source	*Type III Sum of Squares*	df	*Mean Square*	F	*Significance*
Intercept	21,871.211	1	21,871.211	399.011	0.000
Group	774.489	2	387.244	7.065	0.003
Error	1,479.967	27	54.814		

This study design is a 3 × 3 repeated-measures ANOVA, with two independent variables: method and testing time. Method is a between-subjects variable with three levels (keyword, semantic, and combined) and testing time is a within-subjects variable also with three levels (pre- vs. post- vs. delayed). The dependent variable in this study is the score on a 40-item multiple-choice test. Similar to a two-way ANOVA, three null hypotheses are tested in the repeated-measures ANOVA with two independent variables, two for main effects and one for the interaction effect. Definitions for the main effect and the interaction effect for repeated-measures ANOVA remain the same as those given in section 3.2. The researcher is usually most interested in the interaction effect. A significant interaction in this study will reveal that certain strategies for learning new words are more effective and that the effects may also last longer than others. The SPSS output for testing null hypothesis 1 of no group difference, followed by the Scheffé Test, is presented in Tables 2.11 and 2.12. Please note that Group is a between-subjects variable in study.

The output for testing the between-subjects comparison is similar to that for a one-way ANOVA. From Table 2.11 we see that null hypothesis 1 is rejected with $F(2, 27) = 7.065$ with $p = 0.003$, indicating that at least one method is different from the others. The Scheffé test in Table 2.12 shows that the mean for the combined methods (19.63) is listed in a separate column from the other two means, indicating that the combined method yields

TABLE 2.12
SPSS Output from the Scheffé Test for Comparing Three Vocabulary Learning Methods

		Subset for alpha = .05	
Method	N	*1*	*2*
Keyword	10	12.77	
Semantic	10	14.37	
Keyword & Semantic	10		19.63

TABLE 2.13
SPSS Output for Testing Within-Subjects Effects and the Interaction Effect

Source	*Assumption*	*Type III Sum of Squares*	df	*Mean Square*	F	*Significance*
TIME	Sphericity Assumed	6,068.956	2	3,034.478	158.178	0.000
TIME * GROUP	Sphericity Assumed	440.444	4	110.111	5.740	0.001
Error(TIME)	Sphericity Assumed	1,035.933	54	19.184		

significantly higher scores than the methods used separately, with p less than 0.05. The difference between the keyword and the semantic methods is not significant because the two means are listed in the same column.

SPSS output for testing within-subjects effects and the interaction effect is presented in Table 2.13. Null hypothesis 2, testing the effect of the within-subject variable, is also rejected with $F(2, 54) = 158.18$, $p < 0.001$. This finding was expected because we knew that the pretest scores were much lower than the post- and delayed tests regardless of which learning method was used. Paired-samples t tests are often used as post hoc tests for a within-subject variable. The paired-samples t test showed no statistical difference between the scores on the posttest and the delayed test.

Null hypothesis 3 testing the interaction effect of time by method was rejected with $F(4, 54) = 5.74$, $p = 0.001$. The significant interaction effect indicated that the change of the test scores from pre- to posttest, or from post- to delayed test, was different for groups using different methods. As with a two-way ANOVA, an interaction plot could facilitate the understanding of results. We can see from Figure 2.2 that the three groups were not different at the baseline. But at the time of the posttest and the delayed test, the group using combined methods performed much better than the groups using the methods separately. Based on these results, this study is able to conclude not only that the combined method was more effective immediately after the learning session, but that the effect remained after at least 9 days.

5. Correlation and Regressions: Relations between Variables

Correlation methods are often used to examine the possible linear relationship between two variables. For examples, Harley (2000) investigated the relationship between children's age and the accuracy of listening comprehension in L2 English. Harley reported that unlike native speakers, child L2 learners' age was not related to picking up syntactic cues of spoken English. Geva

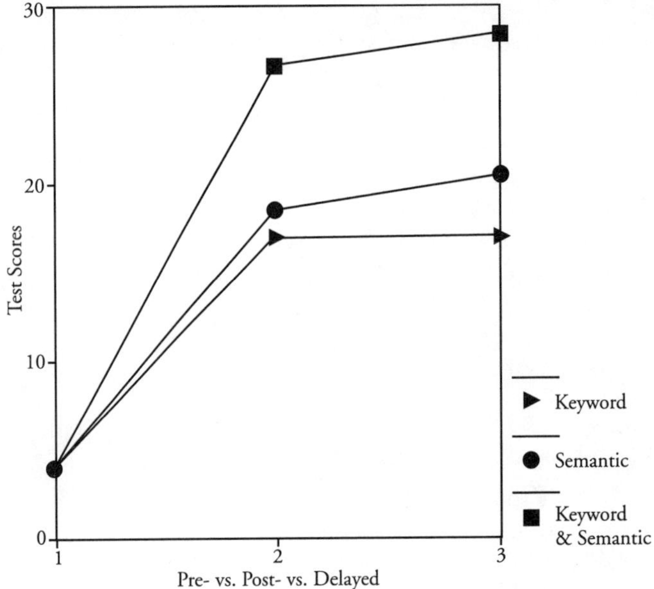

FIGURE 2.2 *Interaction Plot for Group by Testing Time*

(1992) reported positive relationships between performance on academic tasks in L2 and L1 linguistic skills for university students whose L1 was English. Gradman and Hanania (1991) examined the possible social and cognitive factors that could be associated with TOEFL scores for international students admitted to universities. All these studies used the concept of correlation to examine the associations among variables. In most cases, the term *correlation* refers to the Pearson product-moment correlation, which indicates how closely two variables are linearly related. A scatter plot (see Figure 2.3 as an example) is often used to visually present the relationship between two variables. Two variables are linearly related if the dots on a scatter plot are close to a straight line.

Regression is frequently applied for prediction and predictor selection purposes. If two variables are correlated, we are able to use one variable to predict the other. For example, based on the finding (Gradman and Hanania, 1991) that a student's TOEFL score was related to the length of the student's training in intensive English courses, we are able to predict a student's TOEFL score by knowing how many months the student trained in the intensive program. Simple regression has only one predictor, while multiple regression involves more than one predictor. In both cases only one variable is being predicted, and this variable is called a dependent or a criterion variable.

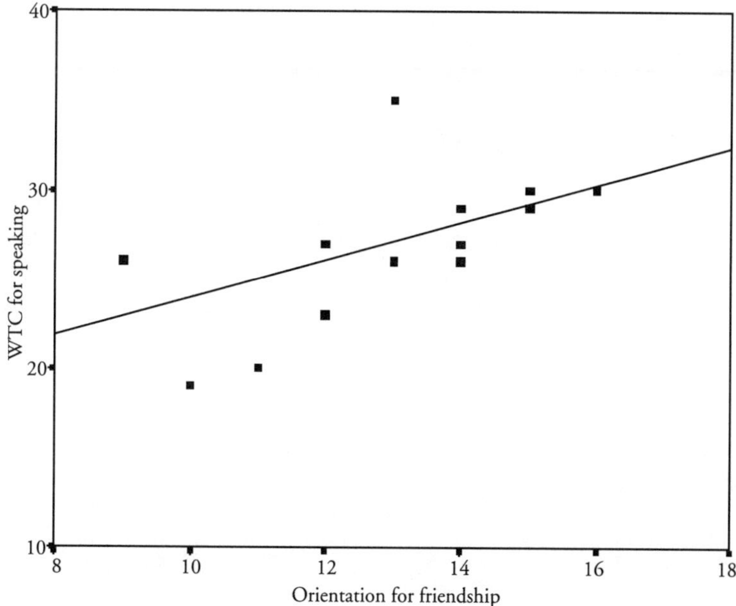

FIGURE 2.3 *Scatter Plot for WTC for Speaking and Orientation for Friendship*

5.1. CORRELATION COEFFICIENT AND THE SCATTER PLOT

MacIntyre and Baker (2001) were interested in the associations between willingness to communicate (WTC) and orientation toward language learning for Grade 9 L2 French learners. WTC was defined as intention to initiate communication when given a choice. Orientation (i.e., reasons for learning French) was classified into five categories: job, travel, friendship, knowledge, and school. It was hypothesized that L2 learners' orientation was positively related to their WTC in the language learning environment. One of the WTC variables, WTC in the classroom, was measured by a questionnaire with eight items, and the students were asked to respond to each item on a 5-point Likert-type scale. Orientation for friendship was measured by three items, each with six choices ranging from strong agreement to strong disagreement. Suppose that we replicated the study and obtained data from 14 students as presented in Table 2.14.

The maximum score for WTC in speaking is 40 (8 items × 5 points) and that for orientation for friendship is 18 (3 items × 6 points). It will be helpful to examine the relationship between the two variables in a scatter plot. From the scatter plot we can see that as the scores for orientation for friendship increase, scores for WTC in speaking tend to increase, revealing a positive

TABLE 2.14
WTC in Speaking and Orientation for Friendship Scores for the 14 Students

Subject	*1*	*2*	*3*	*4*	*5*	*6*	*7*	*8*	*9*	*10*	*11*	*12*	*13*	*14*	*Mean*	*(SD)*
WTC speaking	23	27	29	35	27	26	30	26	19	29	30	26	20	26	26.64	(4.13)
Friendship	12	14	15	13	12	9	16	9	10	14	15	13	11	14	12.64	(2.24)

relationship between the two variables. We can also see that the dots in the diagram are quite close to a straight line, indicating a linear relationship between the two variables. If the dots in a scatter diagram spread out everywhere without showing closeness to a straight line, we may conclude that there is probably no linear relationship between the two variables.

A commonly used index to quantify the linear relationship of two variables with measurement scales is the Pearson product-moment correlation coefficient. One of the formulas to calculate the correlation coefficient is given in (5),

$$(5)\quad r = \frac{\sum Z_x Z_y}{N-1}$$

where Z_x and Z_y are z scores for the two variables and N is the sample size in the study. By using the formula, original scores are transformed into z scores first, and then the product of two z scores for each participant can be calculated. The correlation coefficient r for the sample is the sum of all products divided by the sample size minus 1. Using the data in Table 2.14, we are able to calculate $r = (7.383)/13 = 0.568$.

To test the null hypothesis H_0: $\rho = 0$, where ρ is the population correlation coefficient, we can use the t test with (6):

$$(6)\quad t = \frac{r\sqrt{N-2}}{\sqrt{1-r^2}}$$

with $df = N - 2$. In our example, $r = 0.568$ and $N = 14$, $t = 1.967/0.823 = 2.39$ and $df = 14 - 2$. From the t table presented in Table 2.2, we find that the critical value is 2.179 for df at 12 and p equaling 0.05. Since the observed t value (2.39) is greater than the critical value, the null hypothesis is rejected at the 0.05 level, and we conclude that the WTC in speaking is significantly related to the orientation for friendship in the population.

5.2. SIMPLE REGRESSION

From two correlated variables, we are able to use the information of one variable to predict the values on the other variable. In the previous example, if we know a person's score on the orientation for friendship test, we are able to predict this person's willingness to speak in the L2 classroom. Orientation for friendship serves as an independent variable (also called a *predictor*), and WTC in speaking is the dependent variable (also called a *criterion*). How do we use the knowledge of one variable to predict the values on the other variable? Let us assume we have an equation $Y = 13.4 + 1.05\ X$ (we will show how to obtain the numbers in this equation shortly), where Y is the variable for WTC in speaking and X is orientation for friendship. From the equation, we can calculate the value of Y if X is known. If a person had a score of 10 on the orientation for friendship, we can then use the equation to obtain this person's predicted value on WTC in speaking, 23.9.

Now we will show how to obtain the regression coefficients 13.4 and 1.05 in the above equation. In general, a simple regression equation has the formula $\hat{Y} = a + bX$, where $\hat{Y}$ is the predicted value of Y, a is the intercept, and b is the slope of the regression line. The intercept and slope are regression coefficients calculated using the formulas in (7):

(7) a. $b = r\dfrac{S_y}{S_x}$ b. $a = \bar{Y} - b\bar{X}$

S_y and S_x are sample standard deviations for Y and X, and $\bar{Y}$ and $\bar{X}$ are the means for Y and X, respectively. We already know r equals 0.568 for orientation for friendship and WTC in speaking. Using the data in Table 2.14, we can calculate $b = 0.568 \times (4.13/2.24) = 1.05$ and thus $a = 26.64 - 1.05 \times 12.64 = 13.4$. We can summarize the results in a regression equation: $\hat{Y} = 13.4 + 1.05X$.

The interpretation of the coefficients in a linear regression is straightforward. From the regression equation $\hat{Y} = a + bX$, we can see that when X changes by one unit, the value of Y will change b units accordingly. In our example, the slope $b = 1.05$ indicates that with 1 unit change on the orientation-for-friendship scale, the score on the WTC in speaking is expected to change by 1.05 units. Since the relationship between the two variables is linear, this interpretation for slope b is true on all values on the orientation-for-friendship scale. The interpretation of $a = 13.4$ is that when $X = 0$, the expected score for Y is 13.4.

When interpreting results from a regression analysis, r^2 is often used to indicate the percentage of variance in the dependent variable that is explained (accounted for) by the independent variable(s). In our example, $r^2 = 0.568 \times 0.568 = 0.323 = 32.3\%$. We conclude that about 32% of the variance in WTC in speaking can be explained by the differences in the orientation for friendship. The *R*-square (r^2) is also called the coefficient of determination.

TABLE 2.15
SPSS Output for the *R*-square from Simple Regression Analysis

Model	R	R-*square*	*Adjusted* R-*square*	*Standard error of the estimate*
1	0.568	0.323	0.266	3.53391

Tables 2.15 and 2.16 present the SPSS output for a simple regression using the data in Table 2.14. The output in Table 2.15 shows that r equals 0.568 and r^2 equals 0.323, and in Table 2.16 that the intercept a equals 13.4 and the coefficient b equals 1.046.

From Table 2.16, we also see the results of two t tests testing the null hypotheses that the intercept and the slope equal 0 in the population. The result with t at 2.391 and p at 0.034 indicates that we reject the null hypothesis and conclude that the intercept is significantly different from 0. The null hypothesis of slope at 0 is also rejected with t equaling 2.39 and p at 0.034.

5.3. MULTIPLE REGRESSION

We introduced simple regression that allows the prediction of the dependent variable by one independent variable. But in the real world, one phenomenon is often related to multiple factors. For example, in addition to orientation for friendship, willingness to speak could also relate to the learner's personality, the instructor's teaching method, specific teaching material, and class size. The multiple regression analysis allows the researcher to predict the dependent variable using multiple predictors.

Multiple regression analysis is a flexible statistical procedure that serves different research purposes. Besides prediction, multiple regression analysis is often used for selecting important predictors, controlling covariates, and detecting moderator effects between two variables. In this section, we will introduce multiple regression analysis when the selection of predictors is the major interest of the study.

Gradman and Hanania (1991) noticed that incoming ESL students entering an intensive English program at Indiana University had very different

TABLE 2.16
SPSS Output for Simple Regression Analysis

		Unstandardized coefficients		*Standardized coefficients*		
Model	*Variable*	B	*Standard error*	*Beta*	t	*Significance*
1	(Constant)	13.418	5.613		2.391	0.034
	Friendship	1.046	0.438	0.568	2.390	0.034

English proficiency levels and achieved progress with varying degrees of success. The researchers were interested in identifying what language-learning background factors were associated with students' ESL proficiency levels. Instead of focusing on one type of variable, Gradman and Hanania collected data on different types of variables, such as formal learning variables (e.g., age at start of English learning), attitude and motivation variables (e.g., family encouragement), exposure and use-in-class variables (e.g., native- or nonnative-speaking teacher), and extracurricular exposure variables (e.g., reading outside of class). The dependent variable in this study was the TOEFL score reported when the student entered the program. A major purpose of the study was to identify the most important factors that might have influenced the students' TOEFL scores. Using multiple regression analyses, the study found that extracurricular reading and having native-speaking teachers were among the significant predictors, while oral speaking in and out of class was not important when predicting TOEFL scores. Assume that we have replicated Gradman and Hanania's (1991) study and obtained data from 50 ESL students with the five variables presented in Table 2.17.

Four possible predictors of TOEFL scores were chosen as independent variables in the multiple regression analysis. The variable *reading* was obtained from a survey questionnaire that measured the amount of exposure to extracurricular reading of English literature. The variable *month* indicates how many months the student attended intensive English programs before taking the TOEFL test. *Native* is a categorical variable showing whether or not the student had a native English-speaker as a teacher. The variable *oral* measured students' oral communication ability in and out of the classroom.

Before conducting multiple regression analysis, it is natural to first examine whether the TOEFL score is significantly correlated to each of the potential predictors separately. The correlation matrix for the five variables is presented in Table 2.18, with p values indicating the significance for each Pearson correlation coefficient. For example, having the correlation coefficient r at 0.52 for TOEFL and reading with p less than 0.01 indicates that more exposure to extracurricular reading is associated with higher TOEFL scores.

From Table 2.18 we find that the TOEFL score is also significantly correlated with month and native. But the correlation coefficient between TOEFL and oral is not significant, with r at 0.112 and p at 0.438. Given that we already know from the correlation matrix that the TOEFL scores are significantly correlated with reading, month, and native, the reader may ask why we still need to conduct multiple regression analysis to determine the significant predictors. The answer is that when independent variables are intercorrelated, significant predictors resulting from multiple regression analysis are not necessarily the same as those judging from individual correlations. This is because

TABLE 2.17
Prediction of English Proficiency

TOEFL	Reading	Months	Native	Oral	TOEFL	Reading	Months	Native	Oral
547	9	14	1	9	541	5	15	1	11
649	8	9	1	8	566	9	0	1	7
571	5	14	0	6	538	4	6	1	4
595	9	11	1	7	522	6	4	1	8
560	7	11	1	9	503	5	0	1	8
570	6	12	0	5	521	9	3	1	7
500	6	0	0	10	472	7	0	0	6
491	4	6	1	9	570	5	15	1	9
635	6	9	1	7	581	7	9	1	6
582	10	8	1	6	490	4	8	1	5
453	6	5	0	11	549	9	11	1	6
564	8	4	1	7	533	7	10	1	10
483	2	10	0	7	515	9	8	1	7
545	6	15	0	9	653	11	13	1	4
504	7	14	1	8	596	8	12	1	10
580	7	11	1	2	525	6	10	1	6
610	6	12	1	11	540	2	4	1	8
600	8	15	1	11	559	9	6	1	10
584	5	8	0	7	479	7	10	0	3
503	5	3	0	4	681	11	15	1	8
596	7	11	1	9	481	6	5	1	2
583	8	11	1	6	633	11	15	1	10
544	8	6	1	8	487	6	4	1	9
512	2	4	1	4	636	8	8	1	6
514	7	15	0	7	534	8	2	1	5

Note. Reading = exposure to extracurricular reading; months = number of months attending intensive English program; native = native-speaking teacher coded as 1, nonnative-speaking teacher as 0; oral = use of oral English in and out of classroom.

the portion of variance in the dependent variable explained by each predictor will overlap when the predictors are correlated with each other.

You may also notice that the variable *native* is a dichotomous variable with only two possible values, with 1 indicating having native-speaker teachers and 0 indicating no native-speaker teacher. Dichotomous variables can be used as legitimate predictors in regression analysis with meaningful interpretations. The correlation between a dichotomous variable and a continuous variable (on ratio or interval scales) has a special name: point-biserial correlation. The calculation and the significance testing for point-biserial correlation is the same as for Pearson product-moment correlation (Howell, 1992, p. 267).

Numerical calculation for multiple regression analysis depends on matrix algebra. Since the calculation can be cumbersome, it will not be introduced

TABLE 2.18
Correlation Matrix for the Five Variables Used in the Hypothetical Study

Variable	*Statistics*	*TOEFL*	*Reading*	*Month*	*Native*	*Oral*
TOEFL	Pearson correlation	1	0.520(**)	0.479(**)	0.365(**)	0.112
	Significance (2-tailed)		0.000	0.000	0.009	0.438
	N	50	50	50	50	50
Reading	Pearson correlation	0.520(**)	1	0.228	0.295(*)	0.087
	Significance (2-tailed)	0.000		0.111	0.038	0.550
	N	50	50	50	50	50
Month	Pearson correlation	0.479(**)	0.228	1	0.030	0.200
	Significance (2-tailed)	0.000	0.111		0.836	0.163
	N	50	50	50	50	50
Native	Pearson correlation	0.365(**)	0.295(*)	0.030	1	0.098
	Significance (2-tailed)	0.009	0.038	0.836		0.500
	N	50	50	50	50	50
Oral	Pearson correlation	0.112	0.087	0.200	0.098	1
	Significance (2-tailed)	0.438	0.550	0.163	0.500	
	N	50	50	50	50	50

**Correlation is significant at the 0.01 level. *Correlation is significant at the 0.05 level.

here. Instead we present the SPSS output in Tables 2.19 and 2.20 using the data in Table 2.17. We can see from Table 2.19 that the *R*-square equals 0.464, indicating that almost half of the variance in TOEFL scores can be explained by the four predictors combined.

Using the estimated regression coefficients from Table 2.20, we can construct the regression equation: expected TOEFL score = 432.28 + 8.74 × Reading + 4.51 × Month + 31.40 × Native − 0.51 × Oral. Since the

TABLE 2.19
SPSS Output for *R*-square from Multiple Regression Analysis Predicting TOEFL Scores

Model	R	R-*square*	*Adjusted* R-*square*	*Standard error of the estimate*
1	0.681	0.464	0.416	40.152

TABLE 2.20

SPSS Output for Multiple Regression Analysis Predicting TOEFL Scores

		Unstandardized coefficients		*Standardized coefficients*		
Model	*Variable*	B	*Standard error*	*Beta*	t	*Significance*
1	(Constant)	432.284	25.823		16.740	0.000
	Reading	8.741	2.863	0.358	3.053	0.004
	Month	4.511	1.307	0.394	3.450	0.001
	Native	31.402	14.409	0.250	2.179	0.035
	Oral	−0.507	2.538	−0.022	−0.200	0.842

major interest of the study is to select the important predictors for the TOEFL scores, we need to identify significant predictors from the output. The values in the far right column in Table 2.20 are the p values for evaluating the null hypothesis that the regression coefficient is 0 in the population. From the p values we can determine that reading, month, and native are significant predictors with p less than 0.05, but oral is not a significant predictor for TOEFL scores with p equaling 0.842.

The interpretation of the intercept at 432.28 is that for a student with all four independent variables at 0, the expected TOEFL score for that student is 432.28. Since it is not likely that a student will have all four predictors equaling 0, the intercept does not have a meaningful interpretation in this regression equation, although it is significantly different from 0 with p less than 0.001.

The interpretation of slope in multiple regression involves original measurement units. For example, the slope for month is 4.51, indicating that an increase of one additional month in an intensive English program is associated with an increase of 4.51 points in TOEFL score, while holding other predictors constant. To hold a predictor constant means that the value for that variable is the same for all participants. The slope for reading is 8.74, showing that an increase of one unit on the extracurricular reading questionnaire is associated with an increase of TOEFL score by 8.74 points, holding other predictors constant. The interpretation of the slope for a dichotomous variable is straightforward. Native is a dichotomous variable, and it is a significant predictor with slope at 31.4, indicating that ESL students with native-speaker teachers are expected to have an average 31.4 points higher on TOEFL than ESL students with nonnative-speaker teachers.

Using the regression equation, we are able to calculate the expected TOEFL score for a student using the scores on the four predictors. For example, first student in Table 2.17 has scores of 9 for reading, 14 for month, 1 for native, and 9 for oral. Using the regression equation, we obtain the expected TOEFL score: $432.28 + 8.74 \times 9 + 4.51 \times 14 + 31.40 \times 1 - 0.51 \times 9 = 600.89$.

The correlation between the predicted values and the observed values is called the multiple correlation coefficient. In our example, the multiple correlation coefficient is 0.681. The difference between an obtained value and the predicted value is called a *residual.* For the first student in Table 2.17, the residual is 432.28 − 600.89 = −53.9. The sum of all residuals in the sample is always 0.

Stepwise regression selects the most important predictors one at a time to enter the regression equation and presents a final model with only the significant predictors in the equation. An important predictor is defined as the one which accounts for the biggest variance in the dependent variable compared with other predictors. Stepwise regression starts by calculating the variance explained by each of the predictors, selects the predictor that accounts for the biggest variance, and enters that variable into the regression equation. To select the second predictor, the variance explained by the remaining predictors is compared, and the predictor with the biggest and most significant variance will be chosen to enter into the equation. The procedure continues and then stops at the point where none of the remaining predictors accounts for any significant variance beyond the existing equation. Table 2.21 presents the SPSS output for the stepwise regression using the data in Table 2.17.

From Table 2.21, we see that reading was selected as the first predictor to enter into the equation, followed by month and native. Oral was excluded from the equation because the variance it explained was not significant. The final model resulting from this stepwise regression is that expected TOEFL = 429.29 + 8.73 × Reading + 4.46 × Month + 31.16 × Native. All predictors in the final model resulting from a stepwise regression are statistically significant.

TABLE 2.21
SPSS Stepwise Regression Output for the Prediction of TOEFL Scores

		Unstandardized coefficients		*Standardized coefficient*		
Model	*Variable*	B	*Standard error*	*Beta*	t	*Significance*
1	(Constant)	465.086	21.494		21.638	0.000
	Reading	12.685	3.008	0.520	4.217	0.000
2	(Constant)	442.018	20.789		21.262	0.000
	Reading	10.570	2.814	0.433	3.757	0.000
	Month	4.350	1.320	0.380	3.296	0.002
3	(Constant)	429.291	20.820		20.620	0.000
	Reading	8.732	2.833	0.358	3.082	0.003
	Month	4.461	1.270	0.390	3.512	0.001
	Native	31.158	14.206	0.248	2.193	0.033

6. The Chi-Square (χ^2) Test

When introducing measurement scales in section 2.2, we pointed out that categorical variables are just naming systems. For a categorical variable coded with numbers (e.g., 1 = French language, 2 = Japanese language, and 3 = English language), ANOVA and *t* tests are not appropriate to apply because these tests are based on means and variances that require measurement scales to carry out the calculations. If the data are categorical in nature, we can count the frequency of occurrences and their percentages. Chi-square (χ^2) tests are often used for statistical testing when the data are categorical.

Wharton (2000) administered the Oxford 80-Item Strategy Inventory for Language Learning (SILL) to 678 university students learning Japanese and French as foreign languages in Singapore. The major interest of the study was to examine the possible relationships between L2 learning strategies, proficiency levels, and the gender of L2 learners. The SILL inventory classifies learning strategies into different categories such as social, cognitive, and memory. The proficiency levels of the participants were based on self-reports from a background questionnaire having three categories: good, fair, and poor in L2.

Three categorical variables were collected in this study: learning strategy, proficiency, and gender. One may argue that the variable *proficiency* can be treated on an ordinal scale because the values on this variable are ordered from good to poor. When an ordinal variable has only a few values, such as good versus bad, or passing versus not passing a test, we may also treat the variable as categorical. In Wharton's (2000) study, one research interest was to examine whether students with self-rated good proficiency were more likely to use a particular learning strategy (e.g., keeping language information in a notebook). Are students with good proficiency more likely than students with poor proficiency to use the learning strategy of keeping information in notebooks? The chi-square (χ^2) test was used for testing the null hypotheses since the variables are categorical in nature.

6.1. THE GOODNESS-OF-FIT CHI-SQUARE (χ^2) TEST

Suppose we conducted a study similar to Wharton (2000) and obtained 48 students who were self-rated as having good English proficiency. Among the 48 students, 36 reported that they used a learning strategy of organizing language information in notebooks, and the other 12 students reported that they had never used this learning strategy. The research interest was to examine if students with good proficiency were more likely to use this learning strategy. The data are presented in a one-dimensional table in Table 2.22 with only one variable (used vs. not used). The chi-square test applied to a one-dimensional frequency table is called the goodness-of-fit test.

TABLE 2.22
The Use of a Particular Learning Strategy by Students with Good Proficiency

Frequency	*Used*	*Not Used*	*Total*
Observed	36	12	48
Expected	24	24	48

Following the steps of hypothesis testing introduced in section 2.3, we first state a null hypothesis related to the research interest: For good proficiency students, there will be no difference between the numbers of students who used the learning strategy versus those who didn't. The second step of hypothesis testing is to find out the p value indicating whether the null hypothesis is true. The formula for obtaining this chi-square statistic is given in (8):

(8) $$\chi^2 = \sum \frac{(O - E)^2}{E}$$

In this formula, O represents the observed values and E the expected values. Expected values in our example are the frequencies for the students using and not using the learning strategy under the condition that the null hypothesis is true. If students with good proficiency are not more likely to use the learning strategy, the number of students who used the strategy should be the same as the number of students who did not. With a total of 48 students with good proficiency, the expected number of students in each category is $48/2 = 24$.

Applying the chi-square formula to the data in Table 2.22, we obtain $\chi^2 = (36 - 24)^2/24 + (12 - 24)^2/24 = 12$. To obtain the p value from the χ^2 distribution, we need to know the degrees of freedom for the test. The degrees of freedom for the goodness-of-fit chi-square test are the number of categories $-$ 1. In our example, we have two categories in the one-dimensional table (used vs. not used); thus the degrees of freedom are $2 - 1 = 1$. From a χ^2 distribution table (found in statistics textbooks), we find that the critical value for χ^2 distribution with df equaling 1 is 3.84 at α equaling 0.05 level. Since the observed χ^2 value is 12, which is greater than the critical value, we obtain p at less than 0.05 and reject the null hypothesis. We conclude that significantly more students with good L2 proficiency used the learning strategy of organizing language information in notebooks.

6.2. THE CHI-SQUARE (χ^2) TEST OF INDEPENDENCE

The chi-square test of independence evaluates the hypothesis that two categorical variables are associated in the population. Let's continue to use

TABLE 2.23
Contingency Table for Proficiency, Gender, and Learning Strategy

Gender	*Proficiency* *Poor*	*Fair*	*Good*	*Total*
Male	35 (29.5)	34 (29.9)	32 (41.6)	101
Female	28 (33.5)	30 (34.1)	57 (47.4)	115
Total	63	64	89	216

Note. Frequency (percentage).

Wharton (2000) and suppose that we are interested in the issue of whether gender is associated with proficiency levels for using the learning strategy of organizing language information in notebooks. If proficiency is found to be associated with gender, the interpretation is that at different proficiency levels, the ratio of male versus female students who used this learning strategy is different. It is possible that more female students used the learning strategy than male students at the good proficiency level but not at the other proficiency levels. The hypothetical data are presented in a cross-tabulated table (see Table 2.23) with two categorical variables. The chi-square test used to test the association (or independence) of two categorical variables is called the chi-square test for independence.

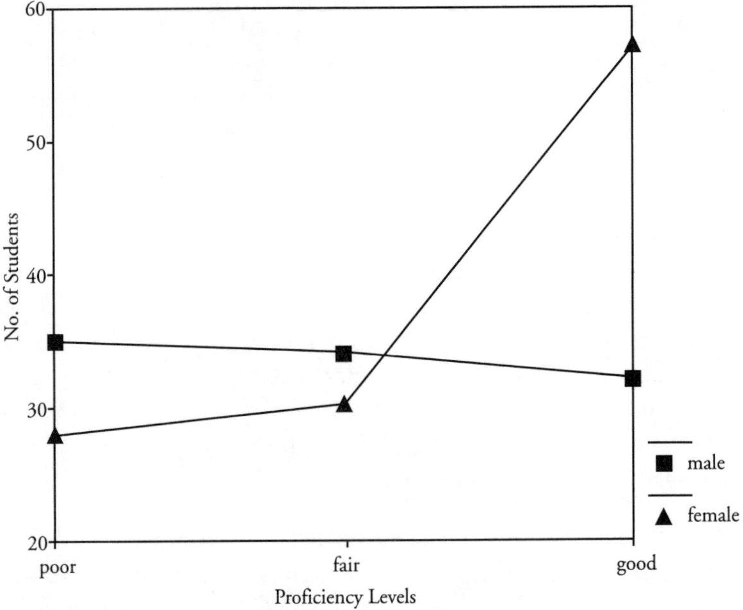

FIGURE 2.4 *Interaction Plot for Gender and Proficiency Level*

The null hypothesis is that there is no association between gender and proficiency for using the learning strategy. The χ^2 formula is the same as that for the goodness-of-fit test introduced in the previous section. We obtain $\chi^2 = (35 - 29.5)^2/29.5 + \ldots + (57 - 47.4)^2 = 7.17$. The degrees of freedom for the test of independence is (number of rows $-$ 1) $\times$ (number of columns $-$ 1). In our example, $df = (2 - 1) \times (3 - 1) = 2$. The critical value for *df* at 2 with α at 0.05 is 5.99. Since the obtained χ^2 of 7.17 is greater than the critical value, we obtain *p* at less than 0.05. The null hypothesis is rejected based on the *p* value, and we conclude that gender and proficiency are associated with using the learning strategy of organizing language information in notebooks.

An interaction plot may facilitate the interpretation of the findings from the χ^2 test of independence. Figure 2.4 is the interaction plot showing how gender and proficiency levels are associated when using the learning strategy. We can see that for male students, the numbers of students using the learning strategy at the three proficiency levels are not very different. But more female students at the good proficiency level used the strategy than those at lower proficiency levels.

7. Summary

This chapter introduced the basic statistical concepts and procedures used by SLA researchers applying quantitative approaches. Since the logic of statistical hypothesis testing is an important issue in learning statistical methods, it has been summarized in three simple steps and illustrated using the statistical procedures introduced in this chapter. This chapter has shown that *t* tests, *F* tests, and χ^2 tests are all based on the same logic of hypothesis testing. This three-step procedure is a simplified version to help the reader to understand the logic of hypothesis testing. Readers interested in more detailed explanations of hypothesis testing are referred to standard textbooks recommended at the end of this chapter.

After learning the statistical procedures introduced in this chapter, a natural question from the reader would be, "What statistical test should I use for my particular research interests?" As a summary of the chapter, three issues addressed below may help the reader to choose an appropriate test. These issues are closely related to specific research interests and the measurement scales of the available data.

In general, there are two types of research interests: comparing group differences and examining relations between variables. The *t* tests and the ANOVA tests introduced in sections 3 and 4 are procedures for group comparisons for mean differences. Correlation, regression, and the χ^2 test for independence introduced in sections 5 and 6 are used to examine the relationships between the variables. However, this dichotomous classification is only useful for the convenience of describing the research interest. It may not be relevant to the nature of research topics. In fact, research that compares means can also be considered as research that examines relationships. In Brown and Perry's (1991) study of the effectiveness of vocabulary learning methods (see section 3), it is possible to view the research interest as comparing group differences. However, it is also possible to state the research interest in the format of a relationship: Is learning method related to vocabulary learning? Therefore the choice of a statistical test based only on group comparison versus relationship may not be very helpful. In fact, the measurement scale on the dependent variable plays an important role in the choice of a test.

For testing the association between two categorical variables, the χ^2 test of independence is a good choice. When one variable is categorical and the other is on a measurement scale (ordinal, internal, or ratio), the independent-samples *t* test or one-way ANOVA can be used with the categorical variable as the independent variable and the variable with the numeric scale as the dependent variable. In the case that the two variables are both on numeric scales, correlation or regression methods are appropriate to examine the relationship between the two variables, as shown by the example introduced in section 5.3 in this chapter.

Another useful guideline for choosing an appropriate statistical test is how many scores are contributed by each participant in the test. With each participant contributing only one score, the independent-samples *t* test, one-way ANOVA, and the factorial ANOVA are appropriate tests because these tests concern between-subject effects. Where each participant contributes multiple scores in the test, the paired-samples *t* test, repeated-measures ANOVA, correlation, and regression analyses apply. Repeated-measures ANOVA applies to situations with multiple within-subject measures with or without between-subject factors.

8. Exercises

The exercises were designed to provide practice to use the quantitative methods introduced in this chapter. In data analysis section 9.1, the research contexts were taken from recently published articles in SLA journals. Numerical data in the exercises were simulated for practice purposes. For each example, the reader is required to state the research interests and the corresponding null hypotheses of the study, conduct data analysis to test the null hypotheses, draw conclusions, and present the findings with appropriate format and with graphs where necessary. In the guided critique section 8.2, the reader is encouraged to read a published article and to address the questions that require the understanding of quantitative methods introduced in this chapter. Author's comments are provided to serve as reference.

8.1. DATA ANALYSIS

1. Cohen and Brooks-Carson (2001) examined the view that thinking through the L1 or even writing out a text first in the L1 may actually enhance the production of good L2 writing. The participants in the study were intermediate learners of French with different L1s, and they were randomly assigned to two groups. Students in Group 1 were asked to write a short essay directly in French, and the students in Group 2 were asked to write the essay in their L1 first and then to translate it into French. The dependent variables measured from students' writing included scores on grammar scales, organizational structures, smoothness of connection, and clarity of points. Assume we conducted a similar study with 10 participants in each group. The scores on the grammar scale are presented in Table 2.24.
2. Kitano (2001) investigated two potential sources of anxiety in Japanese L2 learners in oral practice in the classroom: fear of negative evaluation and self-perceived speaking ability. The researcher was particularly interested in examining whether the effect of self-perceived ability on anxiety was relatively greater for individuals with a stronger fear of negative evaluation. Assume that the anxiety was measured by 20 items, each on a 5-point Likert scale, with a maximum total score of 100. The fear of negative evaluation was self-rated as high and low, and speaking ability was self-rated at three levels: high, intermediate, and low. The obtained data are presented in Table 2.25.
3. Motivation has been identified as an important factor influencing the effectiveness of L2 learning. Noels (2001) investigated whether teachers' communication styles in the classroom would affect L2 students' motivation for learning. The study was conducted with students in lower-level Spanish classes, who completed a questionnaire assessing motivation for learning Spanish. Teachers' communication styles included two subscales: control, with a higher score indicating that a teacher was perceived as more controlling, and informative feedback, with a higher score indicating the provision of more informative feedback from a teacher. Assume that the three selected variables from the study, students' intrinsic motivation, teachers' control, and teachers' feedback, were all measured with five 7-point Likert-type items. The scores for each student are given in Table 2.26.

TABLE 2.24
Scores on the Grammar Scale for the Two Groups

Student	*1*	*2*	*3*	*4*	*5*	*6*	*7*	*8*	*9*	*10*
Direct Writing	8.9	9.3	8.7	8.4	9.2	10.1	9.5	9.7	14.2	11.6
Translated	5.4	8.1	10.9	7.9	8.6	12.8	8.7	8.3	9.8	9.5

TABLE 2.25
Anxiety Scores for Students with Different Levels of Fear of Negative Evaluation and Speaking Ability

S	*Fear*	*Ability*	*Anxiety*	*S*	*Fear*	*Ability*	*Anxiety*	*S*	*Fear*	*Ability*	*Anxiety*
1	H	H	35	13	H	L	63	25	L	M	28
2	H	H	33	14	H	L	74	26	L	M	42
3	H	H	21	15	H	L	48	27	L	M	38
4	H	H	33	16	H	L	42	28	L	M	33
5	H	H	52	17	H	L	63	29	L	M	42
6	H	H	42	18	H	L	59	30	L	M	23
7	H	M	42	19	L	H	24	31	L	L	47
8	H	M	50	20	L	H	39	32	L	L	48
9	H	M	52	21	L	H	33	33	L	L	34
10	H	M	43	22	L	H	21	34	L	L	44
11	H	M	36	23	L	H	46	35	L	L	35
12	H	M	62	24	L	H	37	36	L	L	43

Note. S = Student.

TABLE 2.26
Students' Motivation and Teachers' Communication Style Scores

Student	*Motivation*	*Feedback*	*Control*	*Student*	*Motivation*	*Feedback*	*Control*
1	22	18	16	26	19	29	21
2	16	29	15	27	27	19	19
3	21	21	13	28	21	25	20
4	06	12	21	29	14	14	13
5	13	15	22	30	23	12	14
6	19	16	23	31	15	28	16
7	22	24	16	32	25	21	15
8	16	19	11	33	30	24	09
9	17	18	28	34	09	20	21
10	26	24	15	35	29	33	16
11	11	17	21	36	31	29	07
12	23	26	20	37	30	23	15
13	16	23	17	38	31	27	17
14	18	15	19	39	24	22	15
15	22	30	15	40	22	30	10
16	33	22	13	41	08	22	19
17	15	23	21	42	14	25	16
18	14	21	14	43	12	24	26
19	32	30	12	44	08	19	20
20	12	23	25	45	25	27	13
21	18	23	15	46	20	24	19
22	18	25	16	47	17	22	17
23	26	24	14	48	16	29	12
24	15	27	17	49	24	20	16
25	17	26	15	50	22	13	15

TABLE 2.27
Pretest and Posttest Scores for the Control and Treatment Groups

Control			Treatment		
Student	*Pretest*	*Posttest*	*Student*	*Pretest*	*Posttest*
1	20	55	1	30	61
2	10	43	2	33	57
3	41	54	3	06	14
4	39	48	4	24	31
5	35	27	5	21	30
6	07	24	6	13	44
7	27	59	7	22	44
8	06	09	8	17	52
9	13	41	9	21	40
10	03	18	10	08	26
11	28	57	11	12	34
12	36	49	12	39	47
13	19	57	13	25	35
14	06	21	14	34	40
15	27	34	15	22	37

4. Maxim (2002) investigated whether the reading of authentic texts, defined as materials written to be read by native speakers, would influence the L2 learning of beginning college-level language students. The participants were first-semester L2 learners of German. In the first four weeks of the semester, all participants followed the same standard syllabus. At the end of the fourth week, a pretest that involved reading four short texts and performing a set of tasks was administered to all participants. Starting at the fifth week, the treatment group modified its use of the regular syllabus by reading a 142-page German romance novel, while the control group kept following the standard syllabus. At the end of the semester, a posttest was administered to all participants, who read four short texts and completed a set of tasks related to the four texts. Simulated data for the scores on the pretest and the posttest obtained from 15 participants in each group are presented in Table 2.27.

8.2. GUIDED CRITIQUE

Wharton (2000) has been selected as the published article for a guided critique in this chapter:

Wharton, G. (2000). Language learning strategy use of bilingual foreign language learners in Singapore. *Language Learning, 50,* 203–243.

The study used ANOVA and the χ^2 test for independence as the statistical procedures for testing the null hypotheses related to the research interests. After reading the article, readers may discuss the issues related to the quantitative methodology used in this study by focusing on the following topics:

1. What are the major research interests of the study?
2. Describe the sample of the study.
3. What variables are measured in this study, and what are the measurement scales for these variables?
4. List the null hypotheses tested in the study.
5. What specific statistical procedures were used for testing the null hypotheses? Were these statistical procedures appropriately applied in terms of the measurement scales of the variables and the specific hypotheses being tested?
6. How were the findings of the study presented?
7. Do you have suggestions for improving the presentation of results?

The following comments may serve as reference when discussing the preceding topics.

The major research interest in Wharton (2000) was to investigate how foreign language learners used learning strategies with a particular focus on students with bilingual backgrounds. The author was interested in how learners' background variables, such as proficiency levels and gender, would affect the choices of particular learning strategies.

The sample for the study was 678 university students learning Japanese and French as foreign languages in Singapore. The sample size for the study is relatively large compared with other similar studies in SLA research. The Oxford 80-item Strategy Inventory for Language Learning (SILL) was administered to all participants along with a background questionnaire. SILL is a Likert-type measure with each item on a 5-point ordinal scale ranging from *never use* to *always use;* it indicates the frequency with which a particular learning strategy was used. SILL has five subscales: social compensation, metacognitive, cognitive, memory, and affective. Foreign language proficiency level, an ordinal categorical variable, was self-reported as poor, fair, or good on the background questionnaire. Gender is a dichotomous variable.

The author conducted a series of ANOVAs to test the null hypotheses of no effects of background variables on the use of learning strategies. Based on the results from a one-way ANOVA (see Table 2.2 in Wharton, 2000, p. 218), the author reported that gender had no significant effect on the use of the learning strategies but that proficiency had a significant effect on two of the SILL subscales: compensation ($p < 0.046$) and affect ($p < 0.025$). The author also reported Scheffé post hoc tests showing that for compensation, the fair groups used more learning strategies than the poor group but that there was no significant difference for the three proficiency groups on the affective subscale.

The ANOVA would be a valid test if the dependent variable had been the mean score obtained from each participant across a particular SILL subscale; however, this practice was not clearly indicated in the text. Since the degrees of freedom for ANOVA were not reported in the article, readers may wonder if this was the case. If the dependent variable were the original scores on each item of the SILL subscale, instead of the means for each participant, the ANOVA test would have violated the assumption of independence because scores from the same participant were correlated.

The author also tested the independence of proficiency and gender for each of the particular learning strategies, using separate χ^2 tests for each of the 80 items on the SILL. The rating on each SILL item was converted into high, medium, and low use based on the original 5-point scale, and each χ^2 test was based on a 3×3 contingency table (3 levels of proficiency and 3 levels of frequency of strategy use). The author reported that 39 out of 80 χ^2 tests came out significant, indicating a significant relationship between proficiency and the frequency of the 39 strategies.

For the χ^2 tests, it is not clear why the author did not report the raw frequencies in the contingency tables but only the percentages of users at each proficiency level (see Table 2.3 in Wharton, 2000). Readers could be confused and believe that the χ^2 tests were conducted based on these percentages. The χ^2 test should be conducted on raw occurrences, never on percentages. Another comment on these χ^2 tests is that it is an unacceptable practice to conduct 80 tests simultaneously without protection from making type I errors. The Bonferroni correction or other procedures are available for limiting type I errors when multiple tests are conducted within one study. Readers interested in these procedures may refer to books recommended in the further reading section.

A better data analysis strategy for handling multiple χ^2 tests is to select particular learning strategies that are the most interesting to examine in order to limit the number of total tests. In this way, the power of the analysis will be increased when the necessary correction procedures are used to limit the type I errors.

9. Further Reading

A journey of a thousand miles starts with the first step. By reading this chapter, the reader will have taken the first step in learning quantitative methodology for SLA research. Because of space limitations, some important issues in quantitative methods, such as power analysis, nonparametric procedures, interrater reliability, and agreement indexes, have not been included in this chapter. Further readings are suggested on these topics as well as on more advanced quantitative methods, especially the multivariate procedures used in SLA research.

Howell's (1992) textbook for intermediate learners does not assume knowledge of mathematical derivations and is recommended for readers wishing to learn more details about the procedures introduced in this chapter. This textbook also covers other important topics that have not been addressed in this chapter.

Porte's (2002) textbook, written for students of applied linguistics in research methodology courses, offers detailed procedures of critical analysis of research articles using quantitative approaches. The workbook accompanying the textbook offers guided critiques and constructive appraisals of published articles that readers may find helpful when working on their own research.

Brown's (1991, 1992) articles were written for second and foreign language teachers to better understand statistical methods, with emphasis on the choice of correct statistical procedures, violations of statistical assumptions, and interpretation of findings. Reading these two articles will provide a good review of the statistical procedures presented in this chapter.

Multivariate methods including factor analysis and structural equation modeling are becoming increasingly popular in SLA journals. Tabachnick and Fidell (2001) is recommended for readers interested in learning multivariate statistical methods. Byrne (1994) is recommended for beginners learning structural equation modeling.

Percentages are often used as dependent variables in SLA studies. For appropriate use of percentages, Greer and Dunlap (1997) is an excellent reference. SLA researchers often confuse the concepts of interrater reliability and interrater agreement. Tinsley and Weiss (2000) is recommended for this topic.

Huff and Geis' (1954) classic book *How To Lie with Statistics* is still recommended reading today for keeping a critical viewpoint when reading statistical reports including numbers and figures.

Gardner (2001) is recommended for readers interested in using *SPSS for Windows* for conducting the statistical procedures introduced in this chapter. Green and Salkind's (2004) introduction to SPSS covers both Windows and Macintosh operating systems and the new features offered by SPSS version 13.0. This book provides step-by-step guidelines to many statistical procedures commonly used by behavioral researchers.

Note

1. The Test of English as a Foreign Language (TOEFL) measures the ability of nonnative speakers to use and understand English. U.S. universities require that

international students submit TOEFL scores as a part of their application package. TOEFL is designed and administered by Educational Testing Services (ETS).

References

Arnold, J. (2000). Seeing through listening comprehension exam anxiety. *TESOL Quarterly, 34,* 777–786.

Bateman, B. (2002). Promoting openness toward culture learning: Ethnographic interviews for students of Spanish. *The Modern Language Journal, 86,* 318–331.

Brown, J. D. (1991). Statistics as a foreign language-part 1: What to look for in reading statistical language studies. *TESOL Quarterly, 25,* 569–586.

Brown, J. D. (1992). Statistics as a foreign language-part 2: More things to consider in reading statistical language studies. *TESOL Quarterly, 26,* 629–664.

Brown, T. S., & Perry, F. L., Jr. (1991). A comparison of three learning strategies for ESL vocabulary acquisition. *TESOL Quarterly, 25,* 655–670.

Byrne, B. (1994). *Structural equation modeling with EQS and EQS/Windows: Basic concepts, applications, and programming.* London: Sage.

Cohen, A. D., & Brooks-Carson, A. (2001). Research on direct versus translated writing: Students' strategies and their results. *The Modern Language Journal, 85,* 169–188.

Gardner, R. C. (2001). *Psychological statistics using SPSS for Windows.* Englewood Cliffs, NJ: Prentice Hall.

Geva, E. (1992). The role of conjunctions in L2 text comprehension. *TESOL Quarterly, 26,* 731–747.

Gradman, H. L., & Hanania, E. (1991). Language learning background factors and ESL proficiency. *The Modern Language Journal, 75,* 39–51.

Green, S. B. & Salkind, N. J. (2004) *Using SPSS for Windows and Macintosh: Analyzing and understanding data* (4th ed.). Englewood Cliffs, NJ: Prentice Hall.

Greer, T., & Dunlap, W. P. (1997). Analysis of variance with ipsative measures. *Psychological Methods, 2,* 200–207.

Harley, B. (2000). Listening strategies in ESL: Do age and L1 make a difference? *TESOL Quarterly, 34,* 769–777.

Hayasa, Y. A. (2002). The effects of differential timing in the introduction of Japan syllabaries on early second language development in Japanese interviews for students of Spanish. *The Modern Language Journal, 86,* 318–331.

Honeyfield, J. (1977). Simplification. *TESOL Quarterly, 11,* 431–440.

Howell, D. C. (1992). *Statistical methods for psychology* (3rd ed.). Belmont, CA: Duxbury Press.

Huff, D. & Geis, I. (1954). *How to lie with statistics.* New York: Norton.

Kitano, K. (2001). Anxiety in the college Japanese language classroom. *The Modern Language Journal, 85,* 549–566.

Klingner, J. K., & Vaughn, S. (2000). The helping behaviors of fifth graders while using collaborative strategic reading during ESL content classes. *TESOL Quarterly, 34,* 69–98.

Leow, R. P. (2000). A study of the role of awareness in foreign language behavior: Aware versus unaware learners. *Studies in Second Language Acquisition, 22,* 557–584.

Macias, R. F. (1998). *Summary report of the survey of the states' limited-English proficient students and available educational programs and services 1996–1997.* Washington, DC: U.S. Department of Education, National Clearinghouse for Bilingual Education.

MacIntyre, P. D. & Baker, S. C. (2001). Willingness to communicate, social support, and language-learning orientations of immersion students. *Studies in Second Language Acquisition, 23,* 369–388.

Mackey, A. (1999). Input, interaction, and second language development: An empirical study of question formation in ESL. *Studies in Second Language Acquisition, 21,* 557–587.

Maxim, H. H. (2002). A study into the feasibility and effects of reading extended authentic discourse in the beginning German language classroom. *The Modern Language Journal, 86,* 20–35.

Noels, K. A. (2001). Learning Spanish as a second language: Learners' orientations and perceptions of their teachers' communication style. *Language Learning, 51,* 107–144.

Oh, S. Y. (2001). Two types of input modification and EFL reading comprehension: Simplification versus elaboration. *TESOL Quarterly, 35,* 69–96.

Porte, G. K. (2002). *Appraising research in second language learning: A practical approach to critical analysis of quantitative research.* Amsterdam: JohnBenjamins.

Tabachnick, B. G. & Fidell, L. S. (2001). *Using multivariate statistics* (4th ed.). Boston: Allyn and Bacon.

Tinsley, H. E. A., & Weiss, D. J. (2000). Interrater reliability and agreement. In H. E. A. Tinsley & S.D. Brown (Eds.), *Handbook of applied multivariate statistics and mathematical modeling* (pp. 95–124). New York: Academic Press.

Wharton, G. (2000). Language learning strategy use of bilingual foreign language learners in Singapore. *Language Learning, 50,* 203–243.

Yano, Y., Long, M. H., & Ross, S. (1994). The effects of simplified and elaborated texts on foreign language reading comprehension. *Language Learning, 44,* 189–219.

THREE

Research Methodology: Qualitative Research

REBECCA ADAMS
AKIKO FUJII
ALISON MACKEY

KEY WORDS
Case studies ■ credibility ■ dependability ■ diaries ■ qualitative research ■ questionnaires ■ stimulated recall ■ think-aloud protocols ■ transferability.

1. Introduction

A wide range of empirical research approaches are used in second language acquisition (SLA), including those originating in the fields of linguistics, psychology, anthropology, and education. This range includes quantitative and qualitative approaches to research design, data collection procedures, and methods of data analysis. Although quantitative experimental approaches to research are arguably the dominant paradigm (Lazaraton, 2003; Chen, this volume, chapter 2), the value of employing qualitative methods in SLA studies is being increasingly recognized, particularly in second language (L2) classroom research (Lazaraton, 2000, 2003; Nunan, 1991; Pica, 1997). In the current chapter, we focus specifically on qualitative methods in instructed settings. While quantitative research certainly can shed light on many aspects of learning in L2 classrooms, qualitative research can offer a different perspective grounded in teachers' and learners' views with a more holistic and contextualized view of the many factors that interact in L2 learning. Used in tandem with quantitative research or on its own, qualitative research can yield a clearer understanding of classroom SLA.

The purpose of this chapter is to provide an overview of qualitative approaches to instructed SLA for classroom researchers. We begin with a discussion of theoretical assumptions and methodological characteristics underpinning qualitative research, providing examples of research issues in instructed SLA that have been addressed through qualitative methods. We then outline commonly used methods often associated with qualitative research for gathering data in instructed SLA contexts. These include classroom observations, interviews, case studies and ethnographies, verbal protocols, and diaries or journals, as well as techniques associated with survey-based research such as interviews and questionnaires. We conclude the chapter with a discussion of practical considerations in conducting qualitative research, including issues such as the coding of data, credibility, transferability, and dependability. Our goal in this chapter is to enhance the understanding of qualitative research methodology and techniques in instructed contexts and to prepare readers to make informed decisions about the implementation of qualitative methodology and techniques in instructed SLA research.

2. Qualitative Research and Instructed SLA

This section provides an introduction to the use of qualitative research in L2 contexts. First, qualitative orientations to research are discussed, drawing on research from L2 studies, anthropology, sociology, and other related fields. The introduced aspects of qualitative research are then exemplified through empirical topics that have been addressed using qualitative research.

2.1. PERSPECTIVES ON QUALITATIVE RESEARCH

The term *qualitative research* covers approaches from a range of academic disciplines and research traditions (for a detailed review of representative traditions, see E. Jacob, 1987). Denzin and Lincoln (1994) propose the following general definition, "Qualitative research is multimethod in focus, involving an interpretive and naturalistic approach to its subject matter. This means that qualitative researchers study things in their natural settings, attempting to make sense of, or interpret, phenomena in terms of the meanings people bring to them" (p. 2).

Qualitative research is often contrasted with nonqualitative approaches. L2 researchers have referred to two differing paradigms using a variety of terms including qualitative and quantitative (Larsen-Freeman and Long, 1991; Lazaraton, 1995; Nunan, 1992; Pica, 1997), qualitative and logical-positivistic (Davis, 1995), and qualitative and experimental (Seliger and Shohamy, 1989). Nunan (1992) explains that these paradigms are "underpinned by quite different conceptions of the nature and status of knowledge" (p. 5). Quantitative research has its roots in "the philosophical orientations of mentalism, behaviorism, and individualism" (Davis, 1995, p. 428) and is based on the view that there is an objective reality that can be measured using controlled instrumentation. In contrast, qualitative research is based on the assumption that reality is socially constructed and that the process of research is inherently value-laden (Denzin and Lincoln, 1994, p. 4), meaning that it is grounded in the perspectives of the participants themselves. Therefore, one of the key theoretical assumptions underlying qualitative approaches to SLA is an *emic* perspective, or the use of "categories which are meaningful to members of the speech community under study" (Saville-Troike, 1982, p. 130). This can be distinguished from the use of *etic,* or outsider's, categories and frameworks to interpret behavior. Miller and Ginsberg's (1995) diary study of learning in study-abroad programs, for example, made use of participant terminologies in reporting learning experiences in and out of their classes to create a holistic description of study abroad that considered both learner and researcher perceptions of study abroad as a language-learning context.

In addition, qualitative approaches often emphasize the role of the sociocultural context where language learning occurs (Davis, 1995). Language learning is viewed holistically with a focus on both microlevel phenomena, such as interaction within the classroom, and broader sociocultural phenomena including the experiences of the participants and the ideological orientations of the community. For example, Philips' (1983) ethnographic study of classroom language use in a Native American community compares classroom interactional patterns and nonverbal behavior in Native American classrooms and in Anglo classrooms outside the reservation. In her analysis, Philips draws connections between communicative behavior in the classroom and learners' cultural background. She found that the children's cultural backgrounds strongly influenced their interactional patterns in the classroom, underscoring the importance of a thorough understanding of learners' cultural experiences for interpreting learning behaviors.

While quantitative researchers traditionally seek to maintain impartiality, qualitative researchers may consciously assume ideological positions. Such research is often described as critical (Cumming, 1994) in that the research may have a general agenda, usually the promotion of positive teaching environments or techniques. In classroom action research, which is receiving increasing recognition as a popular research paradigm, teachers and researchers often collaborate with the specific intent to implement change in the classroom in an informed manner (Freeman, 1998; Nunan, 1992). For example, in Tsui's (1996) study of student unwillingness to speak in classes in English as a second language (ESL) in Hong Kong, teachers critically reviewed videotapes of their classes to identify strategies for fostering student involvement, kept diaries chronicling their efforts to implement these strategies, and finally examined new video recordings of their classes to determine whether their teaching strategies had helped learners overcome their reticence.

Philosophical assumptions about the nature of research also dictate the use of certain data collection procedures and methods of analysis. Whereas quantitative research is usually characterized by a focus on certain selected aspects of behavior and controlled data collection, qualitative research is typically concerned with data collected in naturally occurring and nonmanipulated contexts. Quantitative research tends to emphasize measurement and analysis of objective data in terms of variables and the use of statistical analysis and quantification as the primary means for testing prespecified hypotheses. In contrast, qualitative research is often process-oriented, open-ended, or emergent, following a cyclical and inductive path that begins with few preconceptions and is guided by a subsequent gradual narrowing of focus.

Despite seemingly clear-cut distinctions between qualitative and quantitative research, there continues to be a considerable amount of debate about the label *qualitative research* within the field of L2 research (Davis, 1995; Lazaraton, 1995). The term *qualitative* has been used to describe a wide range of classroom SLA studies. At one end of the spectrum are ethnographic studies (Duff, 2002; Hornberger, 1988; J. Jacob, Rottenberg, Patrick, and Wheeler, 1996; Watson-Gegeo and Gegeo, 1995; Willet, 1995; Wong-Fillmore, 1982), which are closest to prototypical descriptions of qualitative research, such as that provided above. At the other extreme are experimental studies (e.g., Adams, 2003; Leow, 1998, 2000; Mackey, Gass, and McDonough, 2000; Mackey, Philp, Egi, Fujii, and Tatsumi, 2002) that, while using controlled experimental designs and quantification, also employ one or more data collection procedures or techniques often used in qualitative research. (Issues related to the qualitative-quantitative distinction, and mixed methods studies, are also discussed in the chapter on qualitative research in Mackey and Gass, 2005.) Some qualitative researchers (e.g., Davis, 1995) suggest that a qualitative study is based on certain philosophical assumptions and should be characterized by an integrated approach to research design, data collection, and analysis. However, it is increasingly common for researchers to report on both quantitative and qualitative findings. For example, in a study of English as a second language (ESL) learners' perceptions of classroom activities, Barkhuizen (1998) used several methods of data collection, including a questionnaire with a rank scale for each item, as well as interviews. The analysis integrates statistical analysis of the questionnaire data with the researcher's interpretations of observations and interviews. Davis recommends making explicit the philosophical, theoretical, and methodological considerations used when reporting on qualitative studies.

Researchers have emphasized the methodological legitimacy of qualitative research (Davis, 1995; Edge and Richards, 1998). However, Edge and Richards (1998) allow that the sheer diversity of qualitative research possibilities can be confusing and argue that researchers must carefully consider the requirements for trustworthy research in the research tradition they follow. And, although guidelines presented in research journals may be useful for some, Lazaraton (2003) points out that existing guidelines are generally tailored towards ethnographic research and "fall short in capturing some of the unique features of specific qualitative research approaches" (p. 6). Lazaraton also calls for constant critical review within the field of standards for valid and acceptable qualitative research.

2.2. L2 TOPICS AND QUALITATIVE RESEARCH

A wide variety of L2 research topics have been addressed through qualitative research. Although space precludes a thorough review, we introduce some sample areas of interest to classroom researchers in the following section.

2.2.1. COGNITIVE PROCESSES

Qualitative research methods have been utilized in studies that focus on a range of L2 learning phenomena and that examine learner interactions to generate insights into interpersonal and mental processes of learning (Storch, 1998; Swain and Lapkin, 2001; Swain, Lapkin, and Smith, 2002). From a Vygotskyan perspective of collaborative learning, Swain and Lapkin (1998) viewed learner language or dialogue as evidence of cognitive activity. Through an in-depth analysis of the dialogue between two learners during a collaborative classroom task, Swain and Lapkin demonstrated that collaborative dialogue can function as a cognitive tool for learning by allowing learners to generate and assess hypotheses about language as well as to apply previously learned knowledge and focus on certain linguistic items.

Studies have also focused more specifically on learners' perceptions about instructional processes such as error correction (Roberts, 1995) and interactional feedback (Mackey, 2000; Mackey et al., 2000) in order to explore learning mechanisms and mental processes involved in recognizing and interpreting corrective feedback. Cognitive processes are usually investigated through introspective verbal protocols, such as stimulated recall and think-aloud protocols. These techniques are discussed in more detail in 2.3.3.

2.2.2. CLASSROOM PROCESSES

Qualitative research has investigated the nature of classroom interaction through observations and analysis of transcripts. Anton (1999) and Musumeci (1996), for example, focused on characterizing teacher-learner interaction in the classroom. Anton (1999) examined contrasting patterns of discourse in two French and Italian university foreign language classrooms, pointing out differences in learner-centered and teacher-centered classrooms and the ways in which communicative moves in learner-centered classrooms facilitated language learning. Musumeci (1996) investigated teacher inferences about meaning in nonnative speech, finding differences between novice and experienced teachers. Other research has focused on the manner in which learners create learning opportunities during classroom research (Storch, 2002; Takahashi, 1998) as well as on the role of the teacher (Lazaraton, 2004; Samuda, 2001).

Qualitative research on classroom processes has also been conducted based on the language socialization approach (Duff, 1996; Ohta, 1994; Willet, 1995). This is a holistic approach to language acquisition that emphasizes sociocultural factors such as discourse competence and identity construction. For example, Willet's (1995) ethnographic study of L2 socialization in a first-grade classroom provided an interpretive account of how four children used interactional routines to construct appropriate social relations, identities, and ideologies. Duff (1996) compared socialization of discourse competence in English-medium and dual-language English classrooms in Hungary, reporting differences in discourse structure and instructional practices such as oral recitation.

Qualitative methods have also been used in investigations of learners' perceptions about learning opportunities in the classroom. A number of studies have used classroom written protocols, sometimes referred to as *uptake charts,* to investigate classroom L2 learning from the learners' points of view (Allwright, 1984; Jones, 1992; Mackey et al., 2000; Palmeira, 1995; Slimani, 1989, 1992). Allwright (1984) and others have used uptake charts to elicit learner perceptions of their classroom learning. These reports have been examined with respect to the relationship between the linguistic items learners reported learning and characteristics of classroom discourse such as who initiated discussion of the item (Slimani, 1989), who supplied the input (Jones, 1992), or whether or not the item had been targeted by the teacher (Palmeira, 1995). D. Block's (1996) study of classroom learning also emphasized participants' perspectives and interpretations, finding significant mismatches in the perceptions of the teacher and one particular learner.

2.2.3. LEARNER VARIABLES

Qualitative methods can also be useful when exploring the role of affective variables such as attitude and motivation in classroom language learning, representing a holistic approach for linking affective factors to the sociocultural context of learning. For example, Syed (2001) used a variety of qualitative procedures, including classroom observation and formal and informal interviewing, to examine the relationship between university students' cultural identity and their motivation for learning Hindi. Spielmann and Radnofsky's (2001) ethnographic study of a seven-week intensive class in a summer French school focused on language anxiety and provided a new perspective on anxiety or tension as a potentially positive or negative dynamic in the cognitive and affective domains. Such research illustrates the way that our understanding of L2 learning in instructed contexts has been enhanced both by traditional qualitative studies and by hybrid studies that employ qualitative methods of data analysis.

2.3. QUALITATIVE APPROACHES TO THE STUDY OF INSTRUCTED SLA

A wide variety of different qualitative techniques are used in the collection and analysis of L2 classroom data. As with all methods, the advantages and disadvantages of each technique should be taken into consideration when deciding how to address a specific research question. In this section, we present an overview of some of the most commonly used qualitative methods in classroom settings, supplemented by brief descriptions of empirical studies. Again, space precludes an exhaustive list, so this is a summary of some of the commonly used qualitative methods.

2.3.1. CLASSROOM OBSERVATIONS

While careful and extensive observations are commonly associated with anthropologists' efforts to document and understand the patterns of human behavior, L2 researchers have also used observational techniques to uncover information about learners and teachers in the classroom (Allwright, 1987; Pica and Doughty, 1985; Wong-Fillmore, 1980, 1982). Classroom observations can be useful in investigating internal and external factors in L2 learning as well as in investigating the relationships between various factors. In classroom observations, researchers endeavor to carefully describe classroom activities without impacting any of the classroom interactions or activities. The data are collected through a combination of audio or visual recordings and field notes. Field notes record the researchers' impressions or questions during the observation. Audio or visual recordings allow researchers to revise and refine their original thoughts, to analyze language use in greater depth, and to make the research available to other researchers who may want to examine and analyze the data. Researchers often choose to use observations to supplement data obtained from interviews, questionnaires, and classroom data, including homework and grading. For example, Bailey (1996) used classroom observations in her study of teacher decision-making processes as an important part of the data on teachers' behaviors. These observations, along with written lesson plans, formed the basis of subsequent in-depth interviews with the teachers.

Observational research may be structured or unstructured. In structured observations, the researcher marks a detailed checklist or rating scale. A structured observation can assist the researcher with keeping track of where, when, and how often certain types of interactions take place in the classroom. Observations can allow researchers to evaluate students' behavior in different contexts in a consistent manner. One example of a structured observation tool based on a checklist is the Communicative Orientation for Language Teaching (COLT) schema, described by Spada and Frohlich (1995), which requires researchers to keep track of 70 categories of classroom interaction phenomena to investigate the organization and the use of language in the classroom. Spada (1990) used the COLT schema to compare classroom interactions in several different French L2 classrooms, finding that the classroom activities differed substantially in traditional grammar-focused classrooms and in communicative classrooms. While it is helpful to contrast structured and nonstructured observations, it is important to recognize that observations can be more or less structured, as appropriate for the research questions and setting. Chaudron (1988) has also pointed out that in utilizing checklists and rating scales, L2 researchers should consider the theoretical basis for such scales. The importance of the suggested categories for the research questions should be considered before employing an observational schema in classroom research. Mackey and Gass (2005) describe several different observation schemas, together with issues to be considered when selecting or adapting schemas.

Most observational research is carried out with the intention of being as unobtrusive as possible; however, the presence of an outsider can affect the behavior of those being observed. This phenomenon is known as the *observer's paradox* (Labov, 1972). Researchers should consider the way they may influence a classroom setting and should take steps to mitigate the effect of their presence in the classroom. For example, researchers can ask to be introduced to the class ahead of time and to observe several classes before they collect data, in order to familiarize the class with their presence. As learners become more accustomed to the researcher's presence, the researcher may be able to blend into the background and interactions may become more natural (Fraenkel and Wallen, 2002). When recording equipment is used, its consistent presence (not recording) in several previous classes can serve the same purpose. As learners become habituated to the presence of the equipment, it may affect them less (Boggs, 1972). As long as appropriate consents have been obtained, concealed cameras might also record a class while researchers watch in another room.

Another option for researchers to be less obtrusive in the classroom is participant observation, where researchers observe a class or group of which they are a member. In this capacity, a researcher can both observe the class and participate fully in classroom activities with other students. Participant observation might reduce the effects of the observer's paradox, but careful observation during participation is difficult. Participant observation is only possible in adult learning contexts where the researcher can reasonably blend in. Some researchers have extended possible contexts for participant observation by participating as teachers. For example, Hardman (1999) studied Cambodian adult learners' community classroom behavior while working in the community center as an

ESL literacy teacher. As a teacher, he was able to study learner production, learning behaviors, and learner concerns that may not have been available to an outside researcher. The degree of participation can vary depending on the researcher and context. In experiments on L2 instruction, researchers operating recording equipment or facilitating group work may also participate as native speaker resources for the class once learners have become accustomed to them (R. Ellis, 1992).

2.3.2. CASE STUDIES AND ETHNOGRAPHIES

Observations can be used with other data collection techniques including questionnaires and interviews. Multiple data collection techniques are used together to create a highly detailed account of a research phenomenon. This process is known as ethnography. Case studies and ethnographies are usually designed along the principle of gathering as much information as possible from multiple sources using a range of data collection techniques with a specific population or setting. Normally ethnographies center around a population of learners while case studies focus on a specific learner, or learning setting. The purpose of both is to present an account that is as complete and accurate as possible of human behaviors, interactions, or learning in the research context.

An ethnography or case study involves several stages of research. Normally researchers identify the group to study, perform observations in the learning context, conduct interviews with the research participants and others connected to them and to the setting, and gather evidence of L2 performance. Watson-Gegeo's (2001) ethnographic work in Hawaiian immersion classrooms involved observing classes and learner behavior outside of class; interviewing students, teachers, parents, and administrators; and collecting learner language production, homework, tests, grades, and writing samples. After assembling information from a wide variety of sources, the researcher sifts through the information looking for trends or interesting issues in the data. Based on the trends identified, the researcher can begin to formulate hypotheses that can be refined through further, more focused data collection.

Case studies can be more or less structured, where structure refers to the degree of consistency. For example, very similar case studies could be conducted with two individual learners or two existing groups of learners for the purpose of comparing and contrasting their behaviors (Fraenkel and Wallen, 2002). Case studies and ethnographies involve intensive research over an extended period of time. They require a commitment to long-term data collection and repeated analysis. However, ethnography and case study research can provide a holistic characterization of language learning and use in a specific population or setting.

2.3.3. VERBAL PROTOCOLS

Classical qualitative methods like classroom observations can provide valuable insights into the learning process, but they usually allow researchers to gather data only on observable behaviors. L2 learning occurs in a social setting (Gass, 1997; Lantolf and Appel, 1994; Swain and Lapkin, 1998, 2001); however, actual learning processes are an internal series of cognitive events that may not be observable from production data alone. Language-learning processes also may be sensitive to individual differences, including levels of anxiety (Foss and Reitzel, 1988), motivation (Dörnyei and Kormos, 2000, 2002), and perceptions about learning in general (Wang, 1999). The specific learning context, including the social setting of the learning and the activities learners engage in, is also relevant. Although there is some dispute about the accessibility of learners' internal processes (see Faerch and Kasper, 1987; Gass and Mackey, 2000), researchers have turned to the collection of introspective data to learn about internal influences to the learning process. Introspective data can be elicited in a number of ways, including the use of questionnaires and interviews (discussed below), as well as diaries and verbal protocols.

Verbal protocols have been used to study characteristics of cognitive processing involved in language acquisition such as noticing (Mackey et al., 2000; Swain and Lapkin, 2002), attention and awareness (Leow, 1998, 2000), or strategy use (Anderson, 1991). Such research makes use of verbal protocols, in which learners verbalize their thoughts during L2 tasks. Verbal protocols can be thought of as simultaneous (or think-aloud) protocols and retrospective (or stimulated recall) protocols.

In simultaneous protocols, learners are asked to verbalize their thoughts while performing a task to investigate the processes of language learning. For example, Anderson (1991) asked ESL learners to vocalize their thoughts while reading academic texts and while completing a reading comprehension test in order to identify processing strategies used by learners in natural reading and language test-taking situations. In addition to reading (Anderson, 1991; E. Block, 1986; Upton, Lee, and Li, 2001), think-aloud protocols have also been used to investigate processes or strategies related to writing (Armengol-Castells, 2001; Cohen and Cavalcanti, 1987) and strategy use in listening (Vandergrift, 2003), as well as the role of attention or awareness (Leow, 1998, 2000; Leow, Egi, Nuevo, and Tsai, 2003).

When think-aloud protocols are implemented in reading or writing tasks, learners are normally asked to report all of their thoughts as they complete the task. As this is not possible when learners complete oral tasks, researchers can create breaks at appropriate intervals throughout speaking and listening tasks, providing learners with time to report their thoughts. Since learners report their thoughts as they occur, think-aloud protocols may not be subject to memory deterioration. However, thinking aloud while performing can seem unnatural. Learners may need training and practice to think aloud during language tasks. The process of thinking aloud itself may also be reactive; it is possible that thinking aloud may influence how learners process language in certain tasks, thereby posing a threat to the validity of the research endeavor (Biggs, Rosman, and Sergenian, 1993; Ericsson and Simon, 1980; Russo, Johnson, and Stephens, 1989).

The use of stimulated recall, or retrospective, protocols may mitigate the possibility of reactivity. For stimulated recall protocols, learners are first recorded completing an L2 activity. Following the activity, learners and researchers review the recording and learners are asked to report the thoughts they had at the time of the activity (Gass and Mackey, 2000). Since learners are asked to remember their thoughts, there is danger of memory deterioration. In order to obtain more accurate data, researchers use a stimulus to help participants remember their thoughts while engaged in L2 work. The stimulus can be audio or visual recordings of the participants engaged in L2 activities or artifacts of L2 production like essays. A stronger stimulus (e.g., video recording as opposed to audio recording) can elicit more accurate and complete responses, as does performing the stimulated recall as soon as possible following engagement in the L2 task. In the stimulated recall session, participants and researchers review the stimulus material together, pausing at times for the participant to share thoughts from their L2 performance.

Stimulated recall can allow researchers and learners to jointly investigate language learning experiences. For example, Swain and Lapkin (2002) used stimulated recall in a study of learning from exposure to reformulated writing. After learners compared their writing with a native speaker reformulation, the learners and researchers engaged in a stimulated recall session, which allowed the researchers to gain insights into the way the learners processed the reformulated writing. In a classroom setting, it is possible for the researcher to schedule individual sessions with learners after the class, where the learners can discuss the thoughts they had during class activities. However, researchers should be cautious in interpreting stimulated recall data. As time passes between the task and the stimulated recall, the quality of the recall may decline because of memory deterioration. When learners have difficulty remembering what they thought during the treatment, they may verbalize what they are thinking at the time of the recall (in order to make sense of their actions) rather than what they were thinking during the treatment. Additionally, when data are collected using stimulated recall, this method of collecting data may also represent an additional learning opportunity (Adams, 2003). In Adams's study, learners engaged in stimulated recall interviews about L2 interactions between the pre- and posttests. She determined that posttest scores were inflated by participation in stimulated recall during the study. For more information on the use of verbal protocols, see Leow and Bowles (this volume, chapter 6).

2.3.4. DIARIES AND JOURNALS

While interviews and questionnaires (discussed below) can help researchers understand learners' experiences, the data collected in them is often decontextualized. Learners' responses are constrained by the questions researchers choose to ask. L2 diaries (also referred to as L2 journals or learner autobiographies) allow learners to write about their language-learning experiences. Since learners are able to record any of their impressions or perceptions about learning, they are not constrained by predetermined areas of interest. This allows researchers to uncover new ideas or trends related to learners' internal processes such as attention and memory, as well as learners' reactions to instructional methods or classroom processes.

The noticing hypothesis of L2 acquisition (Schmidt, 2001; Schmidt and Frota, 1986), for example, emerged following a diary study. Based on Schmidt's introspective descriptions of his learning opportunities and success at learning abroad, Schmidt and Frota were able to determine that he had noticed forms shortly before beginning to use them. They concluded from this that conscious noticing played a role in language learning. Since diaries represent holistic accounts of language learning from a learner's viewpoint, careful analysis of diaries can yield insights into the learning process inaccessible from a researcher's perspective alone. Pavlenko (2001) explains that diaries can provide valuable insights about "learner motivations, experiences, struggles, losses and gains" (p. 213) that are longitudinal and highly personal in nature. For example, Pavlenko (2001) carried out an interpretive analysis of 23 language learning memoirs and autobiographic essays, exploring the role of gender in the construction of narrative voice. She found that male writers tended to highlight language learning as an individual enterprise, while women tended to emphasize values such as interpersonal relationships and commitments.

Diary research requires commitment on the part of the participants to frequently provide detailed accounts of their thoughts on language learning. This is one of the reasons why many researchers participate in their own diary studies (e.g., Liming, 1990; Schmidt and Frota, 1986). While the diaries of L2 researchers have yielded interesting insights, it is important to remember that this is an extremely restricted group and that findings from these studies cannot often be generalized to other contexts. One of the advantages of diaries is the lack of structure imposed on participants. However, this can also complicate data analysis, making it more difficult to find patterns in the data.

2.3.5. QUESTIONNAIRES

Questionnaires can be utilized to gather information that learners are able to report about themselves, such as information about their beliefs about learning or their reactions to learning and classroom instruction and activities. Questions can be open-ended or closed-ended. Closed-ended questions usually require learners to choose an answer from options. In open-ended questions, answer choices are not supplied; learners have more freedom and less direction in expressing their ideas. Obviously, closed-ended questions lead to more uniform data that can be easily compiled and compared, but open-ended questions can allow learners to express what is important to them and can lead to unexpected data. The type of question asked naturally depends on the research questions being addressed in the study. For example, in relatively unstructured research, it may be more appropriate to ask open-ended questions and to allow participant responses to guide hypothesis formation. Once hypotheses are formulated, researchers can ask closed-ended questions to focus in on important concepts. Of course, questionnaires need not be solely open- or closed-ended but can blend different question types depending on the purpose of the research and on what has previously been learned about the research phenomenon. For a more in-depth discussion of considerations as well as a practical guide for the use of questionnaires in L2 research, see Dörnyei (2003).

Questionnaire research has been used to investigate a wide variety of questions in L2 research, including learners' motivations in L2 learning (Dörnyei and Clement, 2001; Gardner, 2001; Gardner and MacIntyre, 1991), learners' L2 learning experiences (Sturman, 1996), and language teachers' perspectives on their teacher education (Adams, 2001; Horwitz, 1996). Questionnaires can allow researchers to investigate phenomena such as perceptions or motivation that are not observable, as well as allowing them to investigate sufficient quantities of an observable phenomenon in a restricted time frame.

When using questionnaires to collect data, researchers should consider a range of issues related to the analysis of questionnaire data. For example, it is possible that responses are inaccurate or incomplete. It is difficult to describe internal phenomena such as perceptions or attitudes, particularly if the questionnaire is completed in the L2 where lower proficiency may interfere. Both learners and native speakers might be able to provide salient details but will usually not be able to paint a complete picture of the research phenomenon. This is particularly important to remember when using open-ended written questionnaires, since participants may be uncomfortable expressing themselves in writing and may choose to provide abbreviated, rather than elaborative, responses. Whenever possible, questionnaires should be administered in the learners' native language, participants should be given ample time to specify their answers, and participants with limited literacy should be given the option of completing the questionnaire orally. In creating questionnaires, simple, uncluttered formats are important, as are unambiguous, answerable questions. Questionnaires should be reviewed by several researchers and piloted among a representative sample of the research population to ensure that the format is user-friendly and the questions are clear.

2.3.6. INTERVIEWS

Like questionnaire data, interviews can allow researchers to investigate cognitive processes such as awareness or constructs such as perceptions or attitudes that are not directly observable. There are many reasons why classroom researchers might choose to conduct interviews rather than use questionnaires or to supplement other data with interview data. Some speakers are less at ease in writing and are more likely to feel comfortable answering questions and providing informative details in a conversational setting. Also, speaking to an interviewer is a more authentic L2 task—learners speak to teachers and other proficient speakers regularly, so the interview context, while not a natural one, may not be as artificial as written questionnaires. In an interview, a researcher can elicit additional data if answers are short or off topic. It should be noted, however, that there are also learners who prefer the extra time, privacy, and low pressure of a questionnaire. Inclusion of multiple methods of data collection (e.g., both questionnaires and interviews) can draw on the strengths of both types of learners.

Like observations, interviews can be more or less structured. When carrying out a highly structured interview, the researcher usually formulates a series of questions before the interview. Structured interviews are similar to verbal questionnaires because the questions are the same, answers from different participants can be compared. Wang (1999), for example, presented the same series of questions about learning English as a second language to Chinese immigrant women in Canada and compared their answers, illustrating the learning beliefs and perceptions of this population. Unstructured interviews are more similar to natural conversations. The researcher begins only with a general area of interest. Together the interviewer and interviewee explore the interviewee's views and experiences. Two unstructured interviews on the same topic might center on very different thoughts and ideas. In this way, unstructured interview findings are not limited by the researcher's beliefs about the area of interest. Scarcella (1983), for example, used unstructured interviews with classroom language learners to explore the learners' attitudes and opinions about L2 oral activities they carried out with their partners in class.

Interviewers may begin with standard questions for all interviewees but still be free to explore interesting or unexpected findings as they arise.

While interviews can provide more detailed data, they are limited by many of the same restrictions as questionnaire data. Participants in interviews are reporting their thoughts and impressions, and these may be neither comprehensive nor accurate. Additionally, good interviewing is a skill. Novice interviewers may need practice or training in gathering interesting data through drawing participants out and encouraging them to express themselves. In interviewing there is also danger of the so-called halo effect (Fraenkel and Wallen, 2002; Mackey and Gass, 2005), which refers to interviewees picking up from the researcher cues related to what they think the researcher wants them to say that potentially influence the learner's responses. Skills such as noncommittal probing (e.g., "Anything else?" "What do you think?" "What do you mean?" or "Could you elaborate or give an example?") and consistent and nonevaluative reactions (e.g. "ok," "I see," rather than "That's a really interesting point") are needed. In addition to these interpersonal interviewing skills, the possibility of crosscultural pragmatic failure exists. Interviewers may need to be sensitive (or matched) to age, gender, and cultural background.

2.4. PRACTICAL CONSIDERATIONS IN QUALITATIVE RESEARCH

In this section we turn to important practical issues for researchers to consider when carrying out qualitative classroom studies, including the analysis, coding, quantification, and reporting of data, as well as the role of credibility, transferability, and dependability.

2.4.1. DATA ANALYSIS

For those used to reading and conducting experimental research, qualitative data analysis techniques can seem quite foreign. Qualitative data analysis is much less constrained than traditional statistical methods of analysis. Davis (1995) explains that "the design of interpretive qualitative studies is constantly emerging" (p. 445), suggesting that restricting analysis to predetermined plans at the onset of research (as is the case in quantitative studies) may also restrict the interpretation to the researcher's viewpoint. The goal of qualitative research is to uncover multiple perspectives in a specific context; because of this, the nature of the data analysis may evolve in the interaction with participants. In order to analyze qualitative data, researchers often make use of cyclical data analysis and grounded theory.

Cyclical data analysis is an analytic process "involving collecting data, conducting data analysis through which hypotheses are formed, testing hypotheses through further, more focused data collection, and so on until redundancy is achieved" (Davis, 1995, p. 444). Hypotheses are tested through focused (or structured) interviews, observations, and systematic analysis such as discourse analysis. The researcher goes through stages of processing the data by increasingly focusing the topic of interest and the hypotheses.

The purpose of grounded theory is to avoid placing preconceived notions on the data (Maxwell, 1996; Strauss and Corbin, 1990, 1994; Watson-Gegeo, 1988). Strauss and Corbin (1994) refer to grounded theory as "a general methodology for developing theory that is grounded in data systematically gathered and analyzed" (p. 273). In this manner, theory "evolves during actual research, and it does this through continuous interplay between analysis and data collection" (p. 273). Grounded theory should account for both the micro- and macrocontextual influences on the data (Davis, 1995; Watson-Gegeo, 1988, 1997). Maxwell (1996) suggests that researchers should consider data from three different vantage points: memo writing, categorizing, and contextualizing. Memo writing refers to keeping track of ideas and emerging theories while examining the data. Categorizing is fracturing and rearranging the data to "facilitate the comparison of data within and between those categories" (p. 78); in other words, sorting the information to find patterns of occurrence. Contextualizing refers to seeking connections between the phenomena observed and the context in which they occur. Maxwell suggests that examining data from these multiple vantage points can provide a more complete account of all the data.

2.4.1.1. *Coding*

In coding data, researchers seek patterns and formulate assertions. In qualitative research, coding should be grounded in the data; in other words, coding schemas should emerge from the data rather than being determined prior to the analysis (Davis, 1995; Maxwell, 1996; Travers, 2001; Watson-Gegeo, 1988; Wolfson, 1984, 1986). Ulichny (1991) advocates beginning coding with a general research question, what Watson-Gegeo (1988) refers to as a topic of focus, to avoid overemphasizing the researcher's perspective on the data. Travers (2001) also recommends proceeding with open coding until initial categories suggest themselves. Then researchers can consider different dimensions of the emerging categories and seek connections among categories. As more data is coded, researchers should also consider the range of variation within any one category. This process can help researchers to refine the coding schema, making it more closely reflect the data.

Without fixed, standardized coding, it can be difficult to compare data across studies and contexts. Watson-Gegeo (1988) points out that while it may not be possible to compare coding between settings on a surface level, it can still be possible on an abstract level. Although a particular event may not occur in two settings, the same communicative need can exist in both. Culturally defined terminology may not be transferable, but the abstract notions and functions described by such terminology can be applied to other situations. Maxwell (1996) also indicates that complementing coding with contextualizing data can facilitate understanding of the interaction of context and findings. This might aid other researchers and teachers in understanding how the findings may apply in their particular context.

As discussed above, one of the characteristics of qualitative research is the use of categories formulated with reference to the participants' understanding of the context. After the data are coded, researchers often seek confirmation of coding schemas with research participants and other representatives of the population as well as with other researchers (Johnson, 1992). For example, in Oliver and Mackey (2003), the researchers observed and analyzed children's ESL classroom interactions and identified feedback behaviors in different contexts. To validate their interpretations of the data, they then consulted the classroom teachers to determine whether the teachers' intuitions were similar to those of the researchers, helping to ensure that the coding had psychological reality outside of the research community and in the actual social context of the language learning.

2.4.1.2. *Quantification*

Much of the discussion of data analysis has centered on finding, describing, and validating patterns in the data. One way that patterns can be verified and reported is through quantification. While qualitative data analysis relies more on patterns of occurrence than actual numbers, quantification can play a role in both hypothesis generation and data reporting (Davis, 1995; Johnson, 1992; Lazaraton, 1995). In the hypothesis-oriented stage of data analysis, frequencies of occurrence can help researchers draw inferences from the data to form hypotheses. Calculating the frequency of occurrence of different linguistic phenomena can help the researcher relate characteristics of language learning and use to the contexts that prompt them.

Quantification is a simple, concise way of reporting general research findings. Descriptions of frequencies (i.e., percentages) can help readers quickly understand both why the researchers drew the inferences they did and how well the proposed theory fits the data (Davis, 1995). Additionally, other researchers can study reported frequencies to quickly ascertain whether the research findings transfer to other contexts (Lazaraton, 1995). Some researchers suggest that when quantification is used in qualitative data analysis, it should not be the focus of the analysis (Ulichny, 1991). As Blot (1991) points out, qualitative research allows researchers to ask questions that fall outside the bounds of quantitative research.

2.4.2. REPORTING

As Ulichny (1991) explains, working hypotheses in qualitative research begin in a thin form. During the cyclical process of data collection, data analysis, and hypothesis refinement, the hypotheses become increasingly developed and detailed. When reporting, researchers can choose between rich and thick description. In rich description, the researcher chronicles the process of hypothesis development. This has also been referred to as narrative reporting (Wolcott, 2001). Rich description necessarily follows the researchers' perspective; thick description, on the other hand, makes use of multiple perspectives to explain the insights. While a rich description consists of the researcher's interpretation of linguistic behavior and communication, thick description takes into account the actors' interpretation of their actions and the speakers' interpretation of their speech.

Davis (1995) divides a thick description into three essential components: particular description (representative examples from the data), general description (information about the patterns in the data), and interpretive commentary (an explanation of the phenomenon researched and an interpretation of the meaning of the findings). The interpretive commentary should connect the research findings to previous research. Davis (1995) points out that the goal of the report is to give the reader enough detail to "become a co-analyst of the data and interpretations presented. Thick descriptions . . . allow the reader to critically evaluate the study and surmise possible applications of grounded theory to their own research or pedagogical interests" (p. 448).

2.4.3. CREDIBILITY

The principle of validity is basic to quantitative research where internal validity (whether the study really investigates what is claimed) and external validity (whether the findings can be extended beyond the population of the study) are important concerns. In qualitative research, the notion of internal validity can be related to credibility and external validity to transferability. This is not just a change in terminology; credibility and transferability differ from quantitative notions of validity in theoretically important ways. Experimental research involves the manipulation of variables to test relationships. The notion of validity rests on the understanding of a single reality and therefore cannot be directly translated into qualitative research, which rests on the assumption of multiple, constructed realities. Thus, rather than determining that their findings are consistent with one single truth, qualitative researchers seek to demonstrate that their findings are credible to their research population.

In order to ensure that the findings are credible, Fraenkel and Wallen (2002) suggest that researchers make use of several techniques, including prolonged engagement, persistent observation, triangulation, and careful documentation. Prolonged engagement refers to collecting data longitudinally in order to ensure that the participants are accustomed to the researchers and are conducting themselves naturally. Persistent observation refers to collecting data in as many contexts and situations as possible to make certain that the picture provided in the research is as full and complete as it can be. Triangulation, using multiple research techniques and multiple sources of data in order to understand the locus of the research from all feasible perspectives, can also enhance credibility. Dörnyei (2003), for example, advocates the integration of questionnaire research with other research methods "to collect background information about the participants . . . or to complement classroom observation data" (p. 131). Among their suggestions for careful documentation, Fraenkel and Wallen suggest that researchers record their own questions to contextualize learner responses, keep notes on their own thoughts and impressions while collecting and analyzing data, and document the basis for the inferences they draw.

2.4.4. TRANSFERABILITY

In quantitative research, external validity is determined by limiting the effects of the research context (for more, see Leow and Bowles, this volume, chapter 6). This is done, for example, by choosing research subjects who are representative of the target population. In qualitative research, the research context is seen as integral to the focus of the research. Denzin and Lincoln (2000) point out that qualitative findings can seldom be transferred directly from one context to another and that the similarity of the context determines the degree to which findings may be transferred to a new context. If researchers report their findings with thick description, including sufficient detail of the context and participants for readers to understand the characteristics of the research context, the burden rests with the reader to compare the research situation with their own and to determine which findings may be appropriately transferred to their setting.

While the responsibility for determining appropriateness of transfer for qualitative findings rests with the reader, researchers can take steps to augment the transferability of their research. For this, Johnson (1992) recommends the use of multisite research, in which a similar phenomenon is observed by several researchers in several different contexts and then compared across contexts. This increases the likelihood of finding appropriate applications for research findings in other contexts and can help elucidate effects of different contexts on the focus of research. When engaged in multisite studies, researchers should endeavor to avoid inconsistency between researchers at different sites and be aware of possible selection effects or mismatches between the population and the construct being researched (Bernard, 1995). Multisite research involves the additional danger of including populations or cultures whose unique contextual characteristics make their experiences inappropriate for comparison.

2.4.5. DEPENDABILITY

In addition to maximizing the credibility and transferability of their findings, qualitative researchers seek to demonstrate that the findings are dependable—that they have reliably characterized the research context and the relationships among the participants. Researchers can establish dependability through several means. For example, peer examination (seeking review by other researchers working in similar contexts) can help researchers draw dependable inferences from the data (Johnson, 1992). In participant evaluation, the researcher presents to the research participants the data patterns and the inferences drawn from them in order to determine whether the participants concur with the assertions the researcher has made based on the data (Davis, 1992). The type and condition of the data can also enhance dependability (Johnson, 1992). Peer examination and participant evaluation are more dependable if the peers or participants have access to high quality representations of the data. Electronically recorded data can help outside researchers, research participants, and the researchers themselves to recreate the data collection context and to make use of all interpretive cues (intonation, pausing, nonverbal cues) to draw inferences. Fraenkel and Wallen (2002) additionally suggest that researchers can enhance the dependability of their studies by comparing different participants' responses to similar questions as well as interviewing participants more than once.

3. Summary

Qualitative research yields valuable insights into the L2 learning process. When appropriate qualitative research methods are chosen to address a particular problem, qualitative research can reliably help us to understand better the nature of L2 learning in a situated classroom context. If proper standards of empirical rigor are met through triangulation of research perspectives, cyclical data collection and analysis, and consideration of emic perspectives to ensure credibility, transferability, and dependability, qualitative research can be a powerful means of enhancing our knowledge of SLA.

4. Exercises

This exercise involves the examination and analysis of excerpts from an ESL classroom observation recorded as part of the data collection for a recent SLA study by Oliver and Mackey (2003).

4.1 DATA ANALYSIS

In the Oliver and Mackey (2003) study, the researchers were interested in how teachers respond to learner errors during different types of classroom activities, such as grammar activities or roll call. Therefore, one of the research questions was to explore the relationship between classroom context and teachers' provision of interactional feedback. The study also investigated the relationship between classroom context and learners' use of interactional feedback. Examples of interactional feedback include repetitions, requests for clarification, and recasts (in a recast a learner's nontargetlike utterance is restated by the teacher in a more targetlike way). Classroom context can be viewed in terms of the content, structure, and characteristics of the interactions. For example, interactions during a grammar activity might differ from interactions during roll call in a variety of ways, including the topic of communication, discourse structure, and instructional goals. The class from which these excerpts are taken is a mixed-grade ESL class at a primary school in Australia. The teacher is a male native speaker of English. The students come from several different ethnolinguistic backgrounds representing several East Asian and European languages.

The excerpts involve student-teacher interactions in the classroom setting. As with any instructional interaction, several interesting phenomena occur throughout the discourse. Read the excerpts, paying attention to learner errors and miscommunications, interactional feedback and learners' responses to the feedback, simplification of input, and teaching strategies. After reading the excerpts, answer the following questions.

1. How are the excerpts similar and how do they differ? Are there cues that suggest that the contexts differ?
2. Develop a coding schema to categorize learner and teacher utterances in these data. How does your coding schema emerge from the data? Try to make the coding schema as complete as possible to account for all the data in the excerpts.
3. Based on the coding schema you developed, form an initial hypothesis about the role of context in the provision of interactional feedback.
   a. How is your hypothesis rooted in the data?
   b. What role did your prior experience with classroom interactions play in shaping your hypothesis?
   c. How do other sources of information (e.g., your knowledge of instructed SLA research) help form your hypotheses?
4. After forming an initial hypothesis, qualitative researchers seek further confirmation through cyclical data analysis and collection.

a. What further information would you gather to clarify your understanding of this phenomenon?
b. How would you collect this information (using what methods)? Consider triangulating to enhance the credibility of your research. How could you collect data from multiple sources using multiple methods to further refine your hypothesis?

Excerpt 1: Date and weather

In this excerpt, the teacher is interacting with the whole class at the beginning of the class. The class is recording the date and weather on a chart they have been keeping throughout the semester.

1 T: Can anybody tell me what um what the date will be today? What is the date? Yes Maishen
2 S: Twenty-five
3 T: No, this was the- the twenty-fifth was Wednesday. So what would be today? Um Kevin?
4 S: Twenty-sixth
5 T: No the twenty-sixth is a Thursday today is a Friday Yang?
6 S: Twenty-five
7 T: No that's going backwards back to Wednesday Franco?
8 S: Twenty-seven
9 T: The twenty-seventh today is the twenty-seventh June Friday the month is June okay? and it's not a very rainy day today put your hands up tell me what kind of a day you think it is yes Xi- um Xixiao
10 S: Sunny
11 T: Yeah quite sunny but-
12 S: Cloudy
13 T: Cloudy and yes?
14 S: Um rainy
15 T: No it didn't rain today yes?
16 S: Sunny
17 T: Cloudy yes cloudy a bit sunny a bit cloudy but it is
18 S: Not raining
19 T: Yeah not raining
20 S: Fine
21 T: Fine, fine day, that's why some people are wearing jumpers yes?
22 S: Cold
23 T: A little bit cold it's a little bit cold that's why we have to wear jumpers

Excerpt 2: News sharing

The teacher divides the class into several smaller groups to share news. Learners volunteer to share recent events in their lives with the group members. Listeners then ask questions about the speaker's event. One student is designated group leader for the week. The group leader designates the next speaker. During the group interactions, the teacher sits with one group and interacts with them, occasionally checking in on the other groups.

1 T: Okay so stand up and go into your news groups okay good nice round circle good very good and you're in a nice round circle here too okay so you can now start your news in your groups off you go now who's the boss? Okay so you say who's got news today?

2 S: Who's got news today?

3 T: Put your hand up no-one? Alright one person has remember to think of questions

4 S: Good morning Kevin

5 S: Yesterday my mum I dance school

6 T: I beg your pardon

7 S: I dancing with school

8 T: Oh did you you go- you went to the disco?

9 S: Got shocolate

10 T: Did you? Why?

11 S: Dancing I got four shocolate

12 T: Anybody else? Has anybody got any more questions to ask Kevin?

13 S: Why disco why you go for dancing- dancing for?

14 S: [unintelligible]

15 T: Well there was a disco wasn't there? There was a special disco and in the disc- at the disco people got here to do dancing and it was for people who are in year four five six and seven Kevin is in year five so he was allowed to go

16 S: Thank you for listening to my news

17 T: Thank you well- he just said thank you for listening to his news

18 Ss: You're welcome Kevin

19 T: Oh wha- you know when you're saying "You're welcome" who do you look at? Do you look at the person at the person over there? Well let's say it nicely now and look at Kevin

20 Ss: You're welcome Kevin

21 T: Good now I was very interested in Kevin's news when Kevin his news- or whoever is saying his news you should look at the person alright yes you w- were very you did a very very good job okay anybody else? Has anybody else got any news?

Excerpt 3: Story discussion

The teacher is interacting with the whole class. They have just finished reading a favorite picture book, a modernized version of *Little Red Riding Hood.* In this segment, individual students are asked to discuss their favorite part of the book with the class.

1 T: You can come up and tell me your favorite part of the story because we've read this lots of times before so you know the story okay what is your- turn around what is your favorite part?
2 S: I like Riding Hood once upon a time
3 T: Yeah what part of the story's do you like the best- do you like the best? Can you- you can remember the story can't you?
4 S: One
5 T: Um Xixiao go and get me the little book over there
6 S: The Red Riding-
7 T: Yeah the Red Riding Hood the little books okay here's the little books select a picture select a picture or select a part of the story that you like okay now what was the story- show the picture- now what was the stor- what was that part of the story?
8 S: Apple pie on the wolf
9 T: Right hit the wolf with what?
10 S: Apple pie
11 T: With an apple pie with a plate and had an apple pie on it right where did the wolf go from there? When he hit the wolf- when Red Riding hit the wolf with an apple pie where did the wolf go to?
12 S: Went to skate board
13 T: Went to where the skate board was and then what happened to the wolf?
14 S: The wolf er out
15 T: Out of the window is that right give her a clap and sit down and somebody else now you can come up now you select a favorite part of the book
16 S: That one
17 T: Okay now you tell us all about that- what that- what that part- part of the picture is about look at that book
18 S: When um Little Red Riding Hood when she at river she saw someone in the woodshed she went deeper deeper in the wood forward and then he ran first into the house the wolf ran first and then Little Riding Hood got first and then he'll knock on the door and Little Riding Hood will know the wolf is there
19 T: Good

4.2. GUIDED CRITIQUE

Harklau, L. (1994). ESL versus mainstream classes: Contrasting L2 learning environments. *TESOL Quarterly, 28,* p. 241–272.

For this exercise, we have selected the article cited above. You can locate a copy of this article at your university library. Many universities have electronic access privileges to journals. After reading the article, try to answer the following questions.

1. Abstract (p. 241)
   a. Qualitative studies typically present a "grand tour" question, which is "a statement of the question being examined in the study in its most general form" (Cresswell, 1994, p. 70), in addition to a range of subquestions. After reading the article and its abstract, identify the "grand tour" question in Harklau's study. Is this question best addressed through qualitative methods? Why?
   b. Qualitative research often has a "clear sociopolitical agenda" (Lazaraton, 2003, p. 3). What can be inferred about the sociopolitical nature of this study?
2. Introduction (pp. 241–243)
   a. How is the research focus justified in the introduction? How does this introduction differ from typical literature reviews in quantitative research?
   b. Identify the specific research questions. In addition to Harklau's approach, what research techniques could be used to address these research questions effectively?
3. Methods (pp. 243–248)
   a. Identify the methods Harklau used for her data collection. Evaluate her data collection techniques. Are there any limitations or problems?
   b. Describe the role of the researcher in the study. How might the role of the researcher have affected the nature of the data collected? Did she take any measures to minimize researcher bias?
   c. Evaluate the credibility and transferability of the results of this study based on the information about the research context, sample, and procedure provided in this section.
4. Discussion (pp. 248–252)
   a. Summarize the important findings concerning oral interaction among students and teachers in mainstream classes. How do the data contribute to an understanding of the research question identified above?
   b. Evaluate the analysis. How does Harklau triangulate different data sources to present her findings? What is the role of research literature

and theory in this section? How is the analysis grounded? What is the role of interpretation?

c. Evaluate the reporting. What reporting technique is used in this section? Can it be characterized as rich or thick? Is it particular, general, or interpretive commentary (Davis, 1995)? What is the role of quantification? Is quantification used appropriately and sufficiently?

d. Based on this part of the discussion, what conclusions can you draw about mainstream classes as an environment for second language learning? What limitations are there in this study and how could this study be extended?

Further Reading

Bailey, K., & Nunan, D. (1996). *Voices from the language classroom: Qualitative research in second language education* (pp.168–194). Cambridge, UK: Cambridge University Press.

Davis, K. A. (1995). Qualitative theory and methods in applied linguistics research. *TESOL Quarterly, 29,* 427–453.

Denzin, N. K., & Lincoln, Y. S. (1994). *Handbook of qualitative research.* London: Sage.

Dörnyei, Z. (2003). *Questionnaires in second language research: Constructing, administering, and processing.* Mahwah, N.J.: Lawrence Erlbaum.

Faerch, C., & Kasper, G. (1987). *Introspection in second language research.* Clevedon, UK: Multilingual Matters.

Fraenkel, J. R., & Wallen, N. (2002). *How to design and evaluate research in education.* New York: McGraw-Hill.

Gass, S. M., & Mackey, A. (2000). *Stimulated recall methodology in second language research.* Mahwah, NJ: Lawrence Erlbaum.

Mackey, A., & Gass, S. (2005). *Second language research: Methodology and design.* Mahwah, NJ: Lawrence Erlbaum.

Maxwell, J. A. (1996). *Qualitative research design: An interactive approach.* London: Sage.

Strauss, A., & Corbin, J. (1990). *Basics of qualitative research: Grounded theory procedures and techniques.* London: Sage.

Toohey, K. (1995). Qualitative research and teacher education. *TESOL Quarterly 29,* 576–581.

References

Adams, R. (2001). *Graduate student teacher education and teacher socialization in an innovative FL curriculum.* Paper presented at the Center for Advanced Research in Language Acquisition Conference, Minneapolis, MN.

Adams, R. (2003). L2 output, reformulation, and noticing: Implications for IL development. *Language Teaching Research, 7,* 347–376.

Allwright, R. (1984). The importance of interaction in classroom language learning. *Applied Linguistics, 5,* 158–171.

Allwright, R. (1987). Classroom observation: Problems and possibilities. In B. K. Das (Ed.), *Patterns of classroom interaction in southeast Asia* (pp. 88–102). Singapore: SEAMEO Regional Language Centre.

Anderson, N. (1991). Individual differences in strategy use in second language reading and testing. *The Modern Language Journal, 75,* 128–143.

Anton, M. (1999). The discourse of a learner-centered classroom: Sociocultural perspectives on teacher-learner interaction in the second language classroom. *The Modern Language Journal, 83,* 303–318.

Armengol-Castells, L. (2001). Text-generating strategies of three multilingual writers: A protocol-based study. *Language Awareness, 10,* 91–106.

Bailey, K. M. (1996). The best-laid plans: Teachers' in-class decisions to depart from their lesson plans. In K. M. Bailey & D. Nunan (Eds.), *Voices from the language classroom* (pp. 15–40). Cambridge, UK: Cambridge University Press.

Barkhuizen, G. (1998). Discovering learner's perceptions of ESL classroom teaching/learning activities in a South African context. *TESOL Quarterly, 32,* 85–108.

Bernard, H. R. (1995). *Research methods in anthropology: Qualitative and quantitative approaches.* Walnut Creek, CA: Altamira Press.

Biggs, S., Rosman, A., & Sergenian, G. (1993). Methodological issues in judgment and decision-making research: Concurrent verbal protocol validity and simultaneous traces of process. *Journal of Behavioral Decision Making, 6,* 187–206.

Block, D. (1996). A window on the classroom: Classroom events viewed from different angles. In K. Bailey & D. Nunan (Eds.), *Voices from the language classroom: Qualitative research in second language education* (pp. 168–194). Cambridge, UK: Cambridge University Press.

Block, E. (1986). The comprehension strategies of second language readers. *TESOL Quarterly, 20,* 463–494.

Blot, R. K. (1991). The role of hypothesis testing in qualitative research. *TESOL Quarterly, 25,* 202–205.

Boggs, S. (1972). The meaning of questions and narratives to Hawaiian children. In C. Cazden, V. John, & D. Hymes (Eds.), *Functions of language in the classroom* (pp. 299–322). New York: Teachers College Press.

Chaudron, C. (1988). *Second language classrooms: Research on teaching and learning.* Cambridge, UK: Cambridge University Press.

Cohen, A. & Cavalcanti, M. (1987). Giving and getting feedback on compositions: A comparison of teacher and student verbal report. *Evaluation and Research in Education, 1,* 63–73.

Cresswell, J. W. (1994). *Research design: Qualitative and quantitative approaches.* Thousand Oaks, CA: Sage.

Cumming, A. (1994). Alternatives in TESOL research: Descriptive, interpretive, and ideological orientations. *TESOL Quarterly, 28,* 673–703.

Davis, K. A. (1992). Validity and reliability in qualitative research on second language acquisition and teaching. *TESOL Quarterly, 26,* 673–703.

Davis, K. A. (1995). Qualitative theory and methods in applied linguistics research. *TESOL Quarterly, 29,* 427–453.

Denzin, N. K., & Lincoln, Y. S. (1994). Introduction: Entering the field of qualitative research. In N. K. Denzin & Y. S. Lincoln (Eds.), *Handbook of qualitative research* (pp. 1–18). London: Sage.

Denzin, N. K., & Lincoln, Y. S. (2000). Introduction: The discipline and practice of qualitative research. In N. K. Denzin & Y. S. Lincoln (Eds.), *Handbook of qualitative research* (pp. 1–25). London: Sage.

Dörnyei, Z. (2003). *Questionnaires in second language research: Construction, administration, and processing.* Mahwah, NJ: Lawrence Erlbaum.

Dörnyei, Z., & Clement, R. (2001). Motivational characteristics of learning different target languages: Results of a nationwide survey. In Z. Dörnyei & R. Schmidt (Eds.), *Motivation and second language acquisition* (pp. 399–432). Honolulu, HI: University of Hawai'i at Manoa, Second Language Teaching and Curriculum Center.

Dörnyei, Z., & Kormos, J. (2000). The role of individual and social variables in oral task performance. *Language Teaching Research, 4,* 275–300.

Dörnyei, Z., & Kormos, J. (2002). *Motivational determinants of the quality and quantity of student performance in communicative language tasks.* Paper presented at the American Association of Applied Linguistics, Salt Lake City, UT.

Duff, P. A. (1996). Different languages, different practices: Socialization of discourse competence in dual language school classrooms in Hungary. In K. Bailey & D. Nunan (Ed.), *Voices from the language classroom: Qualitative research in second language education* (pp. 434–448). Cambridge, UK: Cambridge University Press.

Duff, P. A. (2002). The discursive co-construction of knowledge, identity, and difference: An ethnography of communication in the high school mainstream. *Applied Linguistics, 23,* 289–322.

Edge, J., & Richards, K. (1998). May I see your warrant, please? Justifying outcomes in qualitative research. *Applied Linguistics, 19,* 334–356.

Ellis, R. (1992). Learning to communicate in the classroom: A study of two language learners' requests. *Studies in Second Language Acquisition, 14,* 1–23.

Ericsson, K., & Simon, H. (1980). Verbal reports as data. *Psychological Review, 87,* 215–251.

Faerch, C., & Kasper, G. (1987). From product to process—Introspective methods in second language research. In C. Faerch & G. Kasper (Eds.), *Introspection in second language research* (pp. 5–23). Clevedon, UK: Multilingual Matters.

Foss, K. A., & Reitzel, A. C. (1988). A relational model for managing second language anxiety. *TESOL Quarterly, 22,* 437–454.

Fraenkel, J. R., & Wallen, N. (2002). *How to design and evaluate research in education.* New York: McGraw-Hill.

Freeman, D. (1998). *Doing teacher research: From inquiry to understanding.* Boston: Heinle & Heinle.

Gardner, R. C. (2001). Integrative motivation and second language acquisition. In Z. Dörnyei & R. Schmidt (Eds.), *Motivation in second language learning* (pp. 1–20). Honolulu, HI: University of Hawai'i at Manoa, Second Language Teaching and Curriculum Center.

Gardner, R. C., & MacIntyre, P. D. (1991). An instrumental motivation in language study: Who says it isn't effective? *Studies in Second Language Acquisition, 13,* 57–72.

Gass, S. M. (1997). *Input, interaction, and the second language learner.* Mahwah, NJ: Lawrence Erlbaum.

Gass, S. M., & Mackey, A. (2000). *Stimulated recall methodology in second language research.* Mahwah, NJ: Lawrence Erlbaum.

Hardman, J. C. (1999). A community of learners: Cambodians in an adult ESL classroom. *Language Teaching Research, 3,* 145–166.

Hornberger, N. (1988). Misbehavior, punishment, and put-down: Stress for Quechua children in school. *Language and Education, 2,* 239–253.

Horwitz, E. K. (1996). Meeting the cognitive and emotional needs of foreign language teachers. In Z. Moore (Ed.), *Foreign language teacher education: Multiple perspectives* (pp. 189–199). Lanham, MD: University Press of America.

Jacob, E. (1987). Qualitative research traditions: A review. *Review of Educational Research, 57,* 1–50.

Jacob, J., Rottenberg, L., Patrick, S., & Wheeler, E. (1996). Cooperative learning: Context and opportunities for acquiring academic English. *TESOL Quarterly, 30,* 253–280.

Johnson, D. (1992). *Approaches to research in second language learning.* London: Longman.

Jones, F. (1992). A language teaching machine: Input, uptake, and output in the communicative classroom. *System, 20,* 133–150.

Labov, W. (1972). *Sociolinguistic patterns.* Philadelphia: University of Pennsylvania Press.

Lantolf, J., & Appel, G. (1994). Theoretical framework: An introduction to Vygotskian perspectives on second language research. In J. Lantolf & G. Appel (Eds.), *Vygotskian approaches to second language research* (pp. 1–32). Norwood, NJ: Ablex.

Larsen-Freeman, D. E., & Long, M. (1991). *An introduction to second language acquisition research.* London: Longman.

Lazaraton, A. (1995). Qualitative research in applied lingusitics: A progress report. *TESOL Quarterly, 34,* 174–181.

Lazaraton, A. (2000). Current trends in research methodology and statistics in applied linguistics. *TESOL Quarterly, 29,* 175–181.

Lazaraton, A. (2003). Evaluative criteria for qualitative research in applied linguistics: Whose criteria and whose research? *The Modern Language Journal, 87,* 1–12.

Lazaraton, A. (2004). Gesture and speech in the vocabulary explanations of one ESL teacher: A microanalytic inquiry. *Language Learning, 54,* 79–117.

Leow, R. (1998). Toward operationalizing the process of attention in SLA: Evidence for Tomlin and Villa's (1994) fine-grained analysis of attention. *Applied Psycholinguistics, 19,* 133–159.

Leow, R. (2000). A study of the role of awareness in foreign language behavior: Aware vs. unaware learners. *Studies in Second Language Acquisition, 22,* 557–584.

Leow, R., Egi, T., Nuevo, A. M., & Tsai, Y. (2003). The roles of textual enhancement and types of linguistic items in adult L2 learners' comprehension and intake. *Applied Language Learning, 13,* 93–108.

Liming, Y. (1990). The comprehensible output hypothesis and self-directed learning: A learner's perspective. *TESL Canada Journal, 8,* 9–27.

Mackey, A. (2000). *Feedback, noticing and second language development: An empirical study of L2 classroom interaction.* Paper presented at the Annual Meeting of the British Association for Applied Linguistics, Cambridge, UK.

Mackey, A. (2002). Beyond production: Learners' perceptions about interactional processes. *International Journal of Educational Research, 37,* 379–384.

Mackey, A., & Gass, S. M. (2005). *Second language research: Methodology and design.* Mahwah, NJ: Lawrence Erlbaum.

Mackey, A., Gass, S. M., & McDonough, K. (2000). How do learners perceive interactional feedback? *Studies in Second Language Acquisition, 22,* 471–497.

Mackey, A., Philp, J., Egi, T., Fujii, A., & Tatsumi, T. (2002). Individual differences in working memory, noticing of interactional feedback, and L2 development. In P. Robinson (Ed.), *Individual differences and instructed language learning* (pp. 181–210). Amsterdam: John Benjamins.

Maxwell, J. A. (1996). *Qualitative research design: An interactive approach.* London: Sage.

Miller, L., & Ginsberg, R. B. (1995). Folklinguistic theories of language learning. In B. F. Freed (Ed.), *Foreign language acquisition in a study abroad context* (pp. 293–316). Amsterdam: John Benjamins.

Musumeci, D. (1996). Teacher-learner negotiation in content-based instruction: Communication at cross-purposes. *Applied Linguistics, 17,* 286–325.

Nunan, D. (1991). Methods in second language classroom research: A critical review. *Studies in Second Language Acquisition, 13,* 249–274.

Nunan, D. (1992). *Research methods in language learning.* Cambridge, UK: Cambridge University Press.

Ohta, A. S. (1994). Socializing the expression of affect: An overview of affective particle in the Japanese as a foreign language classroom. *Issues in Applied Lingusitics, 5,* 303–325.

Oliver, R., & Mackey, A. (2003). Interactional context and feedback in child ESL classrooms. *The Modern Language Journal, 87,* 519–533.

Palmeira, W. (1995). A study of uptake by learners of Hawaiian. In R. Schmidt (Ed.), *Attention and awareness in foreign language learning* (Tech. Rep. No. 9, pp. 127–161). Honolulu, HI: University of Hawai'i at Manoa, Second Language Teaching and Curriculum Center.

Pavlenko, A. (2001). "In the world of tradition, I was unimagined": Negotiation of identities in cross-cultural autobiographies. *International Journal of Bilingualism, 5,* 317–344.

Philips, S. (1983). *The invisible culture: Communication in classroom and community on the Warm Springs Indian Reservation.* London: Longman.

Pica, T. (1997). Second language acquisition research methods. In N. Hornberger & D. Corson (Eds.), *Encyclopedia of language and education: Vol. 8. Research methods in language and education* (pp. 89–100). Dordrecht: Kluwer.

Pica, T., & Doughty, C. (1985). Input and interaction in the communicative language classroom: A comparison of teacher-fronted and group activities. In S. M. Gass & C. Madden (Eds.), *Input and second language acquisition* (pp. 115–132). Rowley, MA: Newbury House.

Roberts, M. (1995). Awareness and the efficacy of error correction. In R. Schmidt (Ed.), *Attention and awareness in foreign language learning* (Tech. Rep. No. 3, pp. 163–182). Honolulu, HI: University of Hawai'i at Manoa, Second Language Teaching and Curriculum Center.

Russo, J., Johnson, E., & Stephens, D. (1989). The validity of verbal protocols. *Memory and Cognition, 17,* 759–769.

Samuda, V. (2001). Guiding relationships between form and meaning during task performance: The role of the teacher. In M. Bygate, P. Skehan, & M. Swain (Eds.), *Researching pedagogic tasks: Second language learning, teaching and testing* (pp. 119–140). London: Longman.

Saville-Troike, M. (1982). *The ethnography of communication.* Oxford, UK: Blackwell.

Scarcella, R. C. (1983). Discourse accent in second language performance. In S. M. Gass & L. Selinker (Eds.), *Language transfer in language learning* (pp. 306–326). Rowley, MA: Newbury House.

Schmidt, R. (2001). Attention. In P. Robinson (Ed.), *Cognition and second language instruction* (pp. 3–32). Cambridge, UK: Cambridge University Press.

Schmidt, R., & Frota, S. (1986). Developing basic conversational ability in a second language: A case study of an adult learner of Portuguese. In R. R. Day (Ed.), *Talking to learn: Conversation in second language acquisition* (pp. 237–326). Rowley, MA: Newbury House.

Seliger, H., & Shohamy, E. (1989). *Second language research methods.* Oxford, UK: Oxford University Press.

Slimani, A. (1989). The role of topicalization in classroom language learning. *System, 17,* 223–234.

Slimani, A. (1992). Evaluation of classroom education. In C. Anderson & A. Beretta (Eds.), *Evaluating second language education* (pp. 197–221). Cambridge, UK: Cambridge University Press.

Spada, N. (1990). Observing classroom behaviours and learning outcomes in different second language programs. In J. C. Richards & D. Nunan (Eds.), *Second language teacher education* (pp. 293–310). Cambridge, UK: Cambridge University Press.

Spada, N., & Frohlich, M. (1995). *The communication orientation of language teaching observation scheme: Coding conventions and applications.* Sydney, Australia: Macquarie University, National Centre for English Language Teaching and Research.

Spielmann, G., & Radnofsky, M. L. (2001). Learning language under tension: New directions from a qualitative study. *The Modern Language Journal, 85,* 259–278.

Storch, N. (1998). Comparing second language learners' attention to form across tasks. *Language Awareness, 7,* 176–191.

Storch, N. (2002). Patterns of interaction in ESL pair work. *Language Learning, 52,* 119–158.

Strauss, A., & Corbin, J. (1990). *Basics of qualitative research: Grounded theory procedures and techniques.* London: Sage.

Strauss, A., & Corbin, J. (1994). Grounded theory methodology: An overview. In N. K. Denzin & Y. S. Lincoln (Eds.), *Handbook of qualitative research* (pp. 273–285). London: Sage.

Sturman, P. (1996). Registration and placement: Learner response. In K. Bailey & D. Nunan (Eds.), *Voices from the language classroom* (pp. 338–355). Cambridge, UK: Cambridge University Press.

Swain, M., & Lapkin, S. (1998). Interaction and second language learning: Two adolescent French immersion students working together. *The Modern Language Journal, 82,* 320–337.

Swain, M., & Lapkin, S. (2001). Focus on form through collaborative dialogue: Exploring task effects. In M. Bygate, P. Skehan, & M. Swain (Eds.), *Researching pedagogic tasks: Second language learning, teaching, and testing* (pp. 99–118). London: Longman.

Swain, M., & Lapkin, S. (2002). Talking it through: Two French immersion learners' response to reformuated writing. *International Review of Applied Linguistics, 37,* 285–304.

Swain, M., Lapkin, S., & Smith, M. (2002). Reformulation and the learning of French pronominal verbs in a Canadian French immersion context. *The Modern Language Journal, 86,* 485–507.

Syed, Z. (2001). Notions of self in foreign language learning: A qualitative analysis. In Z. Dörnyei & R. Schmidt (Eds.), *Motivation and second language acquisition* (pp. 127–148). Honolulu, HI: University of Hawai'i at Manoa, Second Language Teaching and Curriculum Center.

Takahashi, E. (1998). Language development in classroom interaction: A longitudinal study of a Japanese FLES program from a sociocultural perspective. *Foreign Language Annals, 31,* 392–406.

Travers, M. (2001). *Qualitative research through case studies.* London: Sage.

Tsui, A. (1996). Reticence and anxiety in second language learning. In K. Bailey & D. Nunan (Eds.), *Voices from the language classroom* (pp. 145–167). Cambridge, UK: Cambridge University Press.

Ulichny, P. (1991). The role of hypothesis testing in qualitative research. *TESOL Quarterly, 25,* 200–202.

Upton, T., Lee, T., & Li, C. (2001). The role of first language in second language reading. *Studies in Second Language Acquisition, 23,* 469–495.

Vandergrift, L. (2003). Orchestrating strategy use: Toward a model of the skilled second language listener. *Language Learning, 53,* 463–496.

Wang, W. (1999). Age and second language acquisition in adulthood: The learning experiences and perceptions of woman immigrants. *TESL Canada Journal, 16,* 1–19.

Watson-Gegeo, K. A. (1988). Ethnography in ESL: Defining the essentials. *TESOL Quarterly, 22,* 575–592.

Watson-Gegeo, K. A. (1997). Classroom ethnography. In N. Hornberger & D. Corson (Eds.), *Encyclopedia of language and education: Vol. 8. Research methods in language and education* (pp. 135–144). Dordrecht: Kluwer.

Watson-Gegeo, K. A. (2001). *Mind, language, and epistemology: Toward a language socialization paradigm for SLA.* Paper presented at the Pacific Second Language Research Forum Conference, Honolulu, HI.

Watson-Gegeo, K. A., & Gegeo, D. (1995). Understanding language and power in the Solomon Islands: Methodological lessons for educational intervention. In

J. Tollefson (Ed.), *Power and inequality in language education* (pp. 59–72). Cambridge, UK: Cambridge University Press.

Willet, J. (1995). Becoming first graders in an L2: An ethographic study of L2 socialization. *TESOL Quarterly, 29,* 473–576.

Wolcott, H. F. (2001). *Writing up qualitative research.* London: Sage.

Wolfson, N. (1984). Pretty is as pretty does: A speech act view of sex roles. *Applied Linguistics, 5,* 236–244.

Wolfson, N. (1986). Research methodology and the question of validity. *TESOL Quarterly, 20,* 689–699.

Wong-Fillmore, L. (1980). Learning a second language: Children in the American classroom. *Georgetown University Round Table on Languages and Linguistics, 1,* 309–325.

Wong-Fillmore, L. (1982). Instructional language as linguistic input: Second language learning in classrooms. In L. C. Wilkinson (Ed.), *Communicating in the classroom* (283–296). New York: Academic Press.

PART 2

Internal Factors

FOUR

Individual Differences: Age, Sex, Working Memory, and Prior Knowledge

HARRIET WOOD BOWDEN
CRISTINA SANZ
CATHERINE A. STAFFORD

KEY WORDS
Aptitude ▪ bilingualism ▪ critical period hypothesis ▪ gender ▪ metalinguistic awareness ▪ rate ▪ route ▪ sex ▪ short-term memory ▪ ultimate attainment ▪ working memory.

1. Introduction

While incomplete acquisition of a first language (L1) is rare and related to cases of severe language deprivation and concomitant problems in cognitive development, achieving nativelike proficiency in a second language (L2) seems to be the exception rather than the norm. Different explanations have been proposed for this significant difference between L1 and L2 acquisition and include type and frequency of input, access to Universal Grammar (or lack thereof), and differential use of general cognitive capacities. Whatever the reason for the difference, there is general agreement that individual differences (IDs) seem to have a greater effect on the acquisition of an L2 than the L1. The nature of the specific IDs and the degree to which they affect specific aspects of L2 acquisition—syntax versus vocabulary, for example—are still debated in the literature.[1] The present chapter focuses on IDs because this is the area where scholarship has grown the most in recent years.

The list of IDs relevant to second language acquisition (SLA) is long and continues to grow as a result of the deconstruction of broad concepts such as aptitude and motivation that took place in the 1990s. Larsen-Freeman and Long's (1991) chapter on IDs includes the following IDs: age, aptitude, motivation, attitude, personality (including self-esteem, extroversion, anxiety, risk-taking, sensitivity to rejection, empathy, inhibition, and tolerance of ambiguity), cognitive style (which includes field independence or dependence, category width, reflectivity or impulsivity, aural or visual learning style, and analytic or gestalt learning style), hemisphere specialization, memory, awareness, will, language disability, interest, sex, birth order, and prior experience.[2] Obviously, a chapter that covers all of these variables would be too long and broad for this volume, thus the need to focus. We have chosen age, sex, working memory, and prior language experience for different reasons. Age has particular relevance for a discussion of IDs because it is the most obvious difference between first and second language acquisition and it is also the one that has produced the highest level of interest and the most research. Sex was selected because new potential explanations are beginning to emerge for behavioral patterns that have been anecdotally observed in the past. Working memory has become a focus of research on what has been referred to historically as *aptitude*.[3] Finally, prior language experience has been selected because, in our view, it deserves more attention than it has received to date, particularly when one considers that bilingualism has become the norm rather than the exception in an age of migration and supranational entities such as the European Union. And, in light of recent research regarding the levels of proficiency at which particular aspects of language are processed (e.g., Gass, Svetics, and Lemelin, 2003) as well as the influence of experience with language study abroad on vocabulary acquisition (e.g., Collentine, 2004), further inquiry in the area of prior language experience certainly appears to be justified.

2. Age

Achieving nativelike competence in an L2 requires that you begin learning as a child. This is an idea that is widely and unquestioningly accepted, and it is echoed around us every day: We assume that immigrant children will speak their L2 much better than their parents, we advocate that foreign language programs begin earlier in schools, our neighbors hire au pairs who speak another language to care for their children. Assumptions and anecdotes following these same lines formed the basis of much early writing on age and SLA from the 1920s until as recently as the 1960s. Singleton's (2001) review article on age and SLA mentions several such papers, where conclusions are based on impressionism, folk wisdom, and personal experience rather than empirical evidence. In scientific terms, these assumptions would point to a critical period for age "beyond which the process of acquiring another language changes in both quality and quantity of presumed success" (Bialystok, 2001, p. 72). Empirical research, however, has not painted nearly so clear a picture.

Terminology related to age effects can be confusing, and some clarification before proceeding is thus in order. A *critical period* necessarily includes an onset and an offset, and it is believed that beyond this period, nativelike success in language learning is impossible. Researchers opting for a weaker interpretation of the phenomenon often refer to a *sensitive period,* during which the organism is especially receptive to learning but beyond which successful learning is not precluded. Hyltenstam and Abrahamsson (2000) contrast the critical and sensitive period stances with what they refer to as the *linear decline hypothesis.* This hypothesis reflects the position of such researchers as Bialystok and Hakuta (1999), Birdsong (1999), and Butler (2000), according to which age effects are not described by a period per se, but rather by a linear decline in performance that persists throughout the lifespan without the salient onset and offset characteristic of a period.

2.1. THE CRITICAL PERIOD HYPOTHESIS

Two sources are generally credited with introducing the concept of a critical period for both L1 and L2 acquisition. The first are Penfield and Roberts (1959), researchers in the field of neuroscience who posited that children have a specific capacity for language learning due to cerebral flexibility that subsides at approximately age 9. The other is Lenneberg (1967), who noted that language recovery after postpubertal brain injury was practically impossible (but who also noted that some adults do learn a foreign language extremely well, given that "the matrix for language skills is present," p. 176). While these researchers did allow for the possibility of successful adult SLA, they were not especially encouraging. In addition, their conclusions were speculative rather than data driven. It should be borne in mind that the notion of a critical period was consistent both with generative linguistic theory's concept of the language acquisition device (LAD) and also with the popular thinking of the late 1950s and 1960s. This state of affairs offers a possible explanation of the initial appeal the critical period hypothesis (CPH) enjoyed and the lack of criticism it faced early on.

The CPH posits that language learning is maturationally limited, that "automatic acquisition from mere exposure to a given language seems to disappear [after puberty], and [that thereafter] foreign languages have to be taught and learned through a conscious and labored effort" (Lenneberg, 1967, p. 176). The hypothesis does not make any explicit claims about the possibility of successful naturalistic L2 acquisition before puberty.

As alluded to above, one issue that tends to complicate interpretation of research on the CPH is what geometry is implied by the term *period.* The conventional geometrical representation of the critical period includes an onset, a peak and an offset (as shown in Figure 4.1); all three components are necessary to be able to account for the entire period of heightened sensitivity (Bornstein, 1989). Crucially, though, a flattening of the function is requisite to indicate where the period ends.

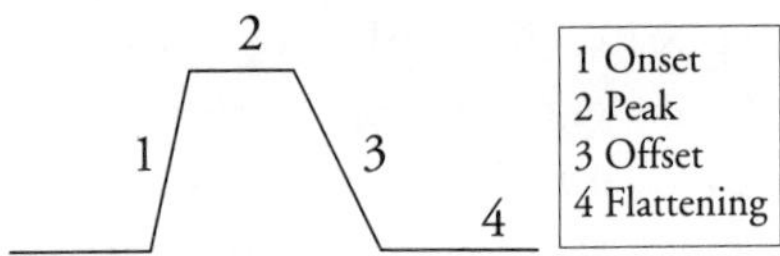

FIGURE 4.1 *Critical Period Geometry*

Because a strong version of the CPH implies the impossibility of achieving native norms in the L2, the issue of ultimate attainment in adult SLA is central. Thus, relevant evidence would come from studies of learners whose L2 development is asymptotic.

Results of empirical research on the CPH have led researchers to quite divergent positions on the likelihood of achieving nativelike L2 proficiency. As Hyltenstam and Abrahamsson (2000) pointed out, such disparity is the result of researchers' focusing on different individual implications of the CPH rather than on a combination of its various implications. For example, while some researchers have investigated the CPH's prediction that younger learners' ultimate attainment will be superior to that of older learners, other researchers have chosen to explore the CPH's prediction that although younger learners can learn an L2 implicitly, older learners will need to invoke explicit learning methods.

In Johnson and Newport (1989) and in DeKeyser's (2000) partial replication of that study, speakers of L2 English with varying ages of arrival (AoA) to the United States completed a grammaticality judgment task in English (for Johnson and Newport, the L1s were Chinese and Korean; for DeKeyser, the L1 was Hungarian). Data analyses revealed a significant negative correlation between AoA and performance through puberty in the Johnson and Newport (1989) data but not in the DeKeyser (2000) data, and no such linear relationship was evident beyond maturation in either study. The researchers interpreted the lack of a systematic relationship after puberty as a leveling off of the age effect. While it is true that statistically there was no linear relationship, it is important to note that this is not the same as a floor effect implied by a strong version of the CPH. Essentially, the distribution of scores is random after puberty, but there are both more successful and less successful learners beyond maturation. Furthermore, the aggregate data (i.e., considered all together) in the DeKeyser study reached significance for age effects, but the disaggregated data (i.e., considered as separate pieces, before and after puberty) showed no significant or systematic relationship. This type of data analysis has led other researchers to call DeKeyser's claim of support for the CPH into question.

These studies are often cited as providing evidence for the CPH, but whether or not one accepts the researchers' claims of support depends on whether or not the absence of a systematic relationship between AoA and L2 performance can be interpreted as the requisite flattening out of the age function signaling the close of the critical period. Other researchers have disagreed with this interpretation and thus have considered the findings of these studies to be counterevidence for the CPH. It is to a representative study from this camp that we now turn.

Birdsong and Molis (2001) replicated the Johnson and Newport (1989) study with the only methodological difference being the participants' L1 (Spanish). The results of the replication were quite different from those of the original study. Participants with an AoA lower than 16 years performed at ceiling (meaning that their scores were so high that they failed to discriminate among participants) and a significant negative correlation between AoA and L2 performance was observed for late arrivals (i.e., after 16 years of age). That is, for these learners, there was an overall linear decline in performance, rather than a leveling off or bottoming out after a certain age. Thus the flattening of the age function that would signify the close of a critical period failed to obtain in this study. In addition, the researchers reported instances of nativelike attainment among late learners, casting doubt upon a strict version of the CPH and offering some evidence that the L1-L2 pairing may have an influence on average level of L2 attainment.

Thus, despite the nagging question of whether or not the CPH can adequately account for the age effects that have been observed in empirical studies, research has shown that the ability to acquire language does indeed deteriorate with age: AoA has been shown to be the best predictor of L2 performance. It is perhaps more appropriate, therefore, to conclude from these data that the success of L2 acquisition is constrained not by a critical period, but rather by *age effects*. And indeed, in a recent attempt to reconcile in a unitary interpretation the facts given by empirical data, Hyltenstam and Abrahamsson (2003) posited a *maturational period* in lieu of a critical period. They qualified the term as one which "implies only that maturation *is going on*" (p. 575), rather than one which implies the characteristic onset, peak, and offset ascribed to the concept of a critical period.

If it is not the closing of a putative critical period that produces age effects in SLA, then to what sources should these effects be attributed? Several factors, both internal and external to the learner, have been proposed in the literature. Some or all of these factors, which may covary with age, could lead to the age effects observed in empirical research.

2.2. AGE EFFECTS: POSSIBLE SOURCES

Biological factors have often been invoked to explain observed differential outcomes in language learning according to age of onset of acquisition. Brain plasticity, or the capacity of neurons in the brain to reorganize or form new connections, for example, is considered central to successful learning outcomes in as far as the strengthening of such connections is the neurobiological foundation of learning (Eubank and Gregg, 1999). Plasticity would appear to differ in L1 and L2 acquisition, given that the former entails the initial organization of a neural architecture that is as yet unspecified, while the latter supposes the reorganization of a neural architecture that has already achieved a steady state with respect to the L1 (Eubank and Gregg, 1999). Other biological explanations that have been forwarded include lateralization (Lenneberg, 1967) and metabolic differences in the brain before and after maturation (Pulvermüller and Schumann, 1994).

Bialystok and Hakuta's (1999) analysis of previous age-related studies pointed to multiple cognitive factors that may lead to age effects on SLA. First, they proposed that L2 literacy skills may have a bearing on L2 proficiency; thus children who are immersed in the L2 speech community at a younger age are likely to achieve superior reading skills due to experience at school. Indeed, some age effects have been attributed, at least in part, to education (Flege, Yeni-Komshian, and Liu, 1999). Bialystok and Hakuta (1999) also reported deterioration over the lifespan of cognitive capacities such as the ability to perform tasks under time pressure, risk taking, establishing long-term memories, and recall of details. These considerations predict a gradual and constant decline in ultimate proficiency over the lifespan, in accordance with the evidence.

Other social and affective factors are likely to vary with age and may favor younger L2 learners. These may include motivation, self-esteem, attitude, and desire to assimilate into the L2 culture (Long, 1990; Singleton, 2001). In addition to these endogenous factors, exogenous factors may affect SLA in a way correlated with but not directly related to age. Namely, it is likely that quality and frequency of language input and use is quite different for a child acquiring language compared to that of an adult. Children may be more likely to be in frequent contact with native speakers of the L2 and to be exposed to more distinct situations and a richer variety of language than adults (Singleton, 2001).

Some researchers (e.g., Bongaerts, Planken, and Schils, 1995; Hyltenstam and Abrahamsson, 2000) suggest that maturational constraints on cognition interact with social-psychological factors, with the latter overtaking the former in the case of late learners of an L2. It seems quite possible that a variety of factors are present and in constant competition with one another throughout the lifespan and that it is the interactions of these factors rather than one factor overtaking the others that produce the age effects observed in empirical research. As stated by Elman and colleagues, "it is interesting to consider the possibility that all the mechanisms are always operating and their relative importance depends only on the state of the system given by [time], rather than invoking some ad hoc change prescribed at a certain time or age" (Elman et al., 1996, pp. 185–6).

2.3. CONCLUSIONS FOR THE ID AGE

In summary, there are a number of age-influenced factors that may have an impact on the success of SLA but that are not caused by the closing of a neurological critical period for language acquisition. It is important to keep several points in mind regarding age effects. First, aging does not involve biological maturation effects alone, since, as Bialystok and Hakuta (1999) pointed out, there are cognitive and social-affective factors that covary with age and that may be responsible for age effects. Second, SLA is not monolithic; the different components of L2 development (e.g., morphosyntax and phonology) may be affected differentially by age, and asymmetrical outcomes are thus to be expected both in the rate of acquisition and in ultimate attainment in SLA. However, studies have produced conflicting results even for phonology (Patkowski, 1994; Bongaerts et al., 1995), where the most inescapable age effects have often been claimed. Finally, under recent accounts of age effects on SLA (e.g., Birdsong, 1992; Birdsong and Molis, 2001), adult learners who attain native norms are not regarded as anomalous; rather, this line of research maintains that while earlier may be better in general, there is no hard and fast window of opportunity for SLA and that successful adult SLA is well within the realm of possibility.

3. Sex Differences

Are there differences between the sexes when it comes to SLA? Sex differences have long been proposed in work on IDs (e.g., Altman, 1980; Larsen-Freeman and Long, 1991; Oxford and Ehrman, 1993). However, there has been surprisingly little research on this issue in the field. It might not be a politically correct question, but it is certainly a legitimate one.

In this section, we will begin by reviewing past research on sex differences in L2. We will then review one new approach that focuses not on performance differences but on processing differences. Finally, we will see what conclusions can be drawn, and what future directions there may be for research on sex differences in SLA.

3.1. RESEARCH ON SEX DIFFERENCES IN SLA

The scant research that has been conducted on sex differences in SLA has revealed a general trend toward higher achievement for females on most tests (Ellis, 1994; Kiss and Nikolov, 2005; Powell, 1979; Oxford and Ehrman, 1993). These results have obtained both for children (Burstall, 1975; Kiss and Nikolov, 2005; Lynn and Wilson, 1992, 1993) and adults (Boyle, 1987).

Similarly, a recent study by Díaz-Campos (2004) revealed that sex was a significant predictor for acquisition of phonology by university-level students, with females making greater gains in accuracy of phonological production. Some research, however, has produced contradictory results. Using various listening and vocabulary measures, some studies have found advantages for males (Boyle, 1987), others for females (Farhady, 1982; Nyikos, 1990), and still others have found no differences between the sexes (Bacon, 1992).

In addition to this research on L2 performance, some research on sex and SLA has focused on differences in learning strategies. This research has revealed that females employ more language-learning strategies (Gass and Varonis, 1986; Politzer, 1983; Ehrman and Oxford, 1989). According to one study, females reported more use of a private, non-oral mode (Bacon and Finnemann, 1992). Oxford, Nyikos, and Ehrman (1988) summarized findings from several studies and concluded that, typically, not only do women use more learning strategies than men, but they also use them more often.

R. Ellis (1994) reported on research that indicated that females may, in general, be more motivated to learn a second language and may have more positive attitudes toward speakers of the L2 (Gardner and Lambert, 1972; Spolsky, 1989). In addition, some research suggests that females may be less anxious than males (Matsuda and Gobel, 2004). Thus it is likely that sex interacts with other variables in determining L2 learning success.[4]

Thus, while females appear to exhibit some advantage over males in terms of learning strategies and motivation, performance differences have not been consistently shown. One possible explanation for the lack of consistent findings in research on sex differences in L2 is that none exists. Another possibility is that there are real differences, but that they have not as yet been clearly revealed because studies have examined the product rather than the process of language learning and use (Ullman et al., 2002). It may be that we need to employ other process-oriented methods for investigating potential sex differences in both L1 and L2. Ullman et al. (2002) reported evidence from several lines of study that support a robust language processing difference between males and females in L1, specifically in the different domains of language. This difference is understood in the light of Ullman's declarative/procedural model for language.

3.2. A NEW APPROACH: THE DECLARATIVE/PROCEDURAL MODEL

This section will give a brief overview of the declarative/procedural model and its claims regarding sex differences in L1 and L2. (For more discussion of the model, see Ullman, this volume, chapter 5.) Like other dual system models, the declarative/procedural model holds that language consists of (at least) two domains: the mental lexicon (which contains memorized word information, such as irregular past tense verb forms like *wrote* and *ran*) and the mental grammar (whose rules underlie the composition of complex words, phrases, and sentences, such as regular past tense verb forms like *walk* + *ed* and *kiss* + *ed*). Unlike other dual system models, this model posits that in the L1 these mental components of language respectively depend on two memory systems that also subserve nonlanguage functions. The mental lexicon relies upon the declarative memory system, which is rooted in bilateral temporal lobe regions and underlies the learning and use of knowledge about facts and events, whereas aspects of the mental grammar rely upon the procedural memory system, which is rooted in frontal and basal ganglia regions and underlies motor and cognitive skills involving sequencing. Several lines of evidence have been offered in support of the model (Ullman, 2001b; Ullman, 2004).

3.2.1. SEX DIFFERENCES IN LI LANGUAGE PROCESSING

We begin by turning to research on sex differences in L1. Again, the results are controversial. While some analyses have concluded that there are no significant differences between males and females in terms of verbal abilities (Hyde and Linn, 1988; Macaulay, 1978), the trend of current evidence suggests that females are better than males at verbal memory—that is, remembering words (Halpern, 2000; Kimura, 1999). Verbal memory appears to depend on declarative memory (Bever, 1992; Pfluger et al., 1999; Ullman, 2004). Ullman and colleagues therefore posited a female advantage at lexical abilities (Ullman, 2004; Ullman et al., 2002). Moreover, they hypothesized that due to their verbal memory advantage, females will tend to memorize previously encountered complex forms (e.g., regular past tense forms) in the declarative system, while males tend to rule-compute them in the procedural system in real time (Ullman, 2004; Ullman et al., 2002; Ullman, Maloof, Hartshorne, Estabrooke, Brovetto, and Walenski, 2005). Both sexes must memorize irregular forms, whereas novel complex forms would be expected to be composed. A range of evidence has been argued to support this prediction, from psycholinguistic studies, neuropsychological patient data, and electrophysiological investigations (Ullman, 2004; Ullman et al., 2002; Ullman et al., 2005).

3.2.2. EXTENSIONS OF THE DECLARATIVE/PROCEDURAL MODEL TO L2

The declarative/procedural model has been applied to adult SLA (Ullman, 2001a; Ullman, this volume, chapter 5). The central claim is that adult L2 learners of both sexes will initially tend to rely very heavily on declarative memory for linguistic processing (more so than women in L1) due to an age-related attenuation of the procedural system's ability to learn or process. Practice, however, is predicted to improve performance in the procedural system, and therefore high-proficiency L2 learners will likely resemble L1 speakers in their reliance on the procedural as well as declarative memory system. Evidence indeed appears to support these claims (Ullman, 2001a). The model predicts that thanks to their superior lexical-declarative memory abilities, women should show an advantage at SLA as compared to men, at least during the initial states of SLA. At high levels of experience and proficiency, such a performance difference would tend to wash out due to the effects of practice on the procedural system.

3.3. CONCLUSIONS AND FUTURE DIRECTIONS FOR SEX DIFFERENCES

Thus it appears that neurological and SLA research may complement each other in informing the question of sex differences in language, both in interpreting past research and in designing new research. Current research indicates that there is indeed a processing difference between males and females and that this processing difference exists in both L1 and at least in highly practiced L2. Future studies in cognition and SLA should include sex as a design factor, and research in each field should be informed by that of the other.

Implications for sex differences in language may be of great importance, especially in the treatment of patients with brain disease or damage that affects one linguistic domain more than another (Ullman et al., 2002; Ullman et al., 2005; Ullman and Pierpont, 2005). Moreover, the sex difference in verbal memory appears to be modulated by estrogen (Phillips and Sherwin, 1992; Sherwin, 1988), which also affects memory for complex forms in L1 (Estabrooke, Mordecai, Maki, and Ullman, 2002). Therefore estrogen may also play a role in SLA, possibly including age or critical period effects (Ullman, 2004; see also Ullman, this volume, chapter 5). Implications for L2 pedagogy will have to be drawn from future research. It seems a good starting point, however, for both educators and researchers to know that robust differences appear to underlie linguistic processing in male and female learners and for them to keep informed of advances in the field.

4. Language Aptitude: Working Memory

Learners approach the task of language learning with a broad spectrum of strategies and with varying aptitude; indeed, the literature is rife with discussions of IDs identified in terms of differences in strategies and aptitude. Studies of the "good language learner" carried out in the 1970s and 1980s (see R. Ellis, 1994, for an overview) attempted to elucidate the strategies employed by successful language learners. Though it is important not to exaggerate the similarities in strategies that are included in successful language learners' repertoires, the collective findings of these studies hit upon several recurrent learning strategies that seem to be conducive to effective language learning. These include an awareness of and active involvement in the learning process, attention to both meaning and form, and flexible use of strategies. Are the strategies employed by successful and unsuccessful L2 learners evidence of varied innate aptitude for language learning?

Aptitude is defined in the literature as a specific talent for foreign language learning that varies from individual to individual. Language aptitude is considered to be a largely stable trait and has been identified as the individual difference most predictive of L2 learning outcomes (Sawyer and Ranta, 2001). The most commonly used test of L2 aptitude is Carroll and Sapon's (1959) Modern Language Aptitude Test (MLAT), a measure consisting of five subtests that were originally intended to evaluate four presumed L2 learning factors: phonetic coding ability, rote learning ability, grammatical sensitivity, and inductive language learning ability. Skehan (1989, 1998) subsequently argued for a collapsing of the latter two factors into one that he called language analytic ability. The MLAT was developed when behaviorist learning theory was prevalent and the audiolingual methodology was popular in the L2 classroom. A new approach seems warranted given the merging of cognitive psychology with linguistic theory and recent associations made between aptitude and psycholinguistic processes (e.g., Skehan, 1998; Dörnyei and Skehan, 2003). A processing approach to SLA, for example, underscores the role of input and its interaction with internal mechanisms responsible for filtering the input in or out, that is, what language learners perceive, attend, and subsequently represent in the developing system. As N. C. Ellis (2001) points out, current models of working memory provide such specialized systems of perception and representation, and are thus a potentially fruitful direction for language aptitude research to take.

4.1. HISTORICAL PERSPECTIVES ON MEMORY

Early accounts of memory (Atkinson and Shiffrin, 1968; Waugh and Norman, 1965; Sternberg, 1966) referred to the hub of encoding, maintenance, and integration of information as short-term memory (STM), which was claimed to consist of structurally independent stores through which information is transferred en route to long-term memory (LTM). Under this traditional view, it is through selective attention that a subset of information in sensory registers is chosen for further processing and this information passes to a short-term store (STS). Information being held in the STS may be retrieved with relatively little effort, but the speed of retrieval depends on the amount of information being held there. The general view is that information in the STS is tenuous and that once it is lost from the STS it is impossible to recover. Thus rehearsal is required to prevent decay of encoded information from the

STS, and it is only after sufficient rehearsal that information may be transferred to a more stable long-term store (LTS), from which subsequent retrieval is possible, albeit slower and more arduous than retrieval from the STS.

An alternate to this structural, or modal, model of memory was a continuous view, which posited working memory as a subset of activated representations within LTM (Norman, 1968). This conceptualization suggested a close relationship between working memory (WM) and attention in which WM capacity refers not to storage capabilities but rather to the ability to control and maintain attention, particularly in the presence of irrelevant or distracting stimuli. An as yet unresolved question for current models of WM is that of the nature of the relationship between WM and LTM (for proposals, see Miyake and Shah, 1999).

4.2. WORKING MEMORY: RECENT THEORETICAL ACCOUNTS

The fundamental difference between traditional views of STM and more recent accounts of WM is that while STM was conceived of commonly as a storage mechanism, WM is considered as both a processing and storage mechanism. Miyake and Shah (1999) formulated a composite definition of WM based on a number of current models of WM as follows: "Working memory is those mechanisms or processes that are involved in the control, regulation, and active maintenance of task-relevant information in the service of complex cognition, including novel as well as familiar, skilled tasks" (p. 450).

Representations of WM vary, but several take as their conceptual starting point the model put forth by Baddeley and his colleagues (Baddeley, 1986; Baddeley and Hitch, 1974; Baddeley and Logie, 1999). The components of the Baddeley model are a central executive, responsible for the control and regulation of attention, and two subsystems, the phonological loop and visuospatial sketchpad. The coordinated functions of the three components are posited to facilitate the performance of complex cognitive tasks. More recently, Baddeley (2000, 2003) has added a fourth component, the episodic buffer, to his model of WM. While the central executive is concerned with attentional control, the episodic buffer is responsible for both the temporary storage of information and the integration of perceptual information from different sources into single, multifaceted episodes. Other models deny the existence of subsystems or characterize their subsystems differently, and opinions vary on whether or not these subsystems are physically separable (e.g., Barnard, 1999; Cowan, 1999; Kieras, Meyer, Mueller, and Seymour, 1999; Schneider, 1999).

Capacity limitations are an aspect of memory that has received a great deal of attention from early accounts through current models of WM. James (1890) partitioned memory into primary and secondary memory. Whereas primary memory is limited in the absolute amount of information that it can manage, secondary memory, the more durable of the two, is unlimited in its capacity. Miller (1956) quantified the capacity limitations, claiming that STM could manage between approximately five and nine chunks of information at a time. Hebb (1949), on the other hand, conceived of the limitations of memory in terms of time limits for the activation of circuits of neurons. More recently, it has been proposed that "capacity limits reflect multiple factors and may even be an emergent property of the multiple processes and mechanisms involved" (Miyake and Shah, 1999, p. 450).

4.3. WORKING MEMORY MEASURES AND L2 RESEARCH

Revised conceptualizations of memory constructs such as that of Miyake and Shah have informed the field of L2 research and led to the development of new ways of assessing memory. Such measurements include "span" tests of verbal working memory and phonological STM (PSTM) measures.

4.3.1. "SPAN" TESTS OF VERBAL WORKING MEMORY

The theoretical shift from STM to WM was motivated in large part by the need to capture the processes involved in the performance of complex cognitive tasks such as language processing. Several research paradigms have verified the importance of WM in the performance of complex cognitive tasks. Hence, designs in SLA research in recent years have included a "span" test of verbal WM that places simultaneous demands on processing and storage, thus emulating the demands theorized to be placed on WM during completion of a complex cognitive task. A span test typically consists of reading or listening to sets of sentences and, in more recent versions, making judgments regarding their grammaticality and/or semantic sense while trying to remember the final word of each sentence. After a given set of two to six sentences is presented, participants recall aloud or in writing the final words for the sentences in that set. Participants in such research are generally classified into different groups based on their performance on the span test or else their scores are correlated with performance on a target language task.

The test that set the standard for research was Daneman and Carpenter's (1980) reading span test. In this test, participants read sentences aloud as they were presented one at a time on cards; this task of reading aloud was considered to satisfy the processing component of WM, but it was not quantified in any way and thus was not taken into account in the ultimate determination of participants' WM spans. After reading a particular set of two to six sentences, participants were required to recall in writing the final words of sentences in that set. Limitations of the reading span test included the questionability of measuring processing with a read-aloud task and the fact that the scoring of the test took only the recall component of WM into account. While the construct of WM was posited to include both processing and recall components, its operationalization included only recall. Furthermore, the reading span test was found to be somewhat unreliable over time (Waters and Caplan, 1996).

Waters and Caplan (1996) developed a sentence span test based on the work of Daneman and Carpenter (1980) in which participants were required to judge the acceptability of sentences while simultaneously trying to remember the final words of sentences. The WM score was a composite *z*-score based on accuracy of sentence processing, recall of sentence-final words, and reaction time.

Results of SLA research using reading or listening span tests and their adaptations are intricate and at times contradictory. Harrington and Sawyer (1992) found a strong correlation between a reading span task administered in the L2 to native Japanese English speakers and participants' TOEFL grammar and reading subtest scores as well as between scores on an L1 reading span task and an L2 reading span task. These findings indicate that a relationship indeed exists between the variables, but they do not specify the direction of the relationship, thus making it impossible to make any claims that one variable causes another. Therefore, the results must be interpreted with caution.

Miyake and Friedman (1998) reported on a study in which native Japanese speakers of English performed a listening span task in both their L1 and L2. Their data pointed to strong causal links between L1 WM and L2 WM as well as between L2 WM and syntactic comprehension in the L2. The researchers cautioned, however, that their results could be attributed to the advanced L2 proficiency of their participants.

In their study of WM, interactional feedback, and L2 development in native Japanese learners of English, Mackey, Philp, Egi, Fujii, and Tatsumi (2002) used three different measures of memory ability. Following previous arguments that the strong predictive validity of aptitude tests such as the MLAT can be attributed to their composite nature (see, for example, Skehan, 1998, 1989), they evaluated memory with measures of L1 and L2 verbal WM as well as with a test of PSTM. Basing themselves on measures used in previous research (Harrington and Sawyer, 1992; Turner and Engle, 1989; Waters and Caplan, 1996), the researchers created listening span tests for the L1 and L2, and operationalized PSTM as the ability to recall sets of nonwords immediately after auditory presentation. In their analysis they considered the L1 and L2 verbal WM and PSTM test scores both independently of one another and as a composite *z*-score. When they analyzed the L1 and L2 verbal WM test results, they found a high positive correlation between L1 and L2 scores, and thus they decided to combine L1 and L2 results in a composite verbal WM score. Participants were classified in groups of low, medium, and high

WM capacity, and the low and high WM groups were compared in terms of their ability to notice and respond to feedback that occurred during an interactive language task. Results showed a marginally significant relationship between composite WM scores and noticing.

Still other studies (e.g., Juffs, 2003; Sagarra, 2000) have found no significant relationship between WM and the higher order cognitive processes implicated in language learning and performance.

4.3.2. PSTM TESTS

Still other researchers claim a particularly important role for PSTM in SLA. PSTM is closely related to the functioning of the phonological loop subsystem of Baddeley's model of WM and has been operationalized as the ability to repeat phonological input accurately immediately after presentation. One such measure, used by Gathercole, Service, Hitch, Adams, and Martin (1999), is the nonword pairs recall test. Pairs of nonwords (i.e., strings of syllables that are phonologically possible in the participants' L1) consisting of two to five syllables each are presented aurally followed by a two-second pause. After the pause, participants are cued to repeat aloud the pair of nonwords.

PSTM capacity has been linked to L2 vocabulary acquisition (e.g., Gathercole and Thorn, 1998; Papagno and Vallar, 1992; Service and Kohonen, 1995) as well as grammar learning (e.g., N. C. Ellis and Schmidt, 1997; N. C. Ellis and Sinclair, 1996; Williams, 1999; Williams and Lovatt, 2003). Papagno and Vallar (1992) conducted a series of experiments to investigate the effects of various types of interference on adult participants' ability to learn pairs of known words and novel pseudowords. Results suggested that the capacity to temporarily store and rehearse verbal material is implicated in the learning of novel words but not of real words for which lexical-semantic representations already exist in LTM. The results must be interpreted with caution, however, in light of the fact that, as Papagno and Vallar acknowledged, the experimental conditions were quite different from real vocabulary learning, which is far less systematic and occurs more gradually over time.

Service and Kohonen (1995) undertook a longitudinal study to investigate whether vocabulary learning at the initial stages of L2 development relies on PSTM, which they operationalized as the ability to accurately repeat pseudowords that followed the phonotactics of the L2 (English) their child participants were starting to learn. Participants were tested once a year for four years on their ability to accurately repeat L1 and L2 pseudowords immediately after their auditory presentation. Results supported the hypothesized relationship between PSTM and the acquisition of foreign-language vocabulary.

N. C. Ellis and Sinclair (1996) undertook research to examine the relationship between PSTM function and the acquisition of L2 syntax. In their study, adult L1 English speakers completed a computerized lesson in Welsh vocabulary and soft mutation, a complex phonological rule system in Welsh. The lesson consisted of four learning trials in which participants attempted to learn 30 target items. Computerized corrective feedback was provided throughout the learning phase and participants completed the lesson in one of three conditions: one in which they were required to repeat aloud each Welsh item every time it was presented, one in which they remained silent, and one in which articulatory suppression (AS) in the form of constant whispered repetition of the numbers 1 through 5 prevented rehearsal of the Welsh items to be learned. Results of posttests revealed no effect of learning condition on accuracy of grammaticality judgments; however, the repetition and silent conditions performed significantly better than the AS condition on both a rule structure test and speech production test. There was no significant difference between performance on the structure test by participants in the repetition and silent conditions, but significant differences in performance between these two groups emerged in the speech production data. As the researchers acknowledged, the findings of their experiment cannot speak to whether the locus of the observed advantages is at the input or output phase of learning, but regardless of the locus of the advantages, the results of this study suggest that rehearsal of L2 utterances is a crucial component of learning. The researchers elaborated on this point and claimed that the rehearsal function of PSTM facilitates the accumulation of words and sequences of words in LTM. According to N. C. Ellis and Sinclair, acquisition of grammar entails the abstraction of regularities from these stored sequences, thus implicating PSTM not only in vocabulary learning but in grammar acquisition as well.

Other researchers, however, deny a direct role for PSTM in the acquisition of L2 grammar. Adams and Willis (2001), for example, claim that while people with greater PSTM capacity are better able to produce complex syntactic structures, this does not necessarily imply a relationship between PSTM and grammar learning.

4.4. CONCLUSIONS AND FUTURE RESEARCH FOR WORKING MEMORY

That the results of empirical research cannot be pieced together in any transparent way may be indicative of the theoretical and empirical work that remains to be done with regard to WM. Great strides have been made in recent years toward theoretical consensus, but the limits of the WM construct have yet to be defined. Recent advances in cognitive neuroscience research are a promising direction for the theory. This line of research has great potential to reveal how different regions of the brain collaborate dynamically during complex cognition and, as Miyake and Shah point out, an incorporation of cognitive psychological and cognitive neuroscience models of WM is critical to continue to move the theory forward (1999, p. 463).[5]

It will be incumbent upon future research to motivate and specify the particular functions and subsystems of WM. While empirical research in SLA certainly has moved forward in establishing the validity and reliability of existing WM measures and continues to refine the instruments used in experimental studies, current operationalizations of the construct will no doubt need to be modified to fit the theory as it evolves as well. As the components and processes of the WM system become more clearly defined in the theory, future research must take care to incorporate these components in new and revised WM measures to ensure that the construct is being operationalized in a manner that approximates as closely as possible real-world complex cognition.

5. Prior Experience

Until the 1960s, research efforts mostly focused on the detrimental effects that bilingualism had on cognition and its development. Methodological limitations were numerous; variables such as socioeconomic status, intelligence, and bilingualism were confounded, and English-based IQ tests were administered to populations with low English proficiency. Changes in general attitudes toward minorities and their rights, increased communication between European and American researchers, and the sudden realization that in our world being bilingual is the norm rather than the exception led to a refocusing of the relationship between bilingualism and cognition. Researchers continued to compare bilinguals and monolinguals, but their research questions and methodologies were finer grained (Peal and Lambert, 1962) and better informed by a growing number of cognitive models; issues of storage and access, for example, moved to the forefront (see Harris, 1992). Unlike previous research, these studies emerged from a new interest in understanding bilingual cognition per se, and did not always feel the need to draw implications for education.

Within studies on bilingual cognition, researchers have investigated the role of prior linguistic experience in the acquisition of an L3. The study of multilingual acquisition is an ideal area for those interested in the role of IDs in language acquisition, as no two bilinguals are the same; they differ in age of L2 acquisition, context and frequency of use of both languages, and degree of bilingualism, for example. An additional consideration is the structural relationship between the learner's L1 and the other, nonprimary languages. Old topics such as transfer are now revisited in the context of multilingual acquisition and the interaction among different IDs (Cenoz, Hufeisen, and Jessner, 2001).

5.1. THE EXPERIENCED LANGUAGE LEARNER: BELIEFS AND ANECDOTES

It is a popular belief that multilinguals learn languages better than monolinguals—that previous practice (being experienced as a language learner) gives you an edge when it comes to learning other languages. This belief is corroborated by informal observations (Larsen-Freeman, 1983, in Zobl, 1992) and by descriptions of "the good language learner" (Ramsey, 1980). Results from this study comparing monolingual and multilingual learners' success at acquisition of a foreign language suggest that multilinguals behave like successful learners in the way they approach the task of learning a language: They look for more sources of input, make early efforts to use the new language, and show self-direction and a positive attitude toward the task. The author concluded that acquiring languages in adulthood results in enhanced creativity and flexibility. While there is a plethora of research on bilingualism that has drawn important conclusions, empirically based research on trilingualism is scarce and has generated contradictory results. The hypothesis that bilinguals are more efficient language learners is intuitively attractive, but what is the evidence?

5.2. EMPIRICAL RESEARCH ON THE EXPERIENCED LANGUAGE LEARNER: THE ACQUISITION OF AN L3

Wagner, Spratt, and Ezzaki (1989) carried out a longitudinal study of literacy acquisition in Berber and Arab children in rural Morocco. The authors compared the acquisition of French literacy by bilingual Berber children illiterate in their L1 but literate in their L2, Arabic, and by monolingual Arabic children who were literate in their L1. Both groups received literacy instruction in Arabic first, followed 4 years later by instruction in French. Results showed no difference between Arabic and Berber groups, but a correlation was found between literacy in Arabic and literacy in French. From this, the authors concluded that children do not need to be taught to read in their L1 to achieve nativelike literacy norms in Arabic or French. Given the high level of attrition (only 50 participants out of the initial group of 166 reached the fifth grade in five years), results have to be considered carefully. The study does not report how many of those 50 students were Berber. However, we might expect that given the importance of literacy for academic success and given that the Arabic children significantly outperformed their Berber classmates in literacy tests every year from first to fourth grade, it is likely that there were few Berber students among those receiving French literacy lessons in grade 4. Consequently, although there is no statistically significant difference between their performance and that of their Arabic classmates, in terms of sheer numbers the difference could be very important.

In contrast with Wagner et al., which was carried out in a developing country, studies by Swain, Lapkin, Rowen, and Hart (1990), Cenoz and Valencia (1994), and Sanz (2000) were conducted in Canada and Spain (specifically, the Basque Country and Catalonia). These studies were conducted in bilingual maintenance programs designed to produce balanced bilinguals, capable of functioning equally well in two languages. Cenoz and Valencia's comparison of achievement on tests of English administered to students instructed in Basque, the minority language, and in Spanish, the majority language, yielded evidence in favor of bilingualism and bilingual education as contributors to foreign-language learning. Furthermore, the positive effects of bilingualism were obtained regardless of cognitive, sociostructural, sociopsychological, and educational variables and independently of the L1; both native speakers of Spanish and native speakers of Basque in the Basque immersion program outperformed the students schooled in the majority language. Sanz (2000) sought to contribute to this line of research by comparing the acquisition of L3 English between bilingual Catalan-Spanish high school students in a Catalan immersion program and a comparable sample from a monolingual Spanish region. Analysis of data from 201 participants revealed that bilingualism indeed had a positive effect on the acquisition of an L3 and that the effect was independent of all other variables, including sex and socioeconomic status (SES).

Swain and colleagues investigated the effect of L1 literacy on L3 learning among 319 eighth graders in Toronto. Participants were of different L1 backgrounds and were schooled in English up to grade 5. After that, they were part of a bilingual English-French program. The study found that literacy in the L1 had a strong impact on performance in French, their L3. This effect was independent of the typological nature (Romance or non-Romance) of the L1. However, knowledge of a heritage language had little facilitative effect without L1 literacy. Results of this study suggest that the crucial factor in successful L3 acquisition is development of heritage language literacy skills, rather than oral skills only. The authors interpreted these results as evidence of transfer of knowledge and processing rather than of specific surface-level aspects from the L1 to the L3. Their conclusion supports Cummins' (1981) linguistic interdependence hypothesis, according to which children learn to use language as a symbolic system in the process of acquiring literacy skills in their L1. The result is the ability to classify, abstract, and generalize linguistic information in a way that can be transferred to subsequent language learning contexts.

The four studies we just reviewed are product oriented and focused on overall language proficiency. Process-oriented research—those studies that look at how learners go about acquiring a specific syntactic parameter, for example—can shed further light on the relationship between bilingualism and L3 acquisition. There is general agreement that while the route followed to acquire an L2 is fairly independent of internal and external variables such as the individual's L1, intelligence, motivation, and context of acquisition, differences in both rate of acquisition and final attainment can be expected as a result of prior experience with language learning. It is possible to hypothesize that bilinguals learning an L3 will form hypotheses and produce errors that are similar to those of monolinguals. However, bilinguals will pick up the new language faster and go farther in the acquisition process than monolinguals. An example studying specific linguistic parameters should help elucidate how this may occur at a lower level. Klein (1995) investigated the effects of prior linguistic experience on the acquisition of the preposition-stranding parameter by a group of 17 monolingual immigrants and 15 multilingual immigrants learning L2 English. Her results showed that both groups of learners produced the same type of errors, which Klein interpreted as evidence that the route leading to acquisition of the parameter was the same. However, the rate at which the groups acquired the parameter was significantly different, with multilinguals resetting the parameter earlier than monolinguals.

5.3. POSITED EXPLANATIONS FOR THE FACILITATIVE EFFECTS OF BILINGUALISM

As we have seen above, studies that have explored bilinguals' and monolinguals' acquisition of a nonprimary language in the form of either general language proficiency or specific parameters suggest an advantage in favor of bilinguals. But why do bilinguals pick up other languages faster? We will review two explanations that have been put forward.

5.3.1. HOW THE INPUT IS PERCEIVED AND ORGANIZED

Neurolinguists describe the bilingual brain as different in structure: more flexible, higher in cerebral plasticity, with a higher number of multiple connections than the monolingual brain. Educational psychologists associate bilingualism with enhanced motivation to learn languages, higher self-esteem when it is accompanied by biliteracy, greater ability to relate to others, and even a more democratic disposition. Cognitive psychologists claim that the bilingual makes more efficient use of STM, has more flexible processing strategies, and, of course, may have a different LTM structure (e.g., are both languages stored together, separately, or neither of the above?). Here we outline different explanations generated by information-processing accounts of the acquisition of nonprimary languages. This research views humans as limited processors but sees bilingual humans as especially efficient users of their limited cognitive resources.

Let's reconsider Klein's study, for example. She differentiated between the acquisition of a syntactic structure and the acquisition of lexical items related to it (the specific verbs and prepositions). She observed that the multilingual group learned more of the lexical items responsible for triggering parameter resetting. Klein interpreted this result as a consequence of enhanced cognitive skill on the part of multilinguals, which helped them pay closer attention to potential triggering data in the input.

In a series of studies on bilingual processing strategies (McLaughlin and Nayak, 1989; Nation and McLaughlin, 1986; Nayak, Hansen, Krueger, and McLaughlin, 1990), McLaughlin and associates' findings on multilingual language learners run parallel to those identified in the literature on acquisition of other skills such as chess and computer programming. Results of these studies suggested that there are differences between experts and novices in the way they process, organize, and restructure information. While experts were able to restructure the elements of the learning task into abstract schemas, novices focused primarily on the surface elements of the task. The researchers observed the following differences in the groups' behavior: (a) Multilingual subjects were found to habitually exert more processing effort in making sense of verbal stimuli, (b) multilingual subjects were better able to shift strategies in order to adapt to the new language and to restructure their language systems, and (c) multilingual subjects used cognitive strategies that facilitated more efficient use of processing resources in the construction of formal rules.

5.3.2. METALINGUISTIC AWARENESS

Compatible with the conclusions drawn by McLaughlin and his colleagues is the explanation advanced by proponents of the weak interface position in SLA (Larsen-Freeman and Long, 1991), which posits a link between explicit knowledge and speed of acquisition. This position maintains that while explicit knowledge cannot be transformed into implicit knowledge, it can facilitate the acquisition process by acting as an advance organizer and focusing the learner's attention on the relevant features of the language. One of the best-documented differences between bilinguals and monolinguals is the degree of metalinguistic awareness each group develops. Research by Bialystok (1986, 1987, 1991); Cummins (1976); Galambos and Hakuta (1988); Galambos and Goldin-Meadow (1990); Yelland, Pollard, and Mercury (1993); and Ricciardelli (1992a, 1992b) has shown that bilinguals have superior explicit knowledge of a target language than do their monolingual counterparts. Although the majority of studies have focused on the relationship between form and meaning at the level of the word (Ben-Zeev, 1977; and Bialystok, 1986, just to name the early studies), there is evidence that the benefits extend to heightened syntactic awareness and even to phonological awareness (Werker, 1986). For example, Galambos and Goldin-Meadow (1990) found that bilingual children outperformed monolinguals on a task that required participants to identify and correct errors. And Bialystok (1987) showed that if an error was formal rather than semantic (e.g., *Girl is swimming* rather than *Ride the picture*), the bilingual group could detect it at an earlier age (4 years 6 months) than monolingual children could (between 5 years 6 months and 6 years). Bialystok (2001, and previous work) interpreted these results as evidence of superiority on the part of bilinguals in their analysis of the language as well as in their control over internal linguistic processes.

5.3.3. WORKING MEMORY

But why is it important that bilinguals use processing strategies more efficiently? A possible answer may lie in WM limitations. WM is a flexible workspace with limited capacity. Available capacity is seen as a trade-off between storage and processing demands. Controlled processes require more processing space. If processes are automatized faster, there is more space available and thus more information can be extracted, segmented, and transformed into intake that will be incorporated later into the L3 system. In conclusion, then, the intuitively attractive notion that bilinguals pick up languages more easily than monolinguals may have a psycholinguistic explanation. We do not propose that the relationship between metalinguistic knowledge, processing flexibility, and WM is the only possible approach to an explanation of the posited advantage of bilingualism in L3 acquisition. Factors such as motivation should also be taken into account.

5.4. CONCLUSION FOR PRIOR EXPERIENCE

Future research should concentrate on explaining the positive relationship that has been observed between bilingualism and the acquisition of an L3 through empirical exploration of the more specific factors implicated in the relationship. For example, research is needed on the effects of prior linguistic experience on the representation of new L3 knowledge (see Ullman, this volume, chapter 5). Also, recent advances in the field of attention and awareness in cognitive psychology and SLA (see Leow and Bowles, this volume, chapter 6) distinguish between awareness at the level of noticing and awareness at the level of understanding. Research on bilingualism and metalinguistic awareness to date has focused exclusively on the latter. Studies such as Klein's (1995), and even this chapter, suggest that it is heightened awareness at the level of noticing which gives experienced language learners the edge. Research on L3 acquisition to date has been very product oriented, so experimental studies that include qualitative data in their design (see Adams, Fujii, and Mackey, this volume, chapter 3) and that compare bilinguals and monolinguals in their processing of input might contribute to an understanding of the ways in which the two groups differ in their processing strategies.

6. Summary

Empirical research since the 1970s has supported the claim that elements of L2 performance decline with increasing age. The question of whether this evidence supports the CPH in its original formulation, however, remains debatable. This state of affairs is largely attributable to researchers' different foci in their investigation of the CPH's implications for L2 learning and to their varied interpretation of the data. In addition, research has identified a significant number of learners whose L2 acquisition began late but who nonetheless achieved nativelike L2 proficiency; thus the evidence from research in this area does not preclude successful L2 acquisition by all late learners.

Recent research on sex differences in language suggests that there may indeed be an underlying difference in processing between males and females, possibly modulated by hormones. Specifically, the declarative/procedural model claims that due to a verbal memory advantage, females tend to memorize previously encountered complex forms (e.g., regular past tense forms) in the declarative system, while males tend to rule-compute them in the procedural system in real time. Recall that no difference is posited in processing of memorized forms, which are subserved by the declarative system in both sexes. This difference has not yet been widely tested, but preliminary evidence does support the notion. Furthermore, these sex differences have important implications for how males and females learn and process an L2 and should be taken into consideration in the analyses of SLA research, especially from a processing perspective.

Memory has long been implicated as an integral part of language learning aptitude. Models of WM that have emerged since the 1970s and 1980s include mechanisms and processes that are closely tied to language acquisition, and thus these models have provided a productive direction for research in both aptitude and language acquisition to take. Experimental studies have shown evidence of a relationship between WM capacity and several aspects of language learning, and the field is moving closer to theoretical consensus on the construct of WM. It is important for future research, however, to define the limits of the construct as well as the functions and subsystems that are implicated in WM. And as the theory evolves in this way, it must continue to inform researchers as they seek to refine the instruments they use to evaluate WM in empirical research.

Just like typists, chess players, and computer programmers, experienced (bilingual) language learners appear to have an advantage when compared to novice (monolingual) learners. As with most complex phenomena, a number of factors need to be brought into the equation in order to be adequately explained. Attitude, motivation, and degree of bilingualism are just a few of those factors. From an information-processing perspective, however, processing strategies, metalinguistic knowledge, and WM capacity are posited to contribute to the superior performance of bilinguals over monolinguals when it comes to learning other languages.

7. Exercises

The exercises that follow are divided into two sections, the first of which focuses on data analysis, and the second of which will help you to practice the basic skill of critical reading. Both sections will require the application of concepts presented in this chapter as well as basic concepts of data analysis and research methodology. Thus, we suggest you revisit Chen (this volume, chapter 2) and Adams, Fujii, and Mackey (this volume, chapter 3).

7.1. DATA ANALYSIS

1. Imagine that you have conducted an experiment to investigate the effects of providing explicit feedback to learners as they complete a language task in which they are trying to induce rules of L2 morphosyntax. Unfortunately, you find no significant differences between the experimental and control groups, and a statistician suggests that differences did not show up because there was a lot of variation within the experimental group, that is, that the provision of feedback had a significant effect on some learners in that group, but no effect on other learners. Fortunately, though, you've administered a test of verbal WM to your participants. For what could you use the WM data? What would you hope to find?
2. You have piloted an L1 WM listening span task that you created. Participants listened to sets of 2 to 5 sentences presented on audiotape with an 8-second pause between sentences. As they listened to each sentence, participants judged whether or not the sentences made sense and recorded their answers on an answer sheet. After presentation of each set of sentences, participants were required to recall aloud the sentence-final words that they could remember from that set. You find that the majority of participants perform at ceiling and conclude that you need to design a more discriminating task. What might you change about the test to better discriminate among participants?
3. The scatterplots shown in Figures 4.2 and 4.3 represent results of correlational analyses of fictitious data on the relationship between participants' AoA to an L2 speech community and their performance in the L2. Interpret each scatterplot and explain what the data might contribute to arguments of either support or refutation of the CPH.
4. Sex differences for language are controversial even in L1 research. Data from brain-damaged patients were briefly mentioned in this chapter as supporting the declarative/procedural model's proposed sex differences in L1. If brain-damaged patients were tested on regular and irregular verb

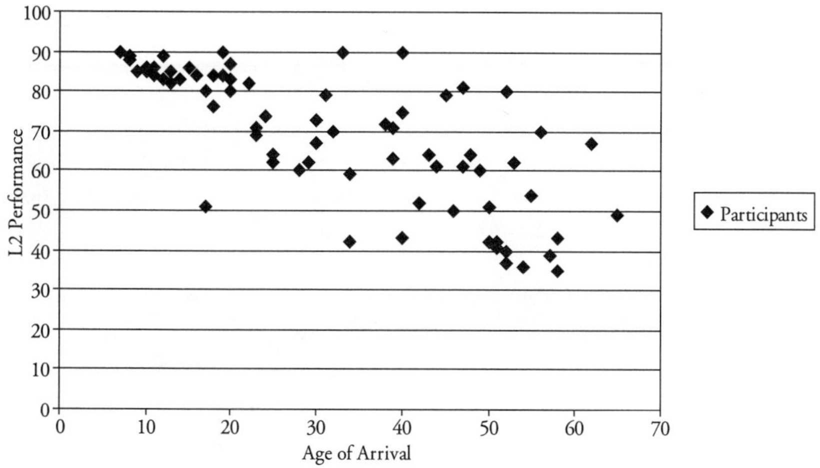

FIGURE 4.2 *L2 Performance by Age of Arrival–Scenario 1*

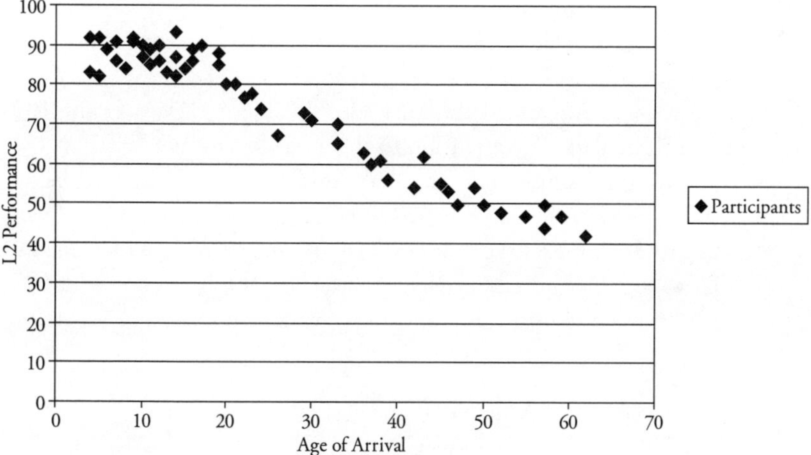

FIGURE 4.3 *L2 Performance by Age of Arrival–Scenario 2*

production, what kind of data would the model predict for (you may need to answer separately for each sex):

a. Men and women with damage to frontal and basal ganglia regions (i.e., the procedural system).
b. Men and women with damage to temporal and parietal regions (i.e., the declarative system).

5. Briefly explain what type of study you might design to test whether the proposed sex differences in processing are found in L2.

6. If the validity of these sex differences, now somewhat tentative in nature, becomes accepted in the field, what applications to pedagogy would you suggest for the L2 classroom? Defend your proposal.
7. Bilinguals as a group show an advantage in L3 acquisition over monolinguals. However, among bilinguals, which ones seem to have a knack for languages? To identify key factors predicting success in L3 acquisition among bilinguals, the data below from a sample of Catalan-Spanish bilinguals were analyzed.
   a. Look at the tables at the end of the exercise. The factors are listed in the left column. Can you explain what they are in your own words?
   b. Read the following research questions (RQs) first and write directional hypotheses based on your intuitions and this chapter's content.
      RQ 1. Which factors best predict grammar test scores?
      RQ 2. Does age of L2 acquisition onset affect the acquisition of L3 grammar?
      RQ 3. Does order of acquisition of the L1 and L2 affect the acquisition of L3 grammar?
      RQ 4. Does the degree of balance of Catalan and Spanish skills affect the acquisition of L3 grammar?
   c. Look at the summary of the analyses in Table 4.1. Answer the RQs based on the data. Pay attention to the asterisks.
   d. Now look at the summary of the analyses in Table 4.2. What are the differences between the two tables? Hints: (a) look at the number of variables in the columns, (b) pay attention to new asterisks, (c) look at the two different r^2s. What do they mean? Answer the RQs based on the data.
   e. Based on these results, can you confirm your hypotheses? reject them?

TABLE 4.1
Multiple Regression of All Variables on English Grammar Scores

Variable	*Parameter Estimate*	*T*	r^2
Sex	.929	.925	
Motivation	.452	3.726**	
Exposure	.005	2.733*	
SES	.339	.756	
L3 Attitudes	.099	1.335	
IQ	−.370	−.897	
Cat/Span Use	.218	2.823*	
Order of Acquisition	.811	.806	
L2 Onset	.072	−.388	
Balance: Literacy Skills	1.338	1.691	
Balance: Oral Skills	−.471	−.576	.36

*$p < .05$. **$p < .01$.

TABLE 4.2
Multiple Regression of English Grammar Scores with Motivation and Exposure Factored Out

Variable	*Parameter Estimate*	*T*	r^2
Sex	.345	.316	
SES	.405	.821	
L3 Attitudes	.250	3.32**	
IQ	−.272	−.591	
Cat/Span Use	.194	2.330*	
Order of Acquisition	.751	.678	
L2 Onset	.071	.356	
Balance: Literacy Skills	1.800	2.082*	
Balance: Oral Skills	.035	.039	.20

*$p < .05$. **$p < .01$.

f. Write a 250-word paragraph summarizing the study as if it were an abstract.

7.2. GUIDED CRITIQUE

The following exercise will help you practice the basic skill of critical reading. As mentioned above, we suggest you revisit Chen (this volume, chapter 2) and Adams, Fujii, and Mackey (this volume, chapter 3) on research methodology as needed and that you provide the information below. It is a good idea to complete forms like this one for every primary source you read in preparation for a research paper or an exam. The article we have chosen is the following:

Wagner, D. A., Spratt, J. E., and Ezzaki, A. (1989). Does learning to read in a second language always put the child at a disadvantage? Some counter evidence from Morocco. *Applied Psycholinguistics, 10,* 31–48.

Read the article, note down the information, and then compare it with your classmates' results. Sort out any differences you might have. Usually readers differ in their interpretations and conclusions, but answers to points 1 through 7 should be pretty much the same.

1. Author(s), title, journal, volume number, pages. We recommend you list the reference according to the *Publication Manual of the American Psychological Association,* so that you familiarize yourself with its style. Most SLA journals follow the APA guidelines for publication.
2. Overall motivation for the study (indicate page number)
3. Hypotheses (or research questions). How many are there? State them in a list with their corresponding supporting literature. This is especially important when the hypothesis is directional (the author states something will happen). Summarize the statements and references (name, year).

4. Methodology
   a. Design: Is the study experimental? quasi-experimental? Is it a case study? cross-sectional? longitudinal? a combination?
   b. Target form, languages involved
   c. Participants: total *N*. List all relevant, specific characteristics (level, L1, naturalistic-classroom learners). Initial sample, final sample. Any explanations for attrition?
   d. Groups? *N* per group?
   e. Instruments
   f. Dependent variables
   g. Independent variables
5. Results
   a. If ANOVA or *t*-test:
      i. Main factors
      ii. Significant correlations
      iii. Post-hocs
   b. If correlation or regression: predicting factors
   c. Revisit the hypotheses and list them again. Next to each, specify whether it was accepted or rejected.
6. Discussion
   a. If any of the hypotheses were rejected, what is the explanation provided by the authors?
   b. What are their supporting references? Specify name, year, and provide a brief statement.
7. Conclusions: Summarize each of the authors' conclusions.
8. Your conclusions. For each of the conclusions in (7) above, specify:
   a. Observations: Do you agree with the authors?
   b. Criticisms: Are any important references missing? Did the authors place more weight on certain studies than others?
   c. Are there any problems with the analysis or methodology (sampling, for example)?
   d. Can their results be interpreted in a different way?
9. Overall statement, interesting points

Further Reading

Bhatia, T. K., & Ritchie, W. (Eds.). (2004). *The handbook of bilingualism.* Oxford, UK: Blackwell.

Birdsong, D. (1999). *Second language acquisition and the critical period hypothesis.* Mahwah, NJ: Lawrence Erlbaum.

Dörnyei, Z., & Skehan, P. (2003). Individual differences in second language learning. In C. J. Doughty & M. H. Long (Eds.), *The handbook of second language acquisition.* Oxford, UK: Blackwell.

Miyake, A., & Shah, P. (Eds.). (1999). *Models of working memory: Mechanisms of active maintenance and executive control.* Cambridge, UK: Cambridge University Press.

Robinson, P. (Ed.). (2002). *Individual differences and instructed language learning.* Amsterdam: John Benjamins.

Notes

1. For classic and recent treatments of IDs in the second language acquisition (SLA) literature, readers are referred to the following volumes: Doughty and Long (2003), R. Ellis (1994), Larsen-Freeman and Long (1991), Robinson (2001).

2. In this chapter, we will refer to *sex* rather than *gender* because we will be concerned with biological rather than social differences. Nonetheless, we recognize that there may indeed be other social factors that correlate with sex and that influence SLA (e.g., motivation).

3. This is not to say, however, that the two constructs are necessarily isomorphic. Many scholars believe that working memory encompasses more than aptitude (for a number of models of working memory, see Miyake and Shah, 1999). Likewise, most scholars will argue that language aptitude goes beyond working memory (see, for example, Dörnyei and Skehan, 2003).

4. For a review of diverse lines of motivation research, see Dörnyei (1998). Also see Dörnyei and Schmidt (2001) for a collection of motivation studies.

5. See, for example, D'Esposito et al. (1995), D'Esposito, Aguirre, Zarahn, Ballard, and Shin (1998), and Owen (1997).

References

Adams, A. M., & Willis, C. (2001). Language processing and working memory: A developmental perspective. In J. Andrade (Ed.), *Working memory in perspective* (pp. 79–100). Hove, UK: Taylor & Francis.

Altman, H. (1980). Foreign language teaching: Focus on the learner. In H. Altman & J. Vaughan (Eds.), *Foreign language teaching: Meeting individual needs* (pp. 30–45). Oxford, UK: Pergamon.

Atkinson, R. C., & Shiffrin, R. M. (1968). Human memory: A proposed system and its control processes. In K. W. Spence & J. T. Spence (Eds.), *The psychology of learning and motivation: Advances in research and theory* (Vol. 2, pp. 89–195). New York: Academic Press.

Bacon, S. (1992). The relationship between gender, comprehension, processing strategies, and cognitive and affective response in second-language listening. *The Modern Language Journal, 76,* 160–178.

Bacon, S., & Finnemann, M. (1992). Sex differences in self-reported beliefs about foreign-language learning and authentic oral and written input. *Journal of Applied Linguistics, 42*(4), 471–495.

Baddeley, A. D. (1986). *Working memory.* Oxford, UK: Oxford University Press.

Baddeley, A. D. (2000). The episodic buffer: A new component of working memory? *Trends in Cognitive Sciences, 4,* 417–423.

Baddeley, A. D. (2003). Working memory and language: An overview. *Journal of Communication Disorders, 36,* 189–208.

Baddeley, A. D., & Hitch, G. J. (1974). Working memory. In G. A. Bower (Ed.), *Recent advances in learning and motivation* (pp. 47–90). New York: Academic Press.

Baddeley, A. D., & Logie, R. H. (1999). Working memory: The multiple-component model. In A. Miyake & P. Shah (Eds.), *Models of working memory: Mechanisms of active maintenance and executive control* (pp. 28–61). Cambridge, UK: Cambridge University Press.

Barnard, P. J. (1999). Interacting cognitive subsystems: Modeling working memory phenomena within a multiprocessor architecture. In A. Miyake & P. Shah (Eds.), *Models of working memory: Mechanisms of active maintenance and executive control* (pp. 298–339). Cambridge, UK: Cambridge University Press.

Ben-Zeev, S. (1977). Mechanisms by which childhood bilingualism affects understanding of language and cognitive structures. In P. A. Hornby (Ed.), *Bilingualism: Psychological, social, and educational implications* (pp. 29–55). New York: Academic Press.

Bever, T. G. (1992). The logical and extrinsic sources of modularity. In M. Gunnar & M. Maratsos (Eds.), *Modularity and constraints in language and cognition* (pp. 179–212). Mahwah, NJ: Lawrence Erlbaum.

Bialystok, E. (1986). Factors in the growth of linguistic awareness. *Child Development, 57,* 498–510.

Bialystok, E. (1987). Words as things: Development of word concept by bilingual children. *Studies in Second Language Learning, 9,* 133–140.

Bialystok, E. (1991). *Language processing in bilingual children.* Cambridge, UK: Cambridge University Press.

Bialystok, E. (2001*). Bilingualism in development: Language, literacy and cognition.* Cambridge, UK: Cambridge University Press.

Bialystok, E., & Hakuta, K. (1999). Confounded age: Linguistic and cognitive factors in age differences for second language acquisition. In D. Birdsong (Ed.), *Second language acquisition and the critical period hypothesis* (p. 161–181). Mahwah, NJ: Lawrence Erlbaum.

Birdsong, D. (1992). Ultimate attainment in second language acquisition. *Language, 68,* 706–755.

Birdsong, D. (Ed.). (1999). *Second language acquisition and the critical period hypothesis.* Mahwah, NJ: Lawrence Erlbaum.

Birdsong, D., & Molis, M. (2001). On the evidence for maturational constraints in second language acquisition. *Journal of Memory and Language, 44,* 1–15.

Bongaerts, T., Planken, B., & Schils, E. (1995). Can late starters attain a native accent in a foreign language? A test of the critical period hypothesis. In D. Singleton & Z. Lengyel (Eds.), *The age factor in second language acquisition* (pp. 30–50). Clevedon, UK: Multilingual Matters.

Bornstein, M. H. (1989). Sensitive periods in development: Structural characteristics and causal interpretations. *Psychological Bulletin, 105,* 179–197.

Boyle, J. (1987). Sex differences in listening vocabulary. *Language Learning, 37,* 273–284.

Burstall, C. (1975). Factors affecting foreign-language learning: A consideration of some relevant research findings. *Language Teaching and Linguistics Abstracts, 8,* 105–125.

Butler, Y. G. (2000). The age effect in second language acquisition: Is it too late to acquire native-level competence in a second language after the age of seven? In Y. Oshima-Takane, Y. Shirai, & H. Sirai (Eds.), *Studies in Language Sciences 1* (pp. 159–169). Tokyo: Japanese Society for Language Sciences.

Carroll, J. B., & Sapon, S. M. (1959). *Modern Language Aptitude Test.* New York: Psychological Corporation.

Cenoz, J., Hufeisen, B., & Jessner, U. (Eds.). (2001). *Cross-linguistic influence in third language acquisition: Psycholinguistic perspectives.* Clevedon, UK: Multilingual Matters.

Cenoz, J., & Valencia, J. F. (1994). Additive trilingualism: Evidence from the Basque Country. *Applied Psycholinguistics, 15,* 195–207.

Collentine, J. (2004). The effects of learning contexts on morphosyntactic and lexical development. *Studies in Second Language Acquisition, 26,* 227–248.

Colombo, J. (1982). The critical period concept: Research, methodology, and theoretical issues. *Psychological Bulletin, 91,* 260–275.

Cowan, N. (1999). An embedded-processes model of working memory. In A. Miyake & P. Shah (Eds.), *Models of working memory: Mechanisms of active maintenance and executive control* (pp. 62–101). Cambridge, UK: Cambridge University Press.

Cummins, J. (1976). The influence of bilingualism on cognitive growth: A synthesis of research findings and explanatory hypothesis. *Working Papers on Bilingualism, 9,* 1–43.

Cummins, J. (1981). The role of primary language development in promoting educational success for language minority students. In *Schooling and language minority students: A theoretical framework, California State Department of Education* (pp. 3–49). Los Angeles: Evaluation, Dissemination, and Assessment Center, California State University.

Daneman, M., & Carpenter, P. (1980). Individual differences in working memory and reading. *Journal of Verbal Learning and Verbal Behavior, 19,* 450–466.

DeKeyser, R. (2000). The robustness of critical period effects in second language acquisition. *Studies in Second Language Acquisition, 22,* 499–533.

D'Esposito, M., Aguirre, G. K., Zarahn, E., Ballard, D., & Shin, R. K. (1998). Functional MRI studies of spatial and non-spatial working memory. *Cognitive Brain Research, 7,* 1–13.

D'Esposito, M., Detre, J. A., Alsop, D. C., Shin, R. K., Atlas, S., & Grossman, M. (1995). The neural basis of the central executive system of working memory. *Nature, 378,* 279–281.

Díaz-Campos, M. (2004). Context of learning in the acquisition of Spanish second language phonology. *Studies in Second Language Acquisition, 26*(2), 249–273.

Dörnyei, Z. (1998). Motivation in foreign and second language learning. *Language Teaching, 31,* 117–135.

Dörnyei, Z., & Schmidt, R. (Eds.). (2001). *Motivation and second language acquisition.* Honolulu, HI: University of Hawai'i at Manoa, Second Language Teaching and Curriculum Center.

Dörnyei, Z., & Skehan, P. (2003). Individual differences in second language learning. In C. J. Doughty & M. H. Long (Eds.), *The handbook of second language acquisition.* Oxford, UK: Blackwell.

Doughty, C. J., & Long, M. H. (Eds.). (2003). *The handbook of second language acquisition.* Oxford, UK: Blackwell.

Ehrman, M., & Oxford, R. (1989). Effects of sex differences, career choice, and psychological type on adult language learning strategies. *The Modern Language Journal, 73*(1), 1–13.

Ellis, N. C. (2001). Memory for language. In P. Robinson (Ed.), *Cognition and second language instruction* (pp. 33–68). Cambridge, UK: Cambridge University Press.

Ellis, N. C., & Schmidt, R. (1997). Morphology and longer distance dependencies: Laboratory research illuminating the A in SLA. *Studies in Second Language Acquisition, 19,* 145–171.

Ellis, N. C., & Sinclair, S. G. (1996). Working memory in the acquisition of vocabulary and syntax: Putting language in good order. *The Quarterly Journal of Experimental Psychology, 49A,* 234–250.

Ellis, R. (1994). *The study of second language acquisition.* Oxford, UK: Oxford University Press.

Elman, J. L., Bates, E. A., Johnson, M. H., Karmiloff-Smith, A., Parisi, D., & Plunkett, K. (1996). *Rethinking innateness: A connectionist perspective on development.* Cambridge, MA: MIT Press.

Estabrooke, I. V., Mordecai, K., Maki, P., & Ullman, M. T. (2002). The effect of sex hormones on language processing [Abstract]. *Brain and Language, 83,* 143–146.

Eubank, L., & Gregg, K. (1999). Critical periods and (second) language acquisition: Divide et impera. In D. Birdsong (Ed.), *Second language acquisition and the critical period hypothesis* (pp. 65–99). Mahwah, NJ: Lawrence Erlbaum.

Farhady, H. (1982). Measures of language proficiency from the learner's perspective. *TESOL Quarterly, 16,* 43–59.

Flege, J. E., Yeni-Komshian, G. H., & Liu, S. (1999). Age constraints on second-language acquisition. *Journal of Memory and Language, 41,* 78–104.

Galambos, S. J., & Goldin-Meadow, S. (1990). The effects of learning two languages on levels of metalinguistic awareness. *Cognition, 34*(1), 1–56.

Galambos, S. J., & Hakuta, K. (1988). Subject-specific and task-specific characteristics of metalinguistic awareness in bilingual children. *Applied Psycholinguistics, 9,* 141–162.

Gardner, R., & Lambert, W. (1972). Attitudes and motivation in second language learning: Course related changes. *The Canadian Modern Language Review, 32,* 243–266.

Gass, S., Svetics, I., & Lemelin, S. (2003). Differential effects of attention. *Language Learning, 53,* 497–545.

Gass, S., & Varonis, E. (1986). Sex differences in NNS/NNS interactions. In R. Day (Ed.), *Talking to learn: Conversation in second language acquisition.* Rowley, MA: Newbury House.

Gathercole, S. E., Service, E., Hitch, G. J., Adams, A. M., & Martin, A. J. (1999). Phonological short-term memory and vocabulary development: Further evidence and the nature of the relationship. *Applied Psycholinguistics, 12,* 349–367.

Gathercole, S. E., & Thorn, A. S. C. (1998). Phonological short-term memory and foreign language learning. In A. F. Healy & L. E. Bourne (Eds.), *Foreign language learning: Psycholinguistic studies on training and retention* (pp. 339–364). Mahwah, NJ: Lawrence Erlbaum.

Halpern, D. F. (2000). *Sex differences in cognitive abilities.* Mahwah, NJ: Lawrence Erlbaum.

Harrington, M., & Sawyer, M. (1992). Second language working memory capacity and second language reading skills. *Studies in Second Language Acquisition, 14,* 25–38.

Harris, J. (Ed.). (1992). *Cognitive processing in bilinguals.* Amsterdam: North-Holland.

Hebb, D. O. (1949). *The organization of behavior.* New York: Wiley.

Hyde, J. S., & Linn, M. C. (1988). Gender differences in verbal ability: A meta-analysis. *Psychological Bulletin 104,* 53–69.

Hyltenstam, K., & Abrahamsson, N. (2000). Who can become native-like in a second language? All, some, or none? On the maturational constraints controversy in second language acquisition. *Studia Linguistica, 54,* 150–166.

Hyltenstam, K., & Abrahamsson, N. (2003). Maturational constraints in SLA. In C. J. Doughty & M. H. Long, (Eds.), *The handbook of second language acquisition.* Oxford, UK: Blackwell.

James, W. (1890). *Principles of psychology.* New York: Holt.

Johnson, J. S., & Newport, E. L. (1989). Critical period effects in second language learning: The influence of maturational state on the acquisition of English as a second language. *Cognitive Psychology, 21,* 60–99.

Juffs, A. (2003, October). Working memory: Understanding issues in mainstream psychology. Paper presented at the meeting of the Second Language Research Forum, Tucson, AZ.

Kieras, D. E., Meyer, D. E., Mueller, S., & Seymour, T. (1999). Insights into working memory from the perspective of the EPIC architecture for modeling skilled perceptual-motor and cognitive human performance. In A. Miyake & P. Shah (Eds.), *Models of working memory: Mechanisms of active maintenance and executive control* (pp. 183–223). Cambridge,UK: Cambridge University Press.

Kimura, D. (1999). *Sex and cognition.* Cambridge, MA: MIT Press.

Kiss, C. & Nikolov, M. (2005). Developing, piloting, and validating an instrument to measure young learners' aptitude. *Language Learning, 55*(1), 99–150.

Klein, E. C. (1995). Second versus third language acquisition: Is there a difference? *Language Learning, 45*(3), 419–465.

Larsen-Freeman, D. (1983). Second language acquisition: Getting the whole picture. In K. M. Bailey, M. Long, & S. Peck (Eds.), *Second language acquisition studies* (pp. 3–22). Rowley, MA: Newbury House.

Larsen-Freeman, D., & Long, M. (1991). *An introduction to second language acquisition research.* London: Longman.

Lenneberg, E. (1967). *Biological foundations of language.* New York: Wiley.

Long, M. (1990). Maturational constraints on language development. *Studies in Second Language Acquisition, 12,* 251–285.

Lynn, R., & Wilson, G. R. (1992). Foreign language ability and its relation to general intelligence. *Research in Education, 47,* 40–53.

Lynn, R., & Wilson, G. R. (1993). Sex differences in second language ability: An Irish study. *School Psychology International, 14*(3), 275–279.

Macaulay, R. K. S. (1978). The myth of female superiority in language. *Journal of Child Language, 5*(2), 353–363.

Mackey, A., Philp, J., Egi, T., Fujii, A., & Tatsumi, T. (2002). Individual differences in working memory, noticing of interactional feedback and L2 development. In

P. Robinson (Ed.), *Individual differences and instructed language learning* (pp. 181–208). Amsterdam: John Benjamins.

Matsuda, S. & Gobel, P. (2004). Anxiety and predictors of performance in the foreign language classroom. *System 32*(1), 21–36.

McLaughlin, B., & Nayak, N. (1989). Processing a new language: Does knowing other languages make a difference? In H. W. Dechert & M. Raupach (Eds.), *Interlingual processes* (pp. 5–16). Tübingen, Germany: Gunter Narr.

Miller, G. (1956). The magical number seven, plus or minus two: Some limits on our capacity for processing information. *Psychological Review, 63,* 81–97.

Miyake, A., & Friedman, N. P. (1998). Individual differences in second language proficiency: Working memory as language aptitude. In A. F. Healy & L. E. Bourne (Eds.), *Foreign language learning: Psychometric studies on training and retention.* Mahwah, NJ: Lawrence Erlbaum.

Miyake, A., & Shah, P. (Eds.). (1999). *Models of working memory: Mechanisms of active maintenance and executive control.* Cambridge, UK: Cambridge University Press.

Nation, R., & McLaughlin, B. (1986). Novices and experts: An information processing approach to the good language learner problem. *Applied Psycholinguistics, 7,* 41–56.

Nayak, N., Hansen, N., Krueger, N., & McLaughlin, B. (1990). Language-learning strategies in monolingual and multilingual adults. *Language Learning, 40*(2), 221–244.

Norman, D. A. (1968). Toward a theory of memory and attention. *Psychological Review, 75,* 522–536.

Nyikos, M. (1990). Sex related differences in adult language learning: Socialization and memory factors. *The Modern Language Journal, 3,* 273–287.

Owen, A. M. (1997). The functional organization of working memory processes within human lateral frontal cortex: The contribution of functional neuroimaging. *European Journal of Neuroscience, 9,* 1329–1339.

Oxford, R. L., & Ehrman, M. (1993). Second language research on individual differences. *Annual Review of Applied Linguistics, 13,* 188–205.

Oxford, R. L., Nyikos, M., & Ehrman, M. (1988). Vive la Difference? Reflections on Sex Differences in Use of Language Learning Strategies. *Foreign Language Annals, 21*(4), 321–329.

Papagno, C., & Vallar, G. (1992). Phonological short-term memory and the learning of novel words: The effect of phonological similarity and item length. *Quarterly Journal of Experimental Psychology, 44A,* 47–67.

Patkowski, M. (1994). The critical age hypothesis and interlanguage phonology. In M. Yavas (Ed.), *First and secondary phonology* (pp. 205–221). San Diego, CA: Singular.

Peal, E., & Lambert, W. E. (1962). The relation of bilingualism to intelligence. *Psychological Monographs: General and Applied, 76*(27), 1–23.

Penfield, W., & Roberts, L. (1959). *Speech and brain mechanisms.* Princeton, NJ: Princeton University Press.

Pfluger, T., Weil, S., Weis, S., Vollmar, C., Heiss, D., Egger, J. et al. (1999). Normative volumetric data of the developing hippocampus in children based on magnetic resonance imaging. *Epilepsia, 40*(4), 414–423.

Phillips, S. M., & Sherwin, B. B. (1992). Effects of estrogen on memory function in surgically menopausal women. *Psychoneuroendocrinology, 17*(5), 485–495.

Politzer, R. (1983). An exploratory study of self-reported language learning behaviors and their relation to achievement. *Studies in Second Language Acquisition, 6,* 54–67.

Powell, R. C. (1979). Sex differences and language learning: A review of the evidence. *Audio Visual Language Journal, 17*(1), 19–24.

Pulvermüller, F., & Schumann, J. H. (1994). Neurobiological mechanisms of language acquisition. *Language Learning, 44,* 681–734.

Ramsey, R. M. G. (1980). Language-learning approach styles of adult multilinguals and successful language learners. *Annals of the New York Academy of Sciences, 345,* 73–96.

Ricciardelli, L. A. (1992a). Bilingualism and cognitive development in relation to threshold theory. *Journal of Psycholinguistic Research, 21*(4), 301–316.

Ricciardelli, L. A. (1992b). Creativity and bilingualism. *Journal of Creative Behavior, 26*(4), 242–254.

Robinson, P. (Ed.). (2001). *Cognition and second language instruction.* Cambridge, UK: Cambridge University Press.

Sagarra, N. (2000). *The longitudinal role of working memory on adult acquisition of L2 grammar.* Unpublished doctoral dissertation, University of Illinois at Urbana-Champaign.

Sanz, C. (2000). Bilingual education enhances third language acquisition: Evidence from Catalonia. (2000). *Applied Psycholinguistics, 21,* 23–44.

Sawyer, M., & Ranta, L. (2001). Aptitude, individual differences, and instructional design. In P. Robinson (Ed.), *Cognition and second language instruction* (pp. 319–353). Cambridge, UK: Cambridge University Press.

Schneider, W. (1999). Working memory in a multilevel hybrid connectionist control architecture (CAP2). In A. Miyake & P. Shah (Eds.), *Models of working memory: Mechanisms of active maintenance and executive control* (pp. 340–374). Cambridge, UK: Cambridge University Press.

Service, E., & Kohonen, V. (1995). Is the relation between phonological memory and foreign language learning accounted for by vocabulary acquisition? *Applied Psycholinguistics, 16,* 155–172.

Sherwin, B. B. (1988). Estrogen and/or androgen replacement therapy and cognitive functioning in surgically menopausal women. *Psychoneuroendocrinology, 13*(4), 345–357.

Singleton, D. (2001). Age and second language acquisition. *Annual Review of Applied Linguistics, 21,* 77–89.

Skehan, P. (1989). *Individual differences in second language learning.* London: Arnold.

Skehan, P. (1998). *A cognitive approach to language learning.* Oxford, UK: Oxford University Press.

Spolsky, B. (1989). *Conditions for second language learning.* Oxford, UK: Oxford University Press.

Sternberg, S. (1966). High speed scanning in human memory. *Science, 153,* 652–654.

Swain, M., Lapkin, S., Rowen, N., & Hart, D. (1990). The role of mother tongue literacy in third language learning. *Language, Culture, and Curriculum, 3*(1), 65–81.

Turner, M. L., & Engle, R. W. (1989). Is working memory task dependent? *Journal of Memory and Language, 28,* 127–154.

Ullman, M. T. (2001a). The neural basis of lexicon and grammar in first and second language: The declarative/procedural model. *Bilingualism: Language and Cognition, 4*(1), 105–122.

Ullman, M. T. (2001b). A neurocognitive perspective on language: The declarative/procedural model. *Nature Reviews Neuroscience, 2,* 717–726.

Ullman, M. T. (2004). Contributions of memory circuits to language: The declarative/procedural model. *Cognition 92,* 231–270.

Ullman, M. T., Estabrooke, I. V., Steinhauer, K., Brovetto, C., Pancheva, R., Ozawa, K., et al. (2002). Sex differences in the neurocognition of language [Abstract]. *Brain and Language, 83,* 141–143.

Ullman, M. T., Maloof, C. J., Hartshorne, J. K., Estabrooke, I. V., Brovetto, C., & Walenski, M. (2005). Sex, regularity, frequency and consistency: A study of factors predicting the storage of inflected forms. Manuscript submitted for publication.

Ullman, M. T., & Pierpont, E. R. (2005). Specific Language Impairment is not specific to language: The procedural deficit hypothesis. *Cortex, 41,* 399–433.

Wagner, D. A., Spratt, J. E., & Ezzaki, A. (1989). Does learning to read in a second language always put the child at a disadvantage? Some counter evidence from Morocco. *Applied Psycholinguistics, 10,* 31–48.

Waters, G. S., & Caplan, D. (1996). The measurement of verbal working memory capacity and its relation to reading comprehension. *The Quarterly Journal of Experimental Psychology, 49A*(1), 51–79.

Waugh, N. C., & Norman, D. A. (1965). Primary memory. *Psychological Review, 72,* 89–104.

Werker, J. 1986. The effect of multilingualism on phonetic perceptual flexibility. *Applied Psycholinguistics, 7,* 141–156.

Williams, J. N. (1999). Memory, attention, and inductive learning. *Studies in Second Language Acquisition, 21,* 1–48.

Williams, J. N., & Lovatt, P. (2003). Phonological memory and rule learning. *Language Learning, 53,* 67–121.

Yelland, G., Pollard, J., & Mercury, A. (1993). The metalinguistic benefits of limited contact with a second language. *Applied Psycholinguistics, 14*(4), 423–444.

Zobl, H. (1992). Prior linguistic knowledge and the conservation of the learning procedure: Grammaticality judgments of unilingual and multilingual learners. In S. M. Gass & L. Selinker (Eds.), *Language transfer in language learning* (pp. 176–196). Amsterdam: John Benjamins.

FIVE

A Cognitive Neuroscience Perspective on Second Language Acquisition: The Declarative/Procedural Model

MICHAEL T. ULLMAN

KEY WORDS

Aphasia ▪ basal ganglia ▪ Broca's area ▪ critical period ▪ declarative memory ▪ ERP ▪ estrogen ▪ explicit ▪ fMRI ▪ frontal lobe ▪ grammar ▪ implicit ▪ language ▪ language processing ▪ lexicon ▪ morphology ▪ neuroimaging ▪ PET ▪ procedural memory ▪ puberty ▪ second language ▪ second language acquisition (SLA) ▪ syntax ▪ temporal lobe.

1. Introduction

The neural, cognitive, and computational (i.e., neurocognitive) bases of second language acquisition and processing are still not well understood. There has been surprisingly little empirical work in this area. Data informing the specific neural substrates of second language and the relations between its neural, cognitive, and computational underpinnings have been especially sparse (e.g., what brain structures play which computational roles and how do they interact?). Given this lack of data, it is not surprising that there have been few attempts to offer integrative neurocognitive theories of second language, particularly in the context of first language and of our broader understanding of the mind and brain.

In this chapter, I discuss a neurocognitive model that begins to address these theoretical gaps. According to this perspective, both first and second languages are acquired and processed by well-studied brain systems that are known to subserve particular nonlanguage functions. These brain systems are posited to play analogous roles in their nonlanguage and language functions. So our independent knowledge of the cognitive, computational, neuroanatomical, physiological, cellular, endocrine, and pharmacological bases of these systems leads to specific testable predictions about both first and second language. The model thus brings the knowledge base and empirical approaches of cognitive neuroscience to bear on the study of second language acquisition (SLA).

This chapter begins by discussing the broader linguistic and neurocognitive issues, along with the neurocognitive model as it pertains to normal early-learned first language (L1). Next, the background, theory, and extant empirical evidence regarding the acquisition and processing of second and subsequent languages are presented, with a focus on later-learned languages, particularly those learned after puberty. (Note that the term *L2* is used in this chapter to refer only to such later-learned languages.) Finally, the chapter concludes with comparisons between the model and other perspectives and with a discussion of implications and issues for further study.

2. The Neurocognition of Lexicon and Grammar

Language depends upon two mental abilities (Chomsky, 1965; Pinker, 1994). First, all idiosyncratic information must be memorized in some sort of mental dictionary, which is often referred to as the mental lexicon. The lexicon necessarily includes all words with arbitrary sound-meaning pairings, such as the noncompositional ("simple") word *cat.* It must also contain other irregular—that is, not entirely derivable—word-specific information, such as whether any arguments must accompany a verb (e.g., *hit* requires a direct object) and whether a word takes any unpredictable related forms (e.g., *teach* takes the irregular past tense *taught*). The mental lexicon may comprise other distinctive information as well, smaller or larger than words: bound morphemes (e.g., the *-ed* or *-ness* suffixes, as in *walked* or *happiness*) and complex linguistic structures whose meanings cannot be transparently derived from their parts (e.g., idiomatic phrases, such as *kick the bucket*) (Di Sciullo and Williams, 1987; Halle and Marantz, 1993).

But language also consists of regularities, which can be captured by rules of grammar. The rules constrain how lexical forms combine to make complex representations and allow us to interpret the meanings of complex forms even if we have not heard or seen them before. Meanings can be derived by rules that underlie the sequential orders and hierarchical relations of lexical items and of abstract categories such as *verb phrase.* Such rule-governed behavior is found in various aspects of language, including phrases and sentences (syntax) and complex words such as *walked* or *happiness* (morphology). The rules are a form of mental knowledge in that they underlie our individual capacity to produce and comprehend complex forms. The learning and use of this knowledge are generally implicit—that is, not available to conscious awareness. Last, although complex representations (e.g., the regular past tense form *walked*) could be computed anew each time (e.g., *walk* + *-ed*), they could in principle also be stored in the mental lexicon.

Numerous theories and empirical studies have probed the neurocognitive bases of lexical and grammatical abilities in L1 (e.g., Damasio and Damasio, 1992; Elman et al., 1996; Friederici, 2002; Gleason and Ratner, 1998; Goodglass, 1993; Pinker, 1994). This research has addressed several interrelated issues, including the following: (a) separability: Do lexicon and grammar depend on distinct components that rely on separable neurocognitive correlates? (b) mechanisms: What mechanisms underlie the learning, representation, computation, and processing of the two linguistic capacities? (c) domain specificity: Are the underlying neurocognitive substrates dedicated to language (domain specific) or do they also subserve nonlanguage functions (that is, are they domain independent)? (d) biological correlates: What are the biological correlates of lexicon and grammar, be they brain structures, neural circuits, or molecular systems? What is the temporal order of their involvement during processing and how do they interact?

Here I focus on one theoretical perspective—the declarative/procedural (DP) model (Ullman, 2001a, 2001c; Ullman, 2004; Ullman et al., 1997)—which addresses these and related issues. The basic premise of the DP model is that aspects of the lexicon-grammar distinction are tied to the distinction between two well-studied brain memory systems (Ullman, 2001c; Ullman, 2004), declarative and procedural memory, that have been implicated in nonlanguage functions in humans and other animals (Mishkin, Malamut, and Bachevalier, 1984; Schacter and Tulving, 1994; Squire and Knowlton, 2000; Squire and Zola, 1996). In the following two sections, I first discuss the nature of the two memory systems and then present the claims and predictions of the DP model as they pertain to L1.

3. Declarative and Procedural Memory

The *declarative memory system* underlies the learning, representation, and use of knowledge about facts (semantic knowledge) and events (episodic knowledge) (Eichenbaum and Cohen, 2001; Mishkin et al., 1984; Schacter and Tulving, 1994; Squire and Knowlton, 2000). This system may be particularly important for learning arbitrary relations (e.g., that fact that Ouagadougou is the capital of Burkina Faso) (Eichenbaum and Cohen, 2001). The knowledge learned in declarative memory is at least partly (but not completely; Chun, 2000) explicit, that is, available to conscious awareness. The memory system is subserved by medial temporal lobe regions (e.g., the hippocampus), which are connected extensively with temporal and parietal neocortical regions (Suzuki and Amaral, 1994). The medial temporal structures consolidate, and possibly retrieve, new memories (Eichenbaum and Cohen, 2001; Mishkin et al., 1984; Schacter and Tulving, 1994; Squire and Knowlton, 2000). Memories seem to eventually become independent of these

(A)

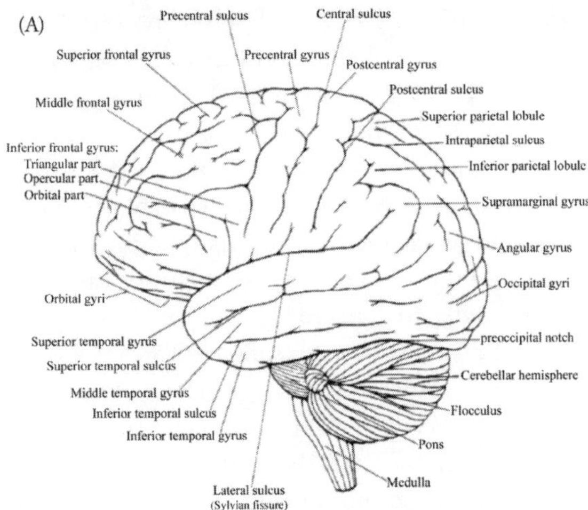

(B)

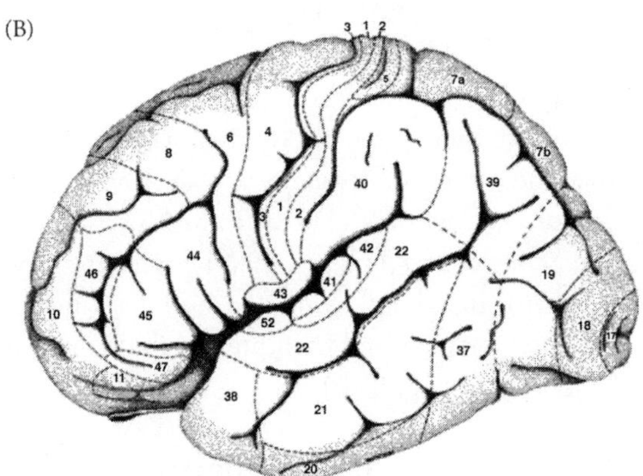

FIGURE 5.1. *Structures and regions of the brain: (A) A lateral view of anatomical structures in the left hemispheres of the cerebrum and the cerebellum. The same structures are found on the right side. There are four lobes in each hemisphere of the cerebrum. The frontal lobe lies anterior to (in front of) the central sulcus, above the lateral sulcus. The temporal lobe lies inferior to (below) the lateral sulcus, going back to the occipital lobe at the back of the brain. The parietal lobe lies posterior to (behind) the central sulcus and superior to (above) the temporal lobe. (B) Brodmann's areas of the lateral aspect of the left hemisphere. The same areas are found in the right hemisphere. Not shown are the Brodmann's areas of the medial aspect of the cerebrum. (C) A whole-head view of certain subcortical structures, including the basal ganglia. In each hemisphere, the basal ganglia consist of several substructures, of which the caudate, putamen, and*

(C)

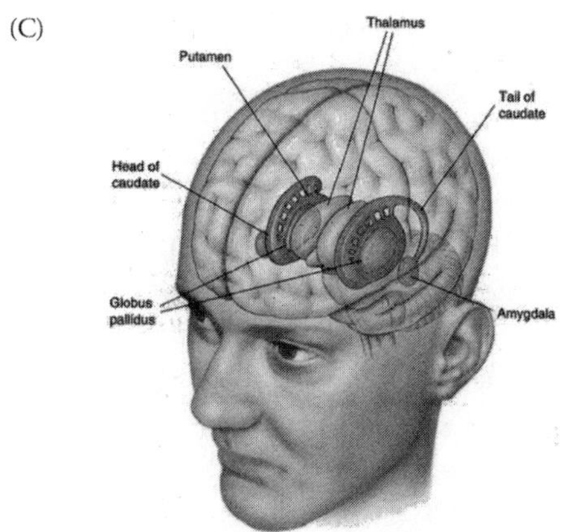

(D)

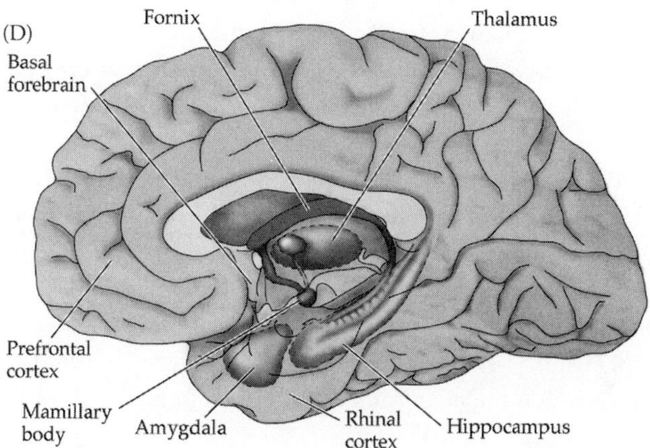

globus pallidus are indicated here. (D) A medial view of the cerebrum, including the hippocampus and various structures to which it is closely connected. Figure 5.1A from the public domain. Figure 5.1B from The human brain: Surface, three-dimensional sectional anatomy, and MRI *(p. 44), by Henri M. Duvernoy, New York: Springer. Copyright 1991. Reprinted with permission. Figure 5.1C from "Human diencephalon," by Jacob L. Drisen, http:// www.driesen.com/ basalganglia-2.jpg. Copyright 2005 by Jacob L. Driesen, PhD. Reprinted with permission. Figure 5.1D from* Neuroscience *(2nd ed.), "Brain areas associated with declarative memory disorders," by Dale Purves, George J. Augustine, David Fitzpatrick, Lawrence C. Katz, Anthony-Samuel LaMantia, James O. McNamara, and S. Mark Williams (Eds.). Sunderland, MA.: Sinauer Associates. Copyright 2001. Reprinted with permission.*

structures and dependent on neocortical regions, particularly in the temporal lobes (Hodges and Patterson, 1997; Martin, Ungerleider, and Haxby, 2000). Other brain structures also play a role in declarative memory. Portions of ventro-lateral prefrontal cortex (corresponding largely to Brodmann's area [BA] 45 and BA 47) seem to play a role in the selection or retrieval of declarative memories, while parts of the right cerebellum may underlie searching for this knowledge (Buckner and Wheeler, 2001; Desmond and Fiez, 1998; Ivry and Fiez, 2000; Wagner et al., 1998). Note that I use the term *declarative memory system* to refer to the entire system involved in the learning and use of the relevant knowledge (Eichenbaum, 2000), not just to those structures underlying memory consolidation.

The declarative memory system has been intensively studied not only from functional and neuroanatomical perspectives but also at cellular and molecular levels (H. V. Curran, 2000; Lynch, 2002). The neurotransmitter acetylcholine plays a particularly important role in declarative memory and hippocampal function (Freo, Pizzolato, Dam, Ori, and Battistin, 2002; Packard, 1998). (Neurotransmitters are molecules that allow communication between neurons.) Evidence also suggests that the declarative memory system is affected by estrogen (Phillips and Sherwin, 1992; Sherwin, 1988), perhaps via the modulation of acetylcholine (Packard, 1998; Shughrue, Scrimo, and Merchenthaler, 2000). For example, estrogen improves declarative memory in women (Maki and Resnick, 2000; Sherwin, 1998) and men (Kampen and Sherwin, 1996; Miles, Green, Sanders, and Hines, 1998), and strengthens the cellular and molecular correlates of long-term hippocampal learning (McEwen, Alves, Bulloch, and Weiland, 1998; Woolley and Schwartzkroin, 1998). Moreover, testosterone, which is the main source of estrogen in men, also improves their memory (Cherrier et al., 2001).

The *procedural memory system* is implicated in the learning of new, and in the control of long-established, motor and cognitive skills and habits, especially those involving sequences (Aldridge and Berridge, 1998; Boecker et al., 2002; Mishkin et al., 1984; Schacter and Tulving, 1994; Squire and Knowlton, 2000; Willingham, 1998). Neither the learning nor the remembering of these procedures appears to be accessible to conscious memory. Thus the system is often referred to as an *implicit memory* system. (I use the term *procedural memory* to refer only to one type of implicit, nondeclarative memory system, Squire and Zola, 1996, not to all such systems; see also section 8 below.) The system is composed of a network of several interconnected brain structures (De Renzi, 1989; Heilman, Watson, and Rothi, 1997; Hikosaka et al., 2000; Jenkins, Brooks, Nixon, Frackowiak, and Passingham, 1994; Mishkin et al., 1984; Rizzolatti, Fogassi, and Gallese, 2000; Schacter and Tulving, 1994; Squire and Zola, 1996). It depends especially on structures in the left hemisphere of the cerebrum (De Renzi, 1989; Heilman et al., 1997; Schluter, Krams, Rushworth, and Passingham, 2001) and is rooted in neural circuits that encompass the frontal lobes and the basal ganglia, which are subcortical structures that are strongly connected to frontal cortex. Evidence suggests that particular neurotransmitters of these circuits, especially dopamine, underlie aspects of procedural learning (Harrington, Haaland, Yeo, and Marder, 1990; Nakahara, Doya, and Hikosaka, 2001; Saint-Cyr, Taylor, and Lang, 1988). Within frontal cortex, two areas play particularly important roles: premotor areas, especially the region of the supplementary motor area (SMA and pre-SMA); and Broca's area, especially posterior portions of this region, corresponding largely to BA 44 (Broca's area is defined here as a part of inferior frontal cortex, including and perhaps limited to cortex corresponding to BA 44 and 45; Amunts et al., 1999). Other brain structures also form part of the procedural system network, including portions of inferior parietal cortex and the cerebellum (Hikosaka et al., 2000; Rizzolatti, Fogassi, and Gallese, 2001; Schacter and Tulving, 1994; Squire and Zola, 1996; Ullman, 2004; Willingham, 1998). Note that I use the term *procedural memory system* to refer to the entire system involved in the learning and use of motor and cognitive skills, not just to those brain structures underlying their acquisition.

The declarative and procedural memory systems interact in a number of ways. Essentially, the systems together form a dynamically interacting network that yields both cooperative and competitive learning and processing, such that memory functions may be optimized (Poldrack and Packard, 2003). First of all, the two systems can complement each other in acquiring the same or analogous knowledge, including knowledge of sequences. As was initially shown in the amnesic patient H.M., the declarative memory system need not be intact for the procedural memory system to learn (Corkin, 1984; Eichenbaum and Cohen, 2001; Squire and Knowlton, 2000). However, when both systems are functioning, they can be used cooperatively to learn a given task (Willingham, 1998). The declarative memory system may be expected to acquire knowledge initially, thanks to its rapid learning abilities, while the procedural system may gradually learn the same or analogous knowledge (Packard and McGaugh, 1996; Poldrack and Packard, 2003). Interestingly, the time course of this shift from declarative to procedural memory can be modulated pharmacologically (Packard, 1999).

Second, animal and human studies suggest that the two systems also interact competitively (for reviews, see Packard and Knowlton, 2002; Poldrack and Packard, 2003; Ullman, 2004). This leads to a "see-saw effect" (Ullman, 2004), such that a dysfunction of one system results in enhanced learning in the other or that learning in one system depresses the functionality of the other (Halbig et al., 2002; McDonald and White, 1993; Mitchell and Hall, 1988; Packard,

Hirsh, and White, 1989; Poldrack and Packard, 2003; Poldrack et al., 2001; Poldrack, Prabhakaran, Seger, and Gabrieli, 1999; Schroeder, Wingard, and Packard, 2002; Ullman, 2004). The see-saw effect may be explained by a number of factors (Ullman, 2004), including direct anatomical projections between the two systems (Sorensen and Witter, 1983) and a role for acetylcholine, which may not only enhance declarative memory but might also play an inhibitory role in brain structures underlying procedural memory (Calabresi, Centonze, Gubellini, Marfia et al., 2000). Estrogen may also contribute to the see-saw effect, perhaps via the modulation of acetylcholine (Ullman, 2004).

The two memory systems display variability in their functioning across individuals. That is, individuals differ in their ability to learn or use knowledge in one or the other system. Of particular interest here is that evidence suggests sex differences in the functionality of the two systems. Women show an advantage over men at verbal memory tasks (Halpern, 2000; Kimura, 1999; Kramer, Delis, Kaplan, O'Donnell, and Prifitera, 1997), which depend on declarative memory (Squire and Knowlton, 2000; Wagner et al., 1998). This sex difference does not seem surprising in light of the higher levels of estrogen in girls and (premenopausal) women than in boys and men (Cutler Jr., 1997; K. Klein, Baron, Colli, McDonnell, and Cutler, 1994; Wilson, Foster, Kronenberg, and Larsen, 1998). Conversely, evidence suggests that men show superior performance at a variety of tasks, such as aimed throwing and mental rotation (Kimura, 1999), which are expected to depend on the procedural system network (Ullman and Pierpont, 2005). Intriguingly, across the menstrual cycle in females, performance on some of these "male" tasks decreases with increasing estrogen and increases with decreasing estrogen (Hampson, 1990; Kimura, 1999), strengthening the view that estrogen may play a role in the see-saw effect.

4. The DP Model and L1

According to the DP model, in L1 the declarative memory system underlies the mental lexicon, whereas the procedural memory system subserves aspects of the mental grammar. (For additional discussion, see Ullman, 2001a, 2001c; Ullman, 2004; Ullman et al., 1997). Each of the two memory systems is posited to play analogous roles in its nonlinguistic and linguistic functions. Declarative memory is an associative memory that stores not only information about facts and events but also lexical knowledge, including the sounds and meanings of words. Learning new words relies largely on medial temporal lobe structures. Eventually the knowledge of words becomes largely independent of the medial temporal lobe and depends upon neocortical areas, particularly in temporal and temporo-parietal regions. Middle and inferior aspects of the temporal lobe may be particularly important for storing word meanings, whereas superior temporal and temporo-parietal regions may be more important in storing phonological word forms and possibly also for stored complex morphological and syntactic structures. These latter regions could thus serve as one type of interface between the declarative and procedural systems. Ventrolateral prefrontal cortex underlies the retrieval or selection of lexical representations stored in the temporal brain regions, while portions of the right cerebellum may underlie searching for that knowledge. Thus these frontal and cerebellar structures may be less important in receptive than in expressive language. Finally, pharmacological manipulations of acetylcholine, and endocrine manipulations of estrogen, should modulate aspects of lexical memory.

The procedural system network of brain structures subserves the implicit learning and use not only of motor and cognitive skills but also aspects of a rule-governed combinatorial grammar. The system is expected to play computationally analogous roles across grammatical subdomains, including morphology, syntax, and possibly phonology. It may be especially important in grammatical structure building—that is, the sequential and hierarchical combination of stored lexical forms (e.g., *walk* + *-ed*) and abstract representations (e.g., verb phrase) into complex structures. Pharmacological manipulations of dopamine, and possibly the modulation of estrogen and acetylcholine, may be expected to affect the acquisition of grammatical knowledge.

The two systems should interact both cooperatively and competitively in the acquisition and use of language. For example, young children should initially learn both idiosyncratic and complex forms in declarative memory, while the procedural system gradually acquires the grammatical knowledge underlying rule-governed combinations. Increased functionality in one system may depress the other and vice versa. Thus the improvements found in declarative memory during childhood (Di Giulio, Seidenberg, O'Leary, and Raz, 1994; Kail and Hagen, 1977; Ornstein, 1978) should not only facilitate lexical acquisition but may also eventually depress the procedural learning of grammatical knowledge.

Individual differences in the acquisition and use of lexical and grammatical knowledge, including sex differences, are expected. Thanks to their advantage at declarative memory, females should show superior lexical abilities as compared to males. In contrast, males may demonstrate better performance at aspects of grammar that depend on the procedural system. This difference in the functionality of the two systems also leads to the prediction that females will tend to memorize complex forms (e.g., *walked*) that men generally compute compositionally in the grammatical-procedural system (e.g., *walk* + *-ed*) (Ullman, 2004; Ullman et al., 2002).

Thus the DP model posits that lexical and grammatical functions are largely separable and are associated with distinct computational and neural substrates that are not dedicated to language but are rather domain independent. These substrates are well-studied brain memory systems, whose functionality may be modulated by particular pharmacological and endocrine substances and which vary with some degree of predictability across the lifespan of and between individuals.

This view contrasts with two competing theoretical frameworks. Although it shares the view of traditional "dual system" or "modular" theories that lexicon and grammar are subserved by two or more distinct systems (Chomsky, 1995; Fodor, 1983; Grodzinsky, 2000; Levelt, 1989; Pinker, 1994), it diverges from their claims that domain-specific components underlie each of the capacities. (For further discussion of the issue of domain specificity, see Ullman, 2004). Conversely, while the DP model agrees with "single mechanism" (e.g., connectionist) theories that the two capacities are subserved by domain-independent mechanisms, it diverges from their claim that both capacities are linked to a single computational mechanism with broad anatomic distribution (Bates and MacWhinney, 1989; Elman et al., 1996; MacDonald, Pearlmutter, and Seidenberg, 1994; Rumelhart and McClelland, 1986; Seidenberg, 1997).

The DP model alone predicts the following double dissociations: One set of links is expected among neurocognitive markers (e.g., neuroimaging activation patterns) of stored linguistic representations, conceptual-semantic knowledge, and declarative memory brain structures. A distinct set of links is expected among neurocognitive markers of grammar (across subdomains, including morphology and syntax), motor and cognitive skills, and procedural memory brain structures. My colleagues and I have previously argued in some depth that converging evidence from a wide range of psycholinguistic, developmental, neurological, electrophysiological, and neuroimaging studies largely supports this view (Ullman, 2001a, 2001c; Ullman, 2004; Ullman et al., 1997).

5. Late-Learned L2

People who learn a language at later ages, particularly after puberty, do not generally acquire the language to the level of proficiency attained by younger learners (Birdsong, 1999; Hyltenstam and Abrahamsson, 2003; Johnson and Newport, 1989; Newport, 1990; Oyama, 1982). However, late language learning does not seem to cause equal difficulties for lexical and grammatical functions. In L1, studies of language-deprived children have shown that late exposure to language results in an apparently irreversible inability to acquire aspects of grammar (particularly in morphology and syntax), whereas lexical acquisition remains relatively spared (S. Curtiss, 1989; S. R. Curtiss, 1977). In L2 the picture appears to be similar. A number of studies have shown that late L2 learning negatively affects the acquisition and/or processing of grammar

(Coppieters, 1987; DeKeyser, 2000; Hahne and Friederici, 2001; Johnson and Newport, 1989; Newport, 1993; Oyama, 1982; Patkowski, 1980; Wartenburger et al., 2003; Weber-Fox and Neville, 1996), while leaving lexical accretion (Eubank and Gregg, 1999) and lexical-conceptual processing (Hahne and Friederici, 2001; Wartenburger et al., 2003; Weber-Fox and Neville, 1996) relatively intact. However, it does not appear to be the case that late learning necessarily precludes nativelike attainment, even of grammatical abilities. Rather, a number of studies have suggested that such attainment is not in fact all that rare, given sufficient exposure to the L2 (Birdsong, 1992; Birdsong and Molis, 2001; Cranshaw, 1997; Van Wuijtswinkel, 1994; White and Genesee, 1996).

6. The DP Model and L2

The DP model makes a somewhat different set of claims and predictions for late-learned L2 than for L1 (see also Ullman, 2001b; Ullman, 2004). At least during early adulthood (see below for a discussion of L2 learning later in the lifespan), the acquisition of grammatical-procedural knowledge is expected to be more problematic than the acquisition of lexical-declarative knowledge, as compared to language learning in young children. This may be due to one or more factors that directly or indirectly affect one or both brain systems, including decreased rule-abstraction abilities due to augmented working memory capacity (see Newport, 1993), the attenuation of procedural memory, and the enhancement of declarative memory. Evidence from humans and animals suggests that motor skill learning associated with the procedural system is subject to early critical period effects (Fredriksson, 2000; Schlaug, 2001; Walton, Lieberman, Llinas, Begin, and Llinas, 1992; Wolansky, Cabrera, Ibarra, Mongiat, and Azcurra, 1999). In contrast, there are clear improvements in declarative memory during childhood, with a possible plateau in adolescence (Campbell and Spear, 1972; Di Giulio et al., 1994; Kail and Hagen, 1977; Meudell, 1983; Ornstein, 1978; Siegler, 1978). The changes in both procedural and declarative memory may be at least partly explained by the increasing levels of estrogen that occur during childhood/adolescence (in boys as well as girls, though estrogen levels are higher in girls) (Ankarberg and Norjavaara, 1999; Cherrier et al., 2001; Cutler Jr., 1997; K. Klein et al., 1994; Klein, Martha, Blizzard, Herbst, and Rogol, 1996), since estrogen may somehow inhibit the procedural memory system as well as enhance declarative memory (Calabresi, Centonze, Gubellini, Pisani, and Bernardi, 2000; Packard, 1998; Phillips and Sherwin, 1992; Sherwin, 1988; Shughrue et al., 2000; Ullman, 2004) (also see discussion above). Additionally, the competitive interaction between the two memory systems, such that learning in one system depresses functionality of the other, leads to the possibility that the improvements in declarative memory during childhood may be accompanied by an attenuation of procedural learning abilities.

Thanks to their relative facility at declarative as compared to procedural learning, young adult L2 learners should tend to rely heavily on declarative memory, even for functions that depend upon the procedural system in L1. In particular, L2 learners should tend to memorize complex linguistic forms (e.g., *walked*) that can be computed compositionally by L1 speakers (e.g., *walk* + *-ed*). Associative properties of lexical memory (Hartshorne and Ullman, in press; Pinker, 1999; Prasada and Pinker, 1993) may lead to productivity in L2. L2 learners can also learn rules in declarative memory (e.g., in a pedagogical context), providing an additional source of productivity. Note that such rules do not depend at all upon grammatical-procedural computations; indeed, what they specify could in principle differ radically from the grammatical-procedural rules of native speakers of the target language.

Memorizing complex forms and rules in declarative memory may be expected to lead to a fairly high degree of proficiency, the level of which should vary according to a number of factors. These include the amount and type of L2 exposure and individual subject differences regarding declarative memory abilities. Thus women's advantage at declarative memory should provide them with advantages at L2 learning. However, not all types of "grammatical" knowledge should be equally learnable in declarative memory. Certain complex forms will be easier to memorize than others, such as those that are shorter or more frequent. Constructions that cannot be easily memorized, such as those that involve long-distance dependencies, should cause particular difficulties. Similarly, not all declarative-memory based rules should be equally easy to learn or apply. The limitations of lexical-declarative memory lead to the expectation that this system alone is unlikely to provide full grammatical proficiency. That is, by itself this system is not predicted to supply all functions subserved by the grammatical-procedural system in L1, and so reliance on this system alone should not lead to nativelike proficiency in all aspects of grammar.

Crucially, however, the complete dysfunction of the grammatical system in L2 is *not* expected. Rather, in accordance with multiple studies of the adult acquisition of nonlinguistic skills by procedural memory (Mishkin et al., 1984; Schacter and Tulving, 1994; Squire and Knowlton, 2000; Squire and Zola, 1996), practice should lead to procedural learning and improved performance. Thus with sufficient experience with L2, the language is expected to become L1-like in its grammatical dependence on the procedural system, with the potential for a high degree of proficiency. Whether or not a given individual acquires a given set of grammatical knowledge in the procedural system will depend on factors such as the type of grammatical knowledge being learned, the nature of the L2 exposure, and characteristics of the learner, such as intrinsic procedural learning abilities. Thus, whereas women should tend to show a faster learning rate than men during early stages of L2 learning (due to females' superior declarative memory abilities), men may show an advantage in later stages (due to a possible male advantage at procedural memory).

The claims and predictions laid out above for young adults differ somewhat for older adults. The ability to learn new information in declarative memory begins to decline in early adulthood, with more notable losses in old age (Park et al., 2002; Prull, Gabrieli, and Bunge, 2000). This pattern may be at least partly explained by the fact that estrogen levels decline with age in both sexes, especially during later years and especially in women (i.e., postmenopausal declines) (Carlson and Sherwin, 2000; Carr, 1998; Ferrini and Barrett-Connor, 1998; Sherman, West, and Korenman, 1976). To complicate matters further, while some forms of procedural learning are spared with aging, others, such as the learning of sequences containing higher level structure, appear to decline gradually across the adult years (Churchill, Stanis, Press, Kushelev, and Greenough, 2003; T. Curran, 1997; Feeney, Howard, and Howard, 2002; Howard, Howard, Dennis, Yankovich, and Vaidya, 2004; Prull et al., 2000). Therefore older adults may have more difficulty than young adults with procedural as well as declarative aspects of L2 acquisition.

Thus the age-of-exposure effects in L2 acquisition that are predicted to occur across childhood and adolescence differ qualitatively from those expected to take place during adulthood. Whereas in the former case the decline in language-learning ability is predicted from a decreasing reliance on procedural memory relative to declarative memory, in the latter case the decline follows primarily from problems with declarative memory, which may be further aggravated by difficulties with procedural memory. Thus age-of-exposure effects in language learning may be explained by more than one mechanism, with different mechanisms at play during different periods of the lifespan.

In sum, at lower levels of L2 experience, declarative memory is posited to subserve the learning and use not only of idiosyncratic lexical knowledge but also of complex linguistic representations. During early adulthood, women should show an advantage at L2 acquisition as compared to men. Due to the attenuation of declarative memory, older learners (especially postmenopausal women) should have particular difficulty acquiring an L2 even to low proficiency. At higher levels of L2 experience, the procedural system should be able to acquire grammatical knowledge (although again, this may be more difficult for older L2 learners), resulting in a neurocognitive pattern similar to that of L1—that is, with idiosyncratic lexical knowledge stored in declarative memory, while rule-governed complex forms are composed by the procedural system.

So dissociations between simple and complex forms are expected in high-experience L2 and in L1 but less so or not at all in low-experience L2. In direct comparisons between L1 and L2 *within* subjects, the use of complex forms should depend more on declarative memory brain structures in low-experience L2 than in L1 or high-experience L2, in which complex forms should show a greater dependence on procedural memory brain structures. In contrast, idiosyncratic lexical knowledge should be stored in declarative memory in all individuals, and therefore no lexical dissociations between L1 and either low- or high-experience L2 are expected.

7. Empirical Evidence on the Neurocognition of L2

Here I present several lines of neurocognitive evidence which speak to a number of the L2-related claims and predictions of the DP model. For further discussion on some of these data, see Ullman (2001b).

Aphasia generally refers to language impairments that result from relatively circumscribed lesions to the brain. In L1, adult-onset damage to neocortical temporal regions often leads to impaired lexical abilities, while the use of grammatically appropriate complex structures remains relatively spared. In contrast, frontal and basal ganglia lesions often produce impaired performance at grammar (across linguistic domains, including syntax and morphology), leaving lexical knowledge largely intact (Goodglass, 1993; Ullman, 2004; Ullman et al., 1997; Ullman et al., 2005).

Brain damage in L2 speakers yields a different pattern. First of all, relatively circumscribed temporal lobe damage can lead to worse grammatical performance in L2 than in L1 (Ku, Lachmann, and Nagler, 1996; Ullman, 2001b). More importantly, left basal ganglia and left frontal lobe lesions have been shown to produce greater grammatical impairments in L1 than L2, as well as in the more proficient L2 as compared to the less proficient L2 (Fabbro, 1999; Fabbro and Paradis, 1995; Ullman, 2001b). This pattern is particularly striking because the damage leads to more severe problems in the earlier learned and the more proficiently spoken languages. However, left frontal or basal ganglia damage does not appear to lead to differences in *lexical* performance between L1 and L2 or between high- and low-proficiency L2s, even in the same patients who show worse grammatical performance in L1 than L2 or in the more proficient L2 (Fabbro, 1999; Fabbro and Paradis, 1995; Ullman, 2001b). Thus frontal and basal ganglia damage appears to be at least somewhat selective, resulting in particular impairments of grammar in L1 and proficient L2.

Positron emission tomography (PET) and functional magnetic resonance imaging (fMRI) measure changes in blood flow or oxygenation levels in the brain. Since these changes are related to changes in neural activity, the techniques provide an indirect method for pinpointing the brain structures that are active during specific cognitive tasks. The representation and/or processing of both lexical knowledge in L1 and nonlinguistic conceptual-semantic information (i.e., knowledge about the world around us) is strongly linked to activation in temporal and temporo-parietal regions (Damasio, Grabowski, Tranel, Hichwa, and Damasio, 1996; Martin et al., 2000; Newman, Pancheva, Ozawa, Neville, and Ullman, 2001; Ullman, 2004). The selection or retrieval of this knowledge reliably leads to activation in ventro-lateral prefrontal cortex, especially in BA 45 and BA 47 (Buckner, 2000; Fiez, 1997; Poldrack, Wagner et al., 1999; Thompson-Schill, D'Esposito, Aguirre, and Farah, 1997). A wide range of tasks designed to probe syntactic processing in both receptive and expressive language have elicited preferential activation in Broca's area, especially in the region of BA 44 (Caplan, Alpert, and Waters, 1998; Embick, Marantz, Miyashita, O'Neil, and Sakai, 2000; Friederici, 2002; Friederici, 2004; Indefrey, Hagoort, Herzog, Seitz, and Brown, 2001; Moro et al., 2001; Ni et al., 2000; Stromswold, Caplan, Alpert, and Rauch, 1996).

In later-learned second languages, tasks that involve *only* lexical-conceptual processing have been found not to yield more activation in L2 than L1 (Chee, Tan, and Thiel, 1999; Illes et al., 1999; Klein, Milner, Zatorre, Zhao, and Nikelski, 1999; Pillai et al., 2003), suggesting a common neurocognitive basis. Such tasks have also elicited greater activation in L2 than L1 in regions that may reflect the greater demands of the less-well learned L2 on articulation (putamen: Klein, Milner, Zatorre, Meyer, and Evans, 1995; Klein, Zatorre, Milner, Meyer, and Evans, 1994), on working memory (left superior BA 44 and SMA: Chee, Hon, Lee, and Soon, 2001), or on lexical retrieval and selection (left BA 45 and BA 47: Chee et al., 2001; De Bleser et al., 2003).

Tasks that are expected to involve grammatical processing (e.g., sentence comprehension) have generally elicited different activation patterns in L2 and L1, in particular in temporal lobe regions, suggesting a greater dependence on these structures in L2 than in L1. Perani et al. (1996) found greater activation in L2 than L1 only in the parahippocampal gyrus, bilaterally. Similarly, in Perani et al. (1998), the only areas of activation that were found in L2 (as compared to baseline) and not in L1 were in the parahippocampal gyrus (bilaterally) and the left middle temporal gyrus. Dehaene et al. (1997) observed greater activation in L2 than in L1 in several right hemisphere temporal neocortical regions, in the left middle temporal gyrus, and in frontal regions implicated in the retrieval of declarative memories (see above; Buckner and Wheeler, 2001; Ullman, 2004). Note that although Kim, Relkin, Lee, and Hirsch (1997) did not discuss temporal lobe activation differences, the paper reported no data outside left posterior superior temporal cortex. Even early L2 learners have shown a pattern of greater temporal lobe involvement in L2 as compared to L1 (e.g., parahippocampal cortex activation in Perani et al.,

1998). However, as would be expected if early-acquired L2 relies on similar neurocognitive correlates as L1, some studies have found no activation differences at all between L1 and very early-acquired L2 (Chee et al., 1999; Wartenburger et al., 2003). Finally, other than the frontal regions associated with retrieval found by Dehaene et al. (1997), greater frontal lobe activation in L2 than L1 has generally *not* been observed (Chee et al., 1999; Kim et al., 1997; Perani et al., 1996; Perani et al., 1998, in neither experiment; Wartenburger et al., 2003, who observed greater frontal activation in late- but not early-acquired L2, as compared to L1, in a grammaticality judgment task).

Intriguingly, a recent fMRI study examining the adult acquisition of an artificial language found that early on during learning, syntactic processing involved the left hippocampus and neocortical temporal regions, including the left middle temporal gyrus (Opitz and Friederici, 2003). However, activation in these brain structures decreased across the experiment (i.e., as experience and proficiency increased), while activation increased in BA 44 within Broca's area. This finding directly supports the DP model's prediction of a shift from the declarative to the procedural system during late L2 learning.

Event-related potentials (ERPs) are scalp-recorded electrical potentials that reflect the real-time electrophysiological brain activity of cognitive processes that are time locked to the presentation of target stimuli, such as words. Lexical processing in L1 and nonlinguistic conceptual processing elicit central-posterior bilateral negativities (N400s) that peak about 400 milliseconds after the presentation of the stimulus (Barrett and Rugg, 1990; Kutas and Hillyard, 1980). The N400 component depends at least in part on temporal lobe structures (McCarthy, Nobre, Bentin, and Spencer, 1995; Nobre, Allison, and McCarthy, 1994; Simos, Basile, and Papanicolaou, 1997) and has been posited to involve the declarative memory system (Ullman, 2001b, 2001c). Lexical stimuli that elicit N400 components in L1 also consistently elicit them in L2, in both low- and high-proficiency speakers (Hahne, 2001; Hahne and Friederici, 2001; McLaughlin, Osterhout, and Kim, 2004; Weber-Fox and Neville, 1996), strengthening the view that lexical-declarative memory is largely available to L2 learners.

In L1, tasks involving the processing of grammatical violations often yield left anterior negativities (LANs) (Friederici, Pfeifer, and Hahne, 1993; Neville, Nicol, Barss, Forster, and Garrett, 1991). LANs have been linked to left frontal cortex and to automatic grammatical processing (Friederici, 2002; Friederici, Hahne, and Mecklinger, 1996; Friederici, Hahne, and von Cramon, 1998). It has been posited that LANs reflect processing by the grammatical-procedural system (Ullman, 2001b, 2001c). In lower proficiency L2, LANs are not found, even when the same violation elicits a LAN in L1 (Hahne, 2001; Hahne and

Friederici, 2001; Weber-Fox and Neville, 1996). Instead of LANs, either no negativities are observed (Hahne, 2001; Hahne and Friederici, 2001), or subjects show more posterior negativities that resemble N400s more than LANs (Ullman, 2001b; Weber-Fox and Neville, 1996). N400s have also been found in very low-proficiency L2 learners for grammatical anomalies that do not elicit a LAN (or an N400) in L1 (Osterhout and McLaughlin, 2000). Together, these findings suggest that grammatical processing in lower proficiency L2 is subserved by brain structures that are at least partially distinct from those subserving grammar in L1 and that overlap, in at least some cases, with those subserving lexical-conceptual processing.

In contrast, an ERP study of adults acquiring an artificial language found that grammatical violations elicited a LAN in highly proficient learners (Friederici, Steinhauer, and Pfeifer, 2002), as would be expected after proceduralization of grammatical knowledge. Similarly, it appears that the only LAN that has been found in a natural language learned as an L2 was elicited by subjects who were proficient in the L2 (Hahne, Muller, and Clahsen, 2003).

Finally, it is interesting to note that the late positive P600 ERP component, which is linked to controlled (that is, not automatic) late syntactic processing in L1 (Friederici et al., 1996) and is *not* posited to depend on procedural processing (Ullman, 2001b, 2001c), is (unlike the LAN) generally displayed by L2 speakers (Hahne, 2001; Osterhout and McLaughlin, 2000; Weber-Fox and Neville, 1996). Its absence in one experiment has been attributed to floor effects, due to higher amplitude positivities in the correct condition in L2 (Hahne and Friederici, 2001).

8. Discussion

In summary, the DP model posits that in the late acquisition of second or subsequent languages, learning grammar in procedural memory is more problematic than learning lexical or other linguistic knowledge in declarative memory, as compared to L1 acquisition. Thus adult second language learners rely particularly heavily on declarative memory, depending on this system not only for storing idiosyncratic lexical knowledge, but also for memorizing complex forms and "rules." However, with sufficient experience with the language, the procedural system should be able to acquire much or perhaps even all of the grammatical knowledge that it subserves in L1. Differences in L2 acquisition abilities are expected across the adult years and between individuals; because learning in declarative memory and possibly procedural memory becomes more problematic with aging during adulthood, particularly in later years, one should find increasing problems with L2 acquisition during this period. Women should tend to be faster than men at L2 acquisition, at least during initial learning stages, thanks to their advantages at declarative memory, although such advantages may be eliminated following menopause. Estrogen is expected to play an important role in a number of these effects.

Existing behavioral evidence, as well as neurocognitive data from brain-damaged patients, neuroimaging, and event-related potentials, largely supports this perspective. However, many gaps in the data remain. For example, neurocognitive experiments have not probed the relation between L2 and either sex differences or the underlying hormonal status and have ignored changes in L2 acquisition abilities later in the lifespan. Moreover, it is important to point out that not all evidence appears to be consistent with the predictions of the DP model. Corpora studies and some research examining highly proficient L2 learners suggest that late L2 acquisition may impact irregular inflected forms and idiosyncratic language features as much as or more than regular inflected forms and abstract grammatical structure (Birdsong, 1992; Birdsong and Flege, 2001; Flege, Yeni-Komshian, and Liu, 1999; Gass and Selinker, 1994). Moreover, whereas a number of studies suggest an L2 performance advantage of females over males, in measures of general language proficiency (Boyle, 1987; Wen and Johnson, 1997), vocabulary memorization (Gardner and Lambert, 1972; Nyikos, 1990), and reading (Chavez, 2001), other investigations have found no sex differences in listening comprehension (Bacon, 1992), in reading comprehension (Phakiti, 2003), and in overall measures of achievement (Spurling and Ilyin, 1985). Still others have reported an advantage for males in certain vocabulary measures (Boyle, 1987; Scarcella and Zimmerman, 1998) and in reading (Bügel and Buunk, 1996). For further discussion on sex differences in SLA, see Bowden, Sanz, and Stafford (this volume, chapter 4).

These empirical gaps and inconsistencies indicate the need for further studies, in particular for ones that are specifically designed to directly test and potentially falsify the L2-related predictions of the DP model. Crucially, these must probe not only performance but also a range of measures of the neurocognitive correlates of the learning and use of L2. Such studies should control for a variety of item, task, and subject factors that are posited to play important roles in the DP model, such as the idiosyncracy versus regularity of items and the sex, age of acquisition, years of exposure, and hormonal status of subjects.

The DP perspective can be directly compared to and contrasted with a number of previous SLA hypotheses. Moreover, it leads to a number of issues for further discussion, has several implications, and suggests a range of questions for further investigation.

First, it is important to emphasize that the model's claims and predictions regarding L2 are largely motivated by our *independent* knowledge of other areas of study, in particular of L1 and cognitive neuroscience, broadly defined. Our understanding of these areas, including the cognitive, computational, anatomical, physiological, cellular, and molecular bases of the two brain systems lead to a wide array of testable predictions. This offers far greater predictive power than hypotheses whose motivations and claims are largely restricted to language itself. Moreover, the two brain systems can be examined with a range of reliable techniques that are widely used in cognitive neuroscience, complementing and greatly strengthening those methods that have traditionally been employed in the study of SLA. Together, the theoretical and empirical advantages of the perspective presented in this chapter provide the potential to make substantial and rapid advances in our understanding of L2 acquisition and processing.

Second, the DP model offers a novel explanatory framework for age-of-exposure effects—that is, for the greater difficulty in learning languages during later years. The model explains these effects largely in terms of biologically based mechanisms that affect one or both memory systems and that vary both with age and across individuals. Importantly, distinct sets of changes are posited to occur prior to and during adulthood, although in both cases the two memory systems are affected, at least in part, as a consequence of modulation by the endocrine system. This testable neurocognitive perspective differs substantially from previous explanations for age-of-exposure effects (Birdsong, 1999), such as the loss of language-specific learning mechanisms (Bley-Vroman, 1990; Pinker, 1994) and earlier learned languages interfering with L2 learning (MacWhinney, 1987; Rohde and Plaut, 1999).

Third, the model's claims that L2 learners can ultimately become L1-like in their proficiency, as well as in their underlying neurocognitive correlates, contradicts the strong form of the critical period hypothesis, which denies both of these assertions (Bley-Vroman, 1990; Clahsen and Muysken, 1986; Hyltenstam and Abrahamsson, 2003; Johnson and Newport, 1989; Meisel, 1991). Importantly, the prediction of L1-like ultimate attainment in both performance and neurocognition is clearly testable using a number of well established methods.

Fourth, the model strongly emphasizes variation in L2 learning aptitude, both within and across individuals. Within individuals, L2 acquisition abilities are expected to vary not only over the lifespan but even across shorter periods. Thus daily as well as seasonal fluctuations in the level of sex hormones (Kimura, 1999) should affect L2 learning and use. Differences across individuals should vary both between groups (e.g., males vs. females) and between individuals within a group, as a consequence of individual variation in the population in factors such as hormone levels. These claims allow one to make specific predictions regarding the rapidity and ultimate attainment of L2 acquisition. Such predictions may be made not only on the basis of general patterns regarding how the memory systems differ over time and between groups but also on the basis of neurocognitive and performance measures of the two memory systems and their biological correlates (e.g., sex hormone levels) in individual subjects. Moreover, this knowledge of group and individual subject characteristics should allow one to make distinct testable predictions for declarative and procedural aspects of L2 acquisition. For example, whereas young women may tend to show more rapid learning than men during early stages of L2 learning, as well as higher eventual levels of idiosyncratic lexical knowledge, young men might be more likely to reach L1-like levels of grammatical proficiency.

Fifth, because the functional and biological characteristics of the two memory systems are reasonably well understood, one should be able to predict how to manipulate them in order to improve the rate and ultimate proficiency levels of L2 learning. For example, one should be able to exploit the functional characteristics of declarative memory, such as promoting learning in rich semantic contexts (Schacter and Tulving, 1994). The DP model also underscores the view that nativelike attainment may be achieved only through extensive practice (i.e., experience). The amount and type of experience that may be necessary to achieve this, and how experience relates to other factors, such as individual subject learning characteristics, remain to be determined. However, one should be able to optimize L2 acquisition by scheduling learning to take advantage of natural fluctuations in the endocrine system (e.g., daily, monthly, seasonal). The model also suggests a potential role for pharmacological agents in SLA. Cholinergic interventions, which can enhance declarative memory (Freo et al., 2002; Packard, 1998), may facilitate the initial stages of learning posited to depend on this system. Dopaminergic interventions, which under certain circumstances can enhance the procedural system (Gerfen, 1995; Jankovic and Tolosa, 1993), might be helpful in promoting the acquisition of grammatical rules by this system. Moreover, as discussed above, the time course of the shift from declarative to procedural memory can also be modulated pharmacologically (Packard, 1999). Further research is clearly needed to investigate these issues.

Sixth, the model may contribute to our understanding of the much-studied distinction between explicit and implicit knowledge in SLA (Bialystok, 1978, 1979; DeKeyser, 2003; N. C. Ellis, 1994, 2002; Krashen, 1985; Krashen, Scarcella, and Long, 1982; Norris and Ortega, 2001). At first blush, this distinction may seem to correspond quite closely to the declarative-procedural distinction proposed by the DP model, given that declarative memory has been claimed to underlie explicit knowledge while procedural memory subserves implicit knowledge. However, there are a number of critical differences. First of all, the DP model is based on claims about neurocognitive systems, whereas the explicit-implicit distinction is premised on claims about awareness. This latter distinction is somewhat problematic in that awareness is difficult not only to define but also to test (DeKeyser, 2003; Doughty, 2003; Schmidt, 1994). In contrast, the distinction between the declarative and procedural brain systems is relatively clear, and the dichotomy can be tested with a variety of methodological approaches.

It is also important to note that the mapping between declarative-procedural memory on the one hand, and explicit-implicit knowledge on the other, is by no means isomorphic (one-to-one). Information stored in declarative memory may very well be explicit (accessible to conscious awareness in some sense), but there is no requirement that it must be, and recent data suggest that at least certain kinds of knowledge acquired by the declarative memory system are not explicit (Chun and Phelps, 1999; Chun, 2000). Additionally, evidence suggests the existence of more than one nondeclarative implicit memory system (Eichenbaum and Cohen, 2001; Squire and Knowlton, 1995). Procedural memory, as it is defined in the DP model and by many memory researchers, refers only to one type of nondeclarative memory system (Eichenbaum and Cohen, 2001; Squire and Knowlton, 1995; Ullman, 2001c; Ullman, 2004; Ullman and Pierpont, 2005). Unfortunately, the term *procedural memory* has sometimes been used interchangeably with *implicit memory,* resulting in quite a confusing situation (Eichenbaum and Cohen, 2001; Schacter and Tulving, 1994). Finally, most previous treatments of explicit-implicit memory in SLA have not focused on, or even clearly acknowledged, the distinction between lexicon and grammar (Bialystok, 1978; N. C. Ellis, 2002; Gass, 1997; Krashen et al., 1982). In sum, it is difficult to draw simple parallels between the explicit-implicit and declarative-procedural distinctions. Nevertheless, the clear and testable dichotomy between declarative and procedural memory and the examination of how these two brain systems relate to lexicon and grammar, across different periods of the lifespan and across individuals, may encourage SLA researchers to consider how these factors relate to the constructs of explicit and implicit knowledge.

Seventh, the DP model can be directly compared to and contrasted with other neurocognitive perspectives of SLA. The model is perhaps most similar to the view espoused by Friederici and her colleagues on the basis of their fMRI and ERP data. They have concluded that low-proficiency L2 learners do not have the neurocognitive abilities of native speakers for automatic parsing and syntactic structure building in sentence comprehension, which are assumed to depend on BA 44 and certain other structures in L1 (Friederici et al., 2002; Hahne, 2001; Hahne and Friederici, 2001; Opitz and Friederici, 2003). Instead, low-proficiency learners initially depend on medial and lateral temporal lobe structures, and possibly on strategy-dependent compensatory right-hemisphere processes (Hahne and Friederici, 2001; Opitz and Friederici, 2003). However, as L2 proficiency increases (with experience with the language), medial and lateral temporal lobe involvement decreases, while BA 44 involvement increases (Opitz and Friederici, 2003). In contrast, conceptual-semantic integration seems to remain largely L1-like in L2 learners (Hahne and Friederici, 2001). Friederici's data and conclusions are thus highly compatible with the DP model. The two views seem to diverge in a number of the details (e.g., the role of the basal ganglia) and in that Friederici's perspective is primarily driven by data from L2 studies, whereas the DP model's claims and predictions follow largely from our independent knowledge of the two memory systems.

The DP model can also be directly compared to the view embraced by Paradis. He has proposed a model that links SLA notions of explicit and implicit knowledge to specific neural structures (Paradis, 1994, 1995, 1997, 1999, 2004). Like the DP model, Paradis emphasizes a greater dependence on declarative than procedural memory in L2 as compared to L1 and in low-proficiency L2 as compared to high-proficiency L2. However, unlike the DP model, Paradis seems to assume a direct correspondence between explicit knowledge and declarative memory and between implicit knowledge and procedural memory (Paradis, 1994, 2004). Moreover, Paradis discusses the increased reliance on procedural memory (in L1 and high-proficiency L2) largely in terms of greater automatization and implicitness across various domains of language, including at least portions of the lexicon. For Paradis, only consciously accessible lexical elements are declarative, in both L1 and L2. This seems to correspond largely to vocabulary items—that is, consciously accessible knowledge of the sound-meaning pairings of words. More abstract lexical knowledge (i.e., lexicalized knowledge of grammatical properties, such as argument structure) is not declarative (Paradis, 2004). Even vocabulary items do not depend on declarative memory when they are processed implicitly (nonconsciously) in sentence contexts (Paradis, 1994). Thus Paradis' claims for the lexicon differ at least partly from those of the DP model: Whereas the DP model assumes that *all* lexical knowledge resides in declarative memory (whether or not the knowledge is available to conscious awareness), Paradis takes seriously the divide between explicit and implicit knowledge, and claims that only the conscious use of lexical knowledge depends on declarative memory. Paradis also diverges somewhat from the DP model with respect to neuroanatomy. He focuses on medial temporal lobe structures for declarative memory and on the basal ganglia, cerebellum, and neocortex for procedural memory; particular neocortical regions do not appear to be implicated, other than left perisylvian areas (Paradis, 1999, 2004). Finally, unlike the DP model, Paradis does not seem to make further predictions based on our independent knowledge of the two memory systems, such as sex differences or modulation by sex hormones. Together these predictions enable Paradis' view to be empirically distinguished from the DP model.

Finally, it is important to point out that a number of theoretical gaps remain to be addressed in the DP perspective of L2 acquisition and processing. For example, the precise relation between late SLA on the one hand, and both native language acquisition and early SLA on the other, remains to be determined. In all cases, declarative memory is predicted to acquire information much faster than procedural memory. Thus even in very young children learning their native language, complex forms as well as idiosyncratic knowledge are predicted to be memorized in declarative memory before grammatical rules are abstracted in procedural memory. Indeed, at least some evidence appears to be consistent with this view (e.g., Marcus et al., 1992). Second and subsequent languages learned during early childhood should follow much the same pattern. However, in both of these cases, the fact that language acquisition occurs early, prior to the posited changes in the two memory systems, leads to the prediction that the grammar will be acquired with greater facility than would occur in later years, particularly following puberty. Other issues, such as the rapidity of vocabulary learning during childhood (Bloom, 2000) and the role of transfer or interference from previously learned languages, also remain to be investigated.

9. Summary

The DP perspective constitutes a novel alternative to previously proposed explanatory hypotheses of SLA. It leads to an array of specific predictions that are largely generated by our independent knowledge of the two memory systems and are directly testable using a range of widely used behavioral and neurocognitive methods. The predictions allow the model to be directly compared against alternative accounts and provide the means for it to be both falsified and further specified. Thus the DP model may provide a useful paradigm for the study of SLA.

10. Exercises

The following exercises are designed to increase your understanding of the neurocognition of SLA.

10.1 QUESTIONS

1. Briefly describe an experiment, using any methodology that you feel is appropriate, that could test one or more of the L2-related predictions of the DP model.

2. According to the DP model, might individual differences in working memory capacity lead to individual differences in SLA? Explain your answer.
3. A monolingual adult male suffers from a stroke that leads to damage to Broca's area, the basal ganglia, and surrounding structures, and to the onset of Broca's aphasia and agrammatism in his L1. Should he be able to learn an L2? Explain your answer. How might pharmacological agents improve his SLA?
4. Adult-onset bilateral damage limited to medial temporal lobe structures leads to an inability to learn new knowledge in declarative memory—that is, information about facts, events, and words. In contrast, such amnesic patients are generally able to acquire new motor and cognitive skills and other procedures, even though they do not remember the individual testing sessions. Should such patients be impaired at SLA? Explain your answer.
5. Specific Language Impairment (SLI) is a congenital disorder that affects language. It generally compromises grammatical abilities more than lexical abilities. It is also associated with a variety of impairments of nonlinguistic functions that are linked to the procedural memory system, while declarative memory appears to be relatively spared (Ullman and Pierpont, 2005). Thus it has been suggested that many individuals with SLI may suffer from abnormalities of brain structures underlying the procedural memory system (Ullman and Pierpont, 2005). Do you think that such individuals should show age-of-exposure period effects in language learning? Why or why not?

10.2 GUIDED CRITIQUE

To practice your skills at reading and critiquing articles on the neurocognition of SLA, please read the following article and answer the questions below.

Weber-Fox, C. M., and Neville, H. J. (1996). Maturational constraints on functional specializations for language processing: ERP and behavioral evidence in bilingual speakers. *Journal of Cognitive Neuroscience, 8*(3), 231–256.

1. Motivations and hypotheses
   a. What are the primary motivations and goals of the study?
   b. What hypothesis or hypotheses are the authors testing?
2. Methodology
   a. ERPs. What are ERPs? What do they reveal about neural and cognitive processes? What are their strengths and weaknesses as compared to other neurocognitive methods?

b. Subjects. What subject groups were examined? What factors (e.g., age, education, etc.) are the subject groups matched or not matched on? Are there confounds between the subject factors of interest (e.g., age of exposure and length of exposure to the L2)?
c. Materials and procedure. Why were both behavioral and ERP measures acquired? Why was only receptive language examined with ERPs? Do you think that 14 electrodes were sufficient in this study? What advantages or disadvantages might such a small number of electrodes confer?
d. List the main strengths and weaknesses of the methods of this study.

3. Results.
   a. Explain the main behavioral results. What do you think are the most important results, and why?
   b. Explain the main ERP results.What do you think are the most important results, and why?
   c. Did one or more of the subject groups yield a pattern of results that was particularly different from that of the others? Why might this be?
4. Discussion and conclusions.
   a. What conclusions do the authors draw from their results?
   b. Are all of their conclusions justified by the data?
   c. Do their data suggest additional questions for study? Suggest one or more experiments to investigate any additional questions of interest.

Further Reading

Birdsong, D. (2004). Second language acquisition and ultimate attainment. In A. Davies & C. Elder (Eds.), *Handbook of Applied Linguistics* (pp. 82–105). Oxford, UK: Blackwell.

Opitz, B., & Friederici, A. D. (2003). Interactions of the hippocampal system and the prefrontal cortex in learning language-like rules. *Neuroimage, 19*(4), 1730–1737.

Paradis, M. (2004). *A neurolinguistic theory of bilingualism.* Amsterdam: John Benjamins.

Ullman, M. T. (2004). Contributions of memory circuits to language: The declarative/procedural model. *Cognition, 92*(1–2), 231–270.

Acknowledgments

This chapter was written with support from NSF SBR-9905273, NIH MH58189, and research grants from the National Alliance for Autism Research, the Mabel Flory Trust, and Pfizer, Inc. I thank David Birdsong, Claudia Bonin, Harriet Wood Bowden, Ivy Estabrooke, Shira Fischer, Matthew Moffa, Kara Morgan-Short, Michel Paradis, Cristina Sanz, Matthew Walenski, and Robbin Wood for helpful comments.

References

Aldridge, J. W., & Berridge, K. C. (1998). Coding of serial order by neostriatal neurons: A "natural action" approach to movement sequence. *The Journal of Neuroscience, 18*(7), 2777–2787.

Amunts, K., Schleicher, A., Burgel, U., Mohlberg, H., Uylings, H., & Zilles, K. (1999). Broca's region revisited: Cytoarchitecture and intersubject variability. *Journal of Comparative Neurology, 412*(2), 319–341.

Ankarberg, C., & Norjavaara, E. (1999). Diurnal rhythm of testosterone secretion before and throughout puberty in healthy girls: Correlation with 17 beta-estradiol and dehydroepiandrosterone sulfate. *Journal of Clinical Endocrinology and Metabolism, 84*(3), 975–984.

Bacon, S. M. (1992). The relationship between gender, comprehension, processing strategies, and cognitive and affective response in foreign language listening. *The Modern Language Journal, 76*(2), 160–178.

Barrett, S. E., & Rugg, M. D. (1990). Event-related potentials and the semantic matching of pictures. *Brain and Cognition, 14*(2), 201–212.

Bates, E., & MacWhinney, B. (1989). Functionalism and the competition model. In B. MacWhinney & E. Bates (Eds.), *The crosslinguistic study of sentence processing* (pp. 3–73). Cambridge, UK: Cambridge University Press.

Bialystok, E. (1978). A theoretical model of second language learning. *Language Learning, 28*(1), 69–83.

Bialystok, E. (1979). An analytical view of second language competence: A model and some evidence. *The Modern Language Journal, 63,* 257–262.

Birdsong, D. (1992). Ultimate attainment in second language acquisition. *Language, 68,* 706–755.

Birdsong, D. (Ed.). (1999). *Second language acquisition and the critical period hypothesis.* Mahwah, NJ: Lawrence Erlbaum.

Birdsong, D., & Flege, J. E. (2001). Regular-irregular dissociations in the acquisition of English as a second language. In A. H.-J. Do, L. Domínguez, & A. Johansen (Eds.), *BUCLD 25: Proceedings of the 25th Annual Boston University Conference on Language Development* (pp. 123–132). Boston, MA: Cascadilla Press.

Birdsong, D., & Molis, M. (2001). On the evidence for maturational constraints in second-language acquisition. *Journal of Memory and Language, 44,* 235–249.

Bley-Vroman, R. (1990). The logical problem of foreign language learning. *Linguistic Analysis, 20,* 3–49.

Bloom, P. (2000). *How children learn the meanings of words.* Cambridge, MA: MIT Press.

Boecker, H., Ceballos-Baumann, A. O., Bartenstein, P., Dagher, A., Forster, K., Haslinger, B., et al. (2002). A H215O positron emission tomography study on mental imagery of movement sequences—the effect of modulating sequence length and direction. *Neuroimage, 17,* 999–1009.

Boyle, J. P. (1987). Sex differences in listening vocabulary. *Language Learning, 37*(2), 273–284.

Buckner, R. L. (2000). Neuroimaging of memory. In M. S. Gazzaniga (Ed.), *The new cognitive neurosciences* (pp. 817–828). Cambridge, MA: MIT Press.

Buckner, R. L., & Wheeler, M. E. (2001). The cognitive neuroscience of remembering. *Nature Review Neuroscience, 2*(9), 624–634.

Bügel, K., & Buunk, B. P. (1996). Sex differences in listening vocabulary. *The Modern Language Journal, 80*(1), 15–31.

Calabresi, P., Centonze, D., Gubellini, P., Marfia, G. A., Pisani, A., Sancesario, G., et al. (2000). Synaptic transmission in the striatum: From plasticity to neurodegeneration. *Progress in Neurobiology, 61,* 231–265.

Calabresi, P., Centonze, D., Gubellini, P., Pisani, A., & Bernardi, G. (2000). Acetylcholine-mediated modulation of striatal function. *Trends in Neurosciences, 23*(3), 120–126.

Campbell, B., & Spear, N. (1972). Ontogeny of memory. *Psychological Review, 79,* 215–236.

Caplan, D., Alpert, N., & Waters, G. (1998). Effects of syntactic structure and propositional number on patterns of regional cerebral blood flow. *Journal of Cognitive Neuroscience, 10*(4), 541–552.

Carlson, L. E., & Sherwin, B. B. (2000). Higher levels of plasma estradiol and testosterone in healthy elderly men compared with age-matched women may protect aspects of explicit memory. *Menopause, 7*(3), 168–177.

Carr, B. R. (1998). Disorders of the ovaries and female reproductive tract. In J. D. Wilson, D. W. Foster, H. M. Kronenberg, & P. R. Larsen (Eds.), *Williams textbook of endocrinology* (9th ed.). Philadelphia: W. B. Saunders.

Chavez, M. (2001). *Gender in the language classroom.* New York: McGraw-Hill.

Chee, M. W., Caplan, D., Soon, C. S., Sriram, N., Tan, E. W., Thiel, T., et al. (1999). Processing of visually presented sentences in Mandarin and English studied with fMRI. *Neuron, 23*(1), 127–137.

Chee, M. W., Hon, N., Lee, H. L., & Soon, C. S. (2001). Relative language proficiency modulates BOLD signal change when bilinguals perform semantic judgments. *Neuroimage, 13*(6), 1155–1163.

Chee, M. W., Tan, E. W., & Thiel, T. (1999). Mandarin and English single word processing studied with functional magnetic resonance imaging. *Journal of Neuroscience, 19*(8), 3050–3056.

Cherrier, M. M., Asthana, S., Plymate, S., Baker, L., Matsumoto, A. M., Peskind, E., et al. (2001). Testosterone supplementation improves spatial and verbal memory in healthy older men. *Neurology, 57*(1), 80–88.

Chomsky, N. (1965). *Aspects of the theory of syntax.* Cambridge, MA: MIT Press.

Chomsky, N. (1995). *The minimalist program.* Cambridge, MA: MIT Press.

Chun, M. M. (2000). Contextual cueing of visual attention. *Trends in Cognitive Science, 4*(5), 170–178.

Chun, M. M., & Phelps, E. (1999). Memory deficits for implicit contextual information in amnesic subjects with hippocampal damage. *Nature Neuroscience, 2*(9), 844–847.

Churchill, J. D., Stanis, J. J., Press, C., Kushelev, M., & Greenough, W. T. (2003). Is procedural memory relatively spared from age effects? *Neurobiology of Aging, 24*(6), 883–892.

Clahsen, H., & Muysken, P. (1986). The availability of universal grammar to adult and child learners—a study of the acquisition of German word order. *Second Language Research, 2,* 93–119.

Coppieters, R. (1987). Competence differences between native and near-native speakers. *Language, 63*(3), 544–573.

Corkin, S. (1984). Lasting consequences of bilateral medial temporal lobectomy: Clinical course and experimental findings in H. M. *Seminars in Neurology, 4*(2), 249–259.

Cranshaw, A. (1997). *A study of Anglophone native and near-native linguistic and metalinguistic performance.* Unpublished doctoral dissertation, Université de Montréal.

Curran, H. V. (2000). Psychopharmacological approaches to human memory. In M. S. Gazzaniga (Ed.), *The new cognitive neurosciences* (pp. 797–804). Cambridge, MA: MIT Press.

Curran, T. (1997). Effects of aging on implicit sequence learning: Accounting for sequence structure and explicit knowledge. *Psychological Research, 60*(1–2), 24–41.

Curtiss, S. R. (1977). *Genie: A psycholinguistic study of a modern-day "wild child."* New York: Academic Press.

Curtiss, S. R. (1989). *The case of Chelsea: A new test case of the critical period for language acquisition.* Unpublished manuscript, University of California, Los Angeles.

Cutler, G. B., Jr. (1997). The role of estrogen in bone growth and maturation during childhood and adolescence. *Journal of Steroid Biochemistry and Molecular Biology, 61*(3–6), 141–144.

Damasio, A. R., & Damasio, H. (1992). Brain and language. *Scientific American, 267*(3), 88–95.

Damasio, H., Grabowski, T., Tranel, D., Hichwa, R., & Damasio, A. (1996). A neural basis for lexical retrieval. *Nature, 380*(6574), 499–505.

De Bleser, R., Dupont, P., Postler, J., Bormans, G., Spellman, D., Mortelmans, L., et al. (2003). The organization of the bilingual lexicon: A PET study. *Journal of Neurolinguistics, 16,* 439–456.

De Renzi, E. (1989). Apraxia. In F. Boller & J. Grafman (Eds.), *Handbook of neuropsychology* (Vol. 2, pp. 245–263). New York: Elsevier Science.

Dehaene, S., Dupoux, E., Mehler, J., Cohen, L., Paulesu, E., Perani, D., et al. (1997). Anatomical variability in the cortical representation of first and second language. *Neuroreport, 8*(17), 3809–3815.

DeKeyser, R. M. (2000). The robustness of critical period effects in second language acquisition. *Studies in Second Language Acquisition, 22,* 499–533.

DeKeyser, R. M. (2003). Implicit and explicit learning. In C. J. Doughty & M. H. Long (Eds.), *The handbook of second language acquisition* (pp. 313–348). Oxford, UK: Blackwell.

Desmond, J. E., & Fiez, J. A. (1998). Neuroimaging studies of the cerebellum: Language, learning, and memory. *Trends in Cognitive Science, 2*(9), 355–362.

Di Giulio, D. V., Seidenberg, M., O'Leary, D. S., & Raz, N. (1994). Procedural and declarative memory: A developmental study. *Brain and Cognition, 25*(1), 79–91.

Di Sciullo, A. M., & Williams, E. (1987). *On the definition of word.* Cambridge, MA: MIT Press.

Doughty, C. J. (2003). Instructed SLA: Constraints, compensation, and enhancement. In C. J. Doughty & M. H. Long (Eds.), *The handbook of second language acquisition* (pp. 256–310). Oxford, UK: Blackwell.

Eichenbaum, H. (2000). A cortical-hippocampal system for declarative memory. *Nature Review Neuroscience, 1*(1), 41–50.

Eichenbaum, H., & Cohen, N. J. (2001). *From conditioning to conscious recollection: Memory systems of the brain.* Oxford, UK: Oxford University Press.

Ellis, N. C. (Ed.). (1994). *Implicit and explicit learning of languages.* New York: Academic Press.

Ellis, N. C. (2002). Reflections on frequency effects in language processing. *Studies in Second Language Acquisition, 24,* 297–339.

Elman, J. L., Bates, E. A., Johnson, M. H., Karmiloff-Smith, A., Parisi, D., & Plunkett, K. (1996). *Rethinking innateness: A connectionist perspective on development.* Cambridge, MA: MIT Press.

Embick, D., Marantz, A., Miyashita, Y., O'Neil, W., & Sakai, K. L. (2000). A syntactic specialization for Broca's area. *Proceedings of the National Academy of Sciences, 97,* 6150–6154.

Eubank, L., & Gregg, K. R. (1999). Critical periods and (second) language acquisition: Divide et impera. In D. Birdsong (Ed.), *Second language acquisition and the critical period hypothesis* (pp. 65–99). Mahwah, NJ: Lawrence Erlbaum.

Fabbro, F. (1999). *The neurolinguistics of bilingualism.* Hove, UK: Psychology Press.

Fabbro, F., & Paradis, M. (1995). Differential impairments in four multilingual patients with subcortical lesions. In M. Paradis (Ed.), *Aspects of bilingual aphasia* (Vol. 3, pp. 139–176). Oxford, UK: Pergamon.

Feeney, J. J., Howard, J. H., & Howard, D. V. (2002). Implicit learning of higher order sequences in middle age. *Psychology and Aging, 17*(2), 351–355.

Ferrini, R., & Barrett-Connor, E. (1998). Sex hormones and age: A cross-sectional study of testosterone and estradiol and their bioavailable fractions in community-dwelling men. *American Journal of Epidemiology, 147*(8), 750–754.

Fiez, J. A. (1997). Phonology, semantics, and the role of the left inferior prefrontal cortex. *Human Brain Mapping, 5*(2), 79–83.

Flege, J. E., Yeni-Komshian, G. H., & Liu, S. (1999). Age constraints on second language acquisition. *Journal of Memory and Language, 41,* 78–104.

Fodor, J. A. (1983). *The modularity of mind: An essay on faculty psychology.* Cambridge, MA: MIT Press.

Fredriksson, A. (2000). Maze learning and motor activity deficits in adult mice induced by iron exposure during a critical postnatal period. *Developmental Brain Research, 119*(1), 65–74.

Freo, U., Pizzolato, G., Dam, M., Ori, C., & Battistin, L. (2002). A short review of cognitive and functional neuroimaging studies of cholinergic drugs: Implications for therapeutic potentials. *Journal of Neural Transmission, 109*(5–6), 857–870.

Friederici, A. D. (2002). Towards a neural basis of auditory sentence processing. *Trends in Cognitive Science, 6*(2), 78–84.

Friederici, A. D. (2004). The neural basis of syntactic processes. In M. S. Gazzaniga (Ed.), *The cognitive neurosciences III* (pp. 789–801). Cambridge, MA: MIT Press.

Friederici, A. D., Hahne, A., & Mecklinger, A. (1996). The temporal structure of syntactic parsing: Early and late effects elicited by syntactic anomalies. *Journal of Experimental Psychology: Learning, Memory, and Cognition, 22*(5), 1219–1248.

Friederici, A. D., Hahne, A., & von Cramon, D. Y. (1998). First-pass versus second-pass parsing processes in a Wernicke's and a Broca's aphasic: Electrophysiological evidence for a double dissociation. *Brain and Language, 62*(3), 311–341.

Friederici, A. D., Pfeifer, E., & Hahne, A. (1993). Event-related brain potentials during natural speech processing: Effects of semantic, morphological, and syntactic violations. *Cognitive Brain Research, 1*(3), 183–192.

Friederici, A. D., Steinhauer, K., & Pfeifer, E. (2002). Brain signatures of artificial language processing: Evidence challenging the critical period hypothesis. *Proceedings of the National Academy of Sciences, 99*(1), 529–534.

Gardner, R. C., & Lambert, W. E. (1972). *Attitudes and motivation in second language learning.* Rowley, MA: Newbury House.

Gass, S. M. (1997). *Input, interaction, and the second language learner.* Mahwah, NJ: Lawrence Erlbaum.

Gass, S. M., & Selinker, L. (1994). *Second language acquisition.* Mahwah, NJ: Lawrence Erlbaum.

Gerfen, C. R. (1995). Dopamine receptor function in the basal ganglia. *Clinical Neuropharmacology, 18,* S162–S177.

Gleason, J. B., & Ratner, N. B. (Eds.). (1998). *Psycholinguistics* (2nd ed.). Fort Worth, TX: Harcourt Brace College.

Goodglass, H. (1993). *Understanding aphasia.* New York: Academic Press.

Grodzinsky, Y. (2000). The neurology of syntax: Language use without Broca's area. *Behavioral and Brain Sciences, 23*(1), 1–71.

Hahne, A. (2001). What's different in second-language processing? Evidence from event-related brain potentials. *Journal of Psycholinguist Research, 30*(3), 251–266.

Hahne, A., & Friederici, A. D. (2001). Processing a second language: Late learners' comprehension strategies as revealed by event-related brain potentials. *Bilingualism: Language and Cognition, 4,* 123–141.

Hahne, A., Muller, J., & Clahsen, H. (2003). Second language learner's processing of inflected words: Behavioral and ERP evidence for storage and decomposition. *Essex Research Reports in Linguistics, 45,* 1–42.

Halbig, T. D., Gruber, D., Scherer, P., Kopp, U. A., Trottenberg, T., & Kupsch, A. (2002). *Subthalamic high frequency stimulation differentially modulates declarative and nondeclarative memory.* Paper presented at the Society for Neuroscience Annual Meeting, Orlando, FL.

Halle, M., & Marantz, A. (1993). Distributed morphology and the pieces of inflection. In K. Hale & S. J. Keyser (Eds.), *The view from Building 20* (pp. 111–176). Cambridge, MA: MIT Press.

Halpern, D. F. (2000). *Sex differences in cognitive abilities* (3rd ed.). Mahwah, NJ: Lawrence Erlbaum.

Hampson, E. (1990). Variations in sex-related cognitive abilities across the menstrual cycle. *Brain and Cognition, 14*(1), 26–43.

Harrington, D. L., Haaland, K. Y., Yeo, R. A., & Marder, E. (1990). Procedural memory in Parkinson's disease: Impaired motor but not visuoperceptual learning. *Journal of Clinical and Experimental Neuropsychology, 12*(2), 323–339.

Hartshorne, J. K., & Ullman, M. T. (in press). Why girls say "holded" more than boys. *Developmental Science.*

Heilman, K. M., Watson, R. T., & Rothi, L. G. (1997). Disorders of skilled movements: Limb apraxia. In T. E. Feinberg & M. J. Farah (Eds.), *Behavioral neurology and neuropsychology* (pp. 227–235). New York: McGraw-Hill.

Hikosaka, O., Sakai, K., Nakahara, H., Lu, X., Miyachi, S., Nakamura, K., et al. (2000). Neural mechanisms for learning of sequential procedures. In M. S. Gazzaniga (Ed.), *The new cognitive neurosciences* (pp. 553–572). Cambridge, MA: MIT Press.

Hodges, J. R., & Patterson, K. (1997). Semantic memory disorders. *Trends in Cognitive Sciences, 1*(2), 68–72.

Howard, J. H., Jr., Howard, D. V., Dennis, N. A., Yankovich, H., & Vaidya, C. J. (2004). Implicit spatial contextual learning in healthy aging. *Neuropsychology, 18,* 124–134.

Hyltenstam, K., & Abrahamsson, N. (2003). Maturational constraints in SLA. In C. J. Doughty & M. H. Long (Eds.), *The handbook of second language acquisition* (pp. 539–588). Oxford, UK: Blackwell.

Illes, J., Francis, W. S., Desmond, J. E., Gabrieli, J. D., Glover, G. H., Poldrack, R., et al. (1999). Convergent cortical representation of semantic processing in bilinguals. *Brain and Language, 70*(3), 347–363.

Indefrey, P., Hagoort, P., Herzog, H., Seitz, R., & Brown, C. (2001). Syntactic processing in left prefrontal cortex is independent of lexical meaning. *Neuroimage, 14*(3), 546–555.

Ivry, R. B., & Fiez, J. A. (2000). Cerebellar contributions to cognition and imagery. In M. S. Gazzaniga (Ed.), *The new cognitive neurosciences* (pp. 999–1011). Cambridge, MA: MIT Press.

Jankovic, J., & Tolosa, E. E. (1993). *Parkinson's disease and movement disorders.* Baltimore: Williams and Wilkins.

Jenkins, I. H., Brooks, D. J., Nixon, P. D., Frackowiak, R. S., & Passingham, R. E. (1994). Motor sequence learning: A study with positron emission tomography. *Journal of Neuroscience, 14*(6), 3775–3790.

Johnson, J. S., & Newport, E. L. (1989). Critical period effects in second language learning: The influence of maturational state on the acquisition of English as a second language. *Cognitive Psychology, 21*(1), 60–99.

Kail, R. V., & Hagen, J. W. (1977). *Perspectives on the development of memory and cognition.* Mahwah, NJ: Lawrence Erlbaum.

Kampen, D. L., & Sherwin, B. B. (1996). Estradiol is related to visual memory in healthy young men. *Behavioral Neuroscience, 110*(3), 613–617.

Kim, K. H. S., Relkin, N. R., Lee, K.-M., & Hirsch, J. (1997). Distinct cortical areas associated with native and second languages. *Nature, 388,* 171–174.

Kimura, D. (1999). *Sex and cognition.* Cambridge, MA: MIT Press.

Klein, D., Milner, B., Zatorre, R. J., Meyer, E., & Evans, A. C. (1995). The neural substrates underlying word generation: A bilingual functional-imaging study. *Proceedings of the National Academy of Sciences of the United States of America, 92*(7), 2899–2903.

Klein, D., Milner, B., Zatorre, R. J., Zhao, V., & Nikelski, J. (1999). Cerebral organization in bilinguals: A PET study of Chinese-English verb generation. *Neuroreport, 10*(13), 2841–2846.

Klein, D., Zatorre, R. J., Milner, B., Meyer, E., & Evans, A. C. (1994). Left putaminal activation when speaking a second language: Evidence from PET. *Neuroreport, 5*(17), 2295–2297.

Klein, K., Baron, J., Colli, M., McDonnell, D., & Cutler, G. (1994). Estrogen levels in childhood determined by an ultrasensitive recombinant cell bioassay. *Journal of Clinical Investigation, 94*(6), 2475–2480.

Klein, K., Martha, P., Blizzard, R., Herbst, T., & Rogol, A. (1996). A longitudinal assessment of hormonal and physical alterations during normal puberty in boys. II. Estrogen levels as determined by an ultrasensitive bioassay. *Journal of Clinical Endocrinology and Metabolism, 81*(9), 3203–3207.

Kramer, J. H., Delis, D. C., Kaplan, E., O'Donnell, L., & Prifitera, A. (1997). Developmental sex differences in verbal learning. *Neuropsychology, 11*(4), 577–584.

Krashen, S. D. (1985). *The input hypothesis.* London: Longman.

Krashen, S. D., Scarcella, R. C., & Long, M. H. (Eds.). (1982). *Child-adult differences in second language acquisition.* Rowley, MA: Newbury House.

Ku, A., Lachmann, E. A., & Nagler, W. (1996). Selective language aphasia from herpes simplex encephalitis. *Pediatric Neurology, 15*(2), 169–171.

Kutas, M., & Hillyard, S. A. (1980). Reading senseless sentences: Brain potentials reflect semantic incongruity. *Science, 207*(1), 203–205.

Levelt, W. J. M. (1989). *Speaking: From intention to articulation.* Cambridge, MA: MIT Press.

Lynch, G. (2002). Memory enhancement: The search for mechanism-based drugs. *Nature Neuroscience, 5*(Supplement), 1035–1038.

MacDonald, M. C., Pearlmutter, N. J., & Seidenberg, M. S. (1994). Lexical nature of syntactic ambiguity resolution. *Psychological Review, 101*(4), 676–703.

MacWhinney, B. (1987). Applying the competition model to bilingualism. *Applied Psycholinguistics, 8,* 415–431.

Maki, P. M., & Resnick, S. M. (2000). Longitudinal effects of estrogen replacement therapy on PET cerebral blood flow and cognition. *Neurobiology of Aging, 21*(2), 373–383.

Marcus, G. F., Pinker, S., Ullman, M., Hollander, M., Rosen, T. J., & Xu, F. (1992). Overregularization in language acquisition. *Monographs of the Society for Research in Child Development, 57*(4, Serial No. 228), 1–165.

Martin, A., Ungerleider, L. G., & Haxby, J. V. (2000). Category specificity and the brain: The sensory/motor model of semantic representations of objects. In M. S. Gazzaniga (Ed.), *The cognitive neurosciences* (pp. 1023–1036). Cambridge, MA: MIT Press.

McCarthy, G., Nobre, A. C., Bentin, S., & Spencer, D. D. (1995). Language-related field potentials in the anterior-medial temporal lobe: I. Intracranial distribution and neural generators. *The Journal of Neuroscience, 15*(2), 1080–1089.

McDonald, R., & White, N. (1993). A triple dissociation of memory systems: Hippocampus, amygdala, and dorsal striatum. *Behavioral Neuroscience, 107*(1), 3–22.

McEwen, B. S., Alves, S. E., Bulloch, K., & Weiland, N. G. (1998). Clinically relevant basic science studies of gender differences and sex hormone effects. *Psychopharmacology Bulletin, 34*(3), 251–259.

McLaughlin, J., Osterhout, L., & Kim, A. (2004). Neural correlates of second-language word learning: Minimal instruction produces rapid change. *Nature Neuroscience, 7*(7), 703–704.

Meisel, J. M. (1991). Principles of Universal Grammar and strategies of language use: On some similarities and differences between first and second language acquisition.

In L. Eubank (Ed.), *Point counterpoint: Universal Grammar in the second language* (pp. 231–276). Amsterdam: John Benjamins.

Meudell, P. R. (1983). The development and dissolution of memory. In A. Mayes (Ed.), *Memory in animals and humans.* New York: Van Nostrand-Reinhold.

Miles, C., Green, R., Sanders, G., & Hines, M. (1998). Estrogen and memory in a transsexual population. *Hormones and Behavior, 34*(2), 199–208.

Mishkin, M., Malamut, B., & Bachevalier, J. (1984). Memories and habits: Two neural systems. In G. Lynch, J. L. McGaugh, & N. W. Weinburger (Eds.), *Neurobiology of learning and memory* (pp. 65–77). New York: Guilford Press.

Mitchell, J. A., & Hall, G. (1988). Caudate-putamen lesions in the rat may impair or potentiate maze learning depending upon availability of stimulus cues and relevance of response cues. *Quarterly Journal of Experimental Psychology B, 40*(3), 243–258.

Moro, A., Tettamanti, M., Perani, D., Donati, C., Cappa, S. F., & Fazio, F. (2001). Syntax and the brain: Disentangling grammar by selective anomalies. *Neuroimage, 13*(1), 110–118.

Nakahara, H., Doya, K., & Hikosaka, O. (2001). Parallel cortico-basal ganglia mechanisms for acquisition and execution of visuomotor sequences—a computational approach. *Journal of Cognitive Neuroscience, 13*(5), 626–647.

Neville, H., Nicol, J. L., Barss, A., Forster, K. I., & Garrett, M. F. (1991). Syntactically based sentence processing classes: Evidence from event-related brain potentials. *Journal of Cognitive Neuroscience, 3*(2), 151–165.

Newman, A. J., Pancheva, R., Ozawa, K., Neville, H. J., & Ullman, M. T. (2001). An event-related fMRI study of syntactic and semantic violations. *Journal of Psycholinguistic Research, 30*(3), 339–364.

Newport, E. L. (1990). Maturational constraints on language learning. *Cognitive Science, 14*(1), 11–28.

Newport, E. L. (1993). Maturational constraints on language learning. In P. Bloom (Ed.), *Language Acquisition* (pp. 543–560). Cambridge, MA: MIT Press.

Ni, W., Constable, R. T., Menci, W. E., Pugh, K. R., Fulbright, R. K., Shaywitz, S. E., et al. (2000). An event-related neuroimaging study distinguishing form and content in sentence processing. *Journal of Cognitive Neuroscience, 12*(1), 120–133.

Nobre, A. C., Allison, T., & McCarthy, G. (1994). Word recognition in the human inferior temporal lobe. *Nature, 372,* 260–263.

Norris, J. M., & Ortega, L. (2001). Does type of instruction make a difference? Substantive findings from a meta-analytic review. *Language Learning, 51*(1), 157–213.

Nyikos, M. (1990). Sex-related differences in adult language learning: Socialization and memory factors. *The Modern Language Journal, 74*(3), 273–287.

Opitz, B., & Friederici, A. D. (2003). Interactions of the hippocampal system and the prefrontal cortex in learning language-like rules. *Neuroimage, 19*(4), 1730–1737.

Ornstein, P. A. (1978). *Memory development in children.* Mahwah, NJ: Lawrence Erlbaum.

Osterhout, L., & McLaughlin, J. (2000). *What brain activity can tell us about second-language learning.* Paper presented at the 13th Annual CUNY Conference on Human Sentence Processing, La Jolla, CA.

Oyama, S. (1982). The sensitive period and comprehension of speech. In S. D. Krashen, R. C. Scarcella, & M. H. Long (Eds.), *Child-adult differences in second language acquisition* (pp. 39–51). Rowley, MA: Newbury House.

Packard, M. G., Hirsh, R., & White, N. (1989). Differential effects of fornix and caudate nucleus lesions on two radial maze tasks: Evidence for multiple memory systems. *The Journal of Neuroscience, 9*(5), 1465–1472.

Packard, M. G. (1998). Posttraining estrogen and memory modulation. *Hormones and Behavior, 34*(2), 126–139.

Packard, M. G. (1999). Glutamate infused posttraining into the hippocampus or caudate-putamen differentially strengthens place and response learning. *Proceedings of the National Academy of Sciences of the United States of America, 96*(22), 12881–12886.

Packard, M. G., & Knowlton, B. J. (2002). Learning and memory functions of the basal ganglia. *Annual Review of Neuroscience, 25,* 563–593.

Packard, M. G., & McGaugh, J. L. (1996). Inactivation of hippocampus or caudate nucleus with lidocaine differentially affects expression of place and response learning. *Neurobiology of Learning and Memory, 65*(1), 65–72.

Paradis, M. (1994). Neurolinguistic aspects of implicit and explicit memory: Implications for bilingualism and SLA. In N. C. Ellis (Ed.), *Implicit and explicit learning of languages* (pp. 393–419). New York: Academic Press.

Paradis, M. (1995). Introduction: The need for distinctions. In M. Paradis (Ed.), *Aspects of bilingual aphasia* (Vol. 3, pp. 1–9). Oxford, UK: Pergamon.

Paradis, M. (1997). The cognitive neuropsychology of bilingualism. In A. M. B. de Groot & J. F. Kroll (Eds.), *Tutorials in bilingualism: Psycholinguistic perspectives* (pp. 331–354). Mahwah, NJ: Lawrence Erlbaum.

Paradis, M. (1999). *Neuroimaging studies of the bilingual brain: Some words of caution.* Paper presented at the 25th Lacus Forum, University of Alberta, Edmonton, Canada.

Paradis, M. (2004). *A neurolinguistic theory of bilingualism.* Amsterdam: John Benjamins.

Park, D. C., Lautenschlager, G., Hedden, T., Davidson, N., Smith, A. D., & Smith, P. (2002). Models of visuospatial and verbal memory across the adult life span. *Psychology and Aging, 16,* 299–320.

Patkowski, M. S. (1980). The sensitive period for the acquisition of syntax in a second language. *Language Learning, 30*(2), 449–472.

Perani, D., Dehaene, S., Grassi, F., Cohen, L., Cappa, S. F., Dupoux, E., et al. (1996). Brain processing of native and foreign languages. *Neuroreport, 7*(15–17), 2439–2444.

Perani, D., Paulesu, E., Galles, N. S., Dupoux, E., Dehaene, S., Bettinardi, V., et al. (1998). The bilingual brain. Proficiency and age of acquisition of the second language. *Brain, 121*(10), 1841–1852.

Phakiti, A. (2003). A closer look at gender and strategy use in L2 reading. *Language Learning, 53*(4), 649–702.

Phillips, S. M., & Sherwin, B. B. (1992). Effects of estrogen on memory function in surgically menopausal women. *Psychoneuroendocrinology, 17*(5), 485–495.

Pillai, J. J., Araque, J. M., Allison, J. D., Suthuraman, S., Loring, D. W., Thiruvaiy, D., et al. (2003). Functional MRI study of semantic and phonological language processing in bilingual subjects: Preliminary findings. *NeuroImage, 19,* 565–576.

Pinker, S. (1994). *The language instinct.* New York: William Morrow.

Pinker, S. (1999). *Words and rules: The ingredients of language.* New York: Basic Books.

Pinker, S., & Ullman, M. T. (2002). The past and future of the past tense. *Trends in Cognitive Sciences, 6*(11), 456–463.

Poldrack, R. A., & Packard, M. G. (2003). Competition among multiple memory systems: Converging evidence from animal and human brain studies. *Neuropsychologia, 41*(3), 245–251.

Poldrack, R. A., Clark, J., Pare-Blagoev, E. J., Shohamy, D., Moyano, J. C., Myers, C., et al. (2001). Interactive memory systems in the human brain. *Nature, 414,* 546–550.

Poldrack, R. A., Prabhakaran, V., Seger, C. A., & Gabrieli, J. D. (1999). Striatal activation during acquisition of a cognitive skill. *Neuropsychology, 13*(4), 564–574.

Poldrack, R. A., Wagner, A. D., Prull, M. W., Desmond, J. E., Glover, G. H., & Gabrieli, J. D. (1999). Functional specialization for semantic and phonological processing in the left inferior prefrontal cortex. *NeuroImage, 10*(1), 15–35.

Prasada, S., & Pinker, S. (1993). Generalization of regular and irregular morphological patterns. *Language and Cognitive Processes, 8*(1), 1–56.

Prull, M. W., Gabrieli, J. D. E., & Bunge, S. A. (2000). Age-related changes in memory: A cognitive neuroscience perspective. In F. I. M. Craik & T. A. Salthouse (Eds.), *The handbook of aging and cognition* (2nd ed.). Mahwah, NJ: Lawrence Erlbaum.

Rizzolatti, G., Fogassi, L., & Gallese, V. (2000). Cortical mechanisms subserving object grasping and action recognition: A new view on the cortical motor functions. In M. S. Gazzaniga (Ed.), *The new cognitive neurosciences* (pp. 539–552). Cambridge, MA: MIT Press.

Rizzolatti, G., Fogassi, L., & Gallese, V. (2001). Neurophysiological mechanisms underlying the understanding and imitation of action. *Nature Review Neuroscience, 2*(9), 661–670.

Rohde, D. L., & Plaut, D. C. (1999). Language acquisition in the absence of explicit negative evidence: How important is starting small? *Cognition, 72*(1), 67–109.

Rumelhart, D. E., & McClelland, J. L. (1986). On learning the past tenses of English verbs. In J. L. McClelland, D. E. Rumelhart, & PDP Research Group (Eds.), *Parallel distributed processing: Explorations in the microstructures of cognition* (Vol. 2, pp. 216–271). Cambridge, MA: MIT Press.

Saint-Cyr, J. A., Taylor, A. E., & Lang, A. E. (1988). Procedural learning and neostriatal dysfunction in man. *Brain, 111*(4), 941–959.

Scarcella, R., & Zimmerman, A. (1998). Academic words and gender: ESL student performance on a test of academic lexicon. *Studies in Second Language Acquisition, 20,* 27–49.

Schacter, D. L., & Tulving, E. (Eds.). (1994). *Memory systems 1994.* Cambridge, MA: MIT Press.

Schlaug, G. (2001). The brain of musicians: A model for functional and structural adaptation. *Annals of the New York Academy of Sciences, 930*(1), 281–299.

Schluter, N. D., Krams, M., Rushworth, M. F. S., & Passingham, R. E. (2001). Cerebral dominance for action in the human brain: The selection of actions. *Neuropsychologia, 39*(2), 105–113.

Schmidt, R. (1994). Implicit learning and the cognitive unconscious: Of artificial grammars and SLA. In N. C. Ellis (Ed.), *Implicit and explicit learning of languages* (pp. 165–209). New York: Academic Press.

Schroeder, J. A., Wingard, J., & Packard, M. G. (2002). Post-training reversible inactivation of the dorsal hippocampus reveals interference between multiple memory systems. *Hippocampus, 12,* 280–284.

Seidenberg, M. S. (1997). Language acquisition and use: Learning and applying probabilistic constraints. *Science, 275,* 1599–1603.

Sherman, B. M., West, J. H., & Korenman, S. G. (1976). The menopausal tradition: Analysis of LH, FSH, estradiol, and progesterone concentrations during menstrual cycles of older women. *Journal of Clinical Endocrinology and Metabolism, 42,* 629–636.

Sherwin, B. B. (1988). Estrogen and/or androgen replacement therapy and cognitive functioning in surgically menopausal women. *Psychoneuroendocrinology, 13*(4), 345–357.

Sherwin, B. B. (1998). Estrogen and cognitive functioning in women. *Proceedings of the Society for Experimental Biology and Medicine, 217*(1), 17–22.

Shughrue, P. J., Scrimo, P. J., & Merchenthaler, I. (2000). Estrogen binding and estrogen receptor characterization (ERalpha and ERbeta) in the cholinergic neurons of the rat basal forebrain. *Neuroscience, 96*(1), 41–49.

Siegler, R. S. (Ed.). (1978). *Children's thinking: What develops?* Mahwah, NJ: Lawrence Erlbaum.

Simos, P. G., Basile, L. F. H., & Papanicolaou, A. C. (1997). Source localization of the N400 response in a sentence-reading paradigm using evoked magnetic fields and magnetic resonance imaging. *Brain Research, 762*(1–2), 29–39.

Sorensen, K., & Witter, M. (1983). Entorhinal efferents reach the caudato-putamen. *Neuroscience Letters, 35*(3), 259–264.

Spurling, S., & Ilyin, D. (1985). The impact of learner variables on language test performance. *TESOL Quarterly, 19,* 283–301.

Squire, L. R., & Knowlton, B. J. (1995). Memory, hippocampus, and brain systems. In M. S. Gazzaniga (Ed.), *The cognitive neurosciences* (pp. 825–837). Cambridge, MA: MIT Press.

Squire, L. R., & Knowlton, B. J. (2000). The medial temporal lobe, the hippocampus, and the memory systems of the brain. In M. S. Gazzaniga (Ed.), *The new cognitive neurosciences* (pp. 765–780). Cambridge, MA: MIT Press.

Squire, L. R., & Zola, S. M. (1996). Structure and function of declarative and nondeclarative memory systems. *Proceedings of the National Academy of Sciences of the United States of America, 93,* 13515–13522.

Stromswold, K., Caplan, D., Alpert, N., & Rauch, S. (1996). Localization of syntactic comprehension by positron emission tomography. *Brain and Language, 52,* 452–473.

Suzuki, W. A., & Amaral, D. G. (1994). Perirhinal and parahippocampal cortices of the macaque monkey: Cortical afferants. *Journal of Comparative Neurology, 350*(4), 497–533.

Thompson-Schill, S. L., D'Esposito, M., Aguirre, G. K., & Farah, M. J. (1997). Role of left inferior prefrontal cortex in retrieval of semantic knowledge: A reevaluation.

Proceedings of the National Academy of Sciences of the United States of America, 94(26), 14792–14797.

Ullman, M. T. (2001a). The declarative/procedural model of lexicon and grammar. *Journal of Psycholinguistic Research, 30*(1), 37–69.

Ullman, M. T. (2001b). The neural basis of lexicon and grammar in first and second language: The declarative/procedural model. *Bilingualism: Language and Cognition, 4*(1), 105–122.

Ullman, M. T. (2001c). A neurocognitive perspective on language: The declarative/procedural model. *Nature Reviews Neuroscience, 2,* 717–726.

Ullman, M. T. (2004). Contributions of memory circuits to language: The declarative/procedural model. *Cognition, 92*(1–2), 231–270.

Ullman, M. T., Corkin, S., Coppola, M., Hickok, G., Growdon, J. H., Koroshetz, W. J., et al. (1997). A neural dissociation within language: Evidence that the mental dictionary is part of declarative memory, and that grammatical rules are processed by the procedural system. *Journal of Cognitive Neuroscience, 9*(2), 266–276.

Ullman, M. T., Estabrooke, I. V., Steinhauer, K., Brovetto, C., Pancheva, R., Ozawa, K., et al. (2002). Sex differences in the neurocognition of language. *Brain and Language, 83,* 141–143.

Ullman, M. T., Izvorski, R., Love, T., Yee, E., Swinney, D., & Hickok, G. (2005). Neural correlates of lexicon and grammar: Evidence from the production, reading, and judgment of inflection in aphasia. *Brain and Language, 93*(2), 185–238.

Ullman, M. T., & Pierpont, E. I. (2005). Specific Language Impairment is not specific to language: The procedural deficit hypothesis. *Cortex, 41,* 399–433.

Van Wuijtswinkel, K. (1994). *Critical period effects on the acquisition of grammatical competence in a second language.* Unpublished BA thesis, Katholieke Universiteit, Nijmegen, The Netherlands.

Wagner, A. D., Schacter, D. L., Rotte, M., Koutstaal, W., Maril, A., Dale, A. M., et al. (1998). Building memories: Remembering and forgetting of verbal experiences as predicted by brain activity. *Science, 281*(5380), 1188–1191.

Walton, K. D., Lieberman, D., Llinas, A., Begin, M., & Llinas, R. R. (1992). Identification of a critical period for motor development in neonatal rats. *Neuroscience, 51*(4), 763–767.

Wartenburger, I., Heekeren, H. R., Abutalebi, J., Cappa, S. F., Villringer, A., & Perani, D. (2003). Early setting of grammatical processing in the bilingual brain. *Neuron, 37,* 159–170.

Weber-Fox, C. M., & Neville, H. J. (1996). Maturational constraints on functional specializations for language processing: ERP and behavioral evidence in bilingual speakers. *Journal of Cognitive Neuroscience, 8*(3), 231–256.

Wen, Q., & Johnson, R. K. (1997). L2 learner variables and English achievements: A study of tertiary-level English majors in China. *Applied Linguistics, 18,* 27–48.

White, L., & Genesee, F. (1996). How native is near-native? The issue of ultimate attainment in adult second language acquisition. *Second Language Research, 12*(3), 233–265.

Willingham, D. B. (1998). A neuropsychological theory of motor skill learning. *Psychological Review, 105*(3), 558–584.

Wilson, J. D., Foster, D. W., Kronenberg, H. M., & Larsen, P. R. (Eds.). (1998). *Williams textbook of endocrinology* (9th ed.). Philadelphia: W. B. Saunders.

Wolansky, M. J., Cabrera, R. J., Ibarra, G. R., Mongiat, L., & Azcurra, J. M. (1999). Exogenous NGF alters a critical motor period in rat striatum. *Neuroreport, 10*(13), 2705–2709.

Woolley, C. S., & Schwartzkroin, P. A. (1998). Hormonal effects on the brain. *Epilepsia, 39*(8), S2–8.

SIX

Attention and Awareness in SLA

RONALD P. LEOW
MELISSA A. BOWLES

KEY WORDS
Attention ▪ awareness ▪ detection ▪ limited capacity processor ▪ noticing ▪ operationalization ▪ verbal reports.

1. Introduction

The 1990s witnessed several major theoretical approaches to the roles of attention and awareness in second or foreign language (L2) learning, mainly in the formal classroom setting (e.g., Robinson, 1995b; Schmidt, 1990, 1993, 1994, 1995, 2001; Tomlin and Villa, 1994). This chapter presents first a brief report of major models of attention in cognitive psychology, followed by a concise review of the important tenets of the major attentional frameworks in second language acquisition (SLA). We then discuss methodological issues associated with the operationalization and measurement of attention and awareness in SLA research methodology, followed by a brief report of several studies that have employed verbal reports to operationalize the constructs of attention and awareness before statistically addressing the effects of attention and awareness on classroom L2 development.

2. Theoretical Models of Attention

Almost all theories of SLA posit some role for attention, but the construct is especially emphasized in cognitivist accounts, where it has been proposed that "attention appears necessary for understanding nearly every aspect of second and foreign language learning" (Schmidt, 2001, p. 6). This view is based in large part on a long-standing and empirically supported position in cognitive psychology that maintains that attention to stimuli is needed for long-term memory storage and that little, if any, learning can take place without attention (Carlson and Dulany, 1985; Carr and Curran, 1994; Nissen and Bullemer, 1987; Posner, 1992; Reber, 1967, 1976, 1989, 1993). A number of theoretical models and hypotheses have been postulated about the specific underpinnings of attention. First, the major models from cognitive psychology will be reviewed, followed by those that have been proposed specifically for SLA.

2.1. MODELS FROM COGNITIVE PSYCHOLOGY

In the classic cognitive psychology literature on attention, the common view was that human attention is of limited capacity by nature and that humans are limited capacity processors (e.g., Broadbent, 1958; Kahneman, 1973). Because this view held that there is a limited supply of attention, it further maintained that attention must be selective. There was disagreement over the exact nature of that selectivity, however. Filter theories of attention proposed that there is a sort of filter or bottleneck that allows only some stimuli to be processed (Broadbent, 1958). This was an "early selection" model, since stimuli are either selected or not early in the process (they are either allowed through the bottleneck or not). This view furthermore held that information is processed serially, in such a way that attention to one message blocked attention to another. Later research (especially dichotic listening studies) led researchers to propose an alternative theory that all information in the input stream is processed in parallel and that selection of what will be attended to happens late. This was a "late selection" model (Deutsch and Deutsch, 1963).

Both the early and the late selection models just discussed share the common view that the human processor is a passive recipient of information. However, more recent models have stressed a more active role for information processors. For instance, Kahneman (1973) proposes that attentional allocation is effortful and although attention is a limited resource, it can vary as a function of arousal. That is, for Kahneman, two tasks can be performed simultaneously as long as there is sufficient arousal and task demands are not too high.

Similar to Kahneman, Wickens (1980, 1984, 1989) assumes that the allocation of attention is effortful. However, his model proposes that there are multiple pools of attentional resources rather than a single pool. Wickens contends that the difficulty of performing two tasks simultaneously depends on whether the necessary attentional resources are being drawn from the same pool (serial processing) or from different pools (parallel processing). According to Wickens, it would be more difficult to perform two tasks drawn from the same pool (e.g., talking to someone and writing an essay) than to perform two tasks drawn from different pools (e.g., driving a car and listening to the radio). He posits that two tasks drawn from the same pool of resources can be performed simultaneously only when one of the tasks has become automatized.[1]

In contrast to the limited capacity theories discussed up to this point, some recent attentional theories contend that human attentional resource capacity is in fact unlimited (Neumann, 1996; Robinson, 2003). These "interference models" maintain that attentional capacity is not at issue but rather that limits on task performance are the result of reduced attention control. "Attention control is constrained to a decision to engage, disengage, and shift attention between tasks and the pursuit of intentions. In interference models the only limited resource is time and its derived scheduling constraints" (Gopher, 1992, as cited in DeKeyser, Salaberry, Robinson, and Harrington, 2002, p. 808).

However, this unlimited capacity interference model has yet to be empirically supported in SLA. On the other hand, the limited capacity models discussed earlier have provided a foundation for theoretical models of attention in SLA, and subsequently such models have been empirically supported. Next, a review of the three major models or hypotheses of attention in SLA is presented.

2.2. MODELS IN SLA

Drawing on the work of Posner (1992), Tomlin and Villa (1994) propose a functionally based, fine-grained analysis of attention. In their model, attention has three components (all of which have neurological correlates): (a) alertness (an overall readiness to deal with incoming stimuli), (b) orientation (the direction of attentional resources to a certain type of stimuli), and (c) detection (the cognitive registration of stimuli). According to Tomlin and Villa, it is detection alone that is necessary for further processing of input and subsequent learning to take place. The other two components can enhance the chances that detection will occur, but neither is necessary. Crucial to understanding Tomlin and Villa's claims is that in their model, detection does not imply awareness. Recently the utility of Tomlin and Villa's model has been questioned, with Schmidt (2001) remarking, ". . . it is self-evidently true that some aspect of language that is not registered in any sense will not lead to learning" (p. 25). That is, Tomlin and Villa's model may be too general to be of use.

In contrast to Tomlin and Villa's (1994) view that awareness is not necessary for learning, the most widely accepted view in SLA is that without awareness, input can be processed only in short-term memory and therefore cannot be deeply processed for learning to occur. According to Schmidt's (1990, 1993, 1994, 1995, 2001) *noticing hypothesis,* attention controls access to awareness and is responsible for noticing, which he says is "the necessary and sufficient condition for the conversion of input into intake" (Schmidt, 1993, p. 209). He views attention as being isomorphic with awareness and rejects the idea of learning without awareness. Awareness, according to Allport (1988), is demonstrated through (a) some resulting behavioral or cognitive change, (b) a report of the experience, or (c) metalinguistic description of an underlying rule. Furthermore, Schmidt proposes that in addition to noticing, there is another, higher level of awareness, which he refers to as awareness at the level of understanding. This level of awareness is marked by the ability to analyze, compare, and test hypotheses, and Schmidt believes that this level of awareness leads to deeper learning marked by restructuring and system learning, whereas awareness at the level of noticing leads to mere intake. Support for the differential effects of levels of awareness on L2 development has been found in a number of SLA studies (e.g., Bowles, 2003; Leow, 1997a, 2001a; Rosa and Leow, 2004a; Rosa and O'Neill, 1999). And although such studies have found support for the beneficial effects of noticing, Schmidt's claim that it is necessary and sufficient for learning may never be proven. As he himself indicates, the difficulty in demonstrating a complete lack of awareness (which would be needed to falsify his claims) may make his model unfalsifiable (Schmidt, 2001).

A third model of attention proposed in SLA is that of Robinson (1995b, 1996a). Robinson's model reconciles Tomlin and Villa's (1994) notion of detection (which does not involve awareness) and Schmidt's (1990, and elsewhere) notion of noticing. Robinson constructs a model in which detection is one early stage in the process, sequentially prior to noticing. Noticing, in Robinson's model, is "detection plus rehearsal in short-term memory, prior to encoding in long-term memory" (Robinson, 1995b, p. 296). To Robinson, noticing does involve awareness, as in Schmidt's model, and it is crucial for learning to take place. That is, Robinson simultaneously supports Tomlin and Villa's notion of detection, simply relegating it to an earlier stage in the learning process, and Schmidt's noticing hypothesis, which he places at a later stage.

More recently, two less developed models have appeared in SLA research. First, Simard and Wong (2001) propose a vaguely defined model of attention even more fine-grained than that of Tomlin and Villa (1994). Although they are not explicit about its details, they recommend "a model of attention that more accurately reflects the complex nature of SLA . . . in which awareness and attentional functions are viewed as being present in graded amounts and whose degree of activation is influenced by the interactions among task type, linguistic items, individual differences, . . . and by any other concurrent cognitive activity competing for processing resources" (Simard and Wong, 2001, p. 119). Second, Robinson (2003) has proposed that the unlimited capacity interference model of attention in cognitive psychology be transferred to SLA. Again, however, this model will need substantial elaboration and empirical support before it can be afforded the status of the limited capacity models (and especially that of the noticing hypothesis, which is backed by substantial empirical evidence in SLA).

3. Awareness and Learning

As can be seen from the different theoretical models of attention, the facilitative role of attention in L2 development is generally accepted, but the role of awareness is not without debate. Specifically, Schmidt's noticing hypothesis and Robinson's model of the relationship between attention and memory posit a crucial role for awareness, whereas Tomlin and Villa's functional model of input processing does not. But what is awareness and how has it been defined in SLA? Awareness is defined as "a particular state of mind in which an individual has undergone a specific subjective experience of some cognitive content or external stimulus" (Tomlin and Villa, 1994, p. 193). So attentional resources may be allocated to a specific linguistic item in the input, but whether learner awareness is required for the grammatical information to be processed by the learner is open to debate. Several researchers have supported a dissociation between learning and awareness (e.g., Carr and Curran, 1994; Curran and Keele, 1994; Hardcastle, 1993; Tomlin and Villa, 1994; Velmans, 1991) while others have rejected this dissociation (Robinson, 1995b; Schmidt, 1990, and elsewhere).

3.1. MEASUREMENT OF AWARENESS: METHODOLOGICAL ISSUES

The operationalization and measurement of what constitutes awareness in SLA is methodologically thorny (see Leow, 1997a, 2001a, for a review of relevant studies). Until recently, most SLA studies have followed a traditional pretest-posttest design, with no operationalization or measurement of attention or awareness. Instead, posttest scores were used to hypothesize about whether the given treatment had indeed led to increased attention to or potential awareness of the targeted item in the L2 data.

Since the late 1980s, however, a number of measures of awareness have been employed in SLA studies conducted in an attentional framework, including off-line questionnaires (Alanen, 1995; Izumi, 1999; Mackey, Philp, Egi, Fujii, and Tatsumi, 2002; Robinson, 1995a, 1996b, 1997a, 1997b), off-line uptake recall charts (Slimani, 1989), on-line uptake charts (Mackey, McDonough, Fujii, and Tatsumi, 2001), free recall of input (Greenslade, Bouden, and Sanz, 1999; VanPatten, 1990), and learning diaries (Altman, 1997; Grabe and Stoller, 1997; Schmidt and Frota, 1986; Warden, Lapkin, Swain, and Hart, 1995). In addition, in some studies students were prompted to take notes while reading an L2 text (Izumi, 1999, 2002) or to underline, circle, or check targeted linguistic structures in written text (Fotos, 1993; Greenslade et al., 1999; Izumi and Bigelow, 2000; Izumi, Bigelow, Fujiwara, and Fearnow, 1999).

Additionally, a line of research has used verbal reports to measure attention and awareness during exposure to L2 input. According to Schmidt (2001), "the clearest evidence that something has exceeded the subjective threshold and been consciously perceived or noticed is concurrent verbal report" (p. 20). We next present a description of verbal reports and a discussion of the issues surrounding their use.

3.1.1. VERBAL REPORTS IN DATA COLLECTION: MEASURING AWARENESS

Verbal reports are one type of introspective method used to elicit data about the thought processes involved in carrying out a task. Verbal reports, simply stated, are verbalizations a subject makes either while carrying out a task or a short time after completing the task.

In their seminal work, Ericsson and Simon (1984, 1993) categorize verbal protocols as either concurrent or retrospective, based on the temporal frame in which the reports are collected. Concurrent protocols are those collected as subjects verbalize while performing the task in question, whereas retrospective protocols are collected when subjects verbalize some time after performing the task. Ericsson and Simon advise that concurrent protocols be collected whenever possible "to avoid [the] problem of accessing information at two different times—first during the actual cognitive processing and then at the time of report" (Ericsson and Simon, 1993, p. xiii).

In addition to categorizing verbal protocols in terms of temporal space, Ericsson and Simon also distinguish between protocols in which subjects verbalize their thoughts freely and those in which subjects verbalize specific information, such as reasons and justifications. Free verbalizations of thoughts are referred to as nonmetalinguistic and those requiring verbalization of additional specific information are referred to as metalinguistic.

Two major issues surrounding the validity of verbal reports surface from this typology. One is veridicality—that is, whether the information in verbal reports accurately represents the thought process it is designed to capture. Some evidence for nonveridicality has been found for retrospective protocols, which can "yield substantial forgetting or fabrication in all tasks" (Russo, Johnson, and Stephens, 1989, p. 759). Concurrent protocols, on the other hand, do not bear the same critique of memory decay, since they are collected during the task. The second issue is reactivity—that is, whether the act of thinking aloud alters the end state of the cognitive process (the accuracy of task performance). Ericsson and Simon's model predicts that requiring subjects to verbalize additional specific information (metalinguistic verbalization) could alter subjects' thought processes and therefore potentially have reactive effects on task performance. However, they caution that if such justifications are "generated as part of the normal process of solution," then such verbalization should not have an effect on task performance (Ericsson and Simon, 1993, p. xxxiii).

Verbal reports have been used for decades in first language (L1) research and other fields. In L1 research, verbal reports have been used extensively, primarily in research on reading and writing. A number of studies have used think-aloud protocols to probe students' reading strategies (e.g., Cohen, 1986, 1987; Earthman, 1992; Folger, 2001; Gordon, 1990) and some have even used verbalization as a technique to compare reading strategies (e.g., Fehrenbach, 1991; McGuire and Yewchuk, 1996). In L1 writing research, verbal protocols have been widely used to investigate the writing process. Studies comparing the cognitive processes involved in writing different kinds of texts (Durst, 1987) and investigating the process of revision and editing (e.g., Breetvelt, 1994; Zellermayer and Cohen, 1996) have been conducted using think-aloud protocols. In recent years, verbal protocols have also been applied to language testing. For a review of verbal protocol methodology in language testing, see Green (1998).

Introspective methods, including verbal reports, have also been used extensively as a data elicitation technique in L2 research. Since SLA was first studied systematically in the early 1970s, there has been some debate over their use, with researchers like Selinker (1972) indicating that researchers should focus analytical attention only on observable data, ". . . the utterances which are produced when a learner attempts to say sentences of a TL [target language]" (p. 213–214). That is, in Selinker's view, only learners' production data should be used in formulating theories and conducting research about SLA. However others, such as Corder (1973), have disagreed with this view, arguing that production data from language learners provides only a small piece of evidence for the language-learning puzzle.

Because verbal reports have the advantage of providing insight into learners' cognitive processes, they have been used in a number of fields in L2 research, ranging from L2 reading and writing (e.g., Cavalcanti and Cohen, 1990; Cohen, 1987; Cohen and Cavalcanti, 1987; Hosenfeld, 1976, 1977, 1979, 1984), comparisons between L1 and L2 strategies (e.g., Chamot and El Dinary, 1999; Davis and Bistodeau, 1993; Nevo, 1989; Yamashita, 2002), L2 test-taking strategies (e.g., Cohen, 2000; Norris, 1992; Warren, 1996), translation (e.g., Enkvist, 1995; Færch and Kasper, 1986; Jaaskelainen, 2000; Kern, 1994), interlanguage pragmatics (e.g., Cohen and Hosenfeld, 1981; Kasper and Blum-Kulka, 1993), and oral interaction research (e.g., Mackey, Gass, and McDonough, 2000; Nabei and Swain, 2002; Philp, 2003), to L2 attention and awareness studies (e.g., Leow, 1997b, 1998a, 1998b, 1999, 2000, 2001a, 2001b; Rosa and Leow, 2004a, 2004b; Rosa and O'Neill, 1999).

Verbal reports have been used as a data elicitation technique in SLA attentional research (studies premised on the role of attention in L2 acquisition) for less than a decade; the first published mention of them occurred in

Alanen (1995), who combined concurrent verbal reports with two other off-line data collection measurements to address the role of noticing in her study. Recently several empirical studies premised on the role of attention in L2 development have begun to employ concurrent verbal reports (e.g., on-line think alouds in Leow, 1997a, 1998a, 1998b, 2000, 2001a, 2001b; Rosa and Leow, 2004a, 2004b; Rosa and O'Neill, 1999) or retrospective verbal reports (e.g., stimulated recalls in Mackey et al., 2000) to gather data on learners' cognitive processes while they interacted with the L2 data. These data were then used to first establish the role of attention or awareness in L2 processing during exposure to the L2 before investigating its effects on L2 development.

Despite the frequency with which verbal reports are gathered in language research, however, their use in SLA has been criticized by a number of sources on the grounds that the requirement to think aloud may be reactive; that is, that verbalization may alter the cognitive process (e.g., R. Ellis, 2001; Jourdenais, 2001; Nisbett and Wilson, 1977; Payne, Braunstein, and Carroll, 1978). The use of verbal reports has been harshly criticized by some who believe that verbalization of thoughts during language tasks imposes an additional processing load on the subjects and is therefore not a pure measure of their thoughts. For instance, Jourdenais (2001) cautions that "the think aloud data collection method itself acts as an additional task which must be considered carefully when examining learner performance" (p. 373). These claims are based largely on anecdotal evidence, however.

3.1.2. INVESTIGATIONS INTO THE REACTIVITY OF VERBAL REPORTS

Research on the effects of verbal reports on problem-solving and decision-making tasks has been conducted in the field of cognitive psychology since at least the 1950s. A synthesis of dozens of studies in cognitive psychology investigating the reactivity of nonmetalinguistic verbal reports indicates that such verbalizations do not seem to influence cognitive processes when compared to silent control groups (Ericsson, 2002). This finding of nonreactivity suggests that nonmetalinguistic verbalization may be a valid method of capturing internal thought processes. With regard to metalinguistic verbalization, an early review of studies (Ericsson and Simon, 1993), found mixed results with regard to reactivity.

In addition, to date there have been two studies (Bowles and Leow, 2005; Leow and Morgan-Short, 2004) that have investigated the reactivity of verbal protocols during L2 reading. Leow and Morgan-Short (2004) found that compared to a silent control group, concurrent nonmetalinguistic verbal reports were not reactive. Expanding on Leow and Morgan-Short (2004), Bowles and Leow (2005) sought to investigate the reactivity of both metalinguistic and nonmetalinguistic protocols. Similar to Leow and Morgan-Short (2004), results indicated that compared to a control group, nonmetalinguistic verbalization did not significantly affect either comprehension or written production of the targeted form. However, metalinguistic verbalization caused a significant decrement in text comprehension but no significant difference for production when compared to either the control or to the nonmetalinguistic group. Furthermore, results indicated that both verbalization groups took significantly more time to read the text and complete the postassessment tasks than the control group and found no significant difference between the nonmetalinguistic and metalinguistic groups in terms of latency.

4. Empirical Research on the Role of Attention (Noticing) in L2 Development

Empirical studies whose results suggest a dissociation between awareness and learning (e.g., Curran and Keele, 1994; Marcel, 1983; Nissen and Bullemer, 1987) together with a few SLA studies (e.g., Alanen, 1995; Robinson, 1996b, 1997a, 1997b) have typically employed postexposure questionnaires or retrospective verbal reports to establish a relationship between learners' awareness during an experimental exposure to some stimuli and their performances after exposure to the stimuli. However, the validity of postexposure questionnaires or retrospective verbal reports is questionable due to the issue of veridicality, that is, the potential of memory decay or of participants providing erroneous information on what they actually became aware of during the exposure (see Leow, 1997a, 2000, 2001a for a discussion of these methodological concerns).

Empirical studies whose results suggest an association between awareness and learning (e.g., Leow, 1997a, 2000, 2001a; Rosa and Leow, 2004a; Rosa and O'Neill, 1999) have attempted to address the above mentioned methodological limitation by employing concurrent data elicitation procedures (e.g., nonmetalinguistic verbal reports) to gather data on whether learners became aware of targeted items in the input. In these studies, participants were asked to think aloud while performing the experimental task without providing an explanation behind the thoughts. In other words, the focus on the completion of the task was primary, while the verbal report was secondary. These think-aloud protocols were recorded for further coding as to whether they demonstrated instances of awareness of these targeted items.

4.1. AN EMPIRICAL STUDY OF TOMLIN AND VILLA'S FINE-GRAINED ANALYSIS OF ATTENTION

The fine-grained analysis of attention proposed by Tomlin and Villa (1994) was empirically tested by Leow (1998a). Leow concurred with Tomlin and Villa's critique that previous SLA research had not addressed the actual role attention played during exposure to the L2 data by pointing out the typical postexposure tasks employed by most SLA studies to operationalize attention (p. 134). The main purposes of the study were to (a) methodologically address the effects of attention in SLA and (b) empirically address the question of which attentional functions or mechanisms were crucial for intake and subsequent processing to take place *while* adult learners interacted with L2 data. To address (a), Leow employed concurrent data elicitation procedures to establish that attention had indeed been paid to the targeted linguistic items in the L2 data. Using a task-based approach at a morphological level to address (b), Leow designed four crossword puzzles to isolate the effects of each of Tomlin and Villa's attentional functions—alertness, orientation, and detection.

In this study, Leow hypothesized that based on Tomlin and Villa's model of input processing, participants who demonstrated detection of targeted forms would take in and produce in writing significantly more targeted forms than participants who did not demonstrate this cognitive registration. Likewise, participants who were alerted to the presence of the targeted forms but did not receive exposure to these targeted forms as expected would not perform as well as those who demonstrated detection. Detection was defined as "some form of cognitive registration of new, targeted grammatical forms as revealed by the learners' performances on a crossword puzzle and in the think-aloud protocols produced while completing this task" (p. 136). It was operationalized as "making a written or verbal correction of the targeted forms (e.g., the learner corrects himself or herself after detecting a mismatch between his or her answer and an answer provided by another clue) and/or commenting on the targeted linguistic forms (including such expression such as 'hmm,' 'I see,' 'OK,' 'interesting,' 'cool,' etc." (p. 136).

Eighty-three first-year students who were not formally exposed to the targeted forms (the irregular third-person singular and plural preterite forms of stem-changing *-ir* verbs in Spanish) participated in the study. They were randomly assigned to one of the following four conditions: [+ alertness, − orientation, − detection], [+ alertness, + orientation, − detection], [+ alertness, + orientation, + detection], [+ alertness, − orientation, + detection]. Leow operationalized alertness as instructions to the participants to complete the crossword puzzle. No knowledge of the targeted forms was required to successfully complete the puzzle. In other words, students could have completed the crossword following the regular verbal paradigm, although the final product would contain errors. To operationalize orientation, Leow added a sentence in boldface to the instructions informing participants that some of the verbs were irregular. To address the inhibitory effects of orientation (that is, orientation without detection), Leow provided participants with a choice of two clues (one correct, one incorrect) with their attention aligned on the incorrect clue. Finally, Leow operationalized detection by drawing learners' attention to the correct targeted form through the creation of a mismatch between the incorrect form and the correct one supplied by another clue known to the learners. For example, participants were encouraged to produce horizontally the (incorrect) regular form of the verb *morir* 'to die,' namely, *morió* 'he died.' However, this verbal form is irregular with a verb stem change, that is, *murió*. The *u* of *murió* came from another clue that was vertical: the *u* of *un* 'a, one' in Spanish, an item already known to these learners.

Leow's hypotheses were confirmed in this study. Results indicated that participants who detected the targeted forms were able to take in and produce in writing significantly more targeted forms than those who did not demonstrate this cognitive registration. This superior effect for detection was also found on the immediate posttest and two delayed posttests administered five and eight weeks after exposure (that is, after completion of the crossword puzzle). These findings lend empirical support for Tomlin and Villa's fine-grained analysis of attention at a morphological level without addressing the issue of the role of awareness at the level of detection.[2]

4.2. EMPIRICAL STUDIES SUPPORTING SCHMIDT'S NOTICING HYPOTHESIS

Subsequently, a number of empirical SLA studies have provided support for Schmidt's noticing hypothesis and specifically for the role of awareness and the differential effects of greater levels of awareness in SLA. Overall, these studies appear to provide empirical support for the facilitative effects of awareness on foreign language behavior and learning. More specifically, the main findings indicate first that awareness at the level of noticing and understanding contributed substantially to a significant increase in learners' ability to take in the targeted form or structure (Leow, 1997a, 2000, 2001a; Rosa and Leow, 2004a; Rosa and O'Neill, 1999) and to produce in writing the targeted form or structure (Leow, 1997a, 2001a; Rosa and Leow, 2004a), including novel exemplars (Rosa and Leow, 2004a). Second, awareness at the level of understanding led to significantly more intake when compared to awareness at the level of noticing (Leow, 1997a, 2001a; Rosa and Leow, 2004a; Rosa and O'Neill, 1999). Third, there was a correlation between awareness at the level of understanding and usage of hypothesis testing or rule formation (Leow, 1997a, 2000, 2001a; Rosa and Leow, 2004a; Rosa and O'Neill, 1999). Fourth, there were correlations between level of awareness and formal instruction and directions to search for rules, respectively (Rosa and O'Neill, 1999). Finally, there was a correlation between awareness at the level of understanding and learning conditions providing an explicit pretask (with grammatical explanation) as well as implicit or explicit concurrent feedback (Rosa and Leow, 2004a).

4.3. LEARNING WITHOUT AWARENESS?

Contrary to these research findings, one recent study (Williams, 2004) has found some limited evidence to support the claim that some language learning may occur without awareness. In Experiment 1 of the study, 37 participants were exposed to an artificial microlanguage (based on Italian) consisting of 8 determiners and 8 nouns. They went through a series of learning trials in which they first listened to each word presented aurally and then performed three tasks: repeating each word aloud, indicating whether each noun referred to a living or nonliving thing, and translating each noun to English. Then, during the test phase participants were presented an English phrase and had to choose between two alternate translations, one with a determiner of the correct animacy and one with the incorrect animacy. Participants were probed after the test phase to determine whether they were aware of the animacy relationship during the study; those who reported awareness were eliminated from the study. Participants who did not demonstrate awareness were found to perform significantly better than chance on the generalization test. However, participants in the study were from various L1 backgrounds, and subsequent analyses found that those who spoke gendered L1 languages performed significantly better than those who did not. Therefore, this study's findings should be interpreted with caution. Experiment 2, reported in the same article, used a different artificial microlanguage which was less similar to natural noun class systems. In this experiment, no evidence of implicit learning of form-meaning connections was found.

5. Summary

This chapter has presented a concise overview of the theoretical and methodological issues surrounding the roles of attention and awareness in adult L2 behavior and learning and provided a brief report of empirical studies that have employed verbal reports to investigate their roles in L2 development in the L2 classroom. The overall findings appear to indicate facilitative effects of attention and awareness on adult L2 learners' subsequent processing, intake, and learning of targeted L2 forms or structures embedded in the L2 data, providing empirical support for Schmidt's noticing hypothesis and the facilitative role of awareness in SLA.

In addition, this chapter has stressed that the role awareness plays in adult L2 development needs to be investigated further, although researchers should be aware of the methodological concerns inherent in both the operationalization and measurement of this slippery construct. While current research findings are indeed promising, more robust research designs are clearly needed to address the issue of L2 development premised on the role of attention or awareness, given the wide variety of variables that can potentially impact learners' processes while interacting with L2 data. The findings can only improve our understanding of the processes involved in language learning.

6. Exercises

This section provides practice in coding think-aloud protocols, establishing interrater reliability, and reporting your findings in relation to level of awareness and L2 learners' subsequent performances. In addition, you will perform a guided critique of a published empirical study in SLA by using a checklist of criteria for internal and external validity.

6.1 DATA ANALYSIS

Recent studies conducted within an attentional framework have begun to employ data elicitation procedures such as think-aloud protocols to gather on-line evidence of attention and awareness being deployed or present while interacting with the L2 input. Leow (1997a, 2001a) reported three levels of awareness based on Tomlin and Villa's (1994) restricted definition and Allport's (1988) criteria for the presence of awareness. In the Appendix, you will find three samples of think-aloud protocols that were gathered concurrently to establish that attention was paid to the targeted linguistic forms in the input (Spanish formal imperatives) before the effects of attention were statistically analyzed. In this exercise, you will be asked to do the following:

1. Use the criteria provided in Table 6.1 (based on Leow, 1997a) to broadly code the three think-aloud protocols in the Appendix into different levels of awareness.
2. Now pair up with another student and compare your codings. It is important to have information on interrater reliability to report when working with qualitative data that are subjectively coded and in order to have confidence in your codings. A simple formula to calculate the interrater reliability between two raters is to determine how many codings are similar and divide this number by the total number of codings. A relatively high reliability is usually over .90.[3]
3. The scores of three participants in the study are presented below:

	pretest		*immediate posttest*		*delayed posttest*	
Participant	*recognition*	*production*	*recognition*	*production*	*recognition*	*production*
1.	0	0	17	14	17	13
2.	0	0	0	0	1	0
3.	0	0	10	0	1	0

Based on these scores, what plausible conclusions can you come up with to relate level of awareness with the participants' subsequent performances on

TABLE 6.1
Samples of Levels of Awareness as Revealed by Think-Aloud Protocols

Particpant 1. Awareness at the level of understanding: + cognitive/behavioral change, + meta-awareness, + morphological rule

- 12 down is *sí* so the stem changes *e* to *i*, *corrigió* . . .
  - looks like all the *e*'s are becoming *i*'s in the stems . . .
    - 4 down (mumble) *tú* so *dormir* is irregular in the third person so that's gotta be *durmió* with a *u* . . .
      - mmm alright, the stems are changing, from *e* to *i* and ah *o* to *u* . . .

Particpant 2. Awareness at the level of reporting: + cognitive/behavioral change, + meta-awareness, − morphological rule

- and the verb to go is *ir* . . . oh cool, so that corrects number 24 across, *repitieron*, so you find out that's *ir* OK . . .
  - number 5 *ellos* of *pedir* . . . *pidieron* and it is good . . .
    - so 11 horizontal would no longer be *mentieron* and is now *mintieron*, so I have to remember that (changes *mentieron* to *mintieron*) . . .

Particpant 3. Awareness at the level of noticing: + cognitive/behavioral change, − meta-awareness, − morphological rule

- 1 down *divirtieron* . . .
  - third person plural *preferió*, *prefirió* . . .
    - 12 down opposite of *no* is *sí* (changes *corregió* to *corrigió*) . . .
      - to go *en español* 25 *ir* (changes *repetieron* to *repitieron*) . . .
        - 17 down, it's *tú* so it turns *se dormieron* to *se durmieron* . . .

(a) the immediate posttests (recognition and written production) and (b) the delayed posttests (recognition and written production)? Fill in your conclusions in the blanks below.

The Relationship between Level of Awareness and Postexposure Performances

	recognition	
	immediate posttest	*delayed posttest*
Participant 1	____________	____________
	____________	____________
Participant 2	____________	____________
	____________	____________
	____________	

Participant 3		

	production	
	immediate posttest	*delayed posttest*
Participant 1		
Participant 2		
Participant 3		

4. Finally, based on the data and plausible explanations above, what would you conclude in regard to the role of awareness in L2 development?

6.2. GUIDED CRITIQUE

Addressing the issues of internal and external validity of empirical studies is an important aspect of any review of relevant research literature. Using the lists of criteria provided in Leow (1999) for internal validity (Table 1, page 64) and external validity (Table 2, page 68), select one of the articles in the references of that article and conduct a checklist of the criteria fulfilled by the study. If you were to replicate the study, which limitations would you address, and how would you address them?

Appendix 6.A

Samples of concurrent think-aloud protocols of three participants; targeted linguistic forms: Spanish formal imperatives

1. Participant 1

Um, OK. Uh, preventative medicine. How to live a healthy life. First, you have to eat well. Um, cada día toma fruta y verduras. Each day eat fruit and vegetables, meat, and uh, pescado, I think that's, um, poultry. Uh, two or three eggs per week, milk or cheese, uh, for dairy food. Um, let's see. Haga y ponga, hmm. Well, ponga kind of looks like pongo which is, um, pon, or poner, ponerse which is able. So, um, and haga kind of looks like uh, kinda looks like uh, hacer or something. So you can list, uh, puerta. I thought that was door, but so you can list in door of nevera. Ok, I don't really know what that sentence means, so I'll put a little star by it or something. Um. I don't really recognize these verb forms either so I better circle any unknown verb forms so I'll circle haga and ponga, except I think ponga is, um, I think ponga might be a tú command. Anyway.

And, hmm. There is a time when adquiera zanahorias. Oh, zanahorias is, uh, I think it's carrots or something. Include other fruit, seco mejor que bollos . . . pan is bread. So include another fruit and some bread. Ok. Um. I don't recognize adquiera.

Um. Physical exercise is also inprescendible . . . probably important. Do not have to convert in, you do not have to convert into a great athlete. Simply suba y baja, simply something and something. Oh, you simply have to like walk the stairs or run the stairs in your casa. Um. I'm not doing to well on these verb forms. Let's see.

Know perfect. Ok. Know perfectamente. Oh you know your preference(?) or something. Know when the habits. When your habits. Hmm. Are habits, then, peligrosos. Isn't that dangerous? But others are not obvious. For example, if it is necessary to work hasta altas horas, if it is necessary to work other hours of the night or to go with your friends in the night, duerma is sleep. Oh, wait, no, I do recognize those verb forms from above. Pon, hmm, well. No, wait, well, whatever. Duerma, I recognize that. Duerma. Um, sleep without interuption for seven or eight hours for organismo, for an organism, pueda, for an organism to recuperate. Ok. So, it's necessary to sleep seven or eight hours for an organism to recuperate. Other habits. Ok, so, so far: physical exercise, food, sleep are important. Other habits, important, have, for you to have or whatever. Um, to go with seguridad, I forget what that means. Use casco if, if, go in a motor or a bicycle. Um, always descansada y, oh, listen to music. Oh no, wait, sin música, isn't that without music? Yeah. Ok. Um, conduzca and use.

Whew! Ok. Puede. You can, um, you are able to evitar muchos, evitar muchos enfermadades. Ok. On occasion, exist in the families antecedentes de enfermedades a las que Ud. puede tener propensión. Um. Ask um, ask your. Ok. Ask the older, elders in your family the hist, the clinical history and discuss the history with, uh, your doctor. Um. Ok. Ok, so. Food, exercise, sleep. Um. Music. And now we gotta find out your history and . . . Obtenga. I think that's obtain. Obtain a biannual check, um. Ok. So go to your doctor, basically and ask your relatives stuff. Um.

Y desde luego evite. Pregunte, pregunte is ask. Ask, discuss. Ok. After, evite. I don't know what that is. Uh. The situations of risk. Siga la calendar of vaccination. No viaje other zones of the world without taking the precautions, vaccination if it is necessary. Drink mineral water and no coma nada en el calle. Ok. I think all these verbs are tú commands but I think that they're the ones that we haven't learned yet 'cause I know that you have to change the last letter for, for like if you're just saying, like for beber you say like beba and that's one of 'em. So yeah. Um.

2. Participant 2

To um, a good life, must be to eat well each day and take in fruits and vegetables, uh, fish or shrimp, two or three eggs por a week, milk or cheese, dairy, diet. Haga y ponga. Make, do, and place a list en la puerta de la nevera. Don't know puerta or nevera. De vez en, once in a while, adquiera, um, add carrots or include some fruit. Major, um, rolls or bread.

Also, um, imprescen, is essential. ? You not have to ? in one grand, simply suba y baje las escaleras de la, de su casa. Suba, no. Baje, escaleras. Ok, it doesn't mean you have to go to an athletic facility, you just have to go, do it in your house. Um, ? habits which, those habits which are dangerous, but others which are not as obvious. For example, if it is necessary to work for hours of the night or to go out with your friends at night, sleep without interruption for seven to eight hours a day. Um, puedo recuperarse. In order that you are something, able to recover your body.

Other habits are important to have, to see, other important habits have to see with your security, securidad. Use casco, use caution if you go on a motorbike or you dri . . . , when you descanada, if you drive, uh, if you're always driving and especially without music. Hmm.

Um, you are able to avoid many sicknesses, and, on occasions exist in your families antecedentes, antece, before uh sicknesses, like a bug, to the which you are able to have propension, proportion, ask the elders in your family the clinical history and discuss this history with your doctor. Um. capicara? do not know that word and this ? Obtain a check—a check—go to the doctor twice a year. Uh, annual, once a year, oh twice a year. And once a month when you're thirty-five to forty. Um.

And desde, when you ? situations of risk, um, siga los calendarios, oh, make a calendar for vacations and don't go to places of the world where there are basic precautions unless you vaccinate. If necessary drink, dri, mineral water and don't eat en el calle.

3. Participant 3

Sí. Primero, tiene un, que comer bien. Cada día tome fruta y verduras, carne o pescado, dos o tres huevos por semana y leche o queso al diario. Cada día tome fruta y verduras. Sí. Haga y ponga un lista en la puerta de nue. Ok. So you have to eat fruits and vegetables, meat and fish, two or three eggs for the week, leche and queso. Um. Place a list in the door. Hmm. Make and place a list in the door, oh in the door to, so that you know what you're doing.

De vez en cuando adquería. Let's see. Hm. I'm not sure about adquería zanahorias. Ok. Include another fruit. So you have to sn, you can snack from time to time on carrots and on some bread. Um. And then it talks about exercise. Um. You don't have to be a good athlete. You simply have to move around to get some exercise.

The second paragraph. You know perfectly da, da, da, uh the dange, uh, you know your habits can be dangerous, I guess if you're not um healthy.

Um. Right, they're obvious. If you work many hours during the night, it's not healthy. If you go out with your friends and don't sleep more than seven or eight hours a day, uh. A moto. Oh, it's some sort of car. Conduzca. Always, uh, or begin always. Conduzca I think is begin, I'm not sure. You say, I wonder why they did that. Hm. Other habits important. Other habit, oh, other habits are important if you are, use something. Casco. No sé. If you always without music. So? driving begin always without music. If you're biking. What? Para, for. Other habits important. Have to see something. (sighs)

You have to avoid sickness. Um. Or illnesses. Well if you have family things or propensities for family illness or heart attack or something. Um, you have to ask your doctor for your medical history. Um, have chequeo bianual, hm. Oh check, check, check-up twice a year if you're thirty-five to forty. Um. Ok.

And the final paragraph. Uh, the ris . . . you have to avoid the situations of risk. Um. You need to travel to other places in the world without having the precautions? What? Oh. If you're going on vacation, don't travel to other worlds without taking the precautions. Oh, I see. Ok. Um. Vacations if necessary, you need to dr, oh, drink bottled water, et cetera. Ok.

??? Athleticism. Part of your diet. Athleticism. Avoiding your danger of sleeping and other habits. Then they went on if you have some other, um, genetic disability. And then they went on to talk about what you should do if you're traveling abroad. Ok. Um. I don't really know this. Condu, conducir, I don't know that. Preguntar, if they had an accent that would work, but they don't. Obtener, again, doesn't work. All the underlines obviously are new forms. I won't . . . Ok. All, mostly underlined verbs. I'm having issues with their endings because they seem to contradict, um, the rules for the -ir and -ar. -Ir goes to -a and the -ar goes to -e. They could be preterites, but they don't have any accents so I don't think that's gonna work out. Hmm. I make a mess of this thing, but I hope people understand what's going on. Ok.

Further Reading

Bowles, M. A., & Leow, R. P. (2005). Reactivity and type of verbal report in SLA research methodology: Expanding the scope of investigation. *Studies in Second Language Acquisition, 27*(3), 415–440.

Rosa, E., & Leow, R. P. (2004a). Awareness, different learning conditions, and L2 development. *Applied Psycholinguistics, 25*(2), 269–292.

Rosa, E., & Leow, R. P. (2004b). Computerized task-based exposure, explicitness, type of feedback, and Spanish L2 development. *The Modern Language Journal, 88*(2), 192–216.

Schmidt, R. (2001). Attention. In P. Robinson (Ed.), *Cognition and second language instruction* (pp. 3–32). Cambridge, UK: Cambridge University Press.

Williams, J. N. (2004). Implicit learning of form-meaning connections. In J. N. Williams, B. VanPatten, S. Rott, & M. Overstreet (Eds.), *Form-meaning connections in second language acquisition* (pp. 203–218). Mahwah, NJ: Lawrence Erlbaum.

Notes

1. In cognitive theory (McLaughlin, 1987), based on the principles and findings of cognitive psychology applied to the field of SLA, L2 learning is viewed as the acquisition of a complex cognitive skill. During the early stages of L2 learning, there is a slow development of the skills that are regulated by *controlled processes.* Controlled processes require a great amount of effort and are considered conscious tasks under voluntary control. These controlled processes are used with any new or inconsistent information learners receive in the input. *Automatic processing* involves "the activation of certain nodes in memory every time the appropriate inputs are present. This activation is a learned response that has been built up through the consistent mapping of the same input to the same pattern of activation over many trials" (p. 134). Once automatic procedures are set up, the controlled processes can be freed up to process new tasks and information.
2. Leow noted that the question of whether the presence of awareness at the level of detection was crucial for further processing to take place was not an issue in this study, since the focus was on the differential effects of Tomlin and Villa's three attentional functions.
3. Not surprisingly, more raters translate into more trust in the codings and higher reliability. To calculate the interrater reliability index for more than two raters, see Hatch and Lazarton (1991, p. 533).

References

Alanen, R. (1995). Input enhancement and rule presentation in second language acquisition. In R. Schmidt (Ed.), *Attention and awareness in foreign language learning* (Tech. Rep. No. 9, pp. 259–302). Honolulu, HI: University of Hawai'i at Manoa, Second Language Teaching and Curriculum Center.

Allport, A. (1988). What concept of consciousness? In A. J. Marcel & E. Bisiach (Eds.), *Consciousness in contemporary science* (pp. 159–182). London: Clarendon Press.

Altman, R. (1997). Oral production of vocabulary: A case study. In J. Coady & T. Huckin (Eds.), *Second language vocabulary acquisition: A rationale for pedagogy* (pp. 69–97). Cambridge, UK: Cambridge University Press.

Bowles, M. A. (2003). The effects of textual input enhancement on language learning: An online/offline study of fourth-semester Spanish students. In P. Kempchinsky & C. E. Piñeros (Eds.), *Theory, practice, and acquisition: Papers from the 6th Hispanic Linguistics Symposium and the 5th Conference on the Acquisition of Spanish and Portuguese* (pp. 395–411). Somerville, MA: Cascadilla Press.

Bowles, M. A., & Leow, R. P. (2005). Reactivity and type of verbal report in SLA research methodology: Expanding the scope of investigation. *Studies in Second Language Acquisition, 27,* 415–440.

Breetvelt, I. (1994). Relations between writing processes and text quality: When and how? *Cognition and Instruction, 12*(2), 103–123.

Broadbent, D. (1958). *Perception and communication.* New York: Academic Press.

Carlson, R. A., & Dulany, D. E. (1985). Conscious attention and abstraction in concept learning. *Journal of Experimental Psychology: Learning, Memory, and Cognition, 11*(1), 45–58.

Carr, T. H., & Curran, T. (1994). Cognitive factors in learning about structured sequences: Applications to syntax. *Studies in Second Language Acquisition, 16*(2), 205–230.

Cavalcanti, M. C., & Cohen, A. D. (1990). Comentarios em composições: Uma comparação dos pontos de vista do professor e do aluno. [Comments in compositions: A comparison of the teacher's and student's viewpoints]. *Trabalhos em Lingüística Aplicada, 15*(Jan.–June), 7–23.

Chamot, A. U., & El Dinary, P. B. (1999). Children's learning strategies in language immersion classrooms. *The Modern Language Journal, 83*(3), 319–338.

Cohen, A. D. (1986). Mentalistic measures in reading strategy research: Some recent findings. *English for Specific Purposes, 5*(2), 131–145.

Cohen, A. D. (1987). Recent uses of mentalistic data in reading strategy research. *Revista de Documentação de Estudos em Lingüística Teorica e Aplicada, 3*(1), 57–84.

Cohen, A. D. (2000). Exploring strategies in test-taking: Fine-tuning verbal reports from respondents. In G. Ekbatani & H. Pierson (Eds.), *Learner-directed assessment in ESL* (pp. 127–150). Mahwah, NJ: Lawrence Erlbaum.

Cohen, A. D., & Cavalcanti, M. C. (1987). Viewing feedback on compositions from the teacher's and the student's perspective. *ESPecialist, 16*(Apr.), 13–28.

Cohen, A. D., & Hosenfeld, C. (1981). Some uses of mentalistic data in second language research. *Language Learning, 31*(2), 285–313.

Corder, S. P. (1973). The elicitation of interlanguage. In J. Svartik (Ed.), *Errata: Papers in error analysis* (pp. 36–48). Lund, Sweden: CKW Geerup.

Curran, T., & Keele, S. (1994). Attentional and nonattentional forms of sequence learning. *Journal of Experimental Psychology: Learning, Memory, and Cognition, 19,* 189–202.

Davis, J., & Bistodeau, L. (1993). How do L1 and L2 reading differ? Evidence from think aloud protocols. *The Modern Language Journal, 77,* 459–472.

DeKeyser, R., Salaberry, R., Robinson, P., & Harrington, M. (2002). What gets processed in processing instruction? A commentary on Bill VanPatten's "Processing instruction: An update." *Language Learning, 52*(4), 805–823.

Deutsch, J. A., & Deutsch, D. (1963). Attention: Some theoretical considerations. *Psychological Review, 70,* 80–90.

Durst, R. K. (1987). Cognitive and linguistic demands of analytic writing. *Research in the Teaching of English, 21*(4), 347–376.

Earthman, E. A. (1992). Creating the virtual work: Readers' processes in understanding literary texts. *Research in the Teaching of English, 26*(4), 351–384.

Ellis, R. (2001). Investigating form-focused instruction. *Language Learning, 51,* 1–46.

Enkvist, I. (1995). Intellectual and linguistic processes in foreign language students: Students' development during their first year of Spanish at a Swedish university. In *Studies of higher education and research* [ED390253]. Washington, DC: ERIC Clearinghouse.

Ericsson, K. A. (2002). Towards a procedure for eliciting verbal expression of nonverbal experience without reactivity: Interpreting the verbal overshadowing effect within the theoretical framework for protocol analysis. *Applied Cognitive Psychology, 16,* 981–987.

Ericsson, K. A., & Simon, H. A. (1984). *Protocol analysis: Verbal reports as data.* Cambridge, MA: MIT Press.

Ericsson, K. A., & Simon, H. A. (1993). *Protocol analysis: Verbal reports as data* (rev. ed.). Cambridge, MA: MIT Press.

Færch, C., & Kasper, G. (1986). One learner–two languages: Investigating types of interlanguage knowledge. In J. House & S. Blum-Kulka (Eds.), *Interlingual and intercultural communication* (pp. 211–227). Tübingen, Germany: Gunter Narr.

Fehrenbach, C. R. (1991). Gifted/average readers: Do they use the same reading strategies? *Gifted Child Quarterly, 35*(3), 125–127.

Folger, T. L. (2001). Readers' parallel text construction while talking and thinking about the reading process. *Dissertation Abstracts International, A: The Humanities and Social Sciences, 62*(4), 1329-A.

Fotos, S. (1993). Consciousness-raising and noticing through focus on form: Grammar task performance versus formal instruction. *Applied Linguistics, 14,* 385–407.

Gopher, D. (1992). Analysis and measurement of mental workload. In G. d'Ydewalle, P. Eelen, & P. Bertelson (Eds.), *International perspectives on psychological science: Vol. 2. State of the art* (pp. 265–291). Mahwah, NJ: Lawrence Erlbaum.

Gordon, C. J. (1990). Modeling an expository text structure strategy in think alouds. *Reading Horizons, 31*(2), 149–167.

Grabe, W., & Stoller, F. (1997). Reading and vocabulary development in a second language. In J. Coady & T. Huckin (Eds.), *Second language vocabulary acquisition: A rationale for pedagogy* (pp. 98–122). Cambridge, UK: Cambridge University Press.

Green, A. J. F. (1998). *Using verbal protocols in language testing research: A handbook.* Cambridge, UK: Cambridge University Press.

Greenslade, T., Bouden, L., & Sanz, C. (1999). Attending to form and content in processing L2 reading texts. *Spanish Applied Linguistics, 3,* 65–90.

Hardcastle, V. G. (1993). The naturalists versus the skeptics: The debate over a scientific understanding of consciousness. *Journal of Mind and Behavior, 14,* 27–50.

Hatch, E., & Lazarton, A. (1991). *The research manual: Design and statistics for applied linguistics.* Rowley, MA: Newbury House.

Hosenfeld, C. (1976). Learning about learning: Discovering our students' strategies. *Foreign Language Annals, 9,* 117–129.

Hosenfeld, C. (1977). A preliminary investigation of the reading strategies of successful and nonsuccessful second language learners. *System, 5*(2), 110–123.

Hosenfeld, C. (1979). Cindy: A learner in today's foreign language classroom. In W. Borne (Ed.), *The foreign language learner in today's classroom environment* (pp. 53–75). Montpelier, VT: Northwest Conference on the Teaching of Foreign Languages.

Hosenfeld, C. (1984). Case studies of ninth grade readers. In J. C. Alderson & A. H. Urquhart (Eds.), *Reading in a foreign language* (pp. 231–249). London: Longman.

Izumi, S. (1999). Promoting noticing and SLA: An empirical study of the effects of output and input enhancement on ESL relativization. *Dissertation Abstracts International, A: The Humanities and Social Sciences, 61*(7), 2683-A.

Izumi, S. (2002). Output, input enhancement, and the noticing hypothesis: An experimental study on ESL relativization. *Studies in Second Language Acquisition, 24*(4), 541–577.

Izumi, S., & Bigelow, M. (2000). Does output promote noticing and second language acquisition? *TESOL Quarterly, 34,* 239–278.

Izumi, S., Bigelow, M., Fujiwara, M., & Fearnow, S. (1999). Testing the output hypothesis: Effect of output on noticing and second language acquisition. *Studies in Second Language Acquisition, 21,* 421–452.

Jaaskelainen, R. (2000). Focus on methodology in think-aloud studies on translating. In S. Tirkkonen Condit & R. Jaaskelainen (Eds.), *Tapping and mapping the processes of translation and interpreting: Outlooks on empirical research* (pp. 71–82). Amsterdam: John Benjamins.

Jourdenais, R. (2001). Cognition, instruction, and protocol analysis. In P. Robinson (Ed.), *Cognition and second language instruction.* Cambridge, UK: Cambridge University Press.

Kahneman, D. (1973). *Attention and effort.* Englewood Cliffs, NJ: Prentice Hall.

Kasper, G., & Blum-Kulka, S. (1993). *Interlanguage pragmatics.* Oxford, UK: Oxford University Press.

Kern, R. G. (1994). The role of mental translation in second language reading. *Studies in Second Language Acquisition, 16*(4), 441–461.

Leow, R. P. (1997a). Attention, awareness, and foreign language behavior. *Language Learning, 47*(3), 467–505.

Leow, R. P. (1997b). The effects of input enhancement and text length on adult L2 readers' comprehension and intake in second language acquisition. *Applied Language Learning, 8*(2), 151–182.

Leow, R. P. (1998a). The effects of amount and type of exposure on adult learners' L2 development in SLA. *The Modern Language Journal, 82*(1), 49–68.

Leow, R. P. (1998b). Toward operationalizing the process of attention in SLA: Evidence for Tomlin and Villa's (1994) fine-grained analysis of attention. *Applied Psycholinguistics, 19*(1), 133–159.

Leow, R. P. (1999). The role of attention in second/foreign language classroom research: Methodological issues. In F. M.-G. J. Gutiérrez-Rexach (Ed.), *Advances in Hispanic linguistics: Papers from the 2nd Hispanic Linguistics Symposium* (pp. 60–71). Somerville, MA: Cascadilla Press.

Leow, R. P. (2000). A study of the role of awareness in foreign language behavior: Aware versus unaware learners. *Studies in Second Language Acquisition, 22*(4), 557–584.

Leow, R. P. (2001a). Attention, awareness, and foreign language behavior. *Language Learning, 51*(Suppl. 1), 113–155.

Leow, R. P. (2001b). Do learners notice enhanced forms while interacting with the L2? An online and offline study of the role of written input enhancement in L2 reading. *Hispania, 84*(3), 496–509.

Leow, R. P., & Morgan-Short, K. (2004). To think aloud or not to think aloud: The issue of reactivity in SLA research methodology. *Studies in Second Language Acquisition, 26*(1), 35–57.

Mackey, A., Gass, S., & McDonough, K. (2000). How do learners perceive interactional feedback? *Studies in Second Language Acquisition, 22*(4), 471–497.

Mackey, A., McDonough, K., Fujii, A., & Tatsumi, T. (2001). Investigating learners' reports about the L2 classroom. *International Review of Applied Linguistics in Language Teaching (IRAL), 39,* 285–308.

Mackey, A., Philp, J., Egi, T., Fujii, A., & Tatsumi, T. (2002). Individual differences in working memory, noticing of interactional feedback and L2 development. In P. Robinson (Ed.), *Individual differences and instructed language learning* (pp. 181–209). Amsterdam: John Benjamins.

Marcel, A. J. (1983). Conscious and unconscious perception: Experiments on visual masking and word recognition. *Cognitive Psychology, 15,* 197–237.

McGuire, K. L., & Yewchuk, C. R. (1996). Use of metacognitive reading strategies by gifted and learning disabled students: An exploratory study. *Journal for the Education of the Gifted, 19*(3), 293–314.

McLaughlin, B. (1987). *Theories of second language learning.* London: Edward Arnold.

Nabei, T., & Swain, M. (2002). Learner awareness of recasts in classroom interaction: A case study of an adult EFL student's second language learning. *Language Awareness, 11,* 43–63.

Neumann, O. (1996). Theories of attention. In O. Neumann & A. Sanders (Eds.), *Handbook of perception and action: Vol. 3. Attention* (pp. 389–446). New York: Academic Press.

Nevo, N. (1989). Test-taking strategies on a multiple-choice test of reading comprehension. *Language Testing, 6*(2), 199–215.

Nisbett, R. E., & Wilson, T. D. (1977). Telling more than we can know: Verbal reports on mental processes. *Psychological Review, 84,* 231–259.

Nissen, M., & Bullemer, P. (1987). Attentional requirements of learning: Evidence from performance measures. *Cognitive Psychology, 19,* 1–32.

Norris, S. P. (1992). A demonstration of the use of verbal reports of thinking in multiple-choice critical thinking test design. *The Alberta Journal of Educational Research, 38*(3), 155–176.

Payne, J. W., Braunstein, M. L., & Carroll, J. S. (1978). Exploring predecisional behavior: An alternative approach to decision research. *Organizational Behavior and Human Performance, 22,* 17–44.

Philp, J. (2003). Nonnative speakers' noticing of recasts in NS-NNS interaction. *Studies in Second Language Acquisition, 25,* 99–126.

Posner, M. I. (1992). Attention as a cognitive and neural system. *Current Directions in Psychological Science, 1,* 11–14.

Reber, A. (1967). Implicit learning of artificial grammars. *Journal of Verbal Learning and Verbal Behavior, 77,* 317–327.

Reber, A. (1976). Implicit learning of synthetic languages: The role of instructional sets. *Journal of Experimental Psychology: Human Learning and Memory, 2,* 88–94.

Reber, A. (1989). Implicit learning and tacit knowledge. *Journal of Experimental Psychology, 118,* 219–235.

Reber, A. (1993). *Implicit learning and tacit knowledge: An essay on the cognitive unconscious* (Oxford psychology series, no. 19). Oxford, UK: Oxford University Press.

Robinson, P. (1995a). Aptitude, awareness, and the fundamental similarity of implicit and explicit second language learning. In R. Schmidt (Ed.), *Attention and awareness in foreign language learning* (Tech. Rep. No. 9, pp. 303–357). Honolulu, HI: University of Hawai'i at Manoa, Second Language Teaching and Curriculum Center.

Robinson, P. (1995b). Attention, memory, and the "noticing" hypothesis. *Language Learning, 45*(2), 283–331.

Robinson, P. (1996a). *Consciousness, rules, and instructed second language acquisition.* New York: Peter Lang.

Robinson, P. (1996b). Learning simple and complex second language rules under implicit, incidental, rule-search, and instructed conditions. *Studies in Second Language Acquisition, 18*(1), 27–67.

Robinson, P. (1997a). Generalizability and automaticity of second language learning under implicit, incidental, enhanced, and instructed conditions. *Studies in Second Language Acquisition, 19*(2), 223–247.

Robinson, P. (1997b). Individual differences and the fundamental similarity of implicit and explicit adult second language learning. *Language Learning, 47*(1), 45–99.

Robinson, P. (2003). Attention and memory in SLA. In C. Doughty & M. Long (Eds.), *Handbook of second language acquisition.* Oxford, UK: Blackwell.

Rosa, E. (1999). A cognitive approach to task-based research: Explicitness, awareness and L2 development. *Dissertation Abstracts International, A: The Humanities and Social Sciences, 60*(12), 4405-A.

Rosa, E., & Leow, R. P. (2004a). Awareness, different learning conditions, and L2 development. *Applied Psycholinguistics, 25*(2), 269–292.

Rosa, E., & Leow, R. P. (2004b). Computerized task-based exposure, explicitness, type of feedback, and Spanish L2 development. *The Modern Language Journal, 88*(2), 192–216.

Rosa, E., & O'Neill, M. D. (1999). Explicitness, intake, and the issue of awareness. *Studies in Second Language Acquisition, 21*(4), 511–556.

Russo, J. E., Johnson, E. J., & Stephens, D. L. (1989). The validity of verbal protocols. *Memory & Cognition, 17,* 759–769.

Schmidt, R. (1990). The role of consciousness in second language learning. *Applied Linguistics, 11*(2), 129–158.

Schmidt, R. (1993). Awareness and second language acquisition. *Annual Review of Applied Linguistics, 13,* 206–226.

Schmidt, R. (1994). Deconstructing consciousness in search of useful definitions for applied linguistics. *AILA Review, 11,* 11–26.

Schmidt, R. (1995). Consciousness and foreign language learning: A tutorial on the role of attention and awareness in learning. In R. W. Schmidt (Ed.), *Attention and awareness in foreign language learning* (Tech. Rep. No. 9, pp. 1–64). Honolulu, HI: University of Hawai'i at Manoa, Second Language Teaching and Curriculum Center.

Schmidt, R. (2001). Attention. In P. Robinson (Ed.), *Cognition and second language instruction* (pp. 3–32). Cambridge, UK: Cambridge University Press.

Schmidt, R., & Frota, S. (1986). Developing basic conversational ability in a second language. In R. Day (Ed.), *Talking to learn* (pp. 237–326). Rowley, MA: Newbury House.

Selinker, L. (1972). Interlanguage. *International Review of Applied Linguistics in Language Teaching (IRAL), 10,* 209–231.

Simard, D., & Wong, W. (2001). Alertness, orientation, and detection: The conceptualization of attentional functions in SLA. *Studies in Second Language Acquisition, 23*(1), 103–124.

Slimani, A. (1989). The role of topicalization in classroom language learning. *System, 17,* 223–234.

Tomlin, R. S., & Villa, V. (1994). Attention in cognitive science and second language acquisition. *Studies in Second Language Acquisition, 16*(2), 183–203.

VanPatten, B. (1990). Attending to form and content in the input: An experiment in consciousness. *Studies in Second Language Acquisition, 12,* 287–301.

Velmans, M. (1991). Is human information processing conscious? *Behavioral and Brain Sciences, 14,* 651–669.

Warden, M., Lapkin, S., Swain, M., & Hart, H. (1995). Adolescent language learners on a three-month exchange: Insights from their diaries. *Foreign Language Annals, 28,* 537–549.

Warren, J. (1996). How students pick the right answer: A 'think aloud' study of the French CAT. *Occasional Papers of the Applied Linguistics Association of Australia, 15,* 79–94.

Wickens, C. D. (1980). The structure of attentional resources. In R. S. Nickerson (Ed.), *Attention and performance VIII* (pp. 239–257). Mahwah, NJ: Lawrence Erlbaum.

Wickens, C. D. (1984). Processing resources in attention. In R. Parasuraman & D. Davies (Eds.), *Varieties of attention* (pp. 63–98). New York: Academic Press.

Wickens, C. D. (1989). Attention and skilled performance. In D. H. Holding (Ed.), *Human skills* (pp. 71–105). New York: John Wiley.

Williams, J. N. (2004). Implicit learning of form-meaning connections. In J. N. Williams, B. VanPatten, S. Rott, & M. Overstreet (Eds.), *Form-meaning connections in second language acquisition* (pp. 203–218). Mahwah, NJ: Lawrence Erlbaum.

Yamashita, J. (2002). Reading strategies in L1 and L2: Comparison of four groups of readers with different reading ability in L1 and L2. *ITL, Review of Applied Linguistics, 135–136,* 1–35.

Zellermayer, M., & Cohen, J. (1996). Varying paths for learning to revise. *Instructional Science, 24*(3), 177–195.

PART 3

External Factors

SEVEN

Input and Interaction

ALISON MACKEY

REBEKHA ABBUHL

KEY WORDS

Implicit ▪ input ▪ interaction ▪ modified output ▪ negative feedback ▪ negotiation ▪ noticing the gap ▪ recasts ▪ task-based learning.

1. The Interaction Hypothesis

The interaction hypothesis (Gass, 1997, 2003; Long, 1996; Pica, 1994) suggests that second language development is facilitated when learners interact with other speakers. In the most recent version of the hypothesis, Long (1996) states that "negotiation work that triggers *interactional* adjustments by the NS [native speaker] or more competent interlocutor facilitates acquisition because it connects input, internal learner capacities, particularly selective attention, and output in productive ways" (pp. 451–452). The major components of this hypothesis—input, feedback, and output—will be discussed in sections 1.1 through 1.3 below.

1.1. INPUT

Input refers to the linguistic forms to which learners are exposed. While exposure to input has been claimed to be sufficient for first language learners to master the syntax, morphology, phonology, and semantics of their native language, simple exposure to the target language rarely has the same outcome for second language (L2) learners. Second language acquisition (SLA) researchers have thus sought to determine how the input needs of L2 learners can be met. For example, researchers have asked whether L2 learners would benefit from *simplified input* (language that has been made less complex so as to be more comprehensible), *baseline input* (unmodified language), or *interactionally modified input* (input that is modified through the course of conversing with an interlocutor).

One of the first SLA researchers to investigate issues related to input, Krashen (1985), proposed that L2 learners require *comprehensible input* (i.e., language that is understandable). More specifically, Krashen hypothesized that when learners understand language at the level of $i + 1$ (i.e., language that is slightly more advanced than their current level of competence), acquisition would automatically occur. However, while this proposal represented a major first step in exploring the relationship between input and acquisition, researchers (e.g., Swain, 1985) have pointed out that input is not sufficient for L2 learning. In other words, while input is obviously a crucial element in acquiring an L2, input alone cannot account for the entire process. The construct of comprehensible input also attracted criticism on theoretical and methodological grounds; for example, the *i* in *i* + *1* was never defined or operationalized (Gregg, 1984; McLaughlin, 1987).

Long (1981, 1983a, 1983b, 1996) shifted the research focus towards the ways in which the structure of interaction itself could be modified to make input more comprehensible for nonnative speakers. In particular, Long (1981) focused on the effects of one type of interaction, negotiation for meaning, on L2 comprehension and development. Negotiation for meaning refers to the efforts learners and their interlocutors make to modify or restructure interaction in order to avoid or overcome difficulties in input comprehensibility. According to Long, negotiation for meaning includes *comprehension* and *confirmation checks* (utterances used to determine whether the interlocutor has understood a previous utterance, e.g., "Do you understand?" and "You said X, right?") and *clarification requests* (appeals to clarify a misunderstood utterance, e.g., "What do you mean?"). Examples of these patterns of negotiation of meaning from discourse involving nonnative speakers (NNS) are provided in examples (1) through (3) below.

(1) Comprehension check (Oliver, 1998)
    NNS: You know what, you know? [OK]?

(2) Confirmation checks (Oliver, 1998)
    NNS 1: Where does the um, glasses go?
    NNS 2: The glasses?

(3) Clarification requests (Oliver, 1998)
    NNS: A little line in the leave.
    NS: A what?

It has been suggested that by using these particular discourse strategies, learners can receive input that is more comprehensible and uniquely suited to their particular developmental needs (Pica, 1994). Empirical studies that have examined links between interaction and input will be reviewed below.

1.1.1. STUDIES EXPLORING INTERACTIONAL INPUT

In order to test claims about the benefits of interaction, a number of researchers have sought to compare the relative effectiveness of input simplification and interactionally modified input on L2 comprehension and acquisition (e.g., Ellis and He, 1999; Ellis, Tanaka, and Yamazaki, 1994; Gass and Varonis, 1994; Loschky, 1994; Mackey, 1999; Pica, 1992; Pica, Young, and Doughty, 1987). For example, Pica et al. (1987) compared the comprehension of 16 learners of English as a second language (ESL) during an object placement task (in which the learners listened to native speaker [NS] directions for choosing and placing felt cutouts on a board) under two conditions. In the first condition, the learners received *premodified input*—that is, simplified input that contained more frequent vocabulary items and less complex sentence structures. In the second condition, the learners were provided with interactionally modified input. Here the learners received unmodified directions but were given the opportunity to interact with the native speaker whenever they experienced difficulties in comprehension. Based on the latter group's higher success rate in choosing and placing the objects correctly, the researchers concluded that "interactional modifications of input did, in fact, lead to significantly greater comprehension than conventional ways of simplifying input" (Pica et al., 1987, p. 745).

In a similar study of learners of Japanese as a second language (JSL), Loschky (1994) sought to determine whether interactionally modified input facilitated the comprehension or acquisition of Japanese vocabulary and locative constructions. Forty-one beginning-level learners of Japanese were assigned to one of the following groups: (a) the unmodified input group, where subjects received baseline descriptions of objects to be located and circled on a picture; (b) the premodified input group, where the descriptions were simplified; and (c) the negotiated (i.e., interactionally modified) input group, where learners were allowed to interact with the NS interlocutor as they listened to the descriptions. The researcher compared pretest and posttest scores on a vocabulary test (in which students were asked to indicate whether certain words were used during the task) and a sentence verification section (in which students indicated whether or not aurally presented sentences matched a set of pictures they were given) and found that the negotiated input group received significantly higher scores on the vocabulary test than both the unmodified and premodified input groups. However, there were no significant differences between groups on the sentence verification test. These results led Loschky to conclude that the interaction had facilitated the comprehension of the vocabulary items but not the acquisition of the grammatical structure.

Mackey's (1999) research, however, suggested that interactionally modified input facilitated the development of question forms in English. Thirty-four adult ESL learners were divided into five groups: (a) *interactors,* who received interactionally modified input while they engaged in three tasks—a picture-drawing task, a story-completion task, and a story-sequencing task; (b) *interactor unreadies,* who received the same input as the interactors, but were at a lower developmental level in terms of English question formation;

(c) *observers,* who were instructed to watch the interaction occurring in the first two groups but did not participate in the interaction; (d) *scripteds,* who received premodified input from the NS; and (e) the control group. Learners' use of question forms was analyzed in both pre- and posttests, using a well established developmental sequence for question forms in which learners pass through specific stages (Pienemann and Johnston, 1987). Mackey found that most of the learners who actively participated in conversational interaction showed stage increases, whereas none of the other groups demonstrated unambiguous evidence of development.

1.1.2. INPUT SUMMARY

Thus, with respect to the question of what kind of input is the greatest facilitator of L2 comprehension and development, there is evidence that interactionally modified input may be more effective than simple input modifications. Proponents of the interaction hypothesis suggest that one reason for this is because interactional modifications allow learners to negotiate the type of input they need at a particular stage in their development, whereas simplified input is determined beforehand and may not cater to individual learners' particular weaknesses, strengths, and real-time communicative needs in relation to the target language.

1.2. FEEDBACK

Feedback refers to information learners receive in response to their communicative efforts. This feedback may be explicit (e.g., direct corrections of nontargetlike utterances, such as "You have to add *-s* to *run* when using it in the third person") or implicit (e.g., discourse moves such as clarification requests that indirectly indicate that a learner's utterance was in some way problematic). Researchers and teachers have long believed that feedback is an important element in the process of learning an L2. Researchers have argued, for instance, that certain relatively subtle aspects of the nonnative grammar are not acquirable from positive evidence alone (White, 1991). For example, a French learner of English may produce sentences such as *He eats slowly the tomatoes,* placing the adverb between the verb and its direct object. In French, this is grammatical; however, in English it results in an ungrammatical sentence. To disconfirm this incorrect overgeneralization, the French learner would have to notice the absence of that particular structure (V Adv Obj) in the L2 positive input. Although this is theoretically possible, researchers have argued that the provision of some sort of negative feedback to the learner (e.g., "You can't place the adverb between the verb and its direct object here" or "You mean, he slowly eats the tomatoes?") would allow learners to "narrow the range of possible hypotheses that can account for the data" (Carroll and

Swain, 1993, p. 358), thus facilitating the SLA process. These issues are further discussed in Gass (2003).

In recent years, several studies have investigated the link between oral feedback, especially implicit negative feedback and SLA (e.g., Braidi, 2002; Han, 2001, 2002; Iwashita, 2003; Leeman, 2003; Long, Inagaki, and Ortega, 1998; Lyster, 1998a, 1998b; Lyster and Ranta, 1997; Mackey, 1999; Mackey, Gass, and McDonough, 2000; Mackey and Philp, 1998; Mackey, Oliver, and Leeman, 2003; Oliver, 1995, 2000; Philp, 2003). Most of these studies have provided evidence that feedback plays at least a facilitative role in L2 development.

1.2.1. EXPLICIT FEEDBACK

In explicit negative feedback, the interlocutor (often a NS or teacher) provides linguistic and metalinguistic information (i.e., information about the language structure itself) to the NNS in order to indicate that an utterance the learner produced was incorrect, incomplete, or somehow nontargetlike (Lin and Hedgcock, 1996).

Early research on explicit feedback, drawing on L1 studies of the frequency of feedback to children, investigated how often explicit correction occurred in NS-NNS conversations, both in the classroom (Allwright, 1975; Bruton and Samuda, 1980; Chaudron, 1977; Fanselow, 1977; Holley and King, 1971; Long, 1988; Swain and Carroll, 1987) and outside (Chun, Day, Chenoweth, and Luppescu, 1982; Crookes and Rulon, 1988; Day, Chenoweth, Chun, and Luppescu, 1984; Gaskill, 1980).

Later studies sought to determine whether the feedback actually affected performance (e.g., Carroll and Swain, 1993; Carroll, Swain, and Roberge, 1992; DeKeyser, 1993; Herron and Tomasello, 1988; Lightbown and Spada, 1990, 1993; Tomasello and Herron, 1989). For example, in one tightly controlled laboratory study, Carroll et al. (1992) examined the effects of explicit written feedback on the learning of word formation rules by learners of French as a second language (FSL). Based on the results of an immediate and a delayed posttest, Carroll et al. concluded that explicit feedback helped the FSL learners to memorize words but not to learn French derivational morphology. However, in similar laboratory experiments (Carroll and Swain, 1991, 1993), Spanish ESL learners who received explicit feedback performed better on the dative alternation rule than learners who were (a) told only that their utterance was incorrect, (b) questioned as to whether they thought their utterance was correct, or (c) given no feedback at all. Carroll and Swain speculated that even though explicit feedback and the detailed grammatical explanations it contains may require specialized vocabulary knowledge, this kind of feedback pinpoints the exact location of the error and is thus more usable than other forms of feedback that require the learner to guess the location. Similar results were also reported in Kubota's (1994) research on Japanese ESL learners and dative alternation. However, DeKeyser (1993), in his study of high school FSL learners, found that error correction benefited only some learners. More specifically, he found that the effectiveness of error correction was related to a number of individual student characteristics such as aptitude, motivation, anxiety, and previous achievement. Sanz and Morgan-Short (this volume, chapter 8) provide more information about explicit feedback.

As Oliver (2000) notes, some researchers and educators have interpreted these less-than-conclusive results to mean that explicit feedback is rarely provided in interaction and that it is at best only indirectly related to L2 development. However, more recent studies have expanded the scope of their research focus to include other forms of feedback, such as clarification requests, elicitations, and especially recasts—all classified as implicit negative feedback. Recasts, the form of implicit feedback that has received the most attention in the literature so far, will be discussed in the next section.

1.2.2. RECASTS

Recasts, as Long (1996) defines them, are utterances that follow and rephrase a language learner's original statement in a more targetlike way, while still maintaining the learner's original meaning. In (4) below, the native speaker provides a recast to the nonnative speaker's original utterance:

(4) NNS: Where did you goed yesterday?
NS: Where did I *go* yesterday? Oh, I went to the store.

Recasts have been gathering increased attention in the L2 literature in recent years (e.g., Braidi, 2002; Han, 2002; Ishida, 2004; Iwashita, 2003; Leeman, 2003; Long, in press; Long, Inagaki, and Ortega, 1998; Lyster, 1998a, 1998b; Lyster and Ranta, 1997; Mackey, Gass, and McDonough, 2000; Mackey and Philp, 1998; Morris and Tarone, 2003; Nabei and Swain, 2002; Nicholas, Lightbown, and Spada, 2001; Ohta, 2000; Oliver, 1995; Ortega and Long, 1997; Panova and Lyster, 2002; Philp, 2003). The topic of recasts has also generated interesting debate, with some researchers maintaining that recasts are too ambiguous to be of significant use in SLA, as they may either go unnoticed or be perceived simply as an alternative way of saying the original utterance (e.g., Lyster, 1998a, 1998b; Lyster and Ranta, 1997; Panova and Lyster, 2002). Others, however, have claimed that recasts can in fact help learners notice a gap (that is, a mismatch between one's own production and the system of the target language). As Gass, Mackey, and Pica (1998) state, recasts "can serve to focus learners' attention on potentially troublesome parts of their discourse, providing them with information that can open the door to IL [interlanguage, the learner's language] modification" (p. 301).

The empirical questions in relation to recasts, then, are whether learners recognize or notice recasts as negative feedback and whether recasts are associated with learning. Many researchers believe that noticing is important for learning. According to Schmidt's noticing hypothesis (Schmidt, 1990, 1995a, 1995b), for example, target language input becomes intake only when it is noticed, where *noticing* refers to the process of consciously becoming aware of some stimulus in the environment and bringing it into focal attention. Similarly, Long (1996) has suggested that in order for recasts to be useful, the learner must notice the element of negative feedback within them, as opposed to regarding the recast as an alternative way of phrasing a previous utterance or as a form of topic continuation on the part of the interlocutor. Although the role of noticing and conscious awareness in SLA has been the subject of much controversy [see Leow and Bowles (this volume, chapter 6) for more on this topic], researchers working in the interaction framework generally seem to agree that interaction can allow learners' attention to be drawn to their interlanguage problems in order for their interlanguage grammars to be revised to more targetlike levels.

One study that examined the issue of recast noticability was Mackey, Gass, and McDonough (2000). In this study, the researchers investigated whether ESL and IFL (Italian as a foreign language) learners perceived implicit negative feedback, including recasts, as negative feedback in task-based interactions with native speakers and whether they were able to identify what had triggered that feedback. Learners participated in task-based dyadic interaction and received recasts on their morphosyntactic, lexical, semantic, and phonological errors. Afterwards the learners watched videotapes of the interactions and were asked to introspect about what their thoughts had been at the time the original interactions were in progress. The researchers found that the learners were relatively accurate in perceiving recasts as negative feedback on their linguistic errors except in relation to morphosyntax, even though 75% of the recasts were in response to morphosyntactic errors. However, as Mackey et al. pointed out, even though the failure to verbalize having noticed something is not equivalent to not having noticed, their study does suggest that the target of the recast may affect its salience.

On the other hand, it has also been suggested that learners may not need to consciously recognize negative feedback as such in order for it to have beneficial effects on language development. Rather, learners may benefit simply because recasts enhance the salience of target forms and thus increase the likelihood that learners will attend to those forms and incorporate them into their interlanguage grammars. To investigate this possibility, Leeman (2003) examined the relationship between recasts and the development of Spanish noun-adjective agreement, a grammatical structure with low perceptual salience and limited communicative value. Seventy-four learners of Spanish as a second language (SSL) were assigned to one of four treatment groups: (a) recasts, (b) explicit feedback, (c) enhanced salience, or (d) control. In the recast group, the researcher reformulated all grammatical errors on noun-adjective agreement. In the explicit feedback group, errors in noun-adjective agreement received direct correction (e.g., "You made a mistake with noun-adjective agreement."), while learners in the enhanced salience group received input that highlighted the target forms through stress and intonation but did not receive feedback. Comparisons of scores on the immediate posttest revealed that the recast and enhanced salience groups outperformed the explicit feedback and control groups on gender and number agreement. On the second posttest, the recast and enhanced salience groups again received significantly higher scores than the other two groups but only for number agreement. Interestingly, on gender agreement, only the enhanced salience group significantly outperformed the control group. Commenting on her results, Leeman noted that "they seem to indicate that there may be no need to attribute the benefits of recasts to negative evidence. Indeed, if the benefits of recasts were due to negative evidence, the negative evidence group should have outperformed the control group [on gender agreement], which it did not" (p. 56).

In addition to investigating the noticeability of recasts, other researchers have focused on whether recasts lead to language development in either the short or long term. For example, in Long and his colleagues' work on recasts (Inagaki and Long, 1999; Long, Inagaki, and Ortega, 1998; Ortega and Long, 1997), pretests and posttests were employed to compare the effectiveness of recasts and models with respect to the short-term development of various grammatical structures in Japanese and Spanish as second languages. In their study of SSL learners, for example, Ortega and Long (1997) found that recasts resulted in participants performing significantly better on adverb placement than those who simply heard models, but that there was no effect for another grammatical structure, object topicalization (which the researchers speculated may have been too difficult for the participants in the study). However, Long, Inagaki, and Ortega (1998) reported that there were no significant differences between groups receiving models and those receiving recasts with respect to two Japanese structures, locative structures and a particular verb form called the *-te* form. As a group, these studies provide at least some evidence that the effects of feedback depend on the targeted language form.

Additional evidence for this conclusion was reported by Iwashita (2003) in her study of JSL learners. Iwashita compared five different types of implicit negative feedback (recasts, clarification requests, confirmation checks, repetitions, and models) and their impact on the short-term development of three grammatical structures in Japanese: the *-te* form of the verb and both word order and particle use in locative-initial constructions. Iwashita noted that both the distribution and the effectiveness of the various implicit negative feedback types depended on the particular linguistic target. For example, comparisons of pretest and immediate posttest scores indicated that recasts promoted learning of the *-te* form but did not seem to facilitate learning of word order or particle use in the locative-initial constructions. Discussing the implications of these results, Iwashita cautioned that future studies will need to look at the effectiveness of various implicit negative feedback types with respect to learner level, individual differences, and specific grammatical constructions.

In one study to take this kind of focus on a specific grammatical construction, Mackey and Philp (1998) examined the relationship between recasts and the development of question forms by adult intermediate- and advanced-level ESL learners of various L1 backgrounds. The learners completed three information gap tasks with a NS partner (story sequencing, story completion, and spot-the-difference). Those learners in the treatment group received recasts whenever they produced a nontargetlike utterance; those in the control group did not. Results showed that advanced learners who received intensive recasts produced more advanced question forms on posttests.

1.2.3. FEEDBACK SUMMARY

This brief review of some of the main studies in the feedback literature suggests that feedback is indeed linked to L2 development. However, their relationship is mediated by various factors, such as the target grammatical structure, and researchers have not come to a consensus on the exact mechanisms underlying the use of feedback in interaction and the role of attention within those interactions.

1.3. OUTPUT

Output is generally understood to be the language that the learner produces. Distinctions are sometimes made between comprehensible output (utterances that are understandable to one's interlocutor) and modified output (utterances that have been modified in response to an interlocutor's signal of noncomprehension). In this chapter, we focus on modified output.

Early researchers assumed that output did not play a significant role in the L2 acquisition process (e.g., Krashen, 1985, 1998) and that output simply served as evidence that acquisition had occurred. However, beginning with Swain's (1985, 1995, 2000) influential work, researchers have become increasingly convinced that learners' output has a number of benefits, including (a) promoting fluency (automatization), (b) drawing learners' attention to their linguistic problems in the L2, (c) encouraging the processing of the L2 syntactically (in terms of linguistic form) rather than simply for meaning, and (d) testing hypotheses about the structure of the target language (Swain, 1995). Each of these functions will be discussed in more depth below.

For teachers accustomed to requiring learners to engage in drills and practice activities, the first function of output—that of aiding fluency and promoting automatization—would seem to be a matter of common sense: the more you practice, the more automatic a skill will become. In recent years, however, researchers have become interested in identifying the precise psycholinguistic mechanisms at work in the output process. For example, de Bot (1996) proposed that frequent opportunities for output can help learners move from an initial stage of *declarative knowledge,* in which isolated facts and rules are acquired and processed in a slow and conscious manner, to a stage of *procedural knowledge,* in which processing is fast, precise, and beyond conscious control (i.e., automatized). When this occurs, learners free up valuable attention, allowing them to focus on higher level concerns such as pragmatics instead of lower level ones (e.g., pronunciation).

In addition to promoting automatization, the act of producing output can lead learners to the second function of output, that of "notic[ing] a gap between what they *want* to say and what they *can* say, leading them to recognize what they do not know, or know only partially" (Swain, 1995, pp. 125–126). In other words, as they struggle to make their words comprehensible, learners may become more aware of what they still need to learn about the L2 and, in turn, may become more receptive to relevant structures in the input. As van den Branden (1997) notes, "in interactional contexts where learners need to produce output that their current IL [interlanguage] system cannot handle, they may be expected to pay close attention to interactional help offered: a learner in search of the right word or structure is a learner who is open to noticing such things in the input" (p. 596). Similarly, Gass and Mackey (2002) claim that in the process of producing output, learners may become more sensitive to patterns and associations in the target language.

The third function of output, that of processing syntactically rather than semantically, refers to the fact that during comprehension (the act of obtaining meaning, i.e., processing semantically), learners may rely solely on pragmatic and contextual cues to get the gist of an interlocutor's message. However, in production, and especially after an interlocutor has signaled lack of understanding, learners may be drawn to pay particular attention to morphosyntactic or phonological accuracy in order to make themselves as comprehensible as possible to their interlocutors (Swain, 1985, 1995). This focus, as Swain and Lapkin (1995) argue, pushes learners beyond their current level of performance, thus extending their linguistic repertoire by either internalizing new linguistic knowledge or consolidating existing knowledge.

Fourth and finally, learners may also use output to test hypotheses on the rules they have constructed about the language, in order to see whether a particular rule leads to successful communication or to negative feedback (Shehadeh, 2003; Swain, 1995, 2000). For example, if learners are unsure about where adverbs can be placed in English, they may try out sentences with their interlocutors, producing, for instance, *He eats slowly tomatoes* to see if it receives either explicit or implicit negative feedback. In this way, learners can revise their rules about the target language and come closer to producing more targetlike utterances.

1.3.1. STUDIES ON OUTPUT AND ACQUISITION

Although most studies investigating the relationship between output and L2 development have focused on the quantity of learner output, as Shehadeh (2002) notes, "there is no evidence, at present, to suggest that quantity (rather than quality or a number of learner and contextual factors) is what matters most" (p. 622). Shehadeh thus suggests that researchers also focus on the relationship between output and language development in either the short- or long-term.

One small-scale study to do so was Nobuyoshi and Ellis (1993). In this study, the researchers assigned six ESL learners to two groups, one in which learners received requests for clarification every time a past tense verb was incorrectly formed or omitted (the experimental group) and one in which learners only received general requests for clarification when the teacher genuinely failed to understand the learner's message (the control group). Use of the past tense in obligatory contexts (e.g., in the sentence *I walked to school yesterday*) was compared between the first and second treatment (one week later) for both groups. Nobuyoshi and Ellis found that two of the three subjects in the experimental group made significant gains in their use of the past tense, whereas none of the three control group members did so. This finding led the researchers to conclude that their results provided "some support for the claim that 'pushing' learners to improve the accuracy of their production results not only in immediate improved performance but also in gains in accuracy over time" (p. 208). In a case study of eight learners, Mackey (1997) similarly found that learners who modified their nontargetlike production of question forms following feedback later increased their production of higher level question forms.

In another study to look at the relationship between output and short-term language development, van den Branden (1997) examined both the quantity and the quality of modified output produced by Dutch-speaking primary school children in various dyad types (NNS-NS peer and NNS-NS adult). He found that those children who had engaged in the interaction (and had thus been given the opportunity to modify their output) produced a significantly greater quantity of output and displayed a greater range of vocabulary on the posttest than did those children in the comparison group. Even though the study did not address the long-term effects of output, he concluded that "it provide[d] a clear indication of the potential effects of negotiation on language acquisition, as well as empirical evidence for the effects of negotiation on subsequent output production" (p. 626).

In a comprehensive study about the value of modified output to learning, McDonough's (2005) research explored the relationship between the production of modified output and L2 question development and past tense usage. In Thailand, 62 learners of English as a foreign language (EFL) carried out a series of communicative tasks with native English speakers in four conditions that provided different feedback and modified output opportunities. The study employed a pretest-posttest design to examine the relationship between the production of modified output and EFL learners' question development and past tense usage. The independent variable, modified output, was learner generated. The treatment conditions manipulated two variables that affected the learners' opportunities to produce modified output: (a) negative feedback in the form of clarification requests and (b) enhanced salience of nontargetlike forms. The treatment materials were information exchange and information gap activities that elicited the target structures. Learners completed an oral production pretest and three posttests. Results showed that modified output involving the target forms was a significant predictor of question development and past-tense improvement. McDonough suggests that both the quantity and quality of modified output may play a role in linguistic development. Her study, like much of the research before it, thus points to the conclusion that there is a relationship between modified output and L2 learning.

1.3.2. OUTPUT SUMMARY

Research on the connections between output and L2 development suggests that output has a number of functions, including promoting automatization, pushing learners to notice gaps in their L2 knowledge, encouraging them to process syntactically rather than just semantically, and providing opportunities for them to test hypotheses they have constructed about the target language. While the production of modified output may be influenced by a number of variables, such as age, whether one's interlocutor is a NS or NNS, and the context of the conversation, there is increasing evidence that opportunities to produce output can facilitate development of the L2.

2. Pedagogical Implications: Task-Based Learning

In light of research on the role of interaction in SLA, researchers have increasingly come to the conclusion that interactionally modified input, feedback, and output can benefit the SLA process. An important practical question relates to how, and perhaps whether, recent work on interaction should be incorporated into the L2 classroom. In their influential articles on the relationship between SLA theory and language pedagogy, both Lightbown (2000) and R. Ellis (1997) have pointed out that given the relative infancy of SLA as a field of inquiry, language teachers should apply the results of both quantitative and qualitative studies carefully in relation to their own classrooms and, at the same time, heed their own counsel regarding what works and what does not work. Nevertheless, R. Ellis (2003) suggests that one potential area of overlap in teachers' and researchers' interests may reside in task-based language teaching.

In both the research and pedagogical literature, tasks have been defined in many ways, ranging from "a piece of work that must be completed" (Gass, 1997, p. 152) to more elaborate operationalizations that include mention of objectives, outcomes, and connections to real-world activities (Bygate, Skehan, and Swain, 2001). As pointed out by Bygate et al., the definition of *task* will vary, depending on whether the focus is pedagogic or research oriented. Generally speaking, however, a task in the pedagogical context refers to a workplan involving information that learners are required to process and use and some instructions relating to what outcome the learners need to achieve (R. Ellis, 2003). More specifically, tasks can be thought of as "bounded classroom activities in which learners use language communicatively to achieve an outcome, with the overall purpose of learning language" (Bygate, 1999, p. 186).

The crucial characteristic of tasks is that they involve some form of learner-learner interaction. In a one-way task, for example, a learner possesses a piece of information (such as a picture) and must convey that information to his or her interlocutor (e.g., by explaining how to draw the picture). Likewise, in a two-way task, learners collaborate to carry out an activity, such as constructing a story from a sequence of pictures. Tasks vary greatly in their complexity, of course, but they all share this emphasis on pair and group work.

The benefits of this kind of in-class interaction include providing learners with opportunities to (a) receive input in the target language, (b) produce and modify their own utterances, (c) shift their attention to form when a problem in comprehension or production arises, and (d) receive feedback on their communicative efforts. Over the years, a body of literature has emerged with respect to various task types (e.g., one-way vs. two-way), task characteristics (e.g., cognitive complexity and topic familiarity), and task implementation (e.g., repetition and planning time) and their differential effects on learner input, output, attention, and opportunities for output (see R. Ellis, 2003, and Pica, Kanagy, and Falodun, 1993, for comprehensive reviews). While this is a relatively new field of investigation, these studies have provided at least preliminary evidence that task-based learning has a promising role to play in promoting learner interaction and thus in helping L2 learners achieve more nativelike proficiency in the L2.

3. Summary

Research has indicated that given the opportunity to interact with interlocutors when a communication problem arises, learners can receive crucial input, including explicit corrections and metalinguistic explanations, as well as more implicit clarification requests, confirmation checks, repetitions, and recasts. These different kinds of input can signal that a learner has produced an ungrammatical utterance and thus provide evidence about what structures are not allowed in the target language. Additionally, interactional features such as recasts can simultaneously provide positive input by reformulating a learner's utterance in a more targetlike manner. Interaction can also make problematic aspects of the learner's interlanguage system salient and thus more open to revision. Helpful interactional patterns, it is also argued, can be facilitated by incorporating task-based activities into the L2 classroom. Of course, as Pica (1994) points out, "no one experience, activity, or endowment can account for all of L2 learning" (p. 517); however, an understanding of research on input and interaction, and its implications for task-based learning, can provide L2 teachers with one more tool in their teaching kits.

4. Exercises

The following exercises involve first analyzing L2 data for evidence of some of the interactional strategies discussed in this chapter, and then doing a guided critique of the study.

4.1. DATA ANALYSIS

The text below is excerpted from a conversation that took place in an intensive ESL classroom. The course was designed to promote conversational fluency while learning about American popular culture. For several weeks of the course, the teacher and students participated in a research study. The goal of this study was to explore the role of interaction in promoting noticing and learning in instructional contexts. During this time, the class viewed popular television shows. In the case of this excerpt, the teacher and students have viewed a show, and the teacher is interacting with the students while they discuss it. Read the excerpt and consider the following questions. (More details of this study are reported in Mackey, 2000.)

1. Are there examples of miscommunication? What evidence is there of nonunderstanding?

2. How is nonunderstanding resolved? Are problematic utterances reformulated?
3. Does the teacher correct nontargetlike utterances? Are corrections implicit or explicit? Are there instances of modified output?
4. How do the learners and teachers collaborate to express meaning?

Excerpt

Learner A: And then go home.
Teacher: And then he goes home? Are you sure it's his house?
Learner A: Perhaps he go spaceship holograph room? Suit?
Teacher: Really?
Learner A: And then he goes back to his planet or to suit?
Teacher: That's more like it then, what do you mean suit?
Learner B: Really? It's his planet? But it is hologram?
Teacher: It has the same houses but look at the three moons. It's not earth.
Learner A: It has houses like earth, made from hologram suit?
Teacher: Driving me nuts. Does the earth have three moons? What do you mean suit?
Learner B: Earth has these type house. He go earth and then his planet.
Teacher: Alternative explanations. Creative. When does he go to earth in this picture?
Learner B: He goes during the break ((laughs))
Learner A: ((laughs)
Teacher: Trying to drive me insane. I get it. Ok, where does he really go?
Learner A: Really, he goes home to his planet by the hologram suit.
Learner B: He go home but maybe not realist have house like earth.
Teacher: You mean the holographic suite? The holodeck? Suite? Suit?
Learner A: I mean suite suite hologram suite like hotel.
Teacher: You had me really confused. Anyway, it's not his planet; he is in the holodeck.

4.2. GUIDED CRITIQUE

Mackey, A., Gass, S. M., & McDonough, K. (2000). How do learners perceive interactional feedback? *Studies in Second Language Acquisition, 22,* 471–497.

1. Read the abstract below.
   a. What was the main goal of this study?
   b. How does the goal relate to the role of feedback in language learning discussed above?

Theoretical claims about the benefits of conversational interaction have been made by Gass (1997), Long (1996), Pica (1994), and others. The Interaction Hypothesis suggests that negotiated interaction can facilitate SLA and that one reason for this could be that, during interaction, learners may receive feedback on their utterances. An interesting issue, which has challenged interactional research, concerns how learners perceive feedback and whether their perceptions affect their subsequent L2 development. The present research addresses the first of these issues—learners' perceptions about interactional feedback. The study, involving 10 learners of English as a second language and 7 learners of Italian as a foreign language, explores learners' perceptions about feedback provided to them through task-based dyadic interaction. Learners received feedback focused on a range of morphosyntactic, lexical, and phonological forms. After completing the tasks, learners watched videotapes of their previous interactions and were asked to introspect about their thoughts at the time the original interactions were in progress. The results showed that learners were relatively accurate in their perceptions about lexical, semantic, and phonological feedback. However, morphosyntactic feedback was generally not perceived as such. Furthermore, the nature as well as the content of the feedback may have affected learners' perceptions.

2. Read the excerpt from the introduction reproduced below. What was the purpose of this section? What assumptions are made about the connections between interaction and language acquisition?

The role of conversational interaction in the acquisition of a second language (L2) is based on a research tradition that covers the past two decades, beginning in the early 1980s. This area of L2 research investigates the role that negotiated interaction (between native [NS] and nonnative [NNS] speakers or between two nonnative speakers) plays in the development of an L2. Negotiated interaction can occur when two speakers work together to arrive at mutual understanding of each other's utterances. Underlying this work is the Interaction Hypothesis, articulated recently by Long (1996): ". . . negotiation of meaning, and especially negotiation work that triggers interactional adjustments by the NS or more competent interlocutor, facilitates acquisition because it connects input, internal learner capacities, particularly selective attention, and output in productive ways" (pp. 451–452). . . .

To make an argument for a connection between interaction and learning, some assumptions need to be made. First, it is assumed that, through interaction, some aspect of learners' attention may become focused on the parts of their language that deviate from target language norms or that, through interaction, attention may be focused on forms not yet in the learners' current repertoire. A second assumption is that this attention, or noticing of the gap (Schmidt & Frota, 1986) between learner language forms and target language forms, is a step toward change.

3. Read the description of the methods below.
   a. Summarize the method for data collection to be used in the study. Given the research questions, is this an appropriate method for gathering data? Are there any potential limitations with this method?
   b. Examine the description of the study participants. How could this information influence the interpretation of the results?
   c. Think about the task employed in the study. Do you think the task was appropriate for the study? What other task types might have also been appropriate?

An investigation of learners' perceptions about interaction is an important aspect of examining the processes by which interaction can lead to L2 development. In this study, we are specifically concerned with the extent to which learners do in fact recognize or perceive (a) feedback provided through interaction and (b) the target of the feedback, that is, what feedback is being provided about.

This study specifically addresses the way second and foreign language learners perceive the feedback they receive in the course of interaction. Thus, the primary question posed by this research was: Do L2 learners accurately perceive feedback that takes place in interaction? By accurately, we mean: Do they perceive the feedback as feedback? and Do they recognize the target of that feedback?

The participants in this study were nonnative speakers in an ESL context and in an Italian as a foreign language (IFL) context. The participants (n = 17) were 11 male and 6 female adult learners enrolled in language courses at a U.S. university. The ESL learners (n = 10) were from a variety of L1 backgrounds including Cantonese, French, Japanese, Korean, and Thai, with an average of 9.3 years of previous English study (ranging from 3 to 15 years). The majority of the students had recently arrived in the country, with an average length of residence of 4.5 months (ranging from 2 to 7 months). The IFL learners (n = 7) had studied or were studying Italian. Their amount of previous study ranged from 6 months to 3 years with an average of 1.8 years. All participants were classified at the beginner or lower-intermediate level by their language programs. . . .

Each learner carried out a communicative task with a native (English) or near-native (Italian) interviewer. The tasks used were two-way information exchange activities. Each participant had a picture that was similar to his or her partner's picture. The tasks involved the learners and interviewers working together to identify the differences between their pictures. Each session lasted for approximately 15–20 minutes and was videotaped. During the interaction, the English and Italian interviewers provided interactional feedback when the participants produced a non-targetlike utterance. The interviewers were instructed to provide interactional feedback wherever it seemed appropriate and in whatever form seemed appropriate during the interaction. Thus, the feedback provided during the task-based interaction occurred in response to errors in morphosyntax, phonology, lexis, or semantics and occurred in the form of negotiation and recasts. A more complete description of the different types of feedback episodes and examples is presented in the section on error and feedback types (pp. 480–481). Not all non-targetlike utterances received feedback from the interviewers. This is probably because excessive (corrective) feedback can lead to dysfluencies or learner irritation (as noted by Aston, 1986), and the goal was to carry out the communicative tasks, providing feedback where appropriate. Also, at times the content-based goals imposed by the task made interactional feedback seem unnatural. Finally, although the tasks provided contexts for a range of linguistic forms to be produced, the errors made by learners could not be tightly controlled, hence neither could the responses. In short, the design of the study required the interviewers to interact, providing feedback (in the form of recasts and negotiation) wherever it seemed natural and appropriate when there were opportunities for such feedback.

Immediately following completion of the task-based activities, the videotape was rewound and played for the learner by a second researcher who also gave the directions for this part of the research to the learner. While watching the videotape, the learners could pause the tape at any time if they wished to describe their thoughts at any particular point in the interaction. The researcher also paused the tape after episodes in which interactional feedback was provided, and asked learners to recall their thoughts at the time the original interaction was going on. These recall sessions, which were audio taped, were conducted in English (the L2 for the ESL participants and the L1 for the IFL participants). This recall procedure was aimed at eliciting learners' original perceptions about the feedback episodes—that is, their perceptions at the time they were taking part in the interaction.

The procedure adopted in this study is generally known as *stimulated recall* (Gass and Mackey, 2000) and its use is well documented in the general L2 literature. It has perhaps most often been used in L2 writing research, where learners introspect about their thoughts while viewing, for example, a videotape of themselves writing, or their written product (drafts or final versions). Stimulated recall is classified as one of the introspective methods, in which learners are asked to articulate their thoughts while performing a task or after the task has been completed. It has been used extensively in information-processing studies, as well as in psychology, education, and, to a lesser extent, SLA. Stimulated recall, like other types of verbal protocols, has been extensively debated in the literature. Some have questioned its validity, whereas others have leapt to its defense. As with all methodologies, it needs to be used cautiously and carefully (for example, specific instructions should be given to learners to orient them to the time of the stimulus), and care should be taken about claims that are made. For example, one limitation on stimulated recall as it is used in this study is that, although it may be sensitive to some of the issues involved in learners' perceptions, it may not be coextensive with perceiving.

4. Read the following excerpt from the data collection section. How will this information be used to address the research questions?

The data set for this study comprises the interactional feedback episodes (n = 192) and the stimulated-recall comments that were provided about the episodes. The number of feedback episodes, including the error and the feedback, ranged from 7 to 18 for each participant, with an average of 11.3. Two separate analyses to code the data were conducted: Both the error and feedback types and the stimulated-recall comments were coded. Definitions and examples of the coding categories for each analysis are given in the following sections.

Error and Feedback Types. Based on the videotapes of the interaction sessions, we transcribed all the episodes of feedback and categorized these episodes based on the error type that had triggered the feedback. The four error types categorized were phonology, morphosyntax, lexis, and semantics. . . .

Stimulated-Recall Comments. In addition to categorizing the original error and feedback types, the participants' perceptions, in the form of their audio taped comments during the stimulated-recall sessions, were transcribed and categorized. The six categories for the stimulated-recall comments [were] lexical, semantic, phonological, morphosyntactic, no content, and unclassifiable. . . . The lexical category was operationalized as containing specific comments about a known or unknown word, including the provision of a synonym and comments about a synonym, or the word itself. . . . The semantic category was operationalized as general comments about communicating meaning, creating understanding, or being unable to express an intended meaning. It also included instances in which the learner provided more detail or elaboration during the recall. . . . The phonological category was operationalized as specific comments about pronunciation. . . . [The] morphosyntax category was operationalized as comments about sentence formation and structure or word order, as well as comments on specific aspects of grammar such as subject-verb agreement and tense. . . . The no content category was operationalized as instances in which the subject participated verbally in the recall, yet said nothing about the content. . . . Coded as unclassifiable were instances in which the learner made comments about specific content, but those comments could not be classified into a particular category. . . .

5. Read the following portion of the discussion section. Summarize the results in your own words. Was there anything unexpected about the results? How might you explain the different patterns revealed by the analysis?

. . . when the feedback provided to the learner during interaction was morphosyntactic in nature, learners recognized the nature of 24% of the feedback. Almost half of the time, they perceived morphosyntactic feedback as being about lexis. The amount of phonological feedback provided to the learners was quite low (18%), with less than a quarter being perceived as related to phonology. In contrast, lexical feedback episodes were perceived to be about lexis almost two-thirds of the time (66%).

In this study of L2 learners' perceptions about feedback in conversational interaction, learners were most accurate in their perceptions about lexical and phonological feedback, and were generally inaccurate in their perceptions about morphosyntactic feedback. Morphosyntactic feedback was often perceived as being about semantics for the ESL learners and about lexis for the IFL learners. Proponents of the Interaction Hypothesis (Gass, 1997; Long, 1996; Pica, 1994) have suggested that interaction can result in feedback that focuses learners' attention on aspects of their language that deviate from the target language. If learners' reports about their perceptions can be equated with attention, then the findings in this study are consistent with the claims of the Interaction Hypothesis, at least with regard to the lexicon and phonology. In terms of morphosyntax, however, these findings are less consistent with researchers' claims about the benefits of interaction, at least at first glance. Exploring the nature of feedback in more detail may shed further light on the findings. It is important to note (as outlined in the Method section) that, in this study, feedback was provided to learners as a natural (non-manipulated) part of task-based interaction. Thus the nature of the feedback type and the forms that attracted feedback varied. Given the results on differing patterns of learner perceptions, we carried out a post hoc analysis to explore the relationship between learners' perceptions, the nature of the interactional feedback, and the linguistic target of the feedback. All of the feedback provided to the learners of the ESL data set was implicit negative feedback (as defined by Long, 1996). We further explored the types of feedback by categorizing and examining the different types of feedback episodes in the data set: recasts, negotiation, and combinations, where negotiation and a recast both occurred in the same episode.

Interestingly, recasts were mostly provided in response to morphosyntactic errors (75% of recasts were in response to morphosyntactic problems, 11% to lexical problems, and 14% to phonological problems).

Negotiation mostly occurred in response to phonological problems (7% of negotiation was related to problems involving morphosyntax, 19% to lexis, and 74% to phonology). Combination episodes also mostly involved phonology (none of the combination episodes involved problems with morphosyntax, 10% involved lexis, and 90% involved phonology). . . . In summary, the finding that morphosyntactic feedback was rarely perceived as being about morphosyntax becomes more interesting when we also note that morphosyntactic feedback was most often provided in the form of a recast.

6. Based on the final part of the discussion reproduced below, what conclusions can you draw about the noticing of feedback by L2 learners? What limitations were there in this study and how might this study be extended?

To summarize, we have shown that morphosyntactic feedback was seldom perceived as being about morphosyntax and was generally provided in the form of recasts. In contrast, feedback on phonology and lexis was perceived more accurately—that is, as being about phonology and lexis—and was generally provided in the form of negotiation and combination episodes. Clearly, the absence of reports of perception does not mean that feedback was not perceived at some level, and perception does not automatically entail or imply L2 development or learning.

Some researchers have expressed cautions about the potential benefits of interactional feedback for different aspects of L2 learning. For example, Pica (1994) claimed that negotiated interaction may be beneficial for lexical learning and for specific L1–L2 contrasts but may be less beneficial for some aspects of L2 morphosyntax. She suggested that this may be due to the focus of interactional feedback, because feedback obtained through negotiated interaction is often provided for lexis or semantics and more rarely for grammar.

The findings reported here shed light on Pica's claims about interaction and grammatical form. In this study, negotiation of meaning seldom involved grammar. However, problem utterances involving morphosyntax were generally recast. Our findings may suggest an additional reason for why interactional feedback may benefit lexis and phonology more than some aspects of grammar. It may be so because, even when morphosyntactic feedback is provided in interaction, through recasts, learners often do not perceive it as such, whereas when phonological and lexical feedback is provided in interaction, they are more likely to perceive it correctly. However, all of these questions need to be addressed by studies that measure development. Another possibility is that, if learners were able to correctly perceive all of the feedback that they received, this would result in a cognitive overload for them; if this is the case, then perceiving a limited amount of feedback at exactly the right developmental time is the optimal condition for the learner. Issues involving the quantity, quality, timing, and nature of feedback and L2 development still need to be carefully isolated and explored. Our findings do suggest that further studies would be worthwhile in the general goal of exploring interaction-driven L2 learning. Finally, we point out that our sample was small and our results should be taken as indicative of the need for further research. For example, individual differences in metalinguistic abilities, working memory, and sensitivity to morphosyntax may have affected perceptions. More focused and finely grained studies (with more participants) are necessary.

Further Reading

Ellis, R. (2003). *Task-based language learning and teaching.* Oxford, UK: Oxford University Press.

Gass, S. M. (1997). *Input, interaction, and the second language learner.* Mahwah, NJ: Lawrence Erlbaum.

Gass, S. M., Mackey, A., & Pica, T. (1998). The role of input and interaction in second language acquisition: Introduction to the special issue. *The Modern Language Journal, 82*(3), 299–307.

Mackey, A. (in press). Interaction and second language development: Perspectives from SLA research. In R. DeKeyser (Ed.), *Practice in second language learning: Perspectives from linguistics and psychology.* Cambridge, UK: Cambridge University Press.

Mackey, A. & Gass, S. M. (2005). *Second language research: Methodology and design.* Mahwah, NJ: Lawrence Erlbaum.

References

Allwright, R. (1975). Problems in the study of the language teacher's treatment of learner error. In M. K. Burt & H. C. Dulay (Eds.), *On TESOL '75: New directions in second language learning, teaching, and bilingual education* (pp. 96–109). Washington, DC: TESOL.

Aston, G. (1986). Trouble-shooting in interaction with learners: The more the merrier? *Applied Linguistics, 7,* 128–143.

Braidi, S. M. (2002). Reexamining the role of recasts in native-speaker/nonnative-speaker interactions. *Language Learning, 52*(1), 1–42.

Bruton, A., & Samuda, V. (1980). Learner and teacher roles in the treatment of oral error in group work. *RELC Journal, 11*(2), 49–63.

Bygate, M. (1999). Quality of language and purpose of task: patterns of learners' language on two oral communication tasks. *Language Teaching Research, 3*(3), 185–214.

Bygate, M., Skehan, P., & Swain, M. (2001). *Researching pedagogic tasks: Second language learning, teaching and testing.* London: Longman.

Carroll, S., & Swain, M. (1991). *Negative evidence in second language learning.* Paper presented at the Second Language Research Forum, University of Southern California, Los Angeles, CA.

Carroll, S., & Swain, M. (1993). Explicit and implicit negative feedback: An empirical study of the learning of linguistic generalizations. *Studies in Second Language Acquisition, 15,* 357–386.

Carroll, S., Swain, M., & Roberge, Y. (1992). The role of feedback in adult second language acquisition: Error correction and morphological generalizations. *Applied Psycholinguistics, 14,* 173–198.

Chaudron, C. (1977). A descriptive model of discourse in the corrective treatment of learners' errors. *Language Learning, 27,* 29–46.

Chun, A., Day, R., Chenoweth, N., & Luppescu, S. (1982). Types of errors corrected in native-nonnative conversations. *TESOL Quarterly, 16,* 537–548.

Crookes, G., & Rulon, K. (1988). Topic and feedback in native-speaker/non-native speaker discourse. *TESOL Quarterly, 22,* 675–681.

Day, R., Chenoweth, A., Chun, A., & Luppescu, S. (1984). Corrective feedback in native-nonnative discourse. *Language Learning, 34*(2), 19–45.

de Bot, K. (1996). The psycholinguistics of the output hypothesis. *Language Learning, 46,* 529–555.

DeKeyser, R. (1993). The effect of error correction on L2 grammar knowledge and oral proficiency. *The Modern Language Journal, 77*(4), 501–514.

Ellis, R. (1997). SLA and language pedagogy: An educational perspective. *Studies in Second Language Acquisition, 20,* 69–92.

Ellis, R. (2003). *Task-based language learning and teaching.* Oxford, UK: Oxford University Press.

Ellis, R., & He, X. (1999). The roles of modified input and output in the incidental acquisition of word meanings. *Studies in Second Language Acquisition, 21,* 285–301.

Ellis, R., Tanaka, Y., & Yamazaki, A. (1994). Classroom interaction, comprehension, and the acquisition of L2 word meanings. *Language Learning, 44,* 449–491.

Fanselow, J. (1977). The treatment of error in oral work. *Foreign Language Annals, 10,* 583–593.

Gaskill, W. (1980). Correction in native speaker-nonnative speaker conversation. In D. Larson-Freeman (Ed.), *Discourse analysis in second language research* (pp. 125–137). Rowley, MA: Newbury House.

Gass, S. M. (1997). *Input, interaction, and the second language learner.* Mahwah, NJ: Lawrence Erlbaum.

Gass, S. M. (2003). Input and interaction. In C. J. Doughty & M. H. Long (Eds.), *The handbook of second language acquisition* (pp. 224–255). Oxford, UK: Blackwell.

Gass, S. M. & Mackey, A. (2000). *Stimulated recall methodology in second language research.* Mahwah, NJ: Lawrence Earlbaum.

Gass, S. M. & Mackey, A. (2002). Frequency effects and second language acquisition. *Studies in Second Language Acquisition, 24,* 249–260.

Gass, S. M., Mackey, A., & Pica, T. (1998). The role of input and interaction in second language acquisition: Introduction to the special issue. *The Modern Language Journal, 82*(3), 299–307.

Gass, S. M., & Varonis, E. M. (1994). Input, interaction, and second language production. *Studies in Second Language Acquisition, 16,* 283–302.

Gregg, K. (1984). Krashen's monitor and Occam's razor. *Applied Linguistics, 5,* 79–100.

Han, Z-H. (2001). Fine-tuning corrective feedback. *Foreign Language Annals, 34,* 582–599.

Han, Z-H. (2002). A study of the impacts of recasts on tense consistency in L2 output. *TESOL Quarterly, 36*(4), 543–572.

Herron, C., & Tomasello, M. (1988). Learning grammatical structures in a foreign language: Modeling versus feedback. *The French Review, 61,* 910–923.

Holley, F. M., & King, J. K. (1971). Imitation and correction in foreign language learning. *The Modern Language Journal, 55,* 494–498.

Inagaki, S., & Long, M. H. (1999). Implicit negative feedback. In K. Kanno (Ed.), *The acquisition of Japanese as a second language* (pp. 9–30). Amsterdam: John Benjamins.

Ishida, M. (2004). Effects of recasts on the acquisition of the aspectual form *-te i-(ru)* by learners of Japanese as a foreign language. *Language Learning, 54*(2), 311–394.

Iwashita, N. (2003). Negative feedback and positive evidence in task-based interaction: Differential effects on L2 development. *Studies in Second Language Acquisition, 25*(1), 1–36.

Krashen, S. D. (1985). *The input hypothesis: Issues and implications.* London: Longman.

Krashen, S. D. (1998). Comprehensible output? *System, 26,* 175–182.

Kubota, M. (1994). The role of negative feedback on the acquisition of the English dative alternation by Japanese college students of EFL. *Institute for Research in Language Teaching Bulletin, 8,* 1–36.

Leeman, J. (2003). Recasts and second language development. *Studies in Second Language Acquisition, 25*(1), 37–63.

Lightbown, P. M. (2000). Anniversary article: Classroom SLA research and second language teaching. *Applied Linguistics, 21*(4), 431–462.

Lightbown, P. M., & Spada, N. (1990). Focus-on-form and corrective feedback in communicative language teaching: Effects on second language learning. *Studies in Second Language Acquisition, 12,* 429–448.

Lightbown, P. M., & Spada, N. (1993). Instruction and the development of questions in L2 classrooms. *Studies in Second Language Acquisition, 15,* 205–224.

Lin, Y., & Hedgcock, J. (1996). Negative feedback incorporation among high-proficiency and low-proficiency Chinese-speaking learners of Spanish. *Language Learning, 46*(4), 567–611.

Long, M. H. (1981). Input, interaction and second language. In H. Winitz (Ed.), *Native language and foreign language acquisition* (pp. 259–278). New York: Annals of the New York Academy of Sciences.

Long, M. H. (1983a). Linguistic and conversational adjustments to nonnative speakers. *Studies in Second Language Acquisition, 5,* 177–194.

Long, M. H. (1983b). Native speaker/non-native speaker conversation and the negotiation of comprehensible input. *Applied Linguistics, 4*(2), 126–141.

Long, M. H. (1988). Instructed interlanguage development. In L. Beebe (Ed.), *Issues in second language acquisition: Multiple perspectives* (pp. 115–141). Rowley, MA: Newbury House.

Long, M. H. (1996). The role of the linguistic environment in second language acquisition. In W. C. Ritchie & T. K. Bhatia (Eds.), *Handbook of second language acquisition: Vol. 2. Second language acquisition* (pp. 413–468). New York: Academic Press.

Long, M. H. (in press). Recasts in SLA: The story so far. In M. H. Long (Ed.), *Problems in SLA.* Mahwah, NJ: Lawrence Erlbaum.

Long, M. H., Inagaki, S., & Ortega, L. (1998). The role of implicit negative feedback in SLA: Models and recasts in Japanese and Spanish. *The Modern Language Journal, 82,* 357–371.

Loschky, L. C. (1994). Comprehensible input and second language acquisition: What is the relationship? *Studies in Second Language Acquisition, 16,* 303–325.

Lyster, R. (1998a). Recasts, repetition, and ambiguity in L2 classroom discourse. *Studies in Second Language Acquisition, 20,* 51–81.

Lyster, R. (1998b). Negotiation of form, recasts, and explicit correction in relation to error types and learner repair in immersion classrooms. *Language Learning, 48,* 183–218.

Lyster, R., & Ranta, L. (1997). Corrective feedback and learner uptake: Negotiation of form in communicative classrooms. *Studies in Second Language Acquisition, 19,* 37–66.

Mackey, A. (1997). *Interactional modifications and the development of questions in English as a second language.* Unpublished manuscript, Michigan State University.

Mackey, A. (1999). Input, interaction, and second language development: An empirical study of question formation in ESL. *Studies in Second Language Acquisition, 21,* 557–587.

Mackey, A. (2000). *Feedback, noticing and second language development. An empirical study of L2 classroom interaction.* Paper presented at BAAL 2000, Cambridge, U.K.

Mackey, A., Gass, S. M., & McDonough, K. (2000). How do learners perceive interactional feedback? *Studies in Second Language Acquisition, 22,* 471–497.

Mackey, A., Oliver, R., & Leeman, J. (2003). Interactional input and the incorporation of feedback: An exploration of NS-NNS and NNS-NNS adult and child dyads. *Language Learning, 53,* 35–66.

Mackey, A., & Philp, J. (1998). Conversational interaction and second language development: Recasts, responses, and red herrings? *The Modern Language Journal, 82,* 338–356.

McDonough, K. (2001). Identifying the impact of negative feedback and learners' response on ESL question development. *Studies in Second Language Acquisition, 27*(1), 79–103.

McLaughlin, B. (1987). *Theories of second language learning.* London: Edward Arnold.

Morris, F. A., & Tarone, E. E. (2003). Impact of classroom dynamics on the effectiveness of recasts in second language acquisition. *Language Learning, 53*(2), 325–368.

Nabei, T., & Swain, M. (2002). Learner awareness of recasts in classroom interaction: A case study of an adult EFL student's second language learning. *Language Awareness, 11*(1), 43–63.

Nicholas, H., Lightbown, P. M., & Spada, N. (2001). Recasts as feedback to language learners. *Language Learning, 51*(4), 719–758.

Nobuyoshi, J., & Ellis, R. (1993). Focused communication tasks and second language acquisition. *ELT Journal, 47,* 203–210.

Ohta, A. S. (2000). Rethinking recasts: A learner-centered examination of correction feedback in the Japanese language classroom. In J. K. Hall & L. S. Verplaetse (Eds.),

Second and foreign language learning through classroom interaction (pp. 47–71). Mahwah, NJ: Lawrence Erlbaum.

Oliver, R. (1995). Negative feedback in child NS/NNS conversation. *Studies in Second Language Acquisition, 17,* 459–483.

Oliver, R. (1998). Negotiation of meaning in child interactions. *The Modern Language Journal, 82,* 372–386.

Oliver, R. (2000). Age differences in negotiation and feedback in classroom and pair work. *Language Learning, 50*(1), 119–151.

Ortega, L., & Long, M. H. (1997). The effects of models and recasts on the acquisition of object topicalization and adverb placement in L2 Spanish. *Spanish Applied Linguistics, 1,* 65–86.

Panova, I. & Lyster, R. (2002). Patterns of corrective feedback and uptake in an adult ESL classroom. *TESOL Quarterly, 36*(4), 573–595.

Philp, J. (2003). Constraints on "noticing the gap": Non-native speakers' noticing of recasts in NS-NNS interaction. *Studies in Second Language Acquisition, 25*(1), 99–126.

Pica, T. (1992). The textual outcomes of native speaker–nonnative speaker negotiation: What do they reveal about second language learning? In C. Kramsch & S. McConnell-Ginet (Eds.), *Text and context: Cross-disciplinary perspectives on language study* (pp. 198–237). Lexington, MA: D. C. Heath.

Pica, T. (1994). Research on negotiation: What does it reveal about second-language learning conditions, processes, and outcomes? *Language Learning, 44,* 493–527.

Pica, T., Kanagy, R., & Falodun, J. (1993). Choosing and using communication tasks for second language instruction and research. In G. Crookes & S. Gass (Eds.), *Tasks and second language learning: Integrating theory and practice* (pp. 9–34). Clevedon, UK: Multilingual Matters.

Pica, T., Young, R., & Doughty, C. (1987). The impact of interaction on comprehension. *TESOL Quarterly, 21,* 738–758.

Pienemann, M., & Johnston, M. (1987). Factors influencing the development of language proficiency. In D. Nunan (Ed.), *Applying second language acquisition research* (pp. 45–141). Adelaide, Australia: National Curriculum Resource Centre.

Schmidt, R. W. (1990). The role of consciousness in second language learning. *Applied Linguistics, 11,* 129–158.

Schmidt, R. W. (Ed.). (1995a). *Attention and awareness in foreign language learning.* Honolulu, HI: Second Language Teaching and Curriculum Center, University of Hawai'i.

Schmidt, R. W. (1995b). Consciousness and foreign language learning: A tutorial on the role of attention and awareness in learning. In R. W. Schmidt (Ed.), *Attention and awareness in foreign language learning* (pp. 1–63). Honolulu, HI: University of Hawai'i at Manoa, Second Language Teaching and Curriculum Center.

Schmidt, R. W., & Frota, S. (1986). Developing basic conversational ability in a second language: A case study of an adult learner of Portuguese. In R. Day (Ed.), *Talking to learn: Conversation in second language acquisition* (pp. 237–326). Rowley, MA: Newbury House.

Shehadeh, A. (2002). Comprehensible output, from occurrence to acquisition: An agenda for acquisitional research. *Language Learning, 52*(3), 597–647.

Shehadeh, A. (2003). Learner output, hypothesis testing, and internalizing linguistic knowledge. *System, 31,* 155–171.

Swain, M. (1985). Communicative competence: Some roles of comprehensible input and comprehensible output in its development. In S. Gass & C. Madden (Eds.), *Input in second language acquisition* (pp. 235–253). Rowley, MA: Newbury House.

Swain, M. (1995). Three functions of output in second language learning. In G. Cook & B. Seidlhofer (Eds.), *Principle and practice in applied linguistics: Studies in honour of H. G. Widdowson* (pp. 125–144). Oxford, UK: Oxford University Press.

Swain, M. (2000). The output hypothesis and beyond: Mediating acquisition through collaborative dialogue. In J. P. Lantolf (Ed.), *Sociocultural theory and second language learning* (pp. 97–114). Oxford, UK: Oxford University Press.

Swain, M., & Carroll, S. (1987). The immersion observation study. In B. Harley, P. Allen, J. Cummins, & M. Swain (Eds.), *The development of bilingual proficiency final report: Classroom treatment* (Vol. 2, pp. 190–342). Toronto, Canada: Modern Language Centre, The Ontario Institute for Studies in Higher Education.

Swain, M., & Lapkin, S. (1995). Problems in output and the cognitive processes they generate: A step towards second language learning. *Applied Linguistics, 16,* 371–391.

Tomasello, M., & Herron, C. (1989). Feedback for language transfer errors. *Studies in Second Language Acquisition, 11,* 384–395.

van den Branden, K. (1997). Effect of negotiation on language learners' output. *Language Learning, 47*(4), 589–636.

White, L. (1991). Adverb placement in second language acquisition: Some effects of positive and negative evidence in the classroom. *Second Language Research, 7,* 133–161.

EIGHT

Explicitness in Pedagogical Interventions: Input, Practice, and Feedback

CRISTINA SANZ

KARA MORGAN-SHORT

KEY WORDS

Explicit and implicit feedback ■ explicit and implicit knowledge ■ explicit and implicit processing ■ manipulated input ■ metalinguistic information ■ pedagogical intervention ■ practice.

1. Introduction

Do adults learn second languages through simple exposure as do children? Do innate or biological mechanisms for language acquisition become constrained with age? Is it possible for adults to reach nativelike accuracy and fluency without exposure to grammar explanation and overt, repeated error correction? Does providing adult learners with information about how the language works (i.e., metalinguistic information) help them (a) by accelerating the process, (b) by enabling it to progress farther than it would in a naturalistic environment, or (c) by both? These are pertinent questions to researchers interested in language and cognition as well as to those whose goal is to optimize second language (L2) teaching.

The language-teaching profession expects applied linguists to provide guidelines for the most effective pedagogical approaches. Information is needed regarding what grammar to explain, when to explain it, whether to correct errors or not, how to correct errors, and how much and what kind of practice to provide L2 learners. Nativist accounts of second language acquisition (SLA) are not helpful points of departure in addressing the above questions because they view all language acquisition as a process driven by internal factors and undisturbed by external manipulations. Information-processing accounts, largely based on cognitive psychology research, do, however, address these issues. Researchers working from this perspective have examined explicitness in the input, in the way the input is processed by the learner, and in the resulting knowledge in order to understand whether external manipulations of both the nature of the input and the way it is presented affect L2 learning.

Degrees of explicitness in the input need to be clearly distinguished from explicit processing of the input as well as from explicit knowledge. While input is an external variable, both processing and knowledge are variables internal to the learner. Hence, while input can be manipulated, recorded, transcribed, and measured, processing and knowledge are abstract psychological realities that are difficult to observe and quantify. SLA researchers who are interested in explicit and implicit L2 processing ask learners to interact with treatments, that is, experimental conditions that vary in their degree of explicitness (e.g., with more or less focus on form, with more or less information about the language). The goal is to see whether external manipulation induces implicit or explicit modes of internal processing, which are differentiated by the presence of awareness on the part of the learner (Schmidt, 2001). Other researchers who are interested in the product of L2 learning evaluate whether external manipulation results in implicit or explicit knowledge. The former is unverbalizable and used without awareness, while the latter is verbalizable and used with awareness (Paradis, 1994). It bears repeating that controlling and measuring the explicitness or implicitness of L2 processing and knowledge is at least extremely difficult and perhaps impossible.

In the 1970s, largely due to Stephen Krashen's (1985) influence, these three factors, input, processing, and knowledge, were seen as working in conjunction: Implicit input (meaningful language) was assumed to be processed implicitly (without attention to form, only to meaning) and to result in implicit knowledge (true linguistic competence). Exposure to explicit evidence (grammar explanation) was considered to be processed explicitly (with attention to form) and to result in learned, explicit knowledge (available only for self-correction). Since then the field has developed in different directions. Researchers (Anderson, 1983, 1992, 1993; DeKeyser, 2003) suggest that language can be learned explicitly and then become implicit through practice, and that both explicit and implicit evidence may be processed with attention to develop knowledge that can be explicit, implicit, or both (Doughty and Williams, 1998; Long and Robinson, 1998; Spada, 1997).

For about thirty years, SLA researchers have utilized pedagogical interventions to attempt to investigate the positions presented above.[1] Pedagogical interventions result when one or more of the following are provided with practice: explicit rule presentation, manipulated input, and feedback. Each of these three variables can be placed along a continuum from more explicit to more implicit: The more metalinguistic the learning condition, the more explicit it is; the more "naturalistic" the learning condition, the more implicit it is considered to be. How these variables change along the continuum can be illustrated by considering manipulated input. The goal of manipulated input is to make the target forms more salient in order to increase the chances of being detected and processed by the language learner (see Mackey and Abbuhl, this volume, chapter 7). We can classify the explicitness of manipulated input by indicating to what degree it is adjusted for use in language instruction. Manipulated input is more implicit when target forms in the input are simply enhanced typographically (Jourdenais, Ota, Stauffer, Boyson, and Doughty, 1995) or prosodically (Leeman, 2003) or when the frequency of the target form is increased, as in *input-flooding* (Trahey and White, 1993). Manipulated input, however, can also be structured, as it is in processing instruction (PI) studies. Structured input is probably the most explicit form of input, as it includes four levels of manipulation: (a) only one form is presented at a time; (b) the key form appears at the beginning of the sentence, increasing its saliency; (c) the frequency of the form is increased; and (d) the input is presented through task-essential activities. In sum, the more one manipulates the L2 input, the more explicit it is considered to be. (See VanPatten, this volume, chapter 9, for details on the theoretical underpinnings of PI and structured input).

A significant amount of evidence based on pedagogical interventions shows positive effects for explicit L2 teaching. Both DeKeyser's (2003) recent review of the literature and Norris and Ortega's (2000) metanalysis conclude that explicit types of instruction are more effective than implicit types. However, the debate on the effectiveness of explicit instruction continues in large part due to the limitation of the measurements used in SLA research. It is not uncommon for researchers who claim to have effected a change in participants' implicit knowledge to be criticized on the basis of their measurements. How can the researchers be sure that participants' performances on the tests were not contaminated by explicit knowledge? How can they be sure of the extent to which learners focused their attention on the critical form? Perhaps learners were aware of a new relationship between form and meaning but chose not to verbalize it, and so their true levels of awareness were not apparent. The problem is obvious: We do not have a window into the mind. This is why some researchers are turning to cognitive neuroscience and brain imaging techniques in search for answers (see Segalowitz, 2003, and Ullman, this volume, chapter 5). Until these techniques prove enlightening, SLA researchers should continue to examine not only group differences within studies and effect sizes across studies but also important differences in the design of the studies. In this light, the present chapter will consider two key factors that have differed between studies and that have been previously ignored: (a) whether studies provided exposure or practice specifically directed at the target form, and (b) what type of practice was provided. The remainder of this section will consider the factor of practice.

As indicated above, SLA research has typically focused on explicit rule presentation, manipulated input, and feedback, rather than the actual practice that contextualizes them. Indeed, one can choose to include rule presentation or feedback in a treatment, but both input and practice—*task* or *activity* in more pedagogical terms[2]—must be present. There is no widely accepted definition of *practice,* a term of common use and in need of careful definition and operationalization. DeKeyser's (2003) discussion of explicit versus implicit processes and Segalowitz's (2003) discussion of automatization make frequent use of the term without providing a definition, even though it is through practice that explicit knowledge is posited to become implicit and that declarative knowledge is posited to be proceduralized. In real life, people talk about *practicing the piano,* meaning using a particular skill repetitively for the purpose of improving it, developing fluency. Cognitive psychologists associate fluency with fast, automatic, effortless, and error-free performance. So at piano practice, we sit and play. To learn a language, do we sit and complete transformational drills, just as we would play scales on a piano? The answer is "probably not," unless we were to adopt a skill acquisition approach to practice—long-term, repetitious, time-consuming, and potentially unmotivating—as described in DeKeyser (1997).

What are the characteristics of practice evident in SLA research? When learners are asked to read and memorize sentences (Robinson, 1996, 1997) or read passages for comprehension (Alanen, 1995), they are exposed to the target forms. Practice requires learners to interact in some way with the target form in the input, to respond to the information. For example, when students are asked to listen to a sentence and choose the picture described (Sanz and Morgan-Short, 2004), this is an instance of *input-based* practice. Practice can also be *output-based.* Output-based activities are always a form of practice in that they require learners to produce the L2 forms; for example, learners are asked to provide instructions to get from A to B on a map (Gass and Varonis, 1994) or to reconstruct a text (Izumi, 2002).

In addition, practice can be more or less explicit depending on the purpose for using the language: to extract meaning or to manipulate form. For example, reading for comprehension is more implicit than a grammatical fill-in-the-blanks exercise. Finally, practice can be *task-essential* or not. Task-essentialness is defined by Loschky and Bley-Vroman (1993, p. 132) as "the most extreme demand a task can place on a structure . . . the task cannot be successfully performed unless the structure is used." They also state that "structural accuracy in comprehension and production should be made essential to meaning in the task" (p. 131). In this chapter, it will become evident that practice interacts with other elements of the treatment (rule explanation and feedback). Practice as a construct needs to be further dissected and its characteristics (whether it is input- vs. output-based, how explicit, how task-essential) revealed in order to explain the differential effects of explicit input found in the studies.[3] Other researchers (Doughty 2003, pp. 267–268) agree with us (Sanz and Morgan-Short, 2004) in calling for greater attention to practice both in SLA research and pedagogy.

The remainder of this chapter is divided into five sections. The first reviews research in cognitive psychology and its relationship to research on explicitness in SLA. It is followed by a section on the effects of explicit rule presentation prior to practice and then by a section on studies on the effects of feedback, specifically explicit feedback. The last section focuses on the interaction between explicit rule presentation, explicit feedback, manipulated input, and practice. The chapter concludes with a summary of the main points.

2. The Issue of Explicit and Implicit Learning in Cognitive Psychology

Cognitive psychology has compared the effectiveness of explicit and implicit learning in controlled empirical studies. One line of such research has examined artificial grammar learning (AGL). Reber (1967, 1976, 1989, 1993) has conducted several AGL investigations. In these studies, participants view strings of letters, which conform to a finite-state rule system, under explicit or implicit learning conditions. In explicit learning conditions, participants are generally asked to search for rules that govern the strings of letters but are sometimes provided with the rules. In implicit learning conditions, in contrast, participants are asked to memorize the strings of input. Hence explicit learning conditions are operationalized as rule search or instruction on how the language works while implicit learning conditions are operationalized as memorization. After exposure to the letter strings, participants are made aware of the fact that a rule system exists and are asked to judge whether both novel and previously encountered letter strings conform to that rule system.

Results from these experiments showed that participants in implicit conditions learned the abstract rules better than those in explicit conditions (Reber, 1967, 1976). In addition, participants in the implicit condition were able to generalize the abstract rules to new letter strings (Reber, 1967). Based on this series of experiments, Reber has concluded that abstract patterns (rules) of artificial finite grammars are implicitly acquired. These conclusions, however, are not uncontroversial. Some researchers account for the results by arguing that participants hold conscious memory of letter strings (i.e., bigrams or trigrams) which allow them to correctly judge the new strings of letters (Knowlton and Squire, 1994; Servan-Schreiber and Anderson, 1990). Other researchers suggest that learners' internal processing strategies may not necessarily match the external explicit or implicit conditions and find that learners under implicit learning conditions develop a conscious rule system, that is, explicit knowledge (Dulany, Carlson, and Dewey, 1984, 1985). Support for implicit learning, however, is reinforced by evidence from amnesic patients, whose impaired declarative memory system precludes explicit learning (see Ullman, this volume, chapter 5, for more information on declarative/procedural memory systems). While amnesic patients cannot recognize letter strings used during AGL training, they perform as well as normal subjects when classifying items as grammatical or nongrammatical (Knowlton and Squire, 1994, 1996).

It is not uncommon for SLA studies investigating explicit and implicit L2 learning to be motivated by cognitive psychology research (DeKeyser, 1997; Robinson, 1996, 1997; Rosa and O'Neill, 1999). However, while studies within cognitive psychology may be informative for SLA, there are sufficient differences between the two fields to merit caution when results are generalized from one to the other. A significant characteristic that distinguishes cognitive psychology research from that of SLA is the nature of the experimental conditions. Cognitive psychology manipulates conditions by assigning each group a different task that purportedly manipulates the learner's internal learning processes. In other words, they attempt to manipulate the way participants process information in order to measure the learning conditions' effects on knowledge that is used to judge a sentence's grammaticality. SLA researchers, however, attempt to manipulate not only internal conditions but external conditions too. While both SLA and cognitive psychology studies have asked participants to look for rules or to memorize the input in an attempt to direct the participants' processing of the task (± explicit) condition, SLA studies more often additionally provide explicit information about the language or manipulate the input to make rules and forms more salient.

In addition, a number of SLA studies differ from cognitive psychology studies in the way they present input. Rather than simply exposing participants to raw evidence, some SLA studies are designed to push participants to react to it under practice conditions, as opposed to exposure-only conditions. The importance of this external manipulation is obvious for pedagogy since having learners respond to input through practice elicits more classroomlike behavior than merely observing or memorizing the language. We will return to this issue at the end of the chapter. A final methodological difference is that SLA studies often use multiple means of assessment to measure effects on learners' abilities to both interpret and produce the L2 while cognitive psychology studies tend to rely on grammaticality judgment tests.

A further difference between the two fields of research lies in the input to be learned. SLA researchers work within a functional framework, which entails the use of natural languages (or, in a few cases, meaning-bearing seminatural or artificial languages) and the study of form-meaning connections. Cognitive psychology research, on the other hand, assesses the learning of artificial grammars, which are devoid of meaning. In addition to the issue of reference, one must also consider other aspects of the grammar rules to be learned in AGL. First, while the rule complexity of a finite grammar may be explained straightforwardly, a multitude of factors must be considered when classifying rules of natural languages. In natural languages, both internal factors (i.e., L1 transfer and cognitive capacity) and external factors (i.e., saliency, frequency, communicative value, and more than one form for one meaning, or vice versa) interact to make a form more or less complex. Indeed, rule complexity may be one possible means of explaining what in principle looks like contradicting results between studies. For example, explicit evidence might not enhance the acquisition of a rule that is too complex or too simple (see Hulstjin and de Graaff, 1994, for discussion). Even within SLA, the definition of simple versus complex forms remains under discussion. For example, DeKeyser, Salaberry, Robinson, and Harrington (2002) claim that the preverbal Spanish direct object clitic system "boils down to a simple morphological alternation" (p. 813, quoted verbatim in DeKeyser, 2003, p. 325). In contrast, Sanz (1999) chooses the same form as an example of a complex, late-acquired Spanish structure that benefits from a focus-on-form treatment. She argues for the complexity of the form based on L1 and L2 acquisition data and knowledge of diachronic and synchronic variations of the form.

Second, in relation to grammar rules, various types should be considered. A growing number of SLA studies look at the relative effects of pedagogical interventions on various aspects of syntax, morphology, and even the lexicon in the same study. Such research often shows that effects vary depending on aspects of the language and rule complexity (de Graaff, 1997; Gass, Svetics, and Lemelin, 2003; Ortega and Long, 1997; Robinson, 2002). Research based on finite-state grammars may not be able to speak to the variety of complexities and types of rules found in natural languages. In fact, it has been argued that important differences between finite-state grammars and natural languages (namely, that finite-state grammars lack movement rules, surface features, and meaning) make it impossible to generalize findings from cognitive psychology to SLA (VanPatten, 1994). In sum, the reader should bear in mind the distinctions between cognitive psychology and SLA research methodology and between finite-state grammars and natural languages, and consider the complexity and features of individual rules when approaching the rest of the chapter. Despite the differences pointed out between the two fields of research, an understanding of relevant cognitive psychology research provides a theoretical foundation from which explicit and implicit issues are often explored in SLA.

3. SLA Research on Explicit Rule Presentation Prior to Input

SLA research has not provided clear evidence regarding the effects of explicit rule presentation presented prior to L2 input. Indeed, results from such research show that explicit rule presentation may lead to positive effects (Alanen, 1995; de Graff, 1997; DeKeyser, 1995; N. C. Ellis, 1993; Robinson, 1996, 1997; Scott, 1989, 1990), no effects (Rosa and O'Neill, 1999; Sanz and Morgan-Short, 2004; VanPatten and Oikkenon, 1996), or even negative effects (Alanen, 1995; Pica, 1983; Robinson, 1996). This section will review studies that show either positive effects, no effects, or negative effects for explicit rule presentation provided prior to exposure to the form and will consider limitations of the methodological design of the studies that hinder the ability to draw strong conclusions from the research.

3.1. POSITIVE EFFECTS

In order to isolate the effects on SLA of explicit rule presentation, researchers have made use of both natural and artificial languages under both exposure and practice conditions. Grammaticality judgments and controlled production task measures of L2 knowledge have generally shown positive effects for explicit rule presentation (Alanen, 1995; DeKeyser, 1995; N. C. Ellis, 1993; Robinson, 1996, 1997). In many of these studies, summarized in Table 8.A (see Appendix), learners are exposed to L2 forms and are generally instructed to read sentences for a variety of purposes (meaning, memorization, or rule search) but do not in fact practice responding to the specific target form in a meaningful manner.

Robinson (1996, 1997) examined the effects of explicit rule presentation and found evidence that explicit rule presentation had a significant effect on learners' abilities to learn target forms, as evidenced by performance on grammaticality judgment tasks, when combined with exposure to input. Alanen (1995) provided evidence that groups receiving explicit instruction performed better on a production measure (i.e., sentence completion tasks) than groups that did not receive explicit information. Participants in this study were exposed to the target forms when reading two passages for meaning. DeKeyser (1995) showed that explicit rule presentation, as opposed to more implicit conditions, had beneficial effects for the acquisition of categorical rules. Furthermore, results indicated that rules were in fact not acquired implicitly since the implicit group did not perform above chance level on the production task. Participants in this study, similar to those in Robinson (1996, 1997) and Alanen (1995), were exposed to L2 forms; they had been trained by viewing written L2 sentences and corresponding pictures. Hence the results from these studies show that explicit information about the language is relevant for learners *exposed* to target forms.

It is probable that explicit rule presentation would have a different effect on learners who interact with L2 forms through practice, given that the practice itself might influence what is learned under any given condition, as evidenced in N. C. Ellis (1993), de Graaff (1997), and Rosa and O'Neill (1999; see section 3.2 below for more discussion). N. C. Ellis (1993) investigated the effects of rule presentation with and without examples and found that explicit instruction, particularly that which contained instances of the target form, facilitated L2 acquisition as measured by grammaticality judgment tasks. During this study's training phase, subjects completed a type of input-based practice: They were asked to translate Welsh phrases into English. This task, however, may be argued to be a mechanical exercise lacking communicative context.

de Graaff (1997) also assessed the effects of explicit rule presentation when participants practiced target forms. His results indicated that when combined with exposure to the input and practice, explicit instruction was beneficial to the process of SLA. These results should be viewed in light of two considerations. First, a confounding factor in this study is that learners were provided with explicit negative feedback in addition to explicit rule presentation. Second, while instruction included seven types of practice activities, only one was reported to require learners to make form-meaning connections during practice. In other words, the great majority of instruction was not characterized by task-essentialness.[4] Thus, the beneficial effects of explicit rule presentation are observed only when combined with practice that is not highly communicative or primarily task-essential. Explicit rule presentation is redundant otherwise.

It would be valuable if laboratory studies, such as those reviewed above, were complemented by classroom research comparing explicit and implicit rule presentation. Unfortunately, studies of this kind that avoid uncontrolled variables are difficult to design. Scott (1989, 1990) and Winitz (1996) conducted studies that were attempts to investigate the effects of explicit and implicit instructional methods in a classroom environment. Winitz found that after a semester, students instructed implicitly performed significantly better on grammaticality judgment tests than students instructed explicitly. Scott's results, on the other hand, indicated an advantage for explicit over implicit instruction for students receiving multiple exposures to a target form. These conflicting results cannot be meaningfully contrasted due to confounding factors, such as uncontrolled amounts of input and use of reference materials, that are inherent to studies with open designs (i.e., those that cover extended periods of time or involve multiple exposures to the target forms). For instance, students in Winitz's implicit group may have consulted reference materials containing explicit information during the course of the semester, invalidating the group as an implicit group. Moreover, the amount of exposure to L2 versus the amount and type of practice with the L2 is not made clear. Other problems specific to these studies are that the types of tests administered are limited, and the test items themselves are few and of a very controlled type. It was found to be statistically significant that Scott's (1989) explicit group improved their score from 7 out of 20 to 8 out of 20 possible points while the implicit group did not improve their average score of 5 out of 20, but these gains are not representative of those that instructors normally strive for. Limitations such as these are regrettable given that effective classroom research would have high ecological validity for instructed SLA.

3.2. NO EFFECTS

Interestingly, some studies have found results indicating that explicit information is not necessary for acquisition of some target forms (Rosa and O'Neill, 1999; Sanz and Morgan-Short, 2004; VanPatten and Oikkenon, 1996). The common factor between such studies, shown in Table 8.B (see Appendix), is that learners are provided with task-essential practice. Rosa and O'Neill (1999) investigated how explicit formal instruction or directions to search for rules affected intake when learners were exposed to a target form through a puzzle task which required that two clauses be matched in order to correctly form a complete sentence and which provided learners with implicit feedback. Their findings contradicted studies that found positive effects for explicit information in that (a) all groups made significant gains, (b) the experimental groups did not outperform the control group, and (c) the instructed groups did not outperform the rule-search group. Based on these results, Rosa and O'Neill concluded that "task demands may have an influence on how L2 input is processed" (p. 546).

This conclusion was further supported by evidence from VanPatten and Oikkenon (1996), which examined the isolated effects of explicit information and structured input in processing instruction (PI) (recall that this is a specific pedagogical intervention that leads learners to make form-meaning connections). Structured input was presented through practice, and it was essential that learners attend to the target form in order to understand the meaning. The findings of this study led the authors to suggest that structured input activities, that is, task-essential practice as opposed to explanation, were primarily responsible for the linguistic benefits found in PI. The findings of this study would be more noteworthy if the methodological design had controlled better the amount of time on task and the feedback offered during treatment. However, the results taken together with other PI studies (Benati, 2004; Wong 2004; VanPatten, 2002) suggest that the element of structured input but not rule explanation may be key to acquisition. Indeed, Sanz and Morgan-Short

(2004) controlled for and examined the effects of feedback and found further evidence for the beneficial role of structured input combined with task-essential practice as compared to explanation. In sum, it seems that with certain tasks, the practice itself and not the explicit condition under which the practice is carried out may lead to acquisition.

3.3. NEGATIVE EFFECTS

As early as 1983, Pica compared naturalistic, classroom, and mixed learners of English as a foreign or second language and identified overuse (the use of morphemes in nonobligatory contexts, e.g., a preterit used when an imperfect is needed) and overgeneralization (e.g., the conjugation of an irregular verb as if it were regular) as two sources of errors characteristic of explicitly instructed learners. In at least one study (Tomasello and Herron, 1988), overgeneralization was assumed to be an aspect of instruction that could be exploited to lead learners to make their hypotheses more accurate. Indeed, some studies that examine the issue of explicit SLA have found additional evidence of the role overgeneralization plays (Alanen, 1995; Robinson, 1996). For instance, an unexpected finding in Alanen (1995) was that her most explicit group, the "Rule & Enhance" group, had lower mean scores on the grammaticality judgment test than the other experimental groups. By analyzing think-aloud data, Alanen was able to attribute that behavior to participants' overgeneralization of a rule. While overuse and overgeneralization may be negative effects of explicit conditions, more research is needed in order to evaluate their possible long-term effects.

4. Research on the Effects of Explicit Feedback

Most studies that address the effects of grammatical explanation generally offer feedback as part of their operationalization of instruction. This use of feedback, when not clearly defined, becomes a confounding variable that may interact with explanation. Complicating matters further, the type of feedback offered varies widely among the studies. Its range includes feedback that is (a) given to an entire class, (b) addressed to an individual in a classroom setting, or (c) provided by a computer program to an individual indicating the correctness of an individual's answer or offering additional explicit information. While most researchers have not isolated feedback as a variable, others have aimed to explore the role of feedback in L2. For the purposes of the present chapter, we will focus on studies that have attempted to isolate the relevant effects of explicit and implicit feedback (see Sanz, 2004, for further discussion of feedback in general and Mackey and Abbuhl, this volume, chapter 6, for an interactionist perspective on feedback). As before, studies will be reviewed in general terms, with more detail available in Table 8.C (see Appendix).

4.1. POSITIVE EFFECTS

Carroll and Swain (1993) investigated effects of different types of feedback. The performance of four experimental feedback groups, including one group that received metalinguistic information and a control group, were compared after a training session during which participants viewed four examples, heard instructions, and produced the target form. Results indicated that all groups receiving feedback performed significantly better than the control group. Also, the group whose feedback included metalinguistic information outperformed all other groups. Carroll and Swain concluded that both direct and indirect forms of feedback could aid L2 learners' mastery of abstract linguistic generalizations, but that explicit feedback was most helpful. This study provides us with further evidence that explicit information is beneficial when learners are primarily exposed to the target form and then asked to produce it.

Nagata (1993; Nagata and Swisher, 1995) also isolated the effects of explicit and implicit written feedback. Nagata's traditional group (T-CALI) received feedback without metalinguistic information while the intelligent group (I-CALI) received feedback consisting of metalinguistic explanations. Participants wrote L2 (Japanese) sentences based on situations which were described to them in their native language (English), a task similar to translation. Analyses showed that after four computer treatment sessions, the type of feedback did not affect production of verbal predicates but that metalinguistic information was beneficial for the production of particles. Considering these findings in light of the type of practice provided, we again are led to conclude that explicit information is beneficial when practice is not task-essential. This conclusion parallels that from the review of studies examining explicit information provided prior to practice; explicit information is beneficial when learners are exposed to L2 forms or when practice does not crucially depend on processing the form for meaning in order to complete the task.

4.2. NO EFFECTS

The literature has not identified negative effects of explicit feedback on learners' L2 production. But is it possible that explicit feedback does not affect L2 development? Sanz (2004) shows that explicit feedback provided for input-decoding performance during online sentence processing does not enhance the acquisition of morphosyntax as measured by interpretation and production tasks. Due to lack of space and because the study is part of a larger project (Sanz and Morgan-Short, 2004), we refer the reader to section 5 for further details. In general, Sanz (2004) concluded that the effects of explicit feedback appear to depend on whether it is provided during production or during practice interpreting input, and in combination with task-essential practice or simple exposure. More experimental research focusing on the differential effects of explicit and implicit feedback is needed.

5. Research on Effects of Both Explicit Rule Presentation and Explicit Feedback

Studies that carefully and systematically control for both grammatical explanation and feedback are few but potentially highly informative. Two studies in particular have controlled for both variables: Sanz and Morgan-Short (2004), and Rosa (1999, published as Rosa and Leow, 2004a, 2004b) (see Table 8.D in the Appendix for details). While both studies examine the effects of explicit explanation and explicit feedback in relation to practice rather than to mere exposure to the target form, they arrive at different conclusions. Rosa and Leow (2004a, 2004b) improved the methodological design and extended Rosa and O'Neill (1999): The task was contextualized and computerized, a written production task was added, and delayed tests were administered. An additional difference was that groups comprised combinations of [± task-essential practice], [± explicit instruction] and [± explicit or implicit feedback] rather than [± formal instruction] and [± rule search]. While Rosa and O'Neill found that all groups, including a control group, made significant gains, Rosa and Leow's results indicated that the experimental groups made significant gains but that the control group, which was only exposed to the forms, did not. There also seemed to be a fundamental difference between one of the experimental groups compared to the other experimental groups. The group that received only implicit feedback did not outperform the control group and was outperformed by the other experimental groups on the recognition of new items and the production of new and old items. In sum, these results seem to indicate that even with task-essential practice, providing at least one form of explicit information (grammatical explanation or feedback) is beneficial.

Upon close consideration of the task itself, however, one might argue that the group receiving only implicit feedback was not able to make form-meaning connections since the meaningful context for the form (whether it referred to a present or past hypothetical situation) was always supplied with the explicit information. Thus it is possible to say that all the experimental groups except the implicit feedback group completed task-essential practice, while the implicit feedback group and control group did not. If this is true, we would expect the implicit feedback group to pattern with the control group, a prediction that is consistent with the results. While the authors concluded that type and degree of explicitness have differential effects (specifically, that more explicit treatments lead to significantly higher levels of linguistic attainment), it appears that the primacy of the task outweighs the advantages of explicit information.

Sanz and Morgan-Short (2004) investigated the effects of explicit information on the acquisition of Spanish word order by comparing four groups: [+ explanation] and [+ explicit feedback], [− explanation] and [− explicit feedback] (i.e., exposure to structured input only), [+ explanation] but [− explicit feedback], and [− explanation] but [+ explicit feedback]. All groups were exposed to structured input through practice tasks. A computer-assisted language learning design was implemented in order to provide feedback that was immediate, individualized, and focused on the target form. This design allowed the study to address a limitation of PI studies (VanPatten and Oikkenon, 1996) as well as other studies focusing on the effects of explicit information (e.g., Alanen, 1995; de Graaff, 1997; N. C. Ellis, 1993; Robinson, 1996, 1997; Rosa and O'Neill, 1999), namely, that feedback was often left as an uncontrolled variable. Results from Sanz and Morgan-Short showed that all groups improved significantly on both interpretation and production tests and that no group significantly outperformed any other group on any test. The authors concluded that exposing L2 learners to structured input through carefully designed task-essential practice is sufficient to promote acquisition. In such a context, providing learners with explicit information on how the language works, either through explanation, feedback, or both, does not significantly add to the knowledge gained through practice.

With the sole exception of Rosa and Leow (2004a, 2004b), SLA studies have not compared the relative effects of explicit treatments and exposure versus explicit treatments and practice. It has been shown that the presence or absence of practice as well as the type of practice interact with rule presentation and feedback. The beneficial effects of explicit rule presentation and feedback in combination with simple L2 exposure are neutralized when combined with exposure to manipulated input presented through task-essential practice (Sanz and Morgan-Short, 2004; Rosa and Leow, 2004a, 2004b). The contradictory results of Carroll and Swain (1993) and Sanz and Morgan-Short (2004) regarding the effects of explicit feedback on the acquisition of L2 syntax may be explained be the type of practice involved—input-based or output-based. Obviously, the issue of practice cannot be overlooked any longer, and in fact some researchers are already paying attention to the issue. Doughty (2003) provides the cognitive underpinnings for a necessary refocusing of the issue of explicitness in pedagogical literature, from the provision of explicit information to the development and testing of tasks (classroom or computer-delivered) that work with the learners' processes in mind. These tasks should promote "the processing of chunks of meaningful language with only perceptual (not metacognitive) attention drawn to redundant and hard-to-notice forms" (Doughty 2004, p. 263), with input elaboration or enhancement, rather than simplification, and task-essentialness as necessary characteristics.

6. Summary and Future Research

This chapter has attempted to shed some light on a key issue in language acquisition. While children acquire one, two, or even more languages through mere exposure to them, SLA research shows that the L2 competence of adult learners seems to benefit from metalinguistic information, that is, from being given information regarding how the language works. Exposure to explicit evidence seems to speed up the process of language acquisition and to further the level of ultimate attainment. The overwhelming majority of experimental studies comparing groups under implicit and explicit conditions show an advantage for the latter.

However, there are several reasons for which caution is necessary when drawing conclusions from studies on the effects of explicit instruction. First, considering that many studies offered only short treatments and assessments tapping explicit knowledge (Norris and Ortega, 2000), it is probable that implicit groups were at a disadvantage. Moreover, studies showing positive effects are generally limited to specific aspects of the language—mostly syntax and some morphology—and to specific forms and rules. It has been posited that explicit instruction might affect the acquisition of simple rules but that its effects might not be as evident for more complex forms (de Graaff, 1997; DeKeyser, 1995; Robinson, 1996). A continuum leading from simple to complex structures and forms based on numerous interrelated criteria would no doubt make this distinction more precise.

Finally, the power of rule presentation and explicit feedback is moderated by the presence or absence of practice and by the type of practice, that is, whether it is task-essential. A distinction needs to be made in future research between treatments that compare the effects of explicit information in combination with exposure to target forms or practice that is not task-essential and those that compare the effects of explicit information in combination with task-essential practice. Results from VanPatten and Oikkenon (1996), Benati (2004), and Wong (2004) show that learners change their processing strategies when practice decoding structured input requires it, but not when they are only told how to decode the input. Similarly, explicit information, when provided before practice, during practice, or both, did not lead to beneficial effects (Sanz and Morgan-Short, 2004). Therefore, further research should isolate and investigate practice, an integral part of pedagogical design almost ignored until recently. Swain's (1995, 1998) work on output practice, along with research on input-decoding practice carried out by VanPatten (1994, 2002, 2004) and VanPatten and Oikkenon (1996), and Rosa and Leow's (2004a, 2004b) work on task-essential practice, are fruitful paths to follow.

Further research is also necessary to understand the underlying mechanisms responsible for making pedagogical interventions more efficient. It might be that they help allocate attention (recall the focus-on-form literature), narrow the number of hypotheses to be formulated by the learner (Swain, 1995, 1998), tune weights in neural networks (McDonald, 1989), or consolidate memory traces (MacWhinney, 1997). The implicit-explicit distinction is too limited a dichotomy; this chapter has argued for a continuum along which to classify input, practice, processes, and knowledge. A change in constructs and definitions will necessarily be correlated with much-needed improvements in the design of treatments and evaluating tools, some of which were suggested a decade ago (Hulstijn and de Graaff, 1994).

7. Exercises

The exercises that follow are divided into two sections, the first of which focuses on some key constructs (i.e., abstract concepts) and their operationalizations (the way the concepts are made concrete for measurement purposes, for example). The last two exercises require attention to data analysis. The second section will help you to practice the basic skill of critical reading. Both sections will require the application of concepts presented in this chapter as well as basic concepts of data analysis and research methodology. Thus, we suggest you revisit Chen (this volume, chapter 2) and Adams, Fujii, and Mackey (this volume, chapter 3).

7.1. DATA ANALYSIS

1. Review the discussion in the introduction of this chapter on the difference between (1) explicit input, (2) implicit input, (3) explicit processing, (4) explicit knowledge, and (5) implicit knowledge. Below are descriptions of operationalizations of these constructs from empirical studies that have investigated the issue of explicitness. Match each description with the appropriate construct listed above. Refer to note 5 at the end of this chapter to check the correctness of your answer.
   a. Rules about the target structure were provided to participants. The participants had the rules available to consult as they subsequently read through exemplar sentences (Robinson, 1996).
   b. Sentences containing exemplars of the rule to be learned were presented. Participants were instructed to memorize the sentences and then answered follow-up questions asking whether certain words had appeared in the sentences (Robinson, 1996).
   c. After having viewed a video of a short story, participants were asked to write a description of the story providing as much detail as possible so that students in other classes could pick out the video based on their written description (Sanz and Morgan-Short, 2004).
   d. Verbal reports collected in the experiment were coded for level of awareness. For example, a participant who explicitly stated the rule, i.e., made a connection between present or past time frames and corresponding

verb forms, was coded as having awareness at the level of understanding (Rosa and O'Neill, 1999).

e. A 45-item sentence judgment and correction task asked participants not only to judge sentences but also to correct any sentence if they had judged it as incorrect and to type it over if they had judged it as correct. They were instructed to take all the time they needed for this task (de Graaff, 1997).

2. Consider the definition of task-essentialness provided in section 1. Based on that definition and the authors' discussion of task-essential practice, decide whether the practice activities below can be considered task-essential. Explain why or why not. Finally, create two tasks that could be considered task-essential practice.

   a. This sample activity is described in Izumi and Bigelow (2000). The target form is the past hypothetical conditional in English.

      Participants were asked to read and underline a short passage with approximately 70% of its sentences containing the past hypothetical conditional, in order to immediately reconstruct the passage as accurately as possible. After the passage was collected, the participants attempted to reconstruct it.

   b. This sample practice activity was taken from Morgan-Short and Bowden (in press). The target form is the preverbal Spanish direct object pronoun.

      Instructions to participant:
      Click on the correct interpretation of the sentence. Keep in mind that Spanish has flexible word order and does not necessarily follow subject-verb-object order like English.

      Participant sees:
      Me llama frecuentemente mi hermana.

      (Translation not available to participant: 'My sister calls me frequently.')
      Who calls whom? a. I call my sister. b. My sister calls me.

      Feedback: Correct/Incorrect

3. One classroom-based feedback study that was not reviewed in this chapter is DeKeyser (1993). Below is the abstract for this study from the *Linguistics and Language Behavior Abstracts* database:

   A study on the parameters in effect of error correction, or no error correction, in the second-language (L2) classroom. Five hypotheses were presented: (1) error correction has no overall significant effect on learning; (2) error correction has a positive effect on students with high pretest scores & a negative effect on students with low pretest scores; (3) students with low scores on a modern language learning aptitude test will benefit from error correction; (4) students with higher extrinsic motivation will improve with error correction; & (5) students with low anxiety will do better with error correction. Native-Dutch-speaking high school seniors (*N* = 35) learning French either received or did not receive error correction treatments for one school year. Analysis of the data showed some support for all of the hypotheses except (3). In general, the hypothesis that error correction does not lead to overall performance improvement is confirmed.

Answer the following questions, basing your answers on the abstract alone:

a. List the types of assessments that would need to be collected in order to test each of the hypotheses.
b. Explain some of the methodological problems mentioned in this chapter that might be limitations for this classroom-based study.
c. Discuss why a study such as this might have low internal validity (i.e., the study itself does not measure what it proposes to measure), or high validity (i.e., the study's findings are generalizable) for the instructed SLA field.

4. The following figure summarizes the means obtained in an empirical study on the effects of explanation (i.e., rule presentation) and explicit feedback (Sanz and Morgan-Short, 2004). Can you interpret the figure? Make sure you understand (a) how many groups were compared, (b) what the treatment for each was, (c) how many tasks were completed and (d) how many

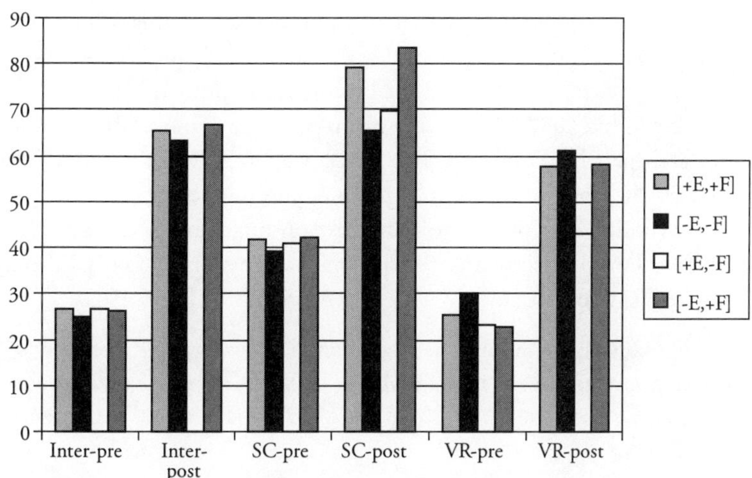

FIGURE 8.1 *Group Means from Assessment Tests*

Inter = interpretation task
SC = sentence completion
VR = video retelling
E = explantion (rule presentation)
F = explicit feedback
Pre = pretest
Post = posttest

TABLE 8.1
ANOVA for Time and Conditions on the Effects of Explanation and Explicit Feedback

Source	df	*SS*	*MS*	F	p
Time	1	47209.35	47209.35	188.42	.00*
Explanation (E)	1	1.17	1.17	.00	.97
Feedback (F)	1	115.76	115.76	.17	.69
E × F	1	17.04	17.04	.02	.88
Time × E	1	167.04	167.04	.67	.42
Time × F	1	172.33	172.33	.69	.41
Time × E × F	1	3.10	3.10	.01	.91
Error	64	16035.24	690.15		

*p < .05.

times each task was administered. What significant differences do you think you can observe across groups and within groups?

5. The previous table summarizes the results from an ANOVA on the same scores as in exercise 4 above. Write a paragraph that describes the results. Be sure to identify the within and across group variable(s), any main effects, and any interactions.

7.2. GUIDED CRITIQUE

The following exercise will help you practice the basic skill of critical reading. To complete the critique, we suggest you revisit Chen (this volume, chapter 2) and Adams, Fujii, and Mackey (this volume, chapter 3) on research methodology and that you provide the information below. It is a good idea to complete forms like this one for every primary source you read in preparation for a research paper or an exam. The article we have chosen is Sanz (2004). Read the article, note down the information, and then compare it with your classmates' results. Sort out any differences you might have. Usually readers differ in their interpretations and conclusions, but answers to points 1 through 7 should be fairly consistent.

Sanz, C. (2004). Computer delivered implicit vs. explicit feedback in processing instruction. In B. VanPatten (Ed.), *Processing instruction: Theory, research, and commentary* (pp. 241–255). Mahwah, NJ: Lawrence Erlbaum.

1. Author(s), year, title, journal, volume number, pages. We recommend you list the reference according to the *Publication Manual of the American Psychological Association,* so that you familiarize yourself with its style. Most SLA journals follow the APA guidelines for publication.

2. Overall motivation for the study (indicate page number)
3. Hypotheses (or Research Questions). How many are there? State them in a list with their corresponding supporting literature. This is especially important when the hypothesis is directional (the author states something will happen). Summarize the statements and references (name, year).
4. Methodology
   a. Design: is the study experimental? quasi-experimental? Is it a case study? cross-sectional? longitudinal? a combination?
   b. Target form, languages involved
   c. Participants: total *N*. List all relevant, specific characteristics (level, L1, naturalistic-classroom learners of X). Initial sample, final sample. Any explanations for attrition?
   d. Groups? *N* per group?
   e. Instruments
   f. Dependent variables
   g. Independent variables
5. Results
   a. ANOVA, *t*-test:
      i. Main factors
      ii. Significant correlations
      iii. Post-hocs
   b. If correlation or regression: predicting factors
   c. Revisit the hypotheses and list them again. Next to each, specify whether it was accepted or rejected.
6. Discussion
   a. If any of the hypotheses were rejected, what is the explanation provided by the authors?
   b. What are their supporting references? Specify name and year and provide a brief statement.
7. Summarize each of the authors' conclusions.
8. Your conclusions. For each of the conclusions in (7) above, specify:
   a. Observations: Do you agree with the authors?
   b. Criticisms: Are any important references missing? Did the authors place more weight on certain studies than others?
   c. Are there any problems with the analysis or methodology (sampling, for example)?
   d. Can their results be interpreted in a different way?
9. Overall statement, interesting points

Appendix 8.A

TABLE 8.A
Summary of Studies Showing Beneficial Effects for Explicit Explanation

	de Graaff (1997)	*Robinson (1997)*	*Robinson (1996)*
Participants	56 undergrads	60 undergrads and grads	104 adults
Language and Forms	eXperanto simple and complex rules, morphological and syntactic rules	English dative alternation	English simple and complex grammatical rules
Training Conditions	EX metalinguistic rules and feedback, IM rehearsed example sentences	IM (memorized), incidental (read for meaning), enhanced forms, instructed (read rules)	IM; (memorized), incidental (read for meaning), rule-search (identify rules), instructed (read rules)
Dependent Variable	GJ task (with or without time pressure), GJ with correction task, gap-filling task	GJ of old and new exemplars, questionnaire asking for noticing, searching, or statement of rules	GJ, questionnaire asking for statement of rules
Training	Dialogs; vocabulary, interpretation, and production exercises	Exposure to 55 exemplar sentences	Exposure to 40 exemplar sentences
Results	*EX did better than IM on all sessions and test types; *interaction between simple and complex syntax and instruction; *no interaction between syntax, morphology, and instruction; *interaction between instruction, time pressure, and structure	*All conditions performed the same on old sentences, *instructed did better than all other conditions on new grammatical sentences, *instructed did better than all other conditions; enhanced did better than IM on new ungrammatical sentences	Simple rules: instructed did better than all other groups, *complex rules: instructed did better than all other groups for grammatical sentences only
Limitations	Confounding factor: feedback (EX or IM) varied with condition, limited task-essential practice	Exposure to forms only, no practice; short exposure; only measured intake	Exposure to forms only, no practice; short exposure; only measured intake

Note. * = result is confirmed statistically. GJ = grammaticality judgment, EX = explicit, IM = implicit.

	DeKeyser (1995)	*Alanen (1995)*	*N. C. Ellis (1993)*
Participants	61 undergrads and grads	36 university students	51 adults
Language and Forms	Implexan categorical rules and prototypicality patterns	Semiartificial Finnish locative suffixes and consonant alternation	Welsh soft mutations
Training Conditions	EX and IM	Rule only (R), enhance only (E), rule and enhance (R & E), control (C)	Rule (explanation), rule and instances (explanation and examples), random (no explanation or examples prior to training), yoked random
Dependent Variable	Concurrent and post-judgment tests for meaning, postproduction task, metalinguistic test, retrospection	Sentence completion, GJ with explanation, think-aloud protocols, and other awareness measures	Rule test, GJ of old and new exemplars
Training	Exposure to sentences and related pictures	Read two passages for meaning	Translation task
Results	*EX did better than IM for categorical rules on new forms, IM conforms better to expected prototypical pattern, *no difference between groups on judgment tests	Sentence completion: *R, R & E did better than E, C; GJ: low mean scores for R & E; *attention correlated with acquisition regardless of group	Rule: EX and some transfer to IM knowledge, rule & instances: EX and IM knowledge, random: some IM knowledge for previously encountered phrases
Limitations	Exposure to forms only, no practice, metalinguistic test given to EX group only	Exposure to forms only, no practice; short exposure, R & E group showed overgeneralization	Practice not communicative

TABLE 8.B
Summary of Studies Showing No Beneficial Effects for Explicit Explanation

	Rosa & O'Neill (1999)	*VanPatten & Oikkenon (1996)*
Participants	67 undergrads	59 high school seniors
Language and Forms	Spanish contrary-to-fact past conditional	Spanish preverbal direct object pronouns
Training Conditions	Formal instruction (FI) and rule-search (RS), FI but no RS, RS but no FI, no FI and no RS, task only	Processing instruction (PI), explanation only (EO), structured input only (SIO)
Dependent Variable	Recognition task and think-aloud protocols	Interpretation task and production task
Training	Multiple-choice jigsaw puzzle	Referential and affective structured input activities
Results	*All groups made gains from pre- to posttest; *no difference between control group and FI groups; *the FI-and-RS group and the FI-but-no-RS group did better than the no-FI-and-no-RS group	Interpretation: *PI and SIO did better than EO; production: all groups improved and PI did better than EO
Limitations	Short exposure; intake measure only; confounding factor: task provided implicit feedback	Amount of exposure not controlled; confounding factor: feedback (explicit or implicit) varied with condition

Note. * = result is confirmed statistically.

TABLE 8.C
Summary of Studies Showing Effects of Explicit Feedback

	Beneficial effects found for explicit feedback		*No beneficial effects found for explicit feedback*
	Carroll & Swain (1993)	*Nagata (1993)*	*Sanz (2004)*
Participants	100 adults	34 undergrads	28 undergrads
Language and Forms	English dative alternation	Japanese passive forms (both particle and verbal)	Spanish preverbal direct object pronouns
Training Conditions	Four feedback groups (metalinguistic information, correct/incorrect, reformulated correct response, asked if sure about response); one control group	Traditional feedback (T-CALI) with no metalinguistic information; intelligent feedback (I-CALI) including metalinguistic information	Explicit feedback but no explanation, no explanation and no explicit feedback
Dependent Variable	Recall (old items) Guessing (new items)	Achievement test Retention test	Interpretation task Production tasks (2)
Training	Exposure to alternate groupings; guessed alternate after viewing stimuli	Write sentences based on situation	Referential and affective structured input activities
Results	*All experimental groups performed better than the control, *the metalinguistic group performed better than all other experimental groups	*I-CALI performed better than T-CALI for particles but not verbal predicates; *I-CALI performed better than T-CALI on retention test	Interpretation: *no differences between groups; production: *no differences between groups
Limitations	No pretest; time on task not controlled	Additional practice with forms provided before retention test; focus on many forms at the same time	Amount of individualized feedback not measured

Note. * = result is confirmed statistically.

TABLE 8.D
Summary of Studies Showing Effects of Explicit Explanation and Explicit Feedback

	Rosa (1999)	*Sanz & Morgan-Short (2004)*
Participants	100 undergrads	69 undergrads
Language and Forms	Spanish contrary-to-fact past conditional	Spanish preverbal direct object pronouns
Training Conditions	Explicit pretask (EP), explicit feedback (EF), and essential task (E); EP, implicit feedback (IF), and E; EF and E; EP; IF and E; control	Explanation and feedback, explanation but no feedback, feedback but no explanation, no explanation and no feedback
Dependent Variable	Recognition task, production task, think-aloud protocols, and questionnaire	Interpretation task and production tasks (2)
Training	Computer-based multiple-choice jigsaw puzzle	Referential and affective structured input activities
Results	*All experimental groups make gains from pre- to post- and delayed tests; *All experimental groups did better than the control (except IFE for new production items); *EPEFE, EPIFE, and EFE did better than IFE for old production and new recognition items; *EPEFE, EPIFE did better than IFE for new production items; *EPEFE did better than EPE for new production items	Interpretation: *no differences between groups, production: *no differences between groups
Limitations	Short exposure; IFE group's treatment may not be as task-essential as for other groups	Amount of individualized feedback not measured; implicit feedback provided to no feedback group due to nature of task

Note. * = result is confirmed statistically.

Further Reading

Doughty, C. & Long, M. H. (Eds.). (2003). *The handbook of second language acquisition.* Oxford, UK: Blackwell.

Ellis, N. C. (Ed.). (1994). *Implicit and explicit learning of languages.* New York: Academic Press.

Norris, J. M., & Ortega, L. (2000). Effectiveness of L2 instruction: A research synthesis and quantitative meta-analysis. *Language Learning, 50*(3), 417–528.

Notes

1. Pedagogical interventions can be provided preemptively or reactively. The typical structural syllabus presents grammar rules preemptively, that is, before it provides learners with practice of the forms to be learned. Reactive pedagogical interventions are often used in task-based approaches to L2 teaching, whereby instructors react to their students' errors either during or after task completion by providing a minilesson on the problematic form, which has come about through the students' performance of the task at hand.

2. In SLA, *practice* and *task* can be used synonymously, but they really stand for different concepts. *Practice* is a more general term, of use both in research and in the classroom. *Task* is a pedagogical term, as in task-based instruction (see Byrnes, this volume, chapter 10). Tasks are implemented to create the context for language use, that is, for practice. The goal is to complete the task (e.g., reading a map or a newspaper) with language as the tool.

3. For more on the concept of practice, see Ellis and Laporte (1997) or Segalowitz (2003).

4. Furthermore, since no examples of practice were provided, we cannot assume that the practice was structured in a way that forced learners to rely in an essential way on the target form in order to interpret the meaning of activities. In other words, we might ask if task-essentialness was truly a characteristic of the practice.

5. The correct answers for exercise 1 in section 7.1 are as follows: a–1, b–2, c–5, d–3, e–4.

References

Alanen, R. (1995). Input enhancement and rule presentation in second language acquisition. In R. Schmidt (Ed.), *Attention and awareness in foreign language learning* (pp. 259–302). Honolulu, HI: University of Hawai'i at Manoa, Second Language Teaching and Curriculum Center.

Anderson, J. R. (1983). *The architecture of cognition.* Mahwah, NJ: Lawrence Erlbaum.

Anderson, J. R. (1992). Automaticity and the ACT* theory. *American Journal of Psychology, 105*(2), 165–180.

Anderson, J. R. (1993). *Rules of the mind.* Mahwah, NJ: Lawrence Erlbaum.

Benati, A. (2004). The effects of structured input activities and explicit information on the acquisition of the Italian future tense. In B. VanPatten (Ed.), *Processing instruction: Theory, research, and commentary* (pp. 187–206). Mahwah, NJ: Lawrence Erlbaum.

Carroll, S., & Swain, M. (1993). Explicit and implicit negative feedback: An empirical study of the learning of linguistic generalizations. *Studies in Second Language Acquisition, 15,* 357–386.

de Graaff, R. (1997). The eXperanto experiment: Effects of explicit instruction on second language acquisition. *Studies in Second Language Acquisition, 19,* 249–276.

DeKeyser, R. (1993). The effect of error correction on L2 grammar knowledge and oral proficiency. *The Modern Language Journal, 77,* 501–514.

DeKeyser, R. (1995). Learning second language grammar rules: An experiment with a miniature linguistic system. *Studies in Second Language Acquisition, 17,* 379–410.

DeKeyser, R. (1997). Beyond explicit rule learning: Automatizing second language morphosyntax. *Studies in Second Language Acquisition, 19,* 195–221.

DeKeyser, R. (2003). Implicit and explicit learning. In C. Doughty & M. H. Long (Eds.), *The handbook of second language acquisition* (pp. 313–347). Oxford, UK: Blackwell.

DeKeyser, R., Salaberry, R., Robinson, P., & Harrington, M. (2002). What gets processed in processing instruction? A commentary on Bill VanPatten's "Processing Instruction: An Update." *Language Learning, 52*(4), 805–823.

Doughty, C. (2003). Instructed SLA: Constraints, compensation, and enhancement. In C. Doughty & M. H. Long (Eds.), *The handbook of second language acquisition* (pp. 256–310). Oxford, UK: Blackwell.

Doughty, C. (2004). Commentary: When PI is focus on form it is very, very good, but when it is focus on forms . . . . In B. VanPatten (Ed.), *Processing instruction: Theory, research, and commentary* (pp. 257–270). Mahwah, NJ: Lawrence Erlbaum.

Doughty, C., & Long, M. H. (Eds.). (2003). *The handbook of second language acquisition.* Oxford, UK: Blackwell.

Doughty, C., & Williams, J. (Eds.). (1998). *Focus on form in classroom second language acquisition.* Cambridge, UK: Cambridge University Press.

Dulany, D., Carlson, R., & Dewey, G. (1984). A case of syntactical learning and judgment: How conscious and how abstract? *Journal of Experimental Psychology, 113,* 541–555.

Dulany, D. Carlson, R., & Dewey, G. (1985). On consciousness in syntactic learning and judgment: A reply to Reber, Allen, and Regan. *Journal of Experimental Psychology, 144,* 25–32.

Ellis, N. C. (1993). Rule and instances in foreign language learning: Interactions of explicit and implicit knowledge. *European Journal of Cognitive Psychology, 5,* 289–318.

Ellis, N. C., & Laporte, N. (1997). Contexts of acquisition: Effects of formal instruction and naturalistic exposure on second language acquisition. In A. de Groot & J. Kroll (Eds.), *Tutorials in bilingualism: Psycholinguistic perspectives* (pp. 53–83). Mahwah, NJ: Lawrence Erlbaum.

Gass, S. M., Svetics, I., & Lemelin, S. (2003). Differential effects of attention. *Language Learning, 53*(3), 497–545.

Gass, S. M., & Varonis, E. M. (1994). Input, interaction, and second language production. *Studies in Second Language Acquisition, 16,* 283–302.

Hulstjin, J., & de Graaff, R. (1994). Under what conditions does explicit knowledge of a second language facilitate the acquisition of implicit knowledge? A research proposal. *AILA Review, 11,* 97–112.

Izumi, S. (2002). Output, input enhancement, and the noticing hypothesis: An experimental study on ESL relativization. *Studies in Second Language Acquisition, 24,* 541–577.

Izumi, S., & Bigelow, M. (2000). Does output promote noticing and second language acquisition? *TESOL Quarterly, 34,* 239–278.

Jourdenais, R., Ota, M., Stauffer, S., Boyson, B., & Doughty, C. (1995). Does textual enhancement promote noticing? A think aloud protocol analysis. In R. Schmidt (Ed.), *Attention and awareness in foreign language learning* (pp. 183–216). Honolulu, HI: University of Hawai'i at Manoa, Second Language Teaching and Curriculum Center.

Knowlton, B. M., & Squire, L. R. (1994). The information acquired during artificial grammar learning. *Journal of Experimental Psychology: Learning, Memory and Cognition, 20,* 79–91.

Knowlton, B. M., & Squire, L. R. (1996). Artificial grammar learning depends on implicit acquisition of both abstract and exemplar-specific information. *Journal of Experimental Psychology: Learning, Memory and Cognition, 22,* 169–181.

Krashen, S. D. (1985). *The input hypothesis: Issues and implications.* London: Longman.

Leeman, J. (2003). Recasts and second language development: Beyond negative evidence. *Studies in Second Language Acquisition, 25,* 37–63.

Long, M. H., & Robinson, P. (1998). Focus on form: Theory, research, and practice. In C. Doughty & J. Williams (Eds.), *Focus on form in classroom second language acquisition* (pp. 15–41). Cambridge, UK: Cambridge University Press.

Loschky, L., & Bley-Vroman, R. (1993). Grammar and task-based learning. In G. Crookes & S. Gass (Eds.), *Tasks and language learning: Integrating theory and practice* (pp. 123–167). Clevedon, UK: Multilingual Matters.

MacWhinney, B. (1997). Implicit and explicit processes: Commentary. *Studies in Second Language Acquisition, 19*(2), 277–284.

McDonald, J. L. (1989). The acquisition of cue-category mappings. In B. MacWhinney & E. Bates (Eds.), *The crosslinguistic study of language processing* (pp. 375–396). Cambridge, UK: Cambridge University Press.

Morgan-Short, K., & Bowden, H. W. (in press). Processing instruction and meaningful output-based instruction: Effects on linguistic development. *Studies in Second Language Acquisition.*

Nagata, N. (1993). Intelligent computer feedback for second language instruction. *The Modern Language Journal, 77*(3), 330–339.

Nagata, N., & Swisher, M. V. (1995). A study of consciousness-raising by computer: The effect of metalinguistic feedback on SLA. *Foreign Language Annals, 28,* 336–347.

Norris, J. M., & Ortega, L. (2000). Effectiveness of L2 instruction: A research synthesis and quantitative meta-analysis. *Language Learning, 50*(3), 417–528.

Ortega, L., & Long, M. H. (1997). The effects of models and recasts on the acquisition of object topicalization and adverb placement in L2 Spanish. *Spanish Applied Linguistics (SAL), 1,* 65–86.

Paradis, M. (1994). Neurolinguistic aspects of implicit and explicit memory: Implications for bilingualism and SLA. In N. C. Ellis (Ed.), *Implicit and explicit learning of languages* (pp. 393–419). New York: Academic Press.

Pica, T. (1983). Adult acquisition of English as a second language under different conditions of exposure. *Language Learning, 33,* 465–497.

Reber, A. (1967). Implicit learning of artificial grammars. *Journal of Verbal Learning and Verbal Behavior, 77,* 317–327.

Reber, A. (1976). Implicit learning of synthetic languages: The role of instructional set. *Journal of Experimental Psychology. Human Learning and Memory, 2,* 88–94.

Reber, A. (1989). Implicit learning and tacit knowledge. *Journal of Experimental Psychology, 118,* 219–235.

Reber, A. (1993). *Implicit learning and tacit knowledge: An essay on the cognitive unconscious.* London: Clarendon Press.

Robinson, P. (1996). Learning simple and complex second language rules under implicit, incidental, rule-search and instructed conditions. *Studies in Second Language Acquisition, 18,* 27–68.

Robinson, P. (1997). Generalizability and automaticity of second language learning under implicit, incidental, enhanced, and instructed conditions. *Studies in Second Language Acquisition, 19,* 223–247.

Robinson, P. (2002). Effect of individual differences in intelligence, aptitude and working memory on adult incidental SLA. In P. Robinson (Ed.), *Individual differences and instructed language learning* (pp. 211–266). Amsterdam: John Benjamins.

Rosa, E. M. (1999). A cognitive approach to task-based research: Explicitness, awareness and L2 development. Unpublished doctoral dissertation, Georgetown University, Washington, DC.

Rosa, E. M., & Leow, R. P. (2004a). Awareness, different learning conditions, and L2 development. *Applied Psycholinguistics, 25,* 269–292.

Rosa, E. M., & Leow, R. P. (2004b). Computerized task-based exposure, explicitness, type of feedback, and Spanish L2 development. *The Modern Language Journal, 88*(2), 192–216.

Rosa, E. M., & O'Neill, M. (1999). Explicitness, intake, and the issue of awareness: Another piece to the puzzle. *Studies in Second Language Acquisition, 21,* 511–556.

Sanz, C. (1999). What form to focus on? Linguistics, language awareness, and the education of L2 teachers. In J. F. Lee & A. Valdman (Eds.), *Meaning and form: Multiple perspectives* (pp. 3–23). Boston: Heinle & Heinle.

Sanz, C. (2004). Computer delivered implicit vs. explicit feedback in processing instruction. In B. VanPatten (Ed.), *Processing instruction: Theory, research, and commentary* (pp. 241–255). Mahwah, NJ: Lawrence Erlbaum.

Sanz, C., & Morgan-Short, K. (2004). Positive evidence versus explicit rule presentation and explicit negative feedback: A computer-assisted study. *Language Learning, 54*(1), 35–78.

Schmidt, R. (2001). Attention. In P. Robinson (Ed.), *Cognition and second language instruction* (pp. 3–32). Cambridge, UK: Cambridge University Press.

Scott, V. M. (1989). An empirical study of explicit and implicit teaching strategies in French. *The Modern Language Journal, 73*(1), 14–22.

Scott, V. M. (1990). Explicit and implicit grammar teaching strategies: New empirical data. *The French Review, 63*(5), 779–789.

Segalowitz, N. (2003). Automaticity and second languages. In C. Doughty & M. H. Long (Eds.), *The handbook of second language acquisition* (pp. 256–310). Oxford, UK: Blackwell.

Servan-Schreiber, E., & Anderson, J. R. (1990). Learning artificial grammars with competitive chunking. *Journal of Experimental Psychology: Learning, Memory and Cognition, 16,* 592–608.

Spada, N. (1997). Form-focused instruction and second language acquisition: A review of classroom and laboratory research. *Language Teaching, 29,* 1–15.

Swain, M. (1995). Three functions of output in second language learning. In G. Cook & B. Seidlhofer (Eds.), *Principles and practice in applied linguistics: Studies in honour of H. Widdowson* (pp. 125–144). Oxford, UK: Oxford University Press.

Swain, M. (1998). Focus on form in classroom through conscious reflection. In C. Doughty & J. Williams (Eds.), *Focus on form in classroom second language acquisition* (pp. 64–81). Cambridge, UK: Cambridge University Press.

Tomasello, M., & Herron, C. (1988). Down the garden path: Inducing and correcting overgeneralization errors in the foreign language classroom. *Applied Psycholinguistics, 9,* 237–246.

Trahey, M., & White, L. (1993). Positive evidence and preemption in the second language classroom. *Studies in Second Language Acquisition, 16,* 183–203.

VanPatten, B. (1994). Evaluating the role of consciousness in second language acquisition: Terms, linguistic features & research methodology. *AILA Review, 11,* 27–36.

VanPatten, B. (2002). Processing instruction: An update. *Language Learning, 52*(4), 755–803.

VanPatten, B. (2004). *Processing instruction: Theory, research, and commentary.* Mahwah, NJ: Lawrence Erlbaum.

VanPatten, B., & Oikkenon, S. (1996). Explanation versus structured input in processing instruction. *Studies in Second Language Acquisition, 18,* 495–510.

Winitz, H. (1996). Grammaticality judgment as a function of explicit and implicit instruction in Spanish. *The Modern Language Journal, 80*(1), 32–46.

Wong, W. (2004). Processing instruction in French: The roles of explicit information and structured input. In B. VanPatten (Ed.), *Processing instruction: Theory, research, and commentary* (pp. 187–206). Mahwah, NJ: Lawrence Erlbaum.

PART 4
Pedagogical Implications

NINE

Processing Instruction

BILL VANPATTEN

KEY WORDS
Focus on form ■ input processing ■ processing instruction ■ structured input.

1. Introduction

Ever since the publication of VanPatten and Cadierno (1993), the field of instructed second language acquisition (SLA) has witnessed increasing interest in what is now called processing instruction (PI). This interest has given rise to an active research agenda on PI and the generalizability of its effects (i.e., do the positive results generalize to all structures in languages?), the interaction of its components (i.e., to what extent do explicit information and feedback play significant roles in the outcomes?), and its long-term effects (e.g., Benati, 2001; Cadierno, 1995; Cheng, 2002; Collentine, 1998; Farley, 2001; Sanz and Morgan-Short, 2004; VanPatten and Oikkenon, 1996; VanPatten and Sanz, 1995; Wong, 2002; and the collection of empirical research articles in VanPatten, 2004a). In addition, the research on PI has led to discussions of theoretical matters in SLA (e.g., Carroll, 2001; Jordens, 1996; Lightbown, 1998; Lightbown and Spada, 1999; Skehan, 1998) as well as lively debate on the interpretation of the results of PI (e.g., Batstone, 2002; DeKeyser, Salaberry, Robinson, and Harrington, 2002; Salaberry, 1998; Sanz and VanPatten, 1998; VanPatten, 2002a, 2002b 2002c, 2004a, 2004d).

In short, PI is a technique that has proven to be worthy of scrutiny in any discussion of focus on form, pedagogical intervention, or computer-assisted language learning. The purpose of the present paper is to briefly describe PI as well as provide an updated set of references for the reader. If not the only one, PI is one of the few pedagogical interventions that are based on psycholinguistic processes occurring during learner comprehension of second language (L2) input. Unlike text enhancement, recasts, and other input-oriented techniques, PI considers the nature of real-time input processing and the ways in which learners make form-meaning connections during comprehension. Thus it attempts to identify particular processing problems and treat them. To this end, it is important to understand L2 input processing. The first section of this chapter provides an outline of the nature of input processing in SLA and the model that informs PI. The subsequent section describes the nature of PI itself. The third offers a brief description of the research on PI.

2. One Model of Input Processing

IP is concerned with how learners derive intake from input regardless of the language being learned and regardless of the context (i.e., instructed or noninstructed). I define *intake* as the linguistic data actually processed from the input and held in working memory for further processing (e.g., VanPatten, 2004b). Thus intake is not equivalent to acquired linguistic form. Of principal concern is the question, "What form-meaning connections do learners make, when do they make them, and why some and not others?" Because we are concerned with what learners do with input, a model of IP attempts to explain how learners get form from input and how they parse sentences during the act of comprehension while their primary attention is on meaning. Form in this model refers to surface features of language (e.g., functors and inflections). This does not mean, however, that IP has little to say about syntax (see VanPatten, 1996, chapter 5, as well as Carroll, 2001). In VanPatten (1996, 2004a) one model of IP is presented. This model consists of a set of principles and corollaries that interact in complex ways in working memory. It is important to point out the role of working memory in this model since the first principles are predicated on a limited capacity for processing information; that is, learners can only do so much in their working memory before attentional resources are depleted, and working memory is forced to dump information to make room for more (incoming) information. The principles are listed in (1). (The reader should be aware that these principles are a revised set of principles; see VanPatten, 2004b.)

(1) Principles of L2 Input Processing (based on VanPatten, 1996, 2004b)

1. The Primacy of Meaning Principle: Learners process input for meaning before they process it for form.
    a. The Primacy of Content Words Principle: Learners process content words in the input before anything else.
    b. The Lexical Preference Principle. Learners will tend to rely on lexical items as opposed to grammatical form to get meaning when both encode the same semantic information.
    c. The Preference for Nonredundancy Principle: Learners are more likely to process nonredundant meaningful grammatical form before they process redundant meaningful forms.

   d. The Meaning Before Nonmeaning Principle: Learners are more likely to process meaningful grammatical forms before nonmeaninful forms irrespective of redundancy.
   e. The Availability of Resources Principle: For learners to process either redundant meaningful grammatical forms or nonmeaningful forms, the processing of overall sentential meaning must not drain available processing resources.
   f. The Sentence Location Principle: Learners tend to process items in sentence-initial position before those in final position and those in medial position.
2. The First Noun Principle: Learners tend to assign subject or agent status to the first (pro)noun they encounter in a sentence.
   a. The Lexical Semantics Principle: Lexical semantics of verbs may attenuate learners' reliance on the first noun principle.
   b. The Event Probabilities Principle: Event probabilities may attenuate learners' reliance on the first noun principle.
   c. The Contextual Constraint Principle: Learners may rely less on the first noun principle if preceding context constrains the possible interpretation of the following clause or sentence.

That learners are driven to get meaning from input has a set of consequences (see Principle 1: The Primacy of Meaning). The first consequence is that words (content lexical items) are processed first (Principle 1a).[1] In the learner's mind—if not in any fluent speaker-listener's—words are the principal source of referential meaning. In addition, L2 learners are different from first language learners in that they come to the task knowing that words exist. They expect, for example, that there are L2 equivalents for *man, work,* and *lazy* (leaving aside cultural differences in the interpretation of these words). At the same time, L2 learners also know that there are such things as temporal reference (e.g., past, present, future), aspect, person-number, case, plurality, and other semantic notions that may be encoded in their languages. However, this does not mean that they immediately search out how the L2 encodes such notions grammatically. Because of the primacy of lexical items in processing, learners will first see if such notions are encoded lexically so that they can grasp the intended meaning of the speaker. This aspect of processing is specified in Principle 1b. This principle holds that when content lexical items and grammatical form both encode the same meaning, and when both are present in an utterance, it is the lexical item that learners rely on for the meaning and not the grammatical form. The following Spanish sentence is an example par excellence: *Ayer mis padres me llamaron para decirme algo importante* 'Yesterday my parents called me to tell me something important.' Here, both the lexical item *ayer* 'yesterday' and the verb inflection *-aron* encode pastness. The learner does not have to allocate attentional resources to a verb form to grasp that the action took place before the present. At the same time, *mis padres* 'my parents' as well as *-aron* encode plurality, and again the learner does not have to allocate attentional resources to an inflection to grasp that the subject is plural.

What these examples help to illustrate is that a great deal of form that is meaning oriented (i.e., related to some semantic concept in the real world, what I call *referential meaning*) may also be expressed by a lexical item or phrase elsewhere in the sentence or the discourse. This observation led me to posit the construct *communicative value* (VanPatten, 1984). Communicative value refers to the meaning that a form contributes to overall sentence meaning and is based on two features: [± inherent semantic value] and [± redundancy]. A given form can have [+ semantic value] and [− redundancy] (e.g., English *-ing*), [+ semantic value] and [+ redundancy] (e.g., subjunctive verb inflections), [− semantic value] and [+ redundancy] (e.g., adjective concord in the Romance languages), and finally [− semantic value] and [− redundancy] (e.g., some complementizers such as *that*). In general, a form's communicative value is greater if it has the characteristics [+ semantic value, − redundancy] than if it has the characteristics [+ semantic value, + redundancy]. In short, if meaning can be retrieved elsewhere and not just from the form itself, then the communicative value of the form is diminished. Forms with [− semantic value] regardless of redundancy contain no communicative value. One should note, however, that redundancy is not absolute; for example, most past tense markers do not always co-occur with a temporal expression in an utterance. One might also hear in the input utterances such as *¿Dónde estudiaste?* 'Where did you study?' in which no lexical item provides clues to tense (or to person-number). But one rarely hears something like the subjunctive without a main clause that triggers it or copular verbs without a predicate of some kind. In short, some forms are more (often) redundant than others. The role of communicative value in terms of forms being meaningful (having semantic information) and/or redundant is captured in Principles 1c and 1d.

Learners may, however, process forms in the input because of shifts in task demands. Input may be simplified or contain short sentences, interactions may somehow modify the input so that a form becomes more salient or more processable because meaning is repeated (e.g., in confirmation requests), and so on. All such aspects of language occurring in communicative contexts may allow learners to redirect processing resources. This idea is captured in Principle 1e. Of course, simply becoming more proficient and having a larger and larger vocabulary that is easily accessed during comprehension would also free up processing resources. Location of a grammatical item in a sentence interacts with the availability of resources. Items in sentence-initial position get the first crack at processing resources since the latter are available at that moment. This is captured in Principle 1f.

Input processing is also concerned with the rudiments of parsing, that is, how nouns are assigned grammatical relationships vis-à-vis the verb. Principle 2, the First Noun Principle, may have important effects on the acquisition of a language that does not follow strict subject-verb-object (SVO) word order. It may also impede the acquisition of noncanonical structures in a language that is not strictly SVO; in other words, structures that appear in noncanonical orders such as OVS may be processed incorrectly. In each of the following sentences in Spanish, the first noun phrase the learner encounters is not a subject, but the learner may very well attempt to encode it as such:

(2) *A Juan no le gusta esta clase mucho.*
to John not to-him pleases this class much
'John does not like this class much.'

(3) *La vi yo en la fiesta anoche.*
her saw-1S I at the party last-night
'I saw her at the party last night.'

(4) *Se levanta temprano.*
self gets-up early
'He/She gets up early.'

(5) *Nos faltan varios libros.*
to-us miss-3P several books
'We are missing several books.'

Research has shown that learners do indeed encode such pronouns and noun phrases as subjects (e.g., *Juan* 'John' as the subject of [2], *la* 'her' as the subject of [3]), thus offering erroneous intake for further processing. In this case, it is not that meaning is gotten elsewhere; it is that meaning is not gotten at all or that it is gotten wrong. Additional problems in processing based on this principle have been found in French (Allen, 2000; VanPatten and Wong, 2004) and German (LoCoco, 1987). Principles 2a through 2c list factors that may attenuate the First Noun Principle.

To summarize, research on IP attempts to describe what linguistic data in the input get processed during comprehension and which do not (or which are privileged and which are not) and what grammatical roles learners assign to nouns. Intake is that subset of filtered input that the learner actually processes and holds in working memory during on-line comprehension.[2] Intake thus contains grammatical information as it relates to the meaning that learners have comprehended (or think they have comprehended). To be sure, IP is only one set of processes related to acquisition; that learners derive some kind of intake from the input does not mean that the data contained in the intake automatically make their way into the developing mental representation of the L2 in the learner's head (i.e., intake is not equivalent to acquisition). In previous work (VanPatten, 1996), accommodation of intake and restructuring are seen as processes separate from IP. In addition, how learners access their developing system to make output is also a distinct set of processes. (For detailed discussion, see VanPatten, 1996, chapters 2 and 5; 2003; and 2004a.)[3]

3. Processing Instruction: A Description

If it is the case that learners' input processing may lead to impoverished intake, a logical question arises: Is there a way to enrich learners' intake using insights from input processing? Another way to ask this question is, to what degree can we either manipulate learner attention during input processing or manipulate input data so that more and better form-meaning connections are made?

As described in VanPatten (1993, 1996), Lee and VanPatten (1995, 2003), and Wong (2004), PI is a type of explicit instruction or focus on form derived from the insights of input processing. It is different from all other input-based approaches to form-focused instruction (e.g., text enhancement or dictogloss) but like them is compatible with all current approaches to communicative language teaching. In this section, I describe the characteristics of PI and what distinguishes it from other approaches to focus-on-form.

3.1. THE BASIC CHARACTERISTICS OF PI

The most salient characteristic of PI is that it uses a particular type of input to push learners away from the nonoptimal processing strategies described in the previous section. As such, PI is not a comprehension-based approach to general language teaching such as Total Physical Response, the Natural Approach, and so on but is rather a complement to them, a technique useful for enhancing grammatical intake. Since the point of PI is to assist the learner in making form-meaning connections during input processing, it is more appropriate to view it as a type of explicit instruction, focus on form, or even input enhancement (Sharwood Smith, 1993). A secondary salient characteristic of PI is that during the instructional phase, learners never produce the target form in question. This does not obviate a role for output, as I have discussed elsewhere (e.g., Lee and VanPatten, 1995, 2003; VanPatten, 2002a, 2003, 2004c). Nonetheless, during PI the learner's job is to process sentences and interpret them correctly while attending to form as well.

PI has three basic features or components:

1. Learners are given information about a linguistic structure or form.
2. Learners are informed about a particular IP strategy that may negatively affect their picking up of the form or structure during comprehension.
3. Learners are pushed to process the form or structure during activities with structured input—input that is manipulated in particular ways so that learners become dependent on form and structure to get meaning (i.e., learners are pulled away from their natural processing tendencies toward more optimal tendencies).

Characteristics 1 through 3 can be exemplified in the case of the French causative with *faire,* which generally takes the form seen in examples (6) and (7).

(6) *Jean fait promener le chien à Marie.*
John makes to walk the dog to Mary
'John makes Mary walk the dog.'

(7) *Mes professeurs me font travailler beaucoup.*
My profs to-me make-3P to-work hard
'My profs make me work hard.'

In (6), there are two verbs and two subjects. The first verb is *fait* 'makes' with its obligatorily preposed subject *Jean.* The second verb is *promener* 'to walk' with its underlying subject, *Marie,* obligatorily placed in postverbal position and marked by the preposition *à* 'to.' It is the underlying subject of the second verb that is the problem for learners of French. When asked "Who walks the dog?" learners overwhelmingly say "Jean," demonstrating their reliance on Principle 2 (since *Jean* is the first noun that appears before the verb). When asked to give a rough translation, learners will say the sentence means something like 'John walks the dog for Mary.' In (7) the causative structure is different because the underlying subject of the second verb appears preverbally but not as a subject pronoun. In this case, it is an indirect object pronoun. When asked "Who works hard?" learners will tend to say "My professors," once again demonstrating reliance on Principle 2. Their overall interpretation of the sentence is something like 'My profs work hard for me.' In short, learners tend to gloss over the verb *faire* 'to make' and process the second verb. At the same time, they assign the first noun as subject of the second verb. Knowing this, a PI supplemental lesson on the causative would first begin with a brief explanation of what the structure is and looks like. Following this, learners would be told that it is natural to process the first noun as the subject of the verb but that this is inappropriate for this structure. Subsequently they would work through written and aural activities in which they are pushed to process sentences correctly. These activities are called *structured input* activities. Here is one example:

(8) Students' instructions: Listen to each sentence. Then indicate who is performing the action by answering each question.
1. Who cleans the room? ______
2. Who packs the bags? ______
etc.

(9) Teacher's script: Read each sentence ONCE. After each sentence, ask for an answer. Do not wait until the end to review answers. Students do not repeat or otherwise produce the structure.[4]
1. Claude fait nettoyer la chambre à Richard.
2. Marc fait les valises pour Jean.
etc.

The above type of activity is called a *referential* structured input activity. Referential activities are those for which there is a right or wrong answer and for which the learner must rely on the targeted grammatical form to get meaning. Normally, a sequence of structured input activities would begin with two or three referential activities. It is important to point out that in the above activities, causative structures with *faire* are mixed in with noncausatives with *faire* (e.g., 'to go skiing' in French is *faire du ski).* In this way, learners are pushed to listen to every sentence and not to apply a strategy that believes all sentences are causative just because that is what they are learning.

Following referential activities, learners are engaged in *affective* structured input activities. These are activities in which learners express an opinion, belief, or some other affective response and are engaged in processing information about the real world. Below is an example of an affective activity that could follow the above referential activities:

(10) In this activity, you will compare and contrast what someone gets a child to do with what someone gets a dog to do. For each item, indicate whether it refers to the small child (*à l'enfant*), the dog (*au chien*), or possibly both (*à tous les deux*).[5]
Un adulte. . .
1. fait chercher l'os à/au ______.
2. fait faire la vaisselle à/au ______.
3. fait manger à certaine heure à/au ______.
4. fait jouer dehors à/au ______.
5. fait se baigner à/au ______.
6. fait dormir au plancher à/au ______.

7. fait se porter bien à/au ______________________ s'il y a des invités.
8. fait boire du lait à/au ______________________.
   Does everyone in class agree?

The construction of structured input activities follows a set of guidelines:

(11) Guidelines for Creating Structured Input Activities
1. One thing at a time.
2. Keep meaning in focus.
3. Learners must do something with the input.
4. Input should be both oral and written.
5. Move from sentences to discourse.
6. Keep the learners' processing strategies in mind.

Space prohibits a discussion of these guidelines but it is worth pointing out that the sixth guideline is the one most often missed or misunderstood. What "keep the learners' processing strategies in mind" is meant to convey is that if the activities are not attempting to alter a processing strategy, then there is no structured input and hence no PI. This is a point I address in the next section.

3.2. PI IS DIFFERENT FROM OTHER TYPES OF INSTRUCTION

To understand why PI works, one needs to understand what is critically different about PI from other treatments that have an input orientation (e.g., textual enhancement, recasts, input flood). The critical difference is that PI first identifies a potentially problematic processing strategy from the model of input processing described in the previous section and then provides activities that push learners away from that strategy. In other words, PI does not just determine what is a problem form or structure but also *why* it is a problem vis-à-vis the processing issues described earlier. To my knowledge, no other instructional treatment does this. The reason this point is worth emphasizing is that some attempted replications of research on PI (e.g., DeKeyser and Sokalski, 1996; Salaberry, 1997) have failed to grasp this important point and their research has failed to yield results similar to the research I have done with colleagues.

As an additional point, the aim of PI is in line with claims of those researchers who assert that acquisition is a failure-driven process (e.g., Carroll, 2001). That is, for acquisition to happen, processing mechanisms must note that the parsing procedure is not getting the learner the right information about the events (e.g., who did what to whom, or when something happened) and must therefore seek alternative procedures for successful interpretation. When these new procedures are successful, they replace the procedures that are not (or exist along with them). PI is designed to cause failure in interpretation at the beginning stages of activities so that the processors can begin to readjust. Because PI uses positive evidence in the form of meaning-based utterances that learners respond to, it is a type of input intervention quite unlike others. To be clear, PI does not manipulate the processors; it manipulates the input data so that the processors can do whatever it is they do to change. In this way, it is also different from the garden path technique, which is failure driven via output practice that involves leading learners to conscious hypotheses about the target structure.[6]

Both input processing and PI have been the subject of some criticism, most notably articulated in DeKeyser et al. (2002). In their discussion, they focus largely on pitfalls in the model of IP, claiming that it lacks true explanatory and predictive ability and is based on several questionable interpretations of constructs borrowed from both cognitive psychology and psycholinguistics. These criticisms were rebutted in VanPatten's (2002b) response, and the reader is directed to both the DeKeyser et al. discussion as well as VanPatten's response for details. In a subsequent publication, VanPatten (2004a), additional commentary on input processing and PI are presented in various reaction papers. Again, most criticism focuses on the model of input processing and not on PI itself, and there are several attempts to suggest revisions to the model (Carroll, 2004; VanPatten, 2004d). However, as VanPatten (2004d) points out, the criticisms on input processing notwithstanding, research on PI has continued to yield robust results. This may suggest that PI does the right thing but that our interpretation of why may need revision. We suspect that as the model of input processing undergoes revision, PI will nonetheless remain unaffected. Recall that guideline 6 for the creation of structured input states, "Keep the learners' processing strategies in mind." When applied to the VanPatten and Cadierno (1993) study (and others), this means that the processing problem may not lie in a general first-noun strategy but on transfer of first-language parsing principles. Either way, the PI materials would look the same, and the general guidelines for creation of structured input activities would remain unchanged.

4. Summary

There is considerable research on PI and its effects. It is clear, for example, that PI is better than traditional approaches to grammar instruction prevalent in many if not most foreign language classes in the United States. (See VanPatten, 2002a; VanPatten, 2004a; and Wong and VanPatten, 2003). It is also clear that the major causative variable in PI is the structured input; that is, explicit information about the target grammatical point is not necessary to bring about substantial gains in performance on certain tasks (Sanz and Morgan-Short, 2004; VanPatten and Oikkenon, 1996; VanPatten 2004a). There is also evidence that the effects of PI can be found in communicatively oriented tasks such as video narration (Sanz, 2004; Sanz and Morgan-Short, 2004; VanPatten and Sanz, 1995). The results of PI are durable (VanPatten and Fernandez, 2004). In short, PI appears to be a viable option among the many emerging approaches to focus-on-form and explicit instruction and is perhaps the only one grounded in an attempt to delineate the learning and processing mechanisms that come into play during comprehension.

We believe, then, that we are on the right path in terms of relating formal instruction to processing issues in SLA (see also the comments in Doughty, 2003). Future research will no doubt push us in certain directions. Nonetheless, we believe that instructional efforts that first ask, "What do learners actually do?" before developing some kind of intervention are better than others in that they logically lead us to the question, "How should we intervene?" It is the *how* that eventually makes the difference.

Further Reading

Doughty, C. (2003). Instructed SLA: constraints, compensation, and enhancement. In C. Doughty & M. H. Long (Eds.), *The handbook of second language acquisition* (pp. 256–310). Oxford, UK: Blackwell. (This chapter contains a detailed critical review of the research on instruction in SLA, including a discussion of the research on PI.)

Farley, A. P. (2004). *Structured input: Grammar instruction for the acquisition-oriented classroom.* New York: McGraw-Hill. (This book is a detailed examination of the various principles of the input-processing model and the implications each has for the creation of structured input activities. Detailed and full of examples, it is an excellent source for those attempting to understand how structured input works.)

VanPatten, B. (Ed.). (2004a). *Processing instruction: Theory, research, and commentary.* Mahwah, NJ: Lawrence Erlbaum. (This volume contains a collection of ten previously unpublished papers plus six commentaries by noted scholars in the field of SLA.)

Wong, W. (2004). *Input enhancement: From theory and research to the classroom.* New York: McGraw-Hill. (This book surveys a variety of input-based approaches to focus on form, thus contextualizing PI. The book includes a critical examination of strengths and weaknesses of the various approaches.)

Notes

1. The term *processing* is used here to mean when learners actually make form-meaning connections, not when they initially perceive or notice something in the input. Thus, under Principle 1a, for example, learners may perceive some formal features of language, but they only process content lexical items (e.g., connect a lexical form to its meaning).

2. *Filtered* here should not be restricted to the meaning 'some stuff didn't get processed' but rather to include that some stuff got processed incorrectly. Principle 2, for example, speaks to how learners may encode the semantic and grammatical meanings of pronouns or nouns incorrectly. It is also possible that learners may encode a form

incorrectly (e.g., learners of English as a second language may initially encode *do* and *did* as particles that indicate yes-no questions rather than as an auxiliary verb that carries person and tense information).

3. So that there is no mistake, it is important to point out once again that a focus on input processing in acquisition does not suggest there is no role for output (in or out of the classroom, a point I have made repeatedly, e.g., VanPatten 2000a, 2000b, 2003, and elsewhere). For a discussion on the research related to output and acquisition, see Sanz and Morgan-Short (this volume, chapter 8). In addition, see Gass (1997). For additional discussion of new directions for a model of IP, see the various papers in VanPatten (2004a). For detailed descriptions of structured input activities, see Farley (2005), Lee and VanPatten (2003), and Wong (2004).

4. The English equivalents of sentences 1 and 2 are *Claude makes Richard clean the room* and *Marc packs* (literally, *makes*) *the bags for Jean.*

5. The English equivalents of sentences 1 through 8 are as follows: *An adult . . . (1) makes _____ go get the bone, (2) makes _____ do the dishes, (3) makes _____ eat at a certain time, (4) makes _____ play outside, (5) makes _____ take a bath, (6) makes _____ sleep on the floor, (7) makes _____ behave nicely if there are guests, (8) makes _____ drink milk.*

6. For more discussion of input-based techniques, see Mackey and Abbuhl (this volume, chapter 7) as well as Leow and Bowles (this volume, chapter 6). In addition, the reader may wish to consult Wong (2005).

References

Allen, L. Q. (2000). Form-meaning connections and the French causative: An experiment in processing instruction. *Studies in Second Language Acquisition, 22,* 69–84.

Batstone, R. (2002). Making sense of new language: a discourse perspective. *Language Awareness, 11,* 14–29.

Benati, A. (2001). A comparative study of the effects of processing instruction and output-based instruction on the acquisition of the Italian future tense. *Language Teaching Research, 5,* 95–127.

Cadierno, T. (1995). Formal instruction in processing perspective: An investigation into the Spanish past tense. *The Modern Language Journal, 79,* 179–194.

Carroll, S. (2001). *Input and evidence: The raw material of second language acquisition.* Amsterdam: John Benjamins.

Carroll, S. (2004). Some general and specific comments on input processing and processing instruction. In B. VanPatten (Ed.), *Processing instruction: Theory, research, and commentary* (pp. 293–323). Mahwah, NJ: Lawrence Erlbaum.

Cheng, A. (2002). The effects of processing instruction on the acquisition of *ser* and *estar. Hispania, 85*(2), 308–323.

Collentine, J. (1998). Processing instruction and the subjunctive. *Hispania, 81,* 576–587.

DeKeyser, R. & Sokalski, K. (1996). The differential role of comprehension and production practice. *Language Learning, 46,* 613–642.

DeKeyser, R., Salaberry, R., Robinson, P., & Harrington, M. (2002). What gets processed in processing instruction? A commentary on Bill VanPatten's "Processing Instruction: An Update." *Language Learning, 52,* 805–823.

Doughty, C. J. (2003). Instructed SLA: Constraints, compensation, and enhancement. In C. J. Doughty & M. H. Long (Eds.), *The handbook of second language acquisition* (pp. 256–310). Oxford, UK: Blackwell.

Farley, A. P. (2001). The effects of processing instruction and meaning-based output instruction. *Spanish Applied Linguistics, 5,* 57–94.

Farley, A. P. (2005). *Structured input: Grammar instruction for the acquisition-oriented classroom.* New York: McGraw-Hill.

Gass, S. M. (1997). *Input and interaction in second language acquisition.* Mahwah, NJ: Lawrence Erlbaum.

Jordens, P. (1996). Input and instruction in second language acquisition. In P. Jordens and J. Lalleman (Eds.), *Investigating second language acquisition,* (pp. 407–449). Berlin: Mouton de Gruyter.

Lee, J., & VanPatten, B. (1995). *Making communicative language teaching happen* (1st ed.). New York: McGraw-Hill.

Lee., J. & VanPatten, B. (2003). *Making communicative language teaching happen* (2nd ed.). New York: McGraw-Hill.

Lightbown, P. (1998). The importance of timing in focus on form. In C. Doughty & J. Williams (Eds.), *Focus on form in classroom second language acquisition* (pp. 177–196). Cambridge, UK: Cambridge University Press.

Lightbown, P. & Spada, N. (1999). *How languages are learned* (Rev. ed.). Oxford, UK: Oxford University Press.

LoCoco, V. (1987). Learner comprehension of oral and written sentences in German and Spanish: The importance of word order. In B. VanPatten, T. R. Dvorak, & J. F. Lee (Eds.), *Foreign language learning: A research perspective* (pp. 119–129). Rowley, MA: Newbury House.

Salaberry, M. R. (1997). The role of input and output practice in second language acquisition. *The Canadian Modern Language Review, 53,* 422–451.

Salaberry, M. R. (1998). On input processing, true language competence, and pedagogical bandwagons: A reply to Sanz and VanPatten. *The Canadian Modern Language Review, 54,* 274–285.

Sanz, C. (2004). Computer delivered implicit vs. explicit feedback in processing instruction. In B. VanPatten (Ed.), *Processing instruction: Theory, research, and commentary* (pp. 241–255). Mahwah, NJ: Lawrence Erlbaum.

Sanz, C. & Morgan-Short, K. (2004). Positive evidence vs. explicit rule presentation and explicit negative feedback: A computer-assisted study. *Language Learning, 54*(1), 35–78.

Sanz, C. & VanPatten, B. (1998). On input processing, processing instruction, and the nature of replication tasks: A response to M. Rafael Salaberry. *The Canadian Modern Language Review, 54,* 263–273.

Sharwood Smith, M. (1993). Input enhancement and instructed SLA: Theoretical bases. *Studies in Second Language Acquisition, 15,* 165–179.

Skehan, P. (1998). *A cognitive approach to language learning.* Oxford, UK: Oxford University Press.

VanPatten, B. (1984). Processing strategies and morpheme acquisition. In F. R. Eckman, L. H. Bell, and D. Nelson (Eds.), *Universals of second language acquisition* (pp. 88–98). Rowley, MA: Newbury House.

VanPatten, B. (1993). Grammar instruction for the acquisition-rich classroom. *Foreign Language Annals, 26,* 225–244.

VanPatten, B. (1996). *Input processing and grammar instruction: Theory and research.* Norwood, NJ: Ablex.

VanPatten, B. (2000a). Thirty years of input (or intake, the neglected sibling). In M. Anderson, C. Klee, F. Morris, E. Tavone, and B. Swierzbin (Eds.), *Interaction of social and cognitive factors in SLA: Selected proceedings of the 1999 Second Language Research Forum* (pp. 287–311). Somerville, MA: Cascadilla Press.

VanPatten, B. (2000b). Processing instruction as form-meaning connections: Issues in theory and research. In J. F. Lee & A. Valdman (Eds.), *Form and meaning in language teaching* (pp. 43–68). Boston: Heinle & Heinle.

VanPatten, B. (2002a). Processing instruction: An update. *Language Learning, 52,* 755–803.

VanPatten, B. (2002b). Processing the content of IP and PI research: A response to DeKeyser, Salaberry, Robinson, and Harrington. *Language Learning, 52,* 825–831.

VanPatten, B. (2002c). Processing instruction, prior awareness, and the nature of second language acquisition: A (partial) response to Batstone. *Language Awareness, 11,* 240–258.

VanPatten, B. (2003). *From input to output: A teacher's guide to second language acquisition.* New York: McGraw-Hill.

VanPatten, B. (Ed.). (2004a). *Processing instruction: Theory, research, and commentary.* Mahwah, NJ: Lawrence Erlbaum.

VanPatten, B. (2004b). Input processing in SLA. In B. VanPatten (Ed.), *Processing instruction: Theory, research, and commentary* (pp. 5–31). Mahwah, NJ: Lawrence Erlbaum.

VanPatten, B. (2004c). On the role(s) of input and output in making form-meaning connections. In B. VanPatten, J. Williams, S. Rott, & M. Overstreet (Eds.), *Form-meaning connections in second language acquisition* (pp. 29–47). Mahwah, NJ: Lawrence Erlbaum.

VanPatten, B. (2004d). Several reflections on why there is good reason to continue researching the effects of processing instruction. In B. VanPatten (Ed.), *Processing instruction: Theory, research, and commentary* (pp. 325–335). Mahwah, NJ: Lawrence Erlbaum.

VanPatten, B. & Cadierno, T. (1993). Explicit instruction and input processing. *Studies in Second Language Acquisition, 15,* 225–243.

VanPatten, B. & Fernández, C. (2004). The long-term effects of processing instruction. In B. VanPatten (Ed.), *Processing instruction: Theory, research, and commentary* (pp. 273–289). Mahwah, NJ: Lawrence Erlbaum.

VanPatten, B. & Oikkenon, S. (1996). Explanation vs. structured input in processing instruction. *Studies in Second Language Acquisition, 18,* 495–510.

VanPatten, B. & Sanz, C. (1995). From input to output: Processing instruction and communicative tasks. In F. Eckman, D. Highland, P. Lee, J. Mileham, & R. Rutkowski Weber (Eds.), *Second language acquisition theory and pedagogy* (pp. 169–185). Mahwah, NJ: Lawrence Erlbaum.

VanPatten, B. & Wong, W. (2004). Processing instruction and the French causative: Another replication. In B. VanPatten (Ed.), *Processing instruction: Theory, research, and commentary* (pp. 87–118). Mahwah, NJ: Lawrence Erlbaum.

Wong, W. (2002). Linking form and meaning: Processing instruction. *The French Review,* 76, 236–264.

Wong, W. (2004). The nature of processing instruction. In B. VanPatten (Ed.) , *Processing instruction: Theory, research, and commentary,* (pp. 33–63). Mahwah, NJ: Lawrence Erlbaum.

Wong, W. (2005). *Input enhancement: From theory and research to the classroom.* New York: McGraw-Hill.

Wong, W. & VanPatten, B. (2003). The evidence is IN and drills are OUT. *Foreign Language Annals, 36,* 403–423.

TEN

Content-Based Foreign Language Instruction

HEIDI BYRNES

KEY WORDS
Advanced-level competence ▪ content-based instruction (CBI) ▪ discourse ▪ extended curricula ▪ foreign languages across the curriculum ▪ form-meaning connections ▪ genre ▪ grammar ▪ language across the curriculum ▪ language for special purposes ▪ literacy ▪ task ▪ test ▪ syllabus.

1. Introduction

Within the present volume's defining interest in theoretical and practical approaches to processing phenomena in instructed SLA, this chapter favors instructional practices as compared with research practices. With its focus on content-based instruction (CBI), it addresses an area that has at best been of tangential concern to second language acquisition (SLA) theorizing and practice precisely because CBI explicitly foregrounds content and not language form. Emphasizing the link between content and language demands an understanding of language that is just now gaining prominence in the field, that of language as a social and discursive phenomenon. Therefore, the challenge for CBI and classroom-based SLA research is this: How can the classroom setting affirm the social embeddedness of language in a way that facilitates learners' acquiring comfortable competence, perhaps even high-level cultural literacy in another language? For in the end, learners should be able to function in a multilingual and multicultural world as individuals who through, with, and in a second or third (or fourth) language alongside their native language, make meaning out of and give meaning to that lived world.

Acquiring language with these complex personal and public goals inherently engages learners over long periods of time. For that reason, the following areas are of concern in this chapter:

1. principles for the development of extended curricula,
2. approaches to pedagogy that support teachers' complex decision making as they guide learners in establishing macro- and microlinks between

meaning and form in ways that facilitate continued development of bilingual capacities over long acquisitional periods, and
3. attainment of advanced levels of second language (L2) capacity, expressed as high levels of literacy.

Accordingly, I begin by characterizing CBI broadly through its deliberate linking of meaning and language form. Because form-meaning connections are also central in recent SLA research, the next section examines the degree of congruence and compatibility between pedagogical approaches and prominent research. The subsequent review of diverse program initiatives in collegiate foreign language departments provides additional detail regarding issues in CBI. I conclude with a proposal for a new conceptualization of CBI in and through advanced learning that incorporates alternative theories of language, develops extended curricula, and reconsiders the notion of task within a genre-based approach to literacy.

2. Locating Content-Based Foreign Language Instruction: General Considerations

For any treatment of CBI, the nature of the link between language and content is central (for an early discussion, see Wesche, 1993; also Grabe and Stoller, 1997). Indeed, in a seminal publication Snow and Brinton (1997) introduce CBI simply in terms of "language and content integration" (p. xi). While this formulation seems uncontroversial on its face, it implicitly acknowledges that both the talking about language teaching and the doing thereof were not typically concerned with content. For that reason, CBI is often described with considerable enthusiasm as a much-needed antidote to the now disfavored focus on formal features and as an impetus for instructional and programmatic innovation (Snow, 1998).

Yet such fervor can easily overlook a serious conceptual flaw that manifests itself when CBI programs are characterized as differing in terms of a greater or lesser emphasis on form or content. Specifically, the literature focuses on questions such as the following (see Met, 1999): (a) Is content taught in L2 with little or no explicit instruction in the foreign language or is it used (in the more instrumentalist meaning of that word) to learn the L2? (b) Does content learning enjoy priority status or does it play an incidental role during language learning, which has priority? (c) Are content objectives determined by course goals or by an overall curricular framework for a subject matter? (d) Conversely, are language objectives determined by a language curriculum organized according to grammatical principles? The resulting array of possible answers is described with a host of terms, among them *content-driven, content-based, content-enriched* (Ballman, 1997), or *content-related language instruction;* or *language-based content instruction.*

Surprisingly, the literature does not identify these models as subverting the very integration of meaning and language that defines CBI. Instead, it mainly follows two paths. The first is to portray weaker and stronger versions of CBI, with weaker forms including "language courses whose main aim is to develop learners' communicative proficiency in the second language through a curriculum organized around the learning of substantive information and skills," and stronger forms including "mainstreaming of second language speakers in classes for native speakers, with some individualized adaptation for their language level" (Wesche and Skehan, 2002, p. 222). The second alternative is to disregard this fundamental dissonance altogether and to praise local approaches for their programmatic variety; their opportunities for collaboration; their staffing, topic, and materials choices; and their creative use of educational resources. Taken together such linking of content and language appears to be more an idealized notion, perhaps even a certain rhetorical positioning: Students continue to be expected to pick up either language or content even when it is not in focus. In that case, the notion of CBI runs the risk of becoming devoid of meaning.

2.1. LOCATING CBI WITHIN RECENT SLA RESEARCH

It is an open question whether one should interpret that compromised stance from a pedagogical perspective and see on it the long shadow of Krashen's comprehensible input hypothesis, coupled with notions of innateness and naturalness, or whether one should choose an epistemological perspective and observe the even longer shadow of a tradition in Western philosophy that has separated language from knowledge, content, and thinking and divorced it from social contexts. However, beyond debate are the consequences of such legacies for the evolution of foreign language study and research in the United States. Pedagogical and research practice is slowly coming to refute an essentially decontextualized, rule-governed, and "scientized" understanding of language, and the specifics of how this is carried out hold the seeds for new ways of imagining how languages are learned, how they are best taught, and what might and should therefore be of interest in and to SLA research.

We can broadly characterize developments in this fashion: In light of extensive research conducted in Canada in the 1980s and 1990s, it became clear that without some attention to the formal features of language, French immersion learners who received a particular kind of content-based teaching retained nontarget-like morphology and syntax even into the higher grades. As a result, the field began to abandon the belief that input-rich communicative teaching is sufficient to allow students to develop target-like proficiency (Harley and Swain, 1984). From that insight, a number of SLA research foci have evolved, the majority of which favor and interpret the learners' side in terms of a strong individualistic and psycholinguistic bent. We speak of the need for output, not only for Krashen's comprehensible input (Swain, 1995), for assistance to enhance the quality of input processing (see Cadierno, 1995; Sanz and Morgan-Short, this volume, chapter 8; VanPatten, this volume, chapter 9; VanPatten, 1996, 2000; VanPatten and Cadierno, 1993; VanPatten and Sanz, 1995), or more generally for input enhancement (e.g., Jourdenais, Ota, Stauffer, Boyson, and Doughty, 1995) and Focus on Form (see in particular Doughty, 1998; Doughty and Williams, 1998a; Leeman, Arteagoitia, Fridman, and Doughty, 1995; Spada, 1997). The constructs of implicitness and explicitness from the standpoint of learners' processing (N. C. Ellis, 1993, 1994), of consciousness raising (Long and Robinson, 1998; Schmidt, 1995b), and of conscious reflection (Swain, 1998), and the related notions of attention, awareness, and noticing (see Leow, 1997; Leow and Bowles, this volume, chapter 6; Schmidt, 1995a) all belong to this line of thinking. On the teacher's side, implicitness and explicitness come into play, frequently expressed as implicit or explicit teaching of "grammar" that is itself understood almost exclusively in terms of sentence-level grammar (but see Celce-Murcia and Olshtain, 2000; Larsen-Freeman, 2003; McCarthy and Carter, 1994) or in terms of teacher feedback (see Carroll and Swain, 1993; R. Ellis, 1994; Ellis and Laporte, 1997; Mackey and Abbuhl, this volume, chapter 7; Sanz and Morgan-Short, this volume, chapter 8). Simultaneously, notions of naturalness and the problematic role of the teacher and the classroom remain alive in the continued need to affirm that instruction makes a difference (Doughty, 1991; Doughty and Williams, 1998b; Norris and Ortega, 2000); otherwise, such a stance would surely be the most commonsensical position in classroom-based SLA and teaching.

In other words, we need to take seriously the foundation of this line of research: Many influential empirical SLA studies published in the last ten years have originated in Canadian immersion instruction contexts in the middle and high school grades, which approximate naturalistic acquisition. Subsequently, their conclusions were applied to instructed settings that bear little resemblance to the Canadian context. Conversely, classroom-based research in the United States typically started out with the assumption of a heavy grammar focus in instruction and with beginning and intermediate levels of acquisition whose limitations were taken to be well understood in the profession. Not surprisingly, a key concern was to prove that instruction that is meaning-focused (as contrasted with form-focused) or that does not simply assume that acquisition will take place by itself (as is presumed for the immersion setting) can make a difference. Thus, in a curious way, both CBI and SLA research as practiced in the United States have been shaped by a kind of intellectual displacement, finding remedies for problems that do not exist and ignoring those that do. In other words, while both the communities of CBI practitioners and of SLA researchers assert the central role of discourse, context, meaning, and content, their actual practices tend to counteract or at least sideline those convictions.

2.2. CBI AS A LOCUS FOR NEW APPROACHES TO LANGUAGE AND KNOWING

Even so, the central concerns of CBI as well as its major program models (e.g., total immersion, partial immersion, sheltered courses, the adjunct model, theme-based courses, and language classes that incorporate content in order to afford language practice, Met, 1998, 1999) usefully point beyond mainstream SLA and mainstream pedagogy. For example, Crandall and Tucker (1990) foreground the integrative aspect of CBI as "drawing topics, texts, and tasks from content or subject-matter classes, but focusing on the cognitive, academic language skills required to participate effectively in content instruction" (p. 83). Although they refer to learning outcomes as skills (much as mainstream pedagogy and SLA research often do), Crandall and Tucker recognize that acquiring and knowing a content area is not about learning a language for expressing preexisting knowledge. It is instead about acquiring and knowing its texts, where such knowing demands and in fact comes about in acquiring and knowing the particular textual language that constitutes them.

If that is so, then specifying how this decidedly textual, not merely grammatical or lexical, focus of CBI instruction will aid learners becomes an important agenda item. The contributions of a textual orientation would also need to be related to the presumed benefits of a primarily oral, interactive, and communicative approach to teaching. And finally, the goals and approaches of foreign and native language learning should be explored for their proximity: Both benefit from explicit instruction throughout precollegiate and collegiate education so that students may learn to handle competently diverse public discourses in both the oral and the written medium. The goal is for all students to become functionally literate, with L2 learners gaining the additional benefit of becoming multiliterate in a multilingual and multicultural society.

In sum, understanding the concerns of CBI in this fashion suggests engaging the construct of literacy, first language literacy and second language literacy, as a possible link between content and form and between knowing and "languaging," to use Becker's (1995) felicitous term (see also Larsen-Freeman's, 2003, use of "grammaring"). In the extensive literature on literacy, Gee (1998) makes a useful distinction between primary discourses of familiarity and secondary discourses of public life, including language use in diverse institutional settings. Literacy is also a prominent concern of systemic-functional linguistics (Halliday 1985/1994), particularly how it might be conceptualized and operationalized in contrast with the heretofore privileged orality. Halliday (1993) refers to two forms of ideation, congruent and synoptic semiosis, and identifies the latter as a central characteristic of literate language. Through the feature of grammatical metaphor in particular, which construes meaning through linguistic means other than those typically used in everyday life (e.g., processes being expressed in terms of nominalized things), disciplinary and institutional discourses present their knowledge in logically condensed and technical ways (see particularly the contributions examining the use of grammatical metaphor in the sciences in Martin and Veel, 1998), a form of meaning construal that is also central to all aspects of schooling (Schleppegrell, 2004).

A pivotal construct for a systemic-functional approach is that of register or, more recently, genre. Though variation exists in the definition of genre—for example, as typification of rhetorical action in Miller (1984), as regularities of staged, goal-oriented social processes in Martin (1993), or as consistency of communicative purposes in Swales (1990)—the key characteristic of genres is that of conventionalization (Bhatia, 2002). That conventionalization enables both an analysis of various textual genres and a genre-based pedagogy that links the prototypicality of textual organization to carefully scaffolded pedagogies (Christie, 1999; Johns, 2002; Kalantzis and Cope, 2000; Richards and Nowicki, 1998a, 1998b; Rothery, 1989).

3. Initiatives in CBI in Collegiate Foreign Language Departments

While a literacy approach has only recently been suggested as a way to overcome the language form and content split (for foreign language [FL] education, see particularly Kern, 2000), past efforts of FL departments are instructive. They can be examined from a programmatic or administrative and from a conceptual side. Given the preoccupations of linguistics as a scientific form of inquiry, of SLA as a relatively young discipline searching for conceptual moorings and intellectual standing, and of pedagogy as existing in various dependency relationships, local and often remarkably creative administrative solutions predominated in the past.

Both routes to innovation encounter two obstacles. The paramount administrative-structural obstacle is the well known programmatic bifurcation of FL curricula into what might benignly be called content-indifferent language courses (usually the first two years and also the required sequence) and language-indifferent content courses (for extensive discussion of this issue and its consequences, see particularly Byrnes, 1998, 2000, 2001). Consequently, the interests of CBI and, more expansively, the notion of an integrated curriculum for which an entire faculty would take responsibility are difficult to realize (Maxim, 2004). The concurrent conceptual obstacle is the recent transformation of most national literature departments into literature-culture departments, a shift that, in line with postmodern thinking in the humanities, has privileged English-language theorizing. Not only has that sociologically grounded shift subdued the otherness to which FL departments earlier on spoke so eloquently, it has denied their essential language foundation (for an extensive discussion, see Byrnes 2002b). For these reasons, initiatives in CBI that target the foreign languages have tended to be sporadic, have been located outside FL departments, and are structurally fragile and highly dependent on energetic individual faculty members for their viability and survival. Only in the rarest of cases did such initiatives influence the praxes of an entire department (Byrnes, 2001).

3.1. PROGRAMS FOR LANGUAGES ACROSS THE CURRICULUM AND THE MOVEMENT FOR FOREIGN LANGUAGES ACROSS THE CURRICULUM

The two most important named initiatives are Languages Across the Curriculum and Foreign Languages Across the Curriculum, both well described by Adams (1996) and in the contributions in Kecht and von Hammerstein (2000) and Krueger and Ryan (1993). By moving into the institution's entire undergraduate curriculum, they have strived to (re-)establish FL study as part of the humanities with its interest in content knowledge, competence, interpretive insight, and critical thinking. That goal has reflected the sense of some faculty that communicative language teaching has become reduced to intellectually questionable practices. Recent instantiations (see Kecht and von Hammerstein, 2000) take a strongly interdisciplinary and global perspective. In line with the shifting demographic, economic, and political order, they highlight complex negotiation of personal and national identity and sovereignty.

3.2. CBI AND IMMERSION INSTRUCTION AT THE COLLEGE LEVEL

The challenges that can be expected to accompany such enlarged educational goals are particularly well demonstrated in an innovative program at the University of Minnesota, the Foreign Language Immersion Program (FLIP) (Klee and Tedick, 1997). Despite careful planning and execution, including preparation of graduate student instructors in the two social science-based courses, the program's deliberate focus on cultural, literary, political, and historical content was difficult to realize under the old paradigm of teaching, learning, and teacher education. Specifically, problems that have generally been attributed to students' missing background knowledge or teachers' and learners' insufficient language proficiency (as though language ability could be usefully described independent of its contexts of use) revealed themselves as unsuitable for understanding the linguistic basis of knowing and the textual basis of language use. Instead, disciplinary ways of knowing need to be explored in terms of the discursive and lexicogrammatical patterns of knowing that express and constitute them, validate and transmit them, hold them together, and allow them to change (see Schleppegrell's, 2004, excellent discussion of what she calls "the language of schooling"). Only when disciplinary practitioners are enabled to become sophisticated and self-aware practitioners will they begin to understand their own particular form of knowledge making through language.

For language professionals at all instructional levels and in all categories of the faculty hierarchy (from graduate TAs to graduate faculty), this insight creates a double need: awareness of the discourse practices of various fields of inquiry or language use (e.g., the various disciplinary areas or institutional discourses) as instantiated in their preferred textual practices, and awareness of pedagogical demands and options that arise from those discourse practices. Nowhere is such metareflection and knowing-in-doing more called for than in fostering upper levels of ability in an L2 (see particularly the contributions in Byrnes and Maxim, 2004; Schleppegrell and Colombi, 2002), traditionally the most obvious place for the linking of language and content.

3.3. LANGUAGE FOR SPECIAL PURPOSES PROGRAMS

Just such considerations are, of course, at the heart of programs in Language for Special Purposes. By now such programs can draw on considerable experience with the teaching of English as a second language. More recently an interest in professional education has also influenced FL programs, particularly in business language courses (for a current rendition, see Weigert, 2004). Among the better known FL projects is the comprehensive program at the University of Rhode Island for a Bachelor of Science in German and engineering (Grandin, 1989). Carefully linking content and language learning throughout the five-year undergraduate program, including a study abroad and an internship component, it is almost completely based on practitioner expertise that found few relevant insights in contemporaneous SLA research.

Interestingly, a retrospective report by Kirchner (2000) notes as a particularly formidable challenge that of the disciplinary identity of engineering students engaged in the learning of German. Just such issues are extensively treated in recent publications that rely on systemic-functional linguistics for their theoretical framework and use its conceptual and analytical tools for the analysis of language in various disciplinary areas and in specific genres (see particularly the volumes by Bazerman, 1988; Halliday and Martin, 1993; Martin and Veel, 1998; Schleppegrell and Colombi, 2002; Swales, 1990).

How fine grained, insightful, and pedagogically translatable such analyses can be is well exemplified in Martin's (1991) exploration of the differential use of nominalizations, a key instance of grammatical metaphor, and of their consequences for clause structures in the sciences and the humanities. As Martin summarizes:

> In science, nominalization is strongly associated with definitions; its function is to accumulate meanings so that a technical term can be defined—in science grammatical metaphor "distills." In history nominalization is strongly associated with realizing events as participants so that logical connections can be realized inside the clause; and at the same time nominalization is deployed to construct layers of thematic and information structures in a text—in history grammatical metaphor "scaffolds." (p. 333)

Similarly, Christie (2002) shows that the production of narrative texts in a native language, the ability to begin to produce literary critical pieces, and the ability to write what she calls *opinionate texts* is intimately related to the control of reference of theme, the ability to handle abstractions and grammatical metaphors, as well as facility with complex nominal groups and diverse forms of circumstantial evidence that nonetheless support the argument. Finally, Colombi (2002) investigates the development of hypotactic clauses in students' expository writing in L2 Spanish as a way to organize an essay, noting in particular the essential need for explicit teaching of such features. In each of these forms of narration, complex decisions are made with regard to what time is to be marked and how, what cause and effect relationships are to be claimed, and what role the evaluation and interpretation of facts inherently plays (see also Byrnes and Sprang, 2004, for the complex movement from time to causality).

4. A Proposal for a New Conceptualization of CBI in and Through Advanced L2 Learning

As already indicated, CBI has particular affinities to the intellectual goals of FL departments, typically located at the more advanced curricular stages. The advantageous development now on our disciplinary horizon is that these intellectual aspirations can in fact be quite directly linked to the previously neglected goal of advanced language acquisition. This is so because the construct of a genre-based literacy as I have outlined it here offers a particularly elegant and rich way for describing advanced attainment in any language, native or nonnative, and is suitable as well as an educational framework for principled curricular and pedagogical decision making and practices (Byrnes, 2002c, 2004). Importantly, a literacy orientation in both environments points beyond language into society and through that explicit reach into sociocultural practice enables a felicitous reconceptualization not only of first and second language teaching and learning, but ultimately of the position of our field within the humanities, and indeed of the nature of any knowing through language.

Specifically, a sociocultural approach to language foregrounds the essential fact that language is a semiotic tool for meaning making and locates language use within the context of social practice (among many other sources, see Lantolf, 2000). Externally, the social, political, and economic environment for which we prepare our students necessitates advanced language literacy capacities. Internally, such a focus encourages us to part company with the still prevalent focus on decontextualized formal features of language that remains viable in no small part because our concerns have been delimited by beginning and intermediate levels of learning rather than advanced literacies. This preoccupation tends to project the recent interest in advanced attainment as little more than the accurate mastery of sentence-level features (i.e., more of the same, but better). By contrast, insights from systemic-functional linguistics, and a genre-based approach compatible with cognitive-semantic notions of processing (as contrasted with cognitive-psycholinguistic processing approaches), and genre-based pedagogies suggest a rich framework for long overdue reconsiderations for CBI, SLA research foci, and curricular and pedagogical practices.

4.1. IDENTIFYING OUTSTANDING ISSUES FOR CBI AND SLA

4.1.1 ALTERNATIVE UNDERSTANDINGS OF LANGUAGE

In the following, I explore possible avenues for such forms of inquiry and reflection in three areas. The first deals with the need for exploring alternative understandings of language. We have already referred to the advantages of a social-semiotic or functional perspective for CBI. Among other advantages, it can overcome prevailing notions of language learning as a skill, even as an academic skill (for broader epistemological issues see Firth and Wagner, 1997, and the responses to it). As Halliday emphasizes in developing a language-based theory of learning, "language is not a *domain* of human knowledge . . . language is the essential condition of knowing, the process by which experience *becomes* knowledge [emphasis in original]" (1993, p. 94). Therefore, because knowledge itself is constructed in varying patterns of discourse, a key way for enhancing mental abilities is through enhancing learners' text-based language patterns.

The kind of cognitive abilities required for thorough engagement with content and language are not abstractly given but develop concurrently through a carefully guided engagement with texts. For example, the learners in an upper-level collegiate German comedy class (Byrnes and Kord, 2002) were asked to think and express in an intellectually and academically valid way the course's challenging content in political and social history, in literary reception history, and in literary analysis. They were able to do so only to the extent that they seized upon the opportunity provided by extensive modeling and feedback regarding certain kinds of chunked language that set the stage for categorical and abstract arguing. This enabled them to leave behind the personal commentary of thinking, believing, discussing, and reacting personally that characterizes so many upper-level classes and to move on to the kind of principled and theorized debate that the community of literary scholars engages in.

Another possibility is through what Mohan (1989) refers to as knowledge structures, such as categorization itself, which represent experience as we acquire it in particular situations and which translate into textual macrostructures. In contrast with genres, which are prototypical structures of specific text types, knowledge structures are situational and ideational semantic structures. In the end, the two approaches (the text-based genre approach and the situation-based knowledge structure approach) are complementary inasmuch as they affect and reflect different aspects of texts and contexts. In a similar vein, principles of information organization at very advanced stages of L2 learning have illuminated how central textual abilities, such as reference introduction, are associated with patterns of grammaticization that are clustered in form-function linkages spread across different domains (e.g., Carroll and Lambert, 2003; Carroll, Murcia-Serra, Watorek, and Bendiscioli, 2000; Carroll and Stutterheim, 2002). Linking psycholinguistic processing with semantic processing, Stutterheim and Lambert (in press) argue against a universalist approach for the processing of conceptualization, as much American SLA research assumes at least implicitly, and argue for a processing that is located at the level of the conceptualizer and therefore subject to the influence of first-language conceptualizations even in very advanced L2 learners.

More generally, a semantic approach affirms Bardovi-Harlig's (2000) finding that meaning-oriented (i.e., semantically oriented) studies, such as those prevalent in European research, are better able to capture the emergent expression of particular concepts (e.g., temporality, spatial relations) across different grammatical categories. Such an approach would, therefore, appear to be of considerable value for CBI and for advanced learning, with their demands for textually creating experience and interpersonal relationships in the multilingual world of the emerging bilingual learner (see Cook, 2002).

A final approach that I mention here for its promise of providing considerable insights for CBI and SLA research is cognitive semantics, particularly as explicated by Langacker (1999), Givón (1998), and Tomasello (1998, 2003). An added advantage is the link to processing research that is both semantically and psycholinguistically informed, such as Slobin (1996a, 1996b). The shared characteristic is a functional perspective that prioritizes cognitive-semantic considerations over formal considerations in order to tease out the correlation between grammatical form and communicative or cognitive function, especially in ways that underscore the centrality of coherence relations in discourse and the adaptive quality of human language and human language use to communicative situations.

4.1.2. THE NEED FOR AN APPROPRIATE CURRICULAR CONTENT

The second area for inquiry and reflection lies in the need for a curricular context for valid pedagogy and for research. A curricular framework recognizes that any pedagogical decision making, be it with regard to content or with regard to language form, is ultimately validated only in terms of long-term development. Far from being merely an educational tool, curricular proposals are a necessity for the SLA research community. Very little is really known about the long-term consequences of instructional choices and particularly about the likelihood that learners will be able to develop discourse-level processing capacities from sentence-level processing practice. In other words, strong notions of developmental sequencing that were posited in a morphemic or at best a sentence-level environment deserve reconsideration, along with their claims for teachability or learnability.

In particular, it is generally held that instruction only speeds up the acquisition of certain features but cannot dramatically alter their sequence (Bardovi-Harlig, 2000). But such a statement presupposes that language features are learned in isolation and that learning in one area does not affect learning in others. For that reason alone, the well-known theoretical postulate of a fixed sequence for highly delimited phenomena (e.g., emergence of word order rules) is at the very least questionable. Similarly fragile are many other research findings that do not report on the curricular and pedagogical context in which a language is learned and learner language produced. As Bardovi-Harlig (1995, p. 153) notes, such practices make fixed acquisitional sequences attractive and lead to a preference for interpreting variation in learning outcomes in different instructional settings in terms of psycholinguistic processing characteristics and not in terms of the nature of classroom discourses. Thus, an educational environment linking language and content in curricular and pedagogical decision making might enable a more expansive interpretation of both the lexical aspect hypothesis and the discourse hypothesis, key constructs for understanding the development of verbal morphology for the expression of temporality (Bardovi-Harlig, 1998), precisely because a discourse-oriented approach should itself affect the acquisition of tense and aspect.

In any case, in the absence of even a preliminary curricular proposal, it is very difficult to hypothesize and test insightfully how the continued complex linkages between meaning and form, from macrotextual to microlexicogrammatical levels, can gradually turn language use at a particular time into the desired language development over time.

4.1.3. THE NEED FOR A CONSTRUCT ABOVE THE TALK-LEVEL

The third and final area for inquiry and reflection is situated in the need for a construct above the task-level. I have already referred to the proximity of interests between CBI and two SLA research foci, communicative language teaching and task-based language teaching (for an excellent discussion of these connections, see Wesche and Skehan, 2002). If one accepts the construct of task as a way of overcoming earlier limitations of analytical syllabus design and structuralist grammars (among many sources, see particularly Crookes and Gass, 1993a, 1993b, and Long, 1994), then the kind of sociocultural orientation and the textual focus I have advocated for CBI also demand an understanding of task that goes beyond any activity not focused on grammar and having specific communicative outcomes, the umbrella under which much task-based teaching is located (for an overview of that orientation, see Skehan, 1998). Instead, a more mature understanding of task is called for, such as that described in the articles in Bygate, Skehan, and Swain (2001) and enhanced by the comprehensive review of the task literature in R. Ellis (2003).

Despite aspirations associated with the construct right from the beginning (e.g., in Long and Crookes, 1992), task has yet to be sufficiently specified to be useful for extended (and by this I mean multiyear) curriculum construction to high levels of ability. Similarly, the recommended needs-assessment inventory that would specify tasks is at the very least problematic for academic instructed settings. And the almost exclusive focus on oral language use that approximates real-world interactive and transactional language, coupled with the ambivalent stance toward explicit teaching, leaves little room for developing the kinds of literate capacities that are so much in demand for CBI and any advanced learning.

In other words, as a unit of analysis for both teaching and SLA research, the notion of task must be both expanded and strengthened through a superordinate construct and subsequently more closely specified in terms of that enlarged conceptual environment. While earlier approaches to CBI took a thematic approach to be sufficient for expressing the content-language link (see, for example, Stoller and Grabe, 1997), we have come to understand that a more linguistic approach is necessary for expressing the crucial link between textuality or discourse, where these terms encompass both oral and written texts or discourses, and pedagogical task, if we are to attain the desired translation into effective and efficient pedagogical practice that fosters advanced levels of L2 attainment.

Even though that orientation might at first appear to demand a radical departure from the major research paradigm in SLA (e.g., comprehensible input, interaction, negotiation, intake, output, Focus on Form) a closer examination provides a more hopeful picture. As Doughty (2000) affirms, the negotiation of meaning that is so fundamental to recent processing-oriented research is a discourse-level process. In that case, specific instructional and learner-focused recommendations like those made in systemic-functional linguistics regarding clause-level phenomena that can be identified within an overall textual focus show important proximities of interest (see particularly Carson, Taylor, and Fredella, 1997; Wesche and Skehan, 2002). Exploring a reconfigured understanding of task from the teacher's standpoint, Samuda (2001) distinguishes between language-activating tasks that simply require the use of certain language forms that already exist in the interlanguage and knowledge-constructing tasks that, in a three-step meaning-form-meaning progression, actually create a need to mean, an inherently discursive effort. Finally, an explicitly textually oriented expansion of the notion of task is proposed by Byrnes and Sprang (2004), who explicate the potential of a cognitivist, genre-based notion of task. As their discussion indicates, deriving pedagogical tasks from diverse textual genres, understood as situated social action that has typified rhetorical forms at all levels of the language system (from the discourse to the sentence to the lexicogrammatical level), affords rich opportunities for making the link between meaning and form and between social setting and individual need to learn, even in a classroom setting. Using the *précis* as a unifying genre, Swaffar (2004) demonstrates its use across major textual environments, such as literary texts, film reviews, and interviews.

A first comprehensive curricular proposal in a collegiate FL department that has chosen this approach is that of the German Department at Georgetown University, called Developing Multiple Literacies (for extensive information on the curricular project, see the department's web site, http://data.georgetown.edu/departments/german/programs/curriculum/). It uses a genre orientation and genre-derived tasks to make decisions for its entire four-year undergraduate curriculum. As a content-based curriculum, it recognizes that instruction must find ways to link content and form in reasonably predictable and overt ways, even if the individual user makes unique choices. It does so in order to organize tasks for their long-term developmental implications with respect to the use of different features of language, for their ability to affect systematically how language is processed, and for their consequences for long-term development toward discursive capacities as they are required in the public forum. Within such a framework, task is used not only to conceptualize, plan, organize, and assess the nature of instructional interventions that link content and language to a sociocultural context of use and do so over long instructional periods; it can also serve as an environment that has high ecological validity for the assessment of learning outcomes (Byrnes, 2002a).

5. Summary

This chapter has presented CBI as a challenge both to pedagogical practice and to SLA research practice. The promises that inhere in this approach, of linking content and language form in a fashion that allow competent use of an L2 in a range of discourse environments, have at this point been only partially fulfilled. Even so, on the basis of a critical evaluation of the evidence, the chapter suggests that important stimuli already exist that can significantly advance the work of both the teacher and the research community. In particular, the chapter suggests that an approach both to constructing an integrated curriculum on the basis of major textual genre and to devising genre-based pedagogical tasks makes possible the integration of cultural content and language and the linkage between language use at a time and language acquisition over time that is at the heart of truly content-based language teaching and learning, particularly toward advanced-level abilities in a second or foreign language.

Further Reading

Cope, B., & Kalantzis, M. (Eds.). (2000). *Multiliteracies. Literacy learning and the design of social futures.* New York: Routledge.

Gee, J. P. (1996). *Social linguistics and literacies: Ideology in discourses.* London: Falmer Press.

Swaffar, J., & Arens, K. (2005). *Remapping the foreign language curriculum: A multiliteracies approach.* New York: Modern Language Association.

Vygotsky, L. (1986). *Thought and language.* Cambridge, MA: MIT Press.

References

Adams, T. M. (1996). Languages across the curriculum: Taking stock. *ADFL Bulletin, 28*(1), 9–19.

Ballman, T. L. (1997). Enhancing beginning language courses through content-enriched instruction. *Foreign Language Annals, 30,* 173–186.

Bardovi-Harlig, K. (1995). The interaction of pedagogy and natural sequences in the acquisition of tense and aspect. In F. Eckman, D. Highland, P. W. Lee, J. Mileham, & R. R. Weber (Eds.), *Second language acquisition theory and pedagogy* (pp. 151–168). Mahwah, NJ: Lawrence Erlbaum.

Bardovi-Harlig, K. (1998). Narrative structure and lexical aspect: Conspiring factors in second language acquisition of tense-aspect morphology. *Studies in Second Language Acquisition, 20,* 471–508.

Bardovi-Harlig, K. (2000). *Tense and aspect in second language acquisition: Form, meaning, and use.* Oxford, UK: Blackwell.

Bazerman, C. (1988). *Shaping written knowledge. The genre and activity of the experimental article in science.* Madison, WI: University of Wisconsin Press.

Becker, A. L. (1995). *Beyond translation: Essays toward a modern philology.* Ann Arbor, MI: University of Michigan Press.

Bhatia, V. K. (2002). A generic view of academic discourse. In J. Flowerdew (Ed.), *Academic discourse* (pp. 21–39). London: Longman.

Bygate, M., Skehan, P., & Swain, M. (Eds.). (2001). *Researching pedagogic tasks: Second language learning, teaching and testing.* Harlow, UK: Pearson Education.

Byrnes, H. (1998). Constructing curricula in collegiate foreign language departments. In H. Byrnes (Ed.), *Learning foreign and second languages: Perspectives in research and scholarship* (pp. 262–295). New York: Modern Language Association.

Byrnes, H. (2000). Languages across the curriculum–intradepartmental curriculum construction: Issues and options. In M. R. Kecht & K. von Hammerstein (Eds.), *Languages across the curriculum: Interdisciplinary structures and internationalized education* (pp. 151–175). Columbus, OH: National East Asian Languages Resource Center, The Ohio State University.

Byrnes, H. (2001). Reconsidering graduate students' education as teachers: It takes a department! *The Modern Language Journal, 85,* 512–530.

Byrnes, H. (2002a). The role of task and task-based assessment in a content-oriented collegiate FL curriculum. *Language Testing, 19,* 419–437.

Byrnes, H. (2002b). The cultural turn in foreign language departments: Challenge and opportunity. *Profession 2002,* 114–129.

Byrnes, H. (2002c). Toward academic-level foreign language abilities: Reconsidering foundational assumptions, expanding pedagogical options. In B. L. Leaver & B. Shekhtman (Eds.), *Developing professional-level language proficiency* (pp. 34–58). Cambridge, UK: Cambridge University Press.

Byrnes, H. (2004). Advanced L2 literacy: Beyond option or privilege. *ADFL Bulletin, 36*(1), 52–60.

Byrnes, H., & Kord, S. (2002). Developing literacy and literary competence: A challenge for foreign language departments. In V. Scott & H. Tuckers (Eds.), *SLA and the literature classroom: Fostering dialogues* (pp. 31–69). Boston: Heinle & Heinle.

Byrnes, H., & Maxim, H. H. (Eds.). (2004). *Advanced foreign language learning: A challenge to college programs.* Boston: Heinle & Heinle.

Byrnes, H., & Sprang, K. A. (2004). Fostering advanced L2 literacy: A genre-based cognitive approach. In H. Byrnes & H. H. Maxim (Eds.), *Advanced foreign language learning: A challenge to college programs* (pp. 47–85). Boston: Heinle & Heinle.

Cadierno, T. (1995). Formal instruction from a processing perspective: An investigation into the Spanish past tense. *The Modern Language Journal, 79,* 179–193.

Carroll, S., & Swain, M. (1993). Explicit and implicit negative feedback: An empirical study of the learning of linguistic generalizations. *Studies in Second Language Acquisition, 15,* 357–386.

Carroll, M., & Lambert, M. (2003). Information structure in narratives and the role of grammaticised knowledge: A study of adult French and German learners of English. In C. Dimroth & M. Starren (Eds.), *Dynamics of first and second language acquisition* (pp. 267–287). Amsterdam: John Benjamins.

Carroll, M., Murcia-Serra, J., Watorek, M., & Bendiscioli, A. (2000). The relevance of information organization to second language acquisition studies: The descriptive discourse of advanced adult learners of German. *Studies in Second Language Acquisition, 22,* 441–466.

Carroll, M., & Stutterheim, C. von (2002). Typology and information organisation: Perspective taking and language-specific effects in the construal of events. In A. G. Ramat (Ed.), *Typology and second language acquisition* (pp. 365–403). Berlin: Mouton de Gruyter.

Carson, J. G., Taylor, J. A., & Fredella, L. (1997). The role of content in task-based EAP instruction. In M. A. Snow & D. M. Brinton (Eds.), *The content-based classroom: Perspectives on integrating language and content* (pp. 367–370). London: Longman.

Celce-Murcia, M., & Olshtain, E. (2000). *Discourse and context in language teaching.* Cambridge, UK: Cambridge University Press.

Christie, F. (1999). Genre theory and ESL teaching: A systemic functional perspective. *TESOL Quarterly, 33*(4), 759–763.

Christie, F. (2002). The development of abstraction in adolescence in subject English. In M. J. Schleppegrell & M. C. Colombi (Eds.), *Developing advanced literacy in first and second languages: Meaning with power* (pp. 45–66). Mahwah, NJ: Lawrence Erlbaum.

Colombi, M. C. (2002). Academic language development in Latino students' writing in Spanish. In M. J. Schleppegrell & M. C. Colombi (Eds.), *Developing advanced literacy in first and second languages: Meaning with power* (pp. 67–86). Mahwah, NJ: Lawrence Erlbaum.

Cook, V. (Ed.). (2002). *Portraits of the L2 user.* Clevedon, UK: Multilingual Matters.

Crandall, J., & Tucker, G. R. (1990). Content-based language instruction in second and foreign languages. In S. Anivan (Ed.), *Language teaching methodology for the nineties* (pp. 83–96). Singapore: SAEMEO Regional Language Centre.

Crookes, G., & Gass, S. M. (Eds.). (1993a). *Tasks and language learning: Integrating theory and practice.* Clevedon, UK: Multilingual Matters.

Crookes, G., & Gass, S. M. (Eds.). (1993b). *Tasks in a pedagogical context: Integrating theory and practice.* Clevedon, UK: Multilingual Matters.

Developing multiple literacies: A curriculum renewal project of the German Department at Georgetown University, 1997–2000. (2000). http://data.georgetown.edu/departments/german/programs/curriculum/.

Doughty, C. (1991). Second language instruction does make a difference. Evidence from an empirical study of SL relativization. *Studies in Second Language Acquisition, 13,* 431–469.

Doughty, C. (1998). Acquiring competence in a second language: Form and function. In H. Byrnes (Ed.), *Learning foreign and second languages: Perspectives in research and scholarship* (pp. 128–156). New York: Modern Language Association.

Doughty, C. (2000). Negotiating the linguistic environment. *University of Hawaii Working Papers in ESL, 19*(2), 45–73.

Doughty, C., & Williams, J. (Eds.). (1998a). *Focus on form in classroom second language acquisition.* Cambridge, UK: Cambridge University Press.

Doughty, C., & Williams, J. (1998b). Pedagogical choices in focus on form. In C. Doughty & J. Williams (Eds.), *Focus on form in classroom second language acquisition* (pp. 197–261). Cambridge, UK: Cambridge University Press.

Ellis, N. C. (1993). The implicit ins and outs of explicit cognitive mediation. In N. C. Ellis (Ed.), *Implicit and explicit learning of languages* (pp. 211–282). New York: Academic Press.

Ellis, N. C. (1994). Consciousness in second language learning: Psychological perspectives on the role of conscious processes in vocabulary acquisition. *AILA Review, 11,* 37–56.

Ellis, N. C., & Laporte, N. (1997). Contexts of acquisition: Effects of formal instruction and naturalistic exposure on second language acquisition. In A. M. B. de Groot & J. F. Kroll (Eds.), *Tutorials in bilingualism* (pp. 53–83). Mahwah, NJ: Lawrence Erlbaum.

Ellis, R. (1994). Implicit/explicit knowledge and language pedagogy. *TESOL Quarterly, 28,* 166–171.

Ellis, R. (2003). *Task-based language learning and teaching.* Oxford, UK: Oxford University Press.

Firth, A., & Wagner, J. (1997). On discourse, communication, and (some) fundamental concepts in SLA research. *The Modern Language Journal, 81,* 285–312.

Gee, J. P. (1998). What is literacy? In V. Zamel & R. Spack (Eds.), *Negotiating academic literacies: Teaching and learning across languages and cultures* (pp. 51–59). Mahwah, NJ: Lawrence Erlbaum.

Givón, T. (1998). The functional approach to grammar. In M. Tomasello (Ed.), *The new psychology of language: Cognitive and functional approaches to language structure* (pp. 41–66). Mahwah, NJ: Lawrence Erlbaum.

Grabe, W., & Stoller, F. L. (1997). Content-based instruction: Research foundations. In M. A. Snow & D. M. Brinton (Eds.), *The content-based classroom: Perspectives on integrating language and content* (pp. 5–21). London: Longman.

Grandin, J. (1989). German and engineering: An overdue alliance. *Die Unterrichtspraxis, 22,* 146–152.

Halliday, M. A. K. (1993). Towards a language-based theory of learning. *Linguistics and Education, 5,* 93–116.

Halliday, M. A. K. (1994). *An introduction to functional grammar.* London: Edward Arnold. (Original work published 1985.)

Halliday, M. A. K., & Martin, J. R. (1993). *Writing science: Literacy and discursive power.* London: Falmer Press.

Harley, B., & Swain, M. (1984). The interlanguage of immersion students and its implications for second language teaching. In A. Davies, C. Criper, & A. P. R. Howatt (Eds.), *Interlanguage* (pp. 291–311). Edinburgh: Edinburgh University Press.

Johns, A. M. (Ed.). (2002). *Genre in the classroom: Multiple perspectives.* Mahwah, NJ: Lawrence Erlbaum.

Jourdenais, R., Ota, M., Stauffer, S., Boyson, B., & Doughty, C. (1995). Does textual enhancement promote noticing? A think-aloud protocol analysis. In R. Schmidt (Ed.), *Attention and awareness in foreign language learning* (Tech. Rep. No. 9, pp. 183–216). Honolulu, HI: University of Hawai'i at Manoa, Second Language Teaching and Curriculum Center.

Kalantzis, M., & Cope, B. (2000). A multiliteracies pedagogy: A pedagogical supplement. In B. Cope & M. Kalantzis (Eds.), *Multiliteracies. Literacy learning and the design of social futures* (pp. 239–248). New York: Routledge.

Kecht, M.-R., & von Hammerstein, K. (Eds.). (2000). *Languages across the curriculum: Interdisciplinary structures and internationalized education.* Columbus, OH: National East Asian Languages Resource Center, The Ohio State University.

Kern, R. (2000). *Literacy and language teaching.* Oxford, UK: Oxford University Press.

Kirchner, D. (2000). Disciplinary fusions: Linking foreign languages and culture studies with engineering. In M.-R. Kecht & K. von Hammerstein (Eds.), *Languages across the curriculum: Interdisciplinary structures and internationalized education* (pp. 227–239). Columbus, OH: National East Asian Languages Resource Center, The Ohio State University.

Klee, C. A., & Tedick, D. (1997). The undergraduate foreign language immersion program in Spanish at the University of Minnesota. S. B. Stryker & B. L. Leaver (Eds.), *Content-based instruction in foreign language education: Models and methods* (pp. 141–173). Washington, DC: Georgetown University Press.

Krueger, M., & Ryan, F. (Eds.). (1993). *Language and content. Discipline and content-based approaches to language study.* Lexington, MA: D. C. Heath.

Langacker, R. W. (1999). *Grammar and conceptualization.* Berlin: Mouton de Gruyter.

Lantolf, J. P. (Ed.). (2000). *Sociocultural theory and second language learning.* Oxford, UK: Oxford University Press.

Larsen-Freeman, D. (2003). *Teaching language: From grammar to grammaring.* Boston: Thomson-Heinle.

Leeman, J., Arteagoitia, I., Fridman, B., & Doughty, C. (1995). Integrating attention to form with meaning: Focus on form in content-based Spanish instruction. In R. Schmidt (Ed.), *Attention and awareness in foreign language learning* (Tech. Rep. No. 9, pp. 217–258). Honolulu, HI: University of Hawai'i at Manoa, Second Language Teaching and Curriculum Center.

Leow, R. P. (1997). Attention, awareness, and foreign language behavior. *Language Learning, 47,* 467–505.

Long, M. H. (1994). On the advocacy of the task-based syllabus. *TESOL Quarterly, 28,* 782–790.

Long, M. H., & Crookes, G. (1992). Three approaches to task-based syllabus design. *TESOL Quarterly, 26,* 27–56.

Long, M. H., & Robinson, P. (1998). Focus on form: Theory, research, and practice. In C. Doughty & J. Williams (Eds.), *Focus on form in classroom second language acquisition* (pp. 15–41). Cambridge, UK: Cambridge University Press.

Martin, J. R. (1991). Nominalization in science and humanities: Distilling knowledge and scaffolding text. In E. Ventola (Ed.). *Functional and systemic linguistics* (pp. 307–337). Berlin: Mouton de Gruyter.

Martin, J. R. (1993). Genre and literacy–modeling context in educational linguistics. *Annual Review of Applied Linguistics, 13,* 141–172.

Martin, J. R., & Veel, R. (Eds.). (1998). *Reading science: Critical and functional perspectives on discourses of science.* New York: Routledge.

Maxim, H. H. (2004). Expanding visions for collegiate advanced foreign language learning. In H. Byrnes & H. H. Maxim (Eds.), *Advanced foreign language learning: A challenge to college programs* (pp. 180–93). Boston: Heinle & Heinle.

McCarthy, M., & Carter, R. (1994). *Language as discourse: Perspectives for language teaching.* London: Longman.

Met, M. (1998). Curriculum decision-making in content-based teaching. In F. Genesee & J. Cenoz (Eds.), *Beyond bilingualism: Multilingualism and multilingual education* (pp. 35–63). Clevedon, UK: Multilingual Matters.

Met, M. (1999). *Content-based instruction: Defining terms, making decisions.* Washington, DC: The National Foreign Language Center.

Miller, C. R. (1984). Genre as social action. *Quarterly Journal of Speech, 70,* 151–167.

Mohan, B. A. (1989). Knowledge structures and academic discourse. *Word,* 40, 99–115.

Norris, J. M., & Ortega, L. (2000). Effectiveness of L2 instruction: A research synthesis and quantitative meta-analysis. *Language Learning, 50,* 417–528.

Richards, D., & Nowicki, U. (1998a). In search of a viable learning theory to support genre-based teaching to adult migrants: Part I. *Prospect, 13*(1), 40–52.

Richards, D., & Nowicki, U. (1998b). In search of a viable learning theory to support genre-based teaching to adult migrants: Part II. *Prospect, 13*(2), 63–77.

Rothery, J. (1989). Learning about language. In R. Hasan & J. R. Martin (Eds.), *Language development: Learning language, learning culture* (pp. 199–256). Norwood, NJ: Ablex.

Samuda, V. (2001). Guiding relationships between form and meaning during task performance: The role of the teacher. In M. Bygate, P. Skehan, & M. Swain (Eds.), *Researching pedagogic tasks: Second language learning, teaching and testing* (pp. 119–140). Harlow, UK: Pearson Education.

Schleppegrell, M. J. (2004). *The language of schooling: A functional linguistics perspective.* Mahwah, NJ: Lawrence Erlbaum.

Schleppegrell, M. J., & Colombi, M. C. (Eds.). (2002). *Developing advanced literacy in first and second languages: Meaning with power.* Mahwah, NJ: Lawrence Erlbaum.

Schmidt, R. (Ed.). (1995a). *Attention and awareness in foreign language learning* (Tech. Rep. No. 9). Honolulu, HI: University of Hawai'i at Manoa, Second Language Teaching and Curriculum Center.

Schmidt, R. (1995b). Consciousness and foreign language learning: A tutorial on the role of attention and awareness in learning. In R. Schmidt (Ed.), *Attention and awareness in foreign language learning* (Tech. Rep. No. 9, pp. 1–63). Honolulu, HI: University of Hawai'i at Manoa, Second Language Teaching and Curriculum Center.

Skehan, P. (1998). A *cognitive approach to language learning.* Oxford, UK: Oxford University Press.

Slobin, D. I. (1996a). From "thought and language" to "thinking for speaking." In J. J. Gumperz & S. C. Levinson (Eds.), *Rethinking linguistic relativity* (pp. 70–96). Cambridge, UK: Cambridge University Press.

Slobin, D. I. (1996b). Two ways to travel: Verbs of motion in English and Spanish. In M. Shibatani & S. A. Thompson (Eds.), *Grammatical constructions: Their form and meaning* (pp. 195–219). Oxford, UK: Clarendon Press.

Snow, M. A. (1998). Trends and issues in content-based instruction. *Annual Review of Applied Linguistics, 18,* 243–267.

Snow, M. A., & Brinton, D. M. (Eds.). (1997). *The content-based classroom: Perspectives on integrating language and content.* London: Longman.

Spada, N. (1997). Form-focussed instruction and second language acquisition: A review of classroom and laboratory research. *Language Teaching, 30,* 73–87.

Stoller, F. L., & Grabe, W. (1997). A six-T's approach to content-based instruction. In M. A. Snow & D. M. Brinton (Eds.), *The content-based classroom: Perspectives on integrating language and content* (pp. 78–94). London: Longman.

Stutterheim, C. von, & Lambert, M. (in press). Crosslinguistic analysis of temporal perspectives in text production. In H. Hendricks (Ed.), *The structure of learner language.* Berlin: Mouton de Gruyter.

Swaffar, J. (2004). A template for advanced learner tasks: Staging genre reading and cultural literacy through the précis. In H. Byrnes & H. H. Maxim (Eds.), *Advanced foreign language learning: A challenge to college programs* (pp. 19–45). Boston: Heinle & Heinle.

Swain, M. (1995). Three functions of output in second language learning. In G. Cook & B. Seidlhofer (Eds.), *Principle and practice in applied linguistics. Studies in honour of H. G. Widdowson* (pp. 125–144). Oxford, UK: Oxford University Press.

Swain, M. (1998). Focus on form through conscious reflection. In C. Doughty & J. Williams (Eds.), *Focus on form in classroom second language acquisition* (pp. 64–81). Cambridge, UK: Cambridge University Press.

Swales, J. M. (1990). *Genre analysis: English in academic and research settings.* Cambridge, UK: Cambridge University Press.

Tomasello, M. (Ed.). (1998). *The new psychology of language: Cognitive and functional approaches to language structure* (Vol. I). Mahwah, NJ: Lawrence Erlbaum.

Tomasello, M. (Ed.). (2003). *The new psychology of language: Cognitive and functional approaches to language structure* (Vol. II). Mahwah, NJ: Lawrence Erlbaum.

VanPatten, B. (1996). *Input processing and grammar instruction in second language acquisition.* Norwood, NJ: Ablex.

VanPatten, B. (2000). Processing instruction as form-meaning connections: Issues in theory and research. In J. Lee & A. Valdman (Eds.), *Form and meaning: Multiple perspectives* (pp. 43–68). Boston: Heinle & Heinle.

VanPatten, B., & Cadierno, T. (1993). Input processing and second language acquisition: A role for instruction. *The Modern Language Journal, 77,* 45–57.

VanPatten, B., & Sanz, C. (1995). From input to output: Processing instruction and communicative tasks. In F. Eckman, D. Highland, P. W. Lee, J. Mileham, & R. R. Weber (Eds.), *Second language acquisition theory and pedagogy* (pp. 169–185). Mahwah, NJ: Erlbaum.

Weigert, A. (2004). What's business got to do with it?: The unexplored potential of business language courses for advanced foreign language learning. In H. Byrnes & H. H. Maxim (Eds.), *Advanced foreign language learning: A challenge to college programs* (pp. 131–150). Boston: Heinle & Heinle.

Wesche, M. B. (1993). Discipline-based approaches to language study: Research issues and outcomes. In M. Krueger & F. Ryan (Eds.), *Language and content. Discipline and content-based approaches to language study* (pp. 57–82). Lexington, MA: D. C. Heath.

Wesche, M. B., & Skehan, P. (2002). Communicative, task-based, and content-based language instruction. In R. B. Kaplan (Ed.), *The Oxford handbook of applied linguistics* (pp. 207–228). Oxford, UK: Oxford University Press.

Contributors

Rebekha Abbuhl (PhD, 2005, Georgetown University) is an assistant professor at California State University, Long Beach. Her research interests include second language writing and the role of feedback in the development of second language writing skills. She has taught English as a foreign language in Hungary, Japan, and Ukraine.

Rebecca Adams (PhD, 2004, Georgetown University) is a lecturer in linguistics and applied language studies at Victoria University of Wellington. Her research interests include classroom second language acquisition, particularly the role of input and interaction on classroom language learning, the role of cognition in second language learning, and qualitative and quantitative research methods in second language research. Her work recently has appeared in *Language Teaching Research* and in an edited book published by Multilingual Matters.

Harriet Wood Bowden is a PhD candidate in second language acquisition in the Department of Spanish and Portuguese at Georgetown University. Her research interests include second language cognition and neurocognition, the roles of attention and instruction in second language acquisition, and second language research methodology. Her recent work includes a coauthored article (along with Kara Morgan-Short) on instruction and SLA that has recently been accepted for publication in *Studies in Second Language Acquisition.*

Melissa Bowles (PhD, 2005, Georgetown University) is assistant professor in the Department of Spanish, Italian, and Portuguese at the University of Illinois, Urbana-Champaign. Her research focuses on individual differences, and specifically on the role of attention in SLA and the various factors that can affect students' attention to form in the L2, including aptitude, provision of immediate feedback, and computer-assisted language learning (CALL) interventions.

Heidi Byrnes (PhD, 1979, Georgetown University) is professor of German at Georgetown University. Her research focus is the acquisition of academic literacy by instructed second language learners, including curriculum development, a discourse-oriented approach to grammar, and the pedagogy of linking content and language acquisition over long instructional sequences. Within her department's genre- and content-oriented, task-based curriculum, she is currently researching the acquisition of writing toward advanced levels of competence. Among her recent publications is a coedited volume *Advanced foreign language learning: A challenge to college programs* (Heinle and Heinle, 2004).

Rusan Chen (PhD, 1993, Tulane University) is a statistician at the Center for New Designs in Learning and Scholarship at Georgetown University. As an adjunct professor, he has offered basic statistics courses to graduate students in psychology, linguistics, biology, and education. He is interested in applying multivariate methods and latent variable modeling in social science research.

Akiko Fujii is a PhD candidate at Georgetown University and a full-time instructor in the English Language Program at the International Christian University in Tokyo, Japan. Her research interests include second language acquisition in classroom contexts, individual differences in second language learning, and English for academic purposes, particularly reading instruction.

Ronald P. Leow (PhD, 1991, University of Illinois, Champaign-Urbana) is associate professor of Spanish applied linguistics and director of Spanish basic language instruction at Georgetown University. His areas of interest include language curriculum development, teacher education, psycholinguistics, second language acquisition research (including computer-based) and research methodology. His articles have appeared in *Studies in Second Language Acquisition, Applied Psycholinguistics, Language Learning, The Modern Language Journal, Applied Language Learning, World Englishes,* and *Hispania.*

Alison Mackey (PhD, 1995, Sydney University) is associate professor of linguistics at Georgetown University. Her research interests focus on second language acquisition, specifically the effects of input and interaction in second language development, and second language research methodologies. Her work appears in *Studies in Second Language Acquisition, Language Learning, The Modern Language Journal, Foreign Language Annals, International Review* *of Applied Linguistics, Language Teaching Research, Language Learning and Technology System,* and *International Journal of Educational Research,* as well as in edited collections published by John Benjamins and Cambridge University Press. With Susan Gass she has published two textbooks on methodology in second language research.

Kara Morgan-Short is a PhD candidate in Spanish applied linguistics at Georgetown University. Her research examines issues in second language acquisition related to explicit and implicit learning of second languages and the use of think-aloud protocols for assessing awareness. Her work has appeared in *Studies in Second Language Acquisition,* including an in press article coauthored with Harriet Wood Bowden, and in *Language Learning.*

Cristina Sanz (PhD, 1994, University of Illinois, Champaign-Urbana) is associate professor of Spanish linguistics at Georgetown University, where she directs the graduate program in Spanish linguistics and the Spanish intensive program, and codirects the Center for the Brain Basis of Cognition. Her research focuses on the interaction between individual variables and types of input in the acquisition of nonprimary languages. She coedited *Spanish Applied Linguistics at the Turn of the Millenium* (2000, Cascadilla Press) and was guest editor of *Cognition and Spanish Bilinguals* (2001), a special volume of *Spanish Applied Linguistics.* Her latest article appeared in *Language Learning* (2004). Dr. Sanz has taught graduate courses in Spain and the Philippines and has been a consultant to the United Nations and the Instituto Cervantes.

Catherine A. Stafford (ABD 2004, Georgetown University) is an assistant professor of Spanish linguistics at the University of Wisconsin, Madison. Her research interests include issues of bilingualism, memory, and age as they relate to the acquisition of nonprimary languages. She has taught Spanish and coordinated the intermediate level of the Spanish language program at Georgetown.

Michael T. Ullman (PhD, 1993, MIT) is associate professor of neuroscience at Georgetown University, where he also holds appointments in linguistics, psychology, and neurology. He directs the Brain and Language Laboratory and codirects the Center for the Brain Basis of Cognition. His research investigates the neural, cognitive, and computational bases of language, and the neurocognitive relations between language and nonlanguage functions, in particular declarative and procedural memory. He examines these issues in both native and nonnative language with psycholinguistic, developmental, neurological, neuroimaging, endocrine, and pharmacological studies, in normal subjects and in individuals with developmental or adult-onset brain disorders. Dr. Ullman publishes in a wide range of journals across several disciplines.

Bill VanPatten (PhD, 1983, The University of Texas at Austin) is professor of Spanish and second language acquisition at the University of Illinois-Chicago. His research interests include cognitive and linguistic aspects of input processing as well as the effects of instruction on second language acquisition. His publications include six books, five textbooks, and over seventy articles and chapters in books. He is currently working on *From Columbus to J. Lo: Truth and Myth about Spanish and Spanish Speakers in the U.S.*

Index

G

Q